FINANCIAL ESSENTIALS
FOR SMALL BUSINESS SUCCESS

FINANCIAL ESSENTIALS FOR SMALL BUSINESS SUCCESS

Accounting, Planning and Recordkeeping Techniques for a Healthy Bottom Line

JOSEPH TABET
and
JEFFREY SLATER

UPSTART PUBLISHING COMPANY, INC.

The Small Business Publishing Company

Dover, New Hampshire

Published by Upstart Publishing Company, Inc.
A Division of Dearborn Publishing Group, Inc.
12 Portland Street
Dover, New Hampshire 03820
(800) 235-8866 or (603) 749-5071

Library of Congress Cataloging-in-Publication Data

Tabet, Joseph
Financial essentials for small business success: accounting, planning and recordkeeping tech-
niques for a healthy bottom line / Joseph Tabet and Jeffrey Slater.
p.   cm.
Includes index.
ISBN 0-936894-45-8
1. Small business—Management.   2. Small business—Accounting.   3. Small business—
Finance. I. Slater, Jeffrey. II. Title.
HD62.7.S565 1994   93-9088
658.15'92—dc20   CIP

Cover design by Pear Graphic Design, Portsmouth, NH.
Text design by Design & Format, Keene, NH.

Printed in the United States of America
10 9 8 7 6 5 4 3

For a complete catalog of Upstart's small business publications, call (800) 235-8866.

CONTENTS

6

TAX OBLIGATIONS: THE RULES OF THE GAME | 96

PREFACE

Just pick up any newspaper. Headlines go on about poor economic conditions, foreclosures, business and bank failures and the difficulties of borrowing. People in small business complain about how they can no longer survive, much less expand. Many of my own friends state, "The day of the small business is over—how can they compete?"

Sure the failure rate of business is high, but let's look at the facts. Many of these businesses would be here today if their owners had taken the time to *plan and to keep accurate records*. This book is an attempt to show small business owners how to succeed in the 1990s. It shows you how, in making your business succeed, to look toward the future, while evaluating the present and not forgetting the past.

This book stresses how important *common sense* is in overcoming the problems of poor recordkeeping and planning. It shows you where to get the information you need. It doesn't talk at you but works *with* you. Are you guilty of *recordkeeping and planning by obstruction?* To ask the same question more simply, do you create or become so immersed in the part of the business that you like that you say, "I have no time for keeping detailed records or creating a business plan?" Owners create their own obstacle, to make it easy for them to avoid their particular areas of incompetence. Don't! Planning and recordkeeping constitute the lifeblood of a business. This sort of attitude reminds me of the heart patient who does *not* accept the need to monitor the condition. If you develop a common-sense approach, through disciplining yourself, planning and recordkeeping can be quite interesting and rewarding. Remember—it is the "bottom line" we are after.

Chapter after chapter takes you step-by-step through the various types of organizations, through the maze of tax obligations, and through other typical small business problems. You will be able to read, as well as to interpret, financial reports. Break-even analysis, budgeting, cash flow, business ratios, projected reports, and bookkeeping procedures will all become invaluable and easy-to-use tools at your disposal. You will see how these tools can make your business in the nineties a profitable operation that is under "control."

After each chapter you get a chance to check your comprehension. At the end of the book, you may take advantage of a wealth of appendix material, including:

1. a programmed review of the book;
2. sample tax forms;
3. where to write for developing a recordkeeping system for your business;
4. how to work with a bank to borrow;
5. watching your profit;
6. a stress-reliever crossword puzzle;
7. a glossary of key terms;
8. a calendar for planning;
9. getting your key phone numbers organized;
10. a small business financial status checklist;
11. a sample of the one-write system.

No book can make you an expert, but this book is an *invaluable tool* in helping to meet the challenges facing small business in the nineties. Its key theme is practicality. You *will* succeed if only you take the time to "set up" as well as to "execute" the plan. Planning, as well as recordkeeping, is work, but the return is well worth the effort. Let's get on to it!

—Joseph L. Tabet and Jeffrey Slater

CREDITS Figures 1-1, 1-3, 1-6, 1-8, 1-9, 1-10, 4-7, and 4-10 are reproduced from *Success and Failure* in Small Business Administrator Management Course Program (Washington, D.C.: Small Business Administration, 1974). This issue is no longer in print.

Figures 1-2, 1-5, 1-7, and 4-16 are reproduced by special permission from Dun and Bradstreet, Inc. For a list of their publications, write to Dun and Bradstreet, 299 Park Ave., New York, New York 10171.

Figures 2-4, 2-6, 2-7, and 2-8 are adapted from Jeffrey Slater, *College Accounting*, 5th Edition (Englewood Cliffs, N.J.: Prentice-Hall, Inc., 1993).

1

A COMMON-SENSE APPROACH TO PLANNING AND RECORDKEEPING

<table>
<tr><td>

1. Identify the track record of small business.
2. List the roadblocks leading to many business failures.
3. Compare and contrast the concept of failing in relation to setting priorities.
4. Identify potential danger signals of financial trouble.
5. Explain the need to plan.
6. Estimate the cash you need to start up.
7. List the disadvantages of the "patching a flat instead of replacing the tire" approach.
8. Explain the practical reasons for having a good accountant.
9. Explain the advantages and disadvantages of a sole proprietorship, partnership, corporation, and S-type corporation.

</td><td>

OBJECTIVES

</td></tr>
</table>

Survival is the name of the game. PETE FREEZE	**CALLING IT THE** **WAY IT IS**

Last week Pete Freeze, owner of the "Pete's Fix-It," came over to our home to fix our dishwasher. Pete has owned his business for the past eighteen months. We had the following conversation:

  JEFF: Pete, I'm writing a book on small business. Any words of wisdom?
  PETE: That's nice, but nobody is going to read it. Who has *time?* No of-
         fense, but people in small business are trying to *survive.* Look at this
         economy . . . I need a new truck. The cost of labor is out of sight . . .

1

I can't invest in more inventory . . . The more money I make, the more expenses I have. I have to cope with rising taxes and increased difficulty in obtaining loans. It's not easy to run a small business.

JEFF: Why do you stay in business?

PETE: I love my independence, but it's not easy wearing so many different hats. My wife and kids would like to see me once in a while. I have little time for myself.

JEFF: How about your records? Do you do them or give them to an accountant?

PETE: I know this is your "cup of tea," but I'm a mechanic, not a bookkeeper. Once a month I sit down with my wife, and we empty the brown bag of slips so we can pay some bills as well as bill my customers. I used to do it once a week, but who has time? I can't afford to pay someone to handle the books.

Figure 1-1: Poor Collections

JEFF: Do you have a plan set up for your business?

PETE: Jeff, you're dreaming. I've got to eat. I don't have time or patience to plan. I hate to say it, but educators are living in a dream world. I'm not a thinker, I'm a doer.

JEFF: What would you say is the worst situation you face?

PETE: The seasonal business. Before Thanksgiving and Christmas, everyone is fixing, but January and February can kill me. I seem to always be out of *cash*.

Although Pete's business is only one situation, his case is not unique; many of his problems and concerns are present in larger businesses.

DON'T TURN YOUR BACK ON THE PAST: THE TRACK RECORD OF A SMALL BUSINESS

Before we develop common-sense solutions to problems like Pete's, let's look at the track record of small business in general. Too often people try to create the wheel again. Yet I believe the best way to succeed is to understand why so many small businesses fail. Taking time to look at the past might make your *road to success* much easier in the future. And you might avoid that one mistake which in a small business can lead to bankruptcy. Depending on how you define a business, there are approximately 17 million small businesses. People don't realize that for every $100 of retail sales, $70 is the result of small business.

Figure 1-2: Failure Trends Since 1927*

Year	Number of failures	Total failure liabilities	Failure rate per 10,000 listed concerns	Average liability per failure
1927	23,146	$520,105,000	106	$22,471
1928	23,842	489,559,000	109	20,534
1929	22,909	483,252,000	104	21,094
1930	26,355	668,282,000	122	25,357
1931	28,285	736,310,000	133	26,032
1932	31,822	928,313,000	154	29,172
1933	19,859	457,520,000	100	23,038
1934	12,091	333,959,000	61	27,621
1935	12,244	310,580,000	62	25,366
1936	9,607	203,173,000	48	21,148
1937	9,490	$183,253,000	46	$19,310
1938	12,836	246,505,000	61	19,204
1939	14,768	182,520,000	70	12,359
1940	13,619	166,684,000	63	12,239
1941	11,848	136,104,000	55	11,488
1942	9,405	100,763,000	45	10,713
1943	3,221	45,339,000	16	14,076
1944	1,222	31,660,000	7	25,908
1945	809	30,225,000	4	37,361
1946	1,129	67,349,000	5	59,654
1947	3,474	$204,612,000	14	$58,898
1948	5,250	234,620,000	20	44,690
1949	9,246	308,109,000	34	33,323
1950	9,162	248,283,000	34	27,099
1951	8,058	259,547,000	31	32,210
1952	7,611	283,314,000	29	37,224
1953	8,862	394,153,000	33	44,477
1954	11,086	462,628,000	42	41,731
1955	10,969	449,380,000	42	40,968
1956	12,686	562,697,000	48	44,356
1957	13,739	615,293,000	52	44,784
1958	14,964	728,258,000	56	48,667
1959	14,053	692,808,000	52	49,300
1960	15,445	$938,630,000	57	$60,772
1961	17,075	1,090,123,000	64	63,843
1962	15,782	1,213,601,000	61	76,898
1963	14,374	1,352,593,000	56	94,100
1964	13,501	1,329,223,000	53	98,454
1965	13,514	1,321,666,000	53	97,800
1966	13,061	1,385,659,000	52	106,091
1967	12,364	1,265,227,000	49	102,332
1968	9,636	940,996,000	39	97,654
1969	9,154	1,142,113,000	37	124,767
1970	10,748	$1,887,754,000	44	$175,638
1971	10,326	1,916,929,000	42	185,641
1972	9,566	2,000,244,000	38	209,099
1973	9,345	2,298,606,000	36	245,972
1974	9,915	3,053,137,000	38	307,931
1975	11,432	4,380,170,000	43	383,150
1976	9,628	3,011,271,000	35	312,762
1977	7,919	3,095,317,000	28	390,872
1978	6,619	2,656,006,000	24	401,270
1979	7,564	2,667,362,000	28	352,639
1980	11,742	$4,635,080,000	42	$394,744
1981	16,794	6,955,180,000	61	414,147
1982	24,908	15,610,792,000	88	626,738
1983	31,334	16,072,860,000	110	512,953
1984	52,078	29,268,646,871	107	562,016
1985	57,253	36,937,369,478	115	645,160
1986	61,616	44,723,991,601	120	725,850
1987	61,111	34,723,831,429	102	568,209
1988	57,097	39,573,030,341	98	693,084
1989	50,361	42,328,790,375	65	840,507
1990	60,747	56,130,073,898	74	923,996
1991	88,140	96,825,314,741	107	1,098,539
1992p	96,857	91,289,379,053	110	942,516

Due to statistical revision, data prior to 1984 are not directly comparable with the new series.

p = preliminary

*From 1991 Business Failure Record, The Dun & Bradstreet Corporation, 1992.

The track record—that is, the number of small businesses that succeed—is not good. Many studies have been undertaken. In general, one out of every three businesses fail within three years of start-up, while as many as half fail within five years. Some studies indicate that, by the end of ten years, nine out of ten fail.

Why? What roadblocks developed?

Figure 1-3: Incompetence

Roadblocks that Led to Many Business Failures

The six roadblocks to success shown in Figure 1-4 should not be looked upon individually but as a whole. Figure 1-5 presents the causes of some of the business failures in 1992 in greater detail.

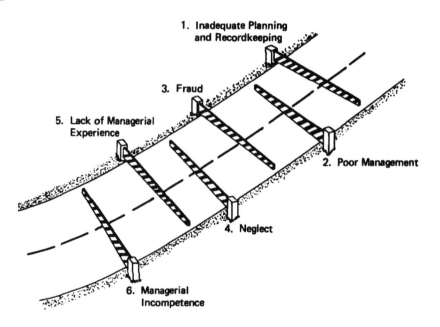

Figure 1-4: Roadblocks Leading to Failure

Despite the statistics, owners of small businesses too often live in a dream world. That's right! They figure things will eventually get better. They enjoy putting out brush fires instead of planning "fire prevention." Then the reality of failure wakes them up. Then they see that many businesses fail because they lack enough money to really get started. Then they complain about inflation, interest rates, wage rates, government

Figure 1-5: Causes of Business Failures in 1992

	Agriculture, forestry & fishing	Mining	Construction	Manufacturing	Transportation & public utilities	Wholesale trade	Retail trade	Finance, insurance & real estate	Services	Total
Neglect Causes	**1.5%**	**2.4%**	**3.9%**	**5.0%**	**4.9%**	**3.6%**	**3.7%**	**9.1%**	**2.2%**	**3.7%**
Business conflicts	0.5%	2.4%	1.9%	2.2%	4.5%	0.4%	2.5%	8.4%	0.8%	2.1%
Family problems	0.5%	0.0%	0.5%	1.6%	0.0%	0.8%	0.3%	0.0%	0.3%	0.4%
Lack of commitments	0.0%	0.0%	0.3%	0.2%	0.0%	0.8%	0.3%	0.0%	0.2%	0.3%
Poor work habits	0.5%	0.0%	1.2%	1.0%	0.4%	1.6%	0.6%	0.7%	0.9%	0.9%
Disaster	**1.9%**	**2.4%**	**4.3%**	**8.3%**	**2.0%**	**4.5%**	**9.0%**	**1.2%**	**2.0%**	**4.5%**
Fraud	**0.5%**	**0.0%**	**1.2%**	**1.6%**	**1.2%**	**6.6%**	**2.2%**	**6.5%**	**1.3%**	**2.2%**
Economic Factors Causes	**86.4%**	**85.7%**	**70.2%**	**57.9%**	**68.4%**	**63.8%**	**63.8%**	**58.4%**	**60.9%**	**64.1%**
High interest rates	0.0%	0.0%	0.1%	0.0%	0.0%	0.0%	0.0%	0.0%	0.0%	0.0%
Inadequate sales	0.0%	0.0%	2.5%	5.0%	2.4%	5.1%	4.8%	0.5%	0.8%	2.6%
Industry weakness	55.4%	40.5%	23.7%	18.4%	19.1%	21.3%	16.5%	17.5%	25.7%	22.7%
Insufficient profits	31.0%	45.2%	43.7%	32.7%	46.3%	34.5%	40.7%	39.9%	34.0%	37.7%
Inventory difficulties	0.0%	0.0%	0.0%	0.2%	0.0%	0.4%	0.2%	0.0%	0.0%	0.1%
Not competitive	0.0%	0.0%	0.1%	1.0%	1.2%	2.1%	0.9%	0.0%	0.2%	0.6%
Poor growth prospects	0.0%	0.0%	0.1%	0.4%	0.4%	0.4%	0.0%	0.5%	0.1%	0.2%
Poor location	0.0%	0.0%	0.0%	0.2%	0.0%	0.0%	0.5%	0.0%	0.1%	0.2%
Experience Causes	**0.0%**	**0.0%**	**0.7%**	**1.6%**	**0.8%**	**1.4%**	**1.2%**	**0.2%**	**0.5%**	**0.8%**
Lack of business knowledge	0.0%	0.0%	0.3%	0.4%	0.0%	0.2%	0.1%	0.2%	0.1%	0.2%
Lack of line experience	0.0%	0.0%	0.2%	0.6%	0.0%	0.4%	0.7%	0.0%	0.2%	0.3%
Lack of managerial experience	0.0%	0.0%	0.2%	0.6%	0.8%	0.8%	0.4%	0.0%	0.2%	0.3%
Finance Causes	**9.9%**	**7.2%**	**18.8%**	**23.9%**	**18.7%**	**17.8%**	**20.1%**	**24.5%**	**32.6%**	**23.9%**
Burdensome institutional debt	2.4%	2.4%	3.6%	6.1%	2.9%	4.9%	4.0%	6.5%	6.4%	5.0%
Heavy operating expenses	6.6%	4.8%	13.4%	12.1%	13.4%	8.8%	13.9%	15.4%	24.7%	16.6%
Insufficient capital	0.9%	0.0%	1.8%	5.7%	2.4%	4.1%	2.2%	2.6%	1.5%	2.3%
Strategy Causes	**0.0%**	**2.4%**	**0.9%**	**1.8%**	**2.8%**	**2.5%**	**0.2%**	**0.2%**	**0.5%**	**0.9%**
Excessive fixed assets	0.0%	0.0%	0.0%	0.0%	0.0%	0.0%	0.0%	0.0%	0.1%	0.1%
Over expansion	0.0%	0.0%	0.2%	0.2%	1.2%	0.2%	0.1%	0.2%	0.1%	0.2%
Receivables difficulties	0.0%	2.4%	0.7%	1.6%	1.6%	2.3%	0.1%	0.0%	0.3%	0.6%

Results based on primary reason for failure.

p = preliminary

Classification failures based on opinion of informed creditors and information in Dun & Bradstreet Reports. From *1991 Business Failure Record*, The Dun & Bradstreet Corporation, 1992.

regulations, and the overall cost of *paperwork*—as well as about the cost of energy today with all its implications.

Figure 1-6: Neglect

The Survival Checklist

So how do you know if your business is going under? You can tell by the signs that your business gives you. These signals of financial trouble or danger to the business are summarized in what we call a "Survival Checklist." Look them over. While many inexperienced business people let these symptoms grow into eventual crises, you will be able to develop common-sense solutions to your own business problems by the time you are through reading this book. You will also have the specific tools needed to make those solutions work. The potential danger signals are as follows:

1. lots of unsold inventory;
2. customers not paying bills on time;
3. not meeting tax obligations on time;
4. writing business checks for personal expenses;
5. bank loan overdue;
6. not paying suppliers on time—paper backlogged;
7. theft unusually high;
8. making lots of money but not enough food on the table;
9. paying bills too early;
10. seasonal slump creating a cash crisis;
11. bank balance and checkbook reconciled once a year;
12. missing many purchase discounts;
13. loans draining the business, sales falling;
14. expenses rising dramatically from previous years;
15. financial reports prepared once a year;
16. bad debts increasing substantially;
17. out of stock—late shipments resulting in "crisis" situations;
18. payroll checks always about three days late;
19. no lawyer or accountant for the business.

THE NEED TO PLAN: A COMMON-SENSE APPROACH

Owners of small businesses cannot be experts in all phases of their businesses. For example, a good auto mechanic doesn't necessarily make a good boss, and many excellent baseball players make poor managers.

	IF YOU OPERATE AT A NET PROFIT OF...				
	2%	3%	4%	5%	6%
TO OFFSET ACTUAL LOSS OF...	THESE ADDITIONAL SALES ARE REQUIRED.				
$ 50.	$ 2,500.	$ 1,666.	$ 1,250.	$ 1,000.	$ 833
100.	5,000.	3,333.	2,500.	2,000.	1,666.
200.	10,000.	6,666.	5,000.	4,000.	3,333.
250.	12,500.	8,333.	6,250.	5,000.	4,166.
300.	15,000.	10,000.	7,500.	6,000.	5,000.
350.	17,500.	11,666.	8,750.	7,000.	5,833.
400.	20,000.	13,333.	10,000.	8,000.	6,666.
450.	22,500.	15,000.	11,250.	9,000.	7,500.
500.	25,000.	16,666.	12,500.	10,000.	8,333.

Figure 1-7: Sales Needed to Offset a Loss

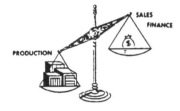

Figure 1-8: Unbalanced Experience

With the time crunch facing them, owners often do what they do best and leave the planning and recordkeeping until "later." They build on their strengths and try to avoid their weaknesses. A *definite mistake!* Owners should *attack* their weaknesses.

Figure 1-9: Lack of Management Experience

History shows that many businesses have failed because the owners did not have a plan. Many owners get so caught up in specific problems that they lose sight of the whole picture. Many are not willing to sacrifice the time to plan; it just isn't on their list of *priorities*. Others are just *afraid to plan*, because a plan represents a potential picture of failure if their expectations are not met. In this respect, the fear of failure can be more hurtful than failure itself. These owners do not plan because they feel incompetent; they are afraid of the result. They never did it before, so why now? "I'm crisis-oriented. Leave me alone. Planning is a waste of my time and energy."

Figure 1-10: Lack of Experience in the Line

Don't fall into this mental trap. Think of a plan as a *roadmap to success*. It allows you to follow your progress. Don't worry if you're not always right. With your plan, which should be in writing, you should try to look ahead for two years. The plan basically sets specific goals, along with a plan of attack to achieve them. Then at points you can evaluate your progress and make modifications. Although you should review the plan every three or six months, some owners do so more frequently.

For example, Jim Spencer opened a "jogging shop" and set a goal of selling 200 pairs of sneakers in the first month. He knew what he wanted to "realistically do." Jim didn't try to recreate the wheel. *He spoke to others in the business for assistance.* Jim used the worksheet shown in Figure 1-11 to estimate his start-up as well as monthly expenses.

Monitoring Your Business

Jim believed that planning for his future really started with the present. He didn't want to get involved with just putting out brush fires—with just patching the flat. He wanted to develop a plan that would provide an early detection system. So Jim's planning system was like putting in a set of smoke detectors. He also wanted his business to develop a sound "track record." Jim felt that disciplining himself to plan (he set aside one evening a week) would provide him with a set of alternatives. He was not just a "doer" but also a thinker.

Jim did not entertain the misconception that planning should be done only by large businesses. This notion is plain false: small businesses have a unique advantage in relation to big firms because they can react to local needs and concerns. Although planning was new to Jim, he was not afraid to fail; the *fear* of failure is worse than failure itself. As good builders need the proper tools, so do owners of small businesses need sound financial planning and recordkeeping. Hence you need some specific tools to monitor your business.

WORKSHEET NO. 2			
ESTIMATED MONTHLY EXPENSES			**What to put in column 2** (These figures are typical for one kind of business. You will have to decide how many months to allow for in your business.)
Item	Your estimate of monthly expenses based on sales of $ _____ per year	Your estimate of how much cash you need to start your business (see column 3)	
	Column 1	Column 2	Column 3
Salary of owner-manager	$	$	2 times column 1
All other salaries and wages			3 times column 1
Rent			3 times column 1
Advertising			3 times column 1
Delivery expense			3 times column 1
Supplies			3 times column 1
Telephone and telegraph			3 times column 1
Other utilities			3 times column 1
Insurance			Payment required by insurance company
Taxes, including Social Security			4 times column 1
Interest			3 times column 1
Maintenance			3 times column 1
Legal and other professional fees			3 times column 1
Miscellaneous			3 times column 1
STARTING COSTS YOU ONLY HAVE TO PAY ONCE			Leave column 2 blank
Fixtures and equipment			Fill in worksheet 3 and put total here
Decorating and remodeling			Talk it over with a contractor
Installation of fixtures and equipment			Talk to suppliers from who you buy these
Starting inventory			Suppliers will probably help you estimate this
Deposits with public utilities			Find out from utilities company
Legal and other professional fees			Lawyer, accountant, and so on
Licenses and permits			Find out from city offices what you have to have
Advertising and promotion for opening			Estimate what you'll use
Accounts receivable			What you need to buy more stock until credit customers pay
Cash			For unexpected expenses or losses, special purchases, etc.
Other			Make a separate list and enter total
TOTAL ESTIMATED CASH YOU NEED TO START WITH	$		Add up all the numbers in column 2

Figure 1-11: Worksheet for Estimating Monthly Expenses

The question is, can you use all the tools yourself? Or do you need outside assistance? Hire a good accountant. I know what you are thinking. You can't afford one! *Wrong!* As I told one of my friends, "If you can't afford to hire an accountant, you probably don't have enough money to go into business." Many accountants are willing to start on the ground floor and to grow with you. The savings and expertise that an accountant brings will pay you back the fees many times over. Doing without professional accounting advice is thus "penny wise and dollar foolish."

The accountant is definitely a "crutch" you need; using one is a common-sense approach to succeeding. Yet to work with accountants effectively, you have to know how to communicate with them. They can aid you in setting up specific records, keeping records, changes in tax regulations, due dates for returns, and so on. Yet you, as the owner, *must* take an active part in the financial process.

The best way to choose an accountant is probably to start with a referral. If you don't already have an accountant that you are comfortable with ask friends or relatives or business associates. You need to find someone who will work with you—after all you are a customer, growth for you means growth for the accountant. Referral is the best method because there are so many firms and types of firms to choose from. For example, big does not always mean better. Many of my clients started out with large firms. They had one or two worthwhile meetings with perhaps a partner or manager who made sure everything got started properly, but later these people were unavailable because the work was delegated to less experienced accountants, and often the person doing their accounting changed from year-to-year. They never really had a good working relationship, and since they were too busy trying to succeed and there were no problems with the taxing agencies, time didn't seem to be available for good tax planning. But, what happened to that working relationship and all that advice that could slip through the cracks?

The key for you, therefore, is your comfort with the accountant, your confidence in the accountant, and of course, the accountant's fee structure.

Finance might or might not be your weak spot, but don't panic! The material presented in the next five chapters provides you with a sound base of information in return for a minimum of time and effort. We will be looking at the following tools to aid you in your financial planning and record-keeping system:

1. A sample bookkeeping system to aid in the recording process, which provides you with a way of accumulating the raw data.
2. How to prepare financial reports, as well as how to read and interpret them.
3. How to prepare a simplified budget.
4. How to make up a simplified cash flow statement: Where is your money going, and what's left?
5. How to do a break-even analysis—at a certain level of sales, what is your profit?
6. How to meet your tax obligations.

Jen Elmo is seriously considering opening a studio where she can give flute, clarinet and oboe lessons. She visited Anne Crystal, a local accountant, for more information on the options open to her.

JEN: Anne, as you know, I'd like to open a music studio. My friends tell me there are three main types of business organizations. Could you briefly explain each? Then I have some specific concerns to discuss.

ANNE: The three forms of business organizations are *sole proprietorships*, *partnerships*, and *corporations*. The sole proprietorship is a business owned by just one person. The partnership is co-owned by two or more people through a legal association. The corporation is a form of business that is owned by shareholders. The corporation, in the eye of the law, is considered a living person, separate and distinct from its owners.

Just one point. There is a potential alternative facing a small business based on specific restrictions.[1] A company may elect to be taxed as an S-type corporation. In simple terms, you get the tax benefit of a proprietorship but retain the limited liability of a corporation. An S-corporation passes its items of income, loss, deduction and credits through to its shareholders to be included on their individual tax returns. The election to be treated as an S-corporation must be made by filing Form 2553 with the Internal Revenue Service. (A sample of Form 2553 is contained in the appendix.) Now that the top individual tax rates are significantly lower, S-corporations have been the organization of choice for many new businesses.

JEN: Of the three types, which will be the most beneficial in keeping my start-up costs low, as well as in avoiding as much red tape as possible?

ANNE: Let me diagram, in simple terms, the pluses and minuses.

Sole Proprietorship	*Partnership*	*Corporation (S-Corporation)*
1. Few organizational costs.	1. Need articles of organization	1. Cost of incorporation expensive.
2. Certain license requirements.	2. Few organizational costs and license requirements.	2. Need corporate charter.
3. Small amount of capital to begin.	3. Sate regulations tend to increase.	3. Close regulations by state and federal government.

JEN: Well, which would best protect my personal assets—my home, my boat, and the like?

ANNE: To answer that question, I have to add a few entries to our diagram.

[1] S-corporation restrictions are (a) a domestic corporation with one class of stock; (b) stock held by no more than 35 shareholders; (c) it must have as shareholders only individuals; (d) shareholders must be U.S. citizens. For more specifics, check Publication 539 (Washington, D.C.: Department of Treasury, Internal Revenue Service, 1991).

Sole Proprietorship	Partnership	Corporation (S-Corporation)
Unlimited liability, if the business fails, your personal assets could be lost.	Unlimited liability for partners. If they are limited partners, they would have limited liabilities.	Liability limited to the amount of your investment.

Concern #3: Taxation

JEN: And the tax burden for each?

ANNE: Tax is a complicated area and continually changing. This is where an accountant is definitely needed, but in simple terms:

Sole Proprietorship	Partnership	Corporation	S-Corporation
Single taxation: The business profit is taxed on your personal income tax return (1040).[2] A schedule C is attached to show the operations of the firm.	Single taxation: The business profit is shown on the personal income taxes forms (1040) of the partners.	Double taxation: You use the corporate tax return (1120), and you pay corporate taxes on the profit.	Single taxation: The business Profit/Loss is shown on the personal income tax forms (1040) of the shareholders.
	Form 1065 (U.S. partnership return of income) must be completed as an informational report.	As an individual, you're taxed on dividends.	Form 1120S (U.S. Small Business Corporation Tax Return) must be completed as an informational report.
		Heavy tax burden.	

Concern #4: Capital

JEN: How about raising more dollars for expansion?

ANNE: From that point of view, our three business forms break down this way:

Sole Proprietorship	Partnership	Corporation (S-Corporation)
Need a track record. Borrowing is possible but could be quite costly.[3]	Credit is usually available. Banks will offer lines of credit. Easier to raise funds than for a sole proprietorship.	Selling of stocks or bonds. Easier to raise funds than for a partnership.

JEN: Since I have had no training in recordkeeping, could you give me a quick overview of the accounting process? I don't want to be an expert, but I want to understand the basics so I can monitor my business.

ANNE: Ok, but let's *clear the air* before we begin. You should be aware of certain misconceptions regarding at least three questions:

[2] Sample of tax forms located in Appendix 8.
[3] We will talk about SBA loans later.

1. What is bookkeeping?
2. Which records are required by law?
3. How long should you retain your records?

We will deal with these questions in upcoming chapters, picking up this discussion again in Chapter 2.

SUMMARY OF KEY POINTS

1. Study the track record of small business. Don't recreate the wheel, just smooth it. Build upon other experiences. Don't be afraid to ask questions.

2. Roadblocks leading to business failure include:
   - inadequate planning and recordkeeping
   - poor management
   - fraud
   - neglect
   - lack of managerial experience
   - managerial incompetence

3. Make planning a priority. Many owners are afraid to plan because they feel incompetent. Yet planning is common sense. It requires self-discipline, and you must make time for it.

4. Go over the survival checklist. Doing so can save you money.

5. Money is well spent hiring an accountant and possibly a lawyer. You can't afford *not* to.

6. Weigh the comparative benefits of each form of business organization (Figure 1-12).

	Few Original Costs	License Regulations	Small Amount of Capital to Begin	Unlimited Liability	Limited Liability	Single Taxation	Raising Funds Difficult	1040 Schedule C	1065	1120 1120S	Double Taxation	Sell Stock
Sole Proprietorship	X	X	X	X		X	X	X				
Partnership	X	X	X	X		X		X	X			
Corporation		X			X					X	X	X
S—Corporation		X			X	X				X		X

Figure 1-12: Forms of Business Organization

This section gives you a chance to check your understanding of the chapter, and it gives us a chance to reemphasize the key points. Following all the questions are the answers.

	True	False
1. Survival is a key goal to many small businesses.	____	____
2. The cash crisis comes whether planning is done or not.	____	____
3. In small businesses an owner must be a "doer" and not think too much about other phases of the business.	____	____
4. In general, 80 to 90 percent of new businesses fail within six months.	____	____
5. Fraud is a concern to many small businesses.	____	____
6. Inadequate planning and recordkeeping are major causes for many small business failures.	____	____
7. Continually putting out brush fires is a sign of good management.	____	____
8. Owners usually try to build on their strengths and try to avoid their weaknesses.	____	____
9. Many owners are afraid to plan.	____	____
10. Paying bills early always shows a company is doing sound financial planning.	____	____
11. Setting goals is a waste of time. The owner has more important things to do.	____	____
12. The fear of failure could be worse than the actual failure.	____	____
13. Not hiring an accountant isn't really "penny wise and dollar foolish."	____	____
14. The owner should leave all the financial matters to the accountant and trust whatever the accountant says.	____	____
15. A corporation is owned by only two people.	____	____
16. A sole proprietorship has unlimited liability.	____	____
17. The corporation is closely regulated only by the federal government.	____	____
18. The sole proprietorship has the heaviest tax burden.	____	____
19. The partnership is based on the concept of double taxation.	____	____
20. S-corporation may be a viable alternative to some small businesses.	____	____

Solutions

1. True	11. False
2. False	12. True
3. False	13. False
4. False	14. False
5. True	15. False
6. True	16. True
7. False	17. False

8. True
9. True
10. False

18. False
19. False
20. True

Column A

Column B

_____ 1. Dun and Bradstreet
_____ 2. An example of self-discipline
_____ 3. Close regulation by state and federal government
_____ 4. Opposite of planning
_____ 5. "Penny wise and dollar foolish."
_____ 6. 1120
_____ 7. Roadblock leading to failure
_____ 8. Form of business with few organizational costs
_____ 9. Why some owners fail to plan
_____10. Corporation
_____11. Priorities
_____12. 1040
_____13. Not meeting tax obligations on time
_____14. Single taxation
_____15. Owner likes to work with hands
_____16. Plan
_____17. Cash crisis
_____18. Domestic corporation
_____19. Sole proprietorship
_____20. Borrowing

A. Lack of managerial experience
B. Lines of credit
C. Afraid to plan
D. Sole proprietorship
E. Limited liability
F. Failure trends since 1920
G. Partnership
H. Setting up the time to plan
I. Schedule C
J. Set aside one evening a week to plan
K. Doer versus thinker
L. Putting out brush fires
M. One owner
N. S-type Corporation
O. Corporation
P. Not hiring an accountant
Q. Corporate tax return
R. Seasonal business
S. Roadmap to success
T. On the survival checklist

Answers

1.	F	11.	H
2.	J	12.	I
3.	O	13.	T
4.	L	14.	G
5.	P	15.	K
6.	Q	16.	S
7.	A	17.	R
8.	D	18.	N
9.	C	19.	M
10.	E	20.	B

2

THE ACCOUNTING PUZZLE: PUTTING THE PIECES TOGETHER

1. Explain the difference between bookkeeping and accounting.
2. List the six basic requirements of a good recordkeeping system.
3. Explain the accounting dilemma.
4. List the retention requirements for your records.
5. Define these terms:
   - assets
   - liabilities
   - owner's investment
   - accounting equation
   - revenue
   - account
   - chart of accounts
   - expense
   - journal
   - ledger
   - rule of debits and credits
   - trial balance
   - income statement
   - balance sheet
6. List the steps of the accounting cycle.
7. Compare and contrast single-entry bookkeeping versus double-entry bookkeeping.

JEN: Aren't bookkeeping and accounting the same thing?

ANNE: No. Bookkeeping is only the recording phase of accounting. Bookkeeping accumulates the data needed in preparing financial reports. Accounting analyzes, interprets, and summarizes as well as reports information. The accountant aids you in making business decisions or planning for the future. Think of accounting as an apple pie and bookkeeping as *one* slice of the pie.

THE ACCOUNTING PROCESS: BOOKS AND RECORDS

Concern #1: Accounting Versus Bookkeeping

Concern #2: Recordkeeping Systems

JEN: My friend told me that there is only one legal way of setting up my records.

ANNE: No. The law does not make such a requirement. What the law states is that your recordkeeping system must be permanent, accurate, and complete. It also requires you to be able to identify your sales, all deductions, employee information, and so on. The key to a good recordkeeping system is that it should be (1) simple to use, (2) easy to understand, (3) reliable, (4) accurate, (5) consistent, and (6) designed to provide information on a timely basis. It's just like a quarterback on a football team. He calls the plays, but the timing of his decision is crucial in executing the play.

JEN: My relative told me I have to keep my records only for the year I work. She said it's good to keep a clean file and dispose of all records after a year.

ANNE: Don't listen to relatives! Their intentions are sound, but their facts are wrong. Let me quote from a government publication:

Availability and Retention of Records[1]
You are required to keep the books and records of your business available at all times for inspection by Internal Revenue officers. The records must be retained as long as their contents may become material in the administration of any Internal Revenue law.

Records supporting items on a tax return should be retained until the statute of limitations for that return expires. Ordinarily, the statute of limitations for an income tax return expires 3 years after the return is due to be filed or 2 years from the date the tax was paid, whichever occurs later. However, in many cases the taxpayer should retain all records indefinitely.

I have seen quite a few cases where people have thrown out important records, only to find themselves in a costly and aggravating situation. Recently a client was called for an audit on his 1989 tax return. He had thrown out all his 1989 cancelled checks and bank statements and of course the IRS wanted to see proof in this case of certain car expenses. The bank

[1] Publication 583, *Recordkeeping for a Small Business* (1988). For more information, *The Guide to Record Retention Requirements* (Washington, D.C.: National Archives and Record Service, GSA) is an annual publication that outlines specific retention requirements for many small-business records.

wanted $250 to reproduce the information. Since he did not want to pay this amount, he had to go to each of the companies in question to ask for a letter stating how much they received from him in 1989. This was a time-consuming process as some of the requests had to be in writing. Even after the letters were received, the IRS auditor was not very cooperative as some letters were not very clear as to dates and amounts. I spent more time at the audit and more time on paperwork, which meant that my fee was unnecessarily higher and the auditor had to spend more time on the case.

Tip: Audits always run smoothly when you are prepared with cancelled checks and documents. If the auditor asks, for example, to see proof of payment for car insurance and you immediately hand him the cancelled checks and invoice and this pattern is followed with other expenses, your audit will run smoothly and the auditor will probably be pleasant. Remember, the auditor has a job to do, chances are if you make his life difficult by being unorganized with confusing or incomplete records, he will not overlook certain items and your audit outcome will not be to your liking.

ANNE: This last section doesn't mean you *must* keep all records indefinitely. By six to ten years, you may dispose of *many* of your records with a high degree of certainty that they will not be needed. There is no absolute rule—except that your relative's rule of one year is what I call "inaccurate." So when in doubt, save your records. Let's turn our attention to the accounting dilemma.

The remainder of this chapter consists of the workshop that Anne ran for Jen.

THE ACCOUNTING DILEMMA

Too many owners of small businesses put the accounting process as a low-priority item. They lack knowledge of it and thus try to avoid it. The truth is that, in our opinion, accounting is nothing more than a common-sense approach to monitoring the direction of your business as well as to making course corrections. So often my clients ask me these questions:

1. How come I earned $15,000 and have only $250 left in the checkbook?
2. How come my sales are up but my profits are down?
3. Where can I cut expenses?
4. Why can't I meet my tax obligations late?
5. What's wrong with my billing system?
6. Where do I really stand in my business?

Learning the Lingo

Part of small business owners' difficulty in understanding what's going on is the language of accounting, which bothers so many people. So before looking at recordkeeping procedures (putting the puzzle together), let's first go over some of the pieces of the puzzle. In other words, let's get to know the language before trying to hold a conversation. At the beginning don't try to put the pieces together. We will do this together, later.

Piece of the Puzzle	Definition	Example(s)
1. Assets	Things of value owned by a business.	Cash, accounts receivable (we hope we're able to receive), supplies, equipment, building, land.
2. Liabilities	What the business owes creditors.	Accounts payable (we hope we're able to pay).
3. Owner's Investment (also sometimes called "owner equity" or "capital")	Difference between assets and liabilities or what the owner has invested in the business (what the business is worth).	Assets $100 Minus Liabilities − 25 Equals owner's equity (capital) $75
4. Accounting Equation	Assets = Liabilities + Owner Equity	Assets = Liabilities + Owner Equity A = L + OE $100 = $25 + $75
5. Revenue	Cash and/or accounts receivable (assets) that come into a business from the sale of goods and services (inward flow of assets).	Sale of merchandise $500 down + 2,000 financed Total revenue $2,500
6. Expense	Day-to-day expenditures in running your business—outward flow of assets.	*Paid heat bill.* Expense is up. Cash, an asset, is down.
7. Account	An accounting device used to record and summarize increases and decreases in an Asset, Liability, Equity, Revenue or Expense item. Each particular item within the above classifications is tracked separately. Accounts are assigned numbers according to classification. For example, all assets begin with the Number 1, Liabilities 2 and so on.	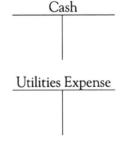

| --- | --- | --- |
8. Chart of Accounts	A list of all account titles within each classification (Asset, Liability, Equity, Revenue, Expense) tailor made for your particular business. (When I meet with a client to help set up a bookkeeping system, one of the first things I do is to construct a Chart of Accounts with my client. By creating a list of day-to-day expenditures and major purchases, an initial chart of accounts suited just for that particular business is developed.)	Acct. # Assets 110 Cash 112 Accounts Receivable 115 Equipment 　　　 Liabilities 210 Accounts Payable 220 Salaries Payable 　　　 Equity 310 J. Elmo, Capital 　　　 Revenue 410 Studio Fees 　　　 Expenses 610 Rent Expense 620 Utilities Expense 630 Advertising Expense
9. Journal	A book for recording business transactions in chronological order. (Think of it as a diary.)	See Figure 2-1, page 23.
10. Ledger	A book for accumulating information about business transactions. The ledger contains all the individual accounts of the business. The transfer of information from the journal to the ledger is called "posting."	Assets, liabilities, owner equity, revenue, and expense. All found in ledger. One per page. See Figure 2-2, page 23.
11. Rules of Debit and Credit	A set of *arbitrary* rules telling you which side to place the information in the journals and ledger. See Figure 2-3, page 23. Notice that the debit is defined as the left side of any account, while credit is defined as the right-hand side. Don't think of debit or credit as something good or bad. Think of debits or credits as rules, though quite arbitrary, allowing us to *accumulate* information so we can eventually prepare our financial reports. In the next section, we will "play the game," and the rules will make more sense as the pieces of the puzzle come together.	John buys a desk for $100 cash.

Piece of the Puzzle	Definition	Example(s)

Analysis

a. By buying a desk—an asset—your assets "go up" (⌃).

b. By giving up cash—another asset—your assets "go down" (⌄).

In terms of the rules, the desk, an asset, is a debit, so put information on the left.

Desk	
Debit	Credit
100	

And cash, an asset, goes down, so you "credit" cash, that is, put information on the right.

Cash	
Debit	Credit
	100

12. Trial Balance

A list of all the accounts in the ledger with their most current balance used to prove the accuracy of recording business transactions. Don't worry about the debit and credit. We will do an entire case coming up. For now, just get the idea that the trial balance helps build the financial reports in the two entries coming up.

Jen Elmo
Music Studio
Trial Balance
September 30, 19xx

	Debit	Credit
Cash	$21,800	
Accounts receivable	1,000	
Equipment	1,200	
Salaries payable		$ 200
J. Elmo Capital		20,000
Studio fees		6,000
Salary expense	1,200	
Rent	800	
Heat expense	200	
	$26,200	$26,200

13. Income Statement

A financial report that compares revenues earned versus expenses incurred over a given period. We are looking at the inward flow minus the business's outward flow.

See page 28.

Piece of the Puzzle	Definition	Example(s)

13. Income Statement (*cont.*)

Jen Elmo
Music Studio
Income Statement
For Month Ended
September 30, 19xx

Revenue		
Studio fees		$6,000
Less Expenses		
Salary	$1,200	
Rent	800	
Heat	20	
Total expenses		2,200
Net income		$3,800

14. Balance Sheet

The financial report, as of a specific date, that lists the assets, liabilities, and owner equity of a company. The assets show what the business *owns*; the liabilities show what it *owes*. The difference between the assets and liabilities remains to the owner.

$$A = L + C$$
$$A - L = C$$

Jen Elmo
Music Studio
Balance Sheet
September 30, 19xx

Assets		*Liabilities*	
Cash	$21,800		
Accounts receivable	1,000	Salary payable	$ 200
Equipment	1,200	*Owner Equity*	
		J. Elmo	
		capital	
	____	9/30/xx	23,800
		Total liabilities	
		and owner's	
Total Assets	$24,000	equity	$24,000

Assets – Liabilities = Owner Equity
$24,000 – 200 = $23,800

DATE		ACCOUNT TITLES AND EXPLANATION	PR	DEBIT	CREDIT

Figure 2-1: General Journal

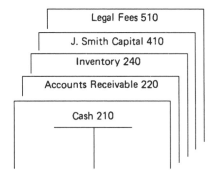

Figure 2-2: Ledger

Assets	=	Liabilities	+	Owner Equity	+	Revenue	−	Expenses	
Dr.	Cr.	Dr.	Cr.	Dr.	Cr.	Dr.	Cr.	Dr.	Cr.
+	−	−	+	−	+	−	+	+	−
The + side of any account is the balance side.									

Figure 2-3: Rules of Debit and Credit

A Case: Russell Smith

Now before we look at a case study of Russell Smith, let's try to visualize what we are doing. We are going to put together the seven steps shown in Figure 2-4 by looking at Russell Smith, attorney-at-law. Russell is opening up a law office to be operational in September.

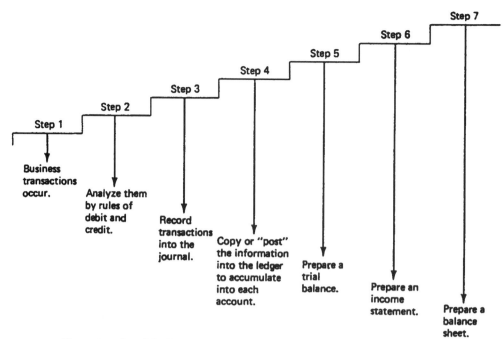

Figure 2-4: Simplified Steps of the Accounting Cycle

STEPS 1 AND 2 *Business transactions occur and are analyzed by the rules of debits and credits.* (These rules are reproduced in Figure 2-5 for your convenience.) Figure 2-6 is a chronological summary of transactions for Russell—but not a journal, as defined for accounting purposes. For each transaction that Russell completes, we have listed the date, an explanation, the accounts affected, the relevant accounting category, and finally how the debit-credit rules apply. Remember: All accounting transactions involve the use of at least two accounts. Your first task it to ask yourself *what* accounts are affected and then ask *how* they are affected. For example, on August 28, when Russell invested $10,000 in the business, the analysis shows which accounts are affected (these titles come from the ledger book or chart of accounts) and whether they are going up or down. After you know which accounts are affected you must determine whether the accounts are increasing or decreasing, you can then apply the rules of debits and credits. For the August 28 transaction, the two accounts affected are cash and R. Smith, capital you can see that an *increase* to cash (↑), which is an asset, is a debit (which says put this information on the left side). The owner's rights (R. Smith Capital) in the business are also going up (↓), and the rule says an increase in owner equity is a credit, so put it on the right side.

Assets	=	Liabilities	+	Owner Equity	+	Legal Fees Revenue	−	Expenses
Dr. | Cr.		Dr. | Cr.		Dr. | Cr.		Dr. | Cr.		Dr. | Cr.
+ | −		− | +		− | +		− | +		+ | −

The + side of any account is the balance side.

Figure 2-5: Rules of Debit and Credit

	DATE	EXPLANATION	ACCOUNTS AFFECTED	CATEGORY	↑↓	RULE
A.	August 28	Russel invested $10,000 into the business	Cash R. Smith, capital	Asset Owner equity	↑ ↑	Dr. Cr.
B.	August 29	Bought equipment, $500. Paid cash.	Equipment Cash	Asset Asset	↑ ↓	Dr. Cr.
C.	August 30	Bought equipment on account, $100	Equipment Accounts payable	Asset Liability	↑ ↑	Dr. Cr.
D.	Month of September	Legal services for cash, $2,000	Cash Legal fees	Asset Revenue	↑ ↑	Dr. Cr.
E.	Month of September	Legal services on credit, $1,000	Accounts receivable Legal fees	Asset Revenue	↑ ↑	Dr. Cr.
F.	Month of September	Received $500 from previously earned revenues	Cash Accounts receivable	Asset Asset	↑ ↓	Dr. Cr.
G.	Month of September	Paid $600 of salaries	Salaries expense Cash	Expense Asset	↑ ↓	Dr. Cr.
H.	Month of September	Paid rent expense, $400	Rent expense Cash	Expense Asset	↑ ↓	Dr. Cr.
I.	Month of September	Paid supplies expense, $100	Supplies expense Cash	Expense Asset	↑ ↓	Dr. Cr.

Figure 2-6: Steps 1 and 2—Analysis of Transactions for Russell Smith Case

CASH		R. Smith Capital	
Dr.	Cr.	Dr.	Cr.
+	−	−	+
10,000			10,000

Some readers might be wondering how both categories can go up or how the books will "balance" unless one category goes down to offset the one that goes up. When we get to step 5, you'll note that the rules work out beautifully. You'll see that, for each individual transaction, the total of all the debits will equal the total of all the credits, depending on where the debit or credit falls on the trial balance in step 5. The key is choosing the proper accounts and determining how they are affected ↑↓. Any transaction can have an increase and a decrease, two increases or two decreases.

STEPS 3 AND 4 *Journalize and post information to the ledger.* Once the analysis of the transactions is done, the information is placed into a journal (the book of original entry) and then posted (or copied) to the ledger (the book of final entry). See Figure 2-7. The August 28 transaction and analysis are repeated here so you can follow the process.

Analyze the transaction

DATE	EXPLANATION	ACCOUNTS AFFECTED	CATEGORY	↓↑	RULE
August 28	Russel invested $10,000 into the business	Cash R. Smith, capital	Asset Owner equity	↓ ↓	Dr. Cr.

Journalize the transaction

Russell Smith, Attorney-at-Law
General Journal

Date		PR	Debit	Credit
19XX				
Aug. 28	Cash	110	10,000	
	R. Smith, capital	510		10,000

Post the transaction

CASH		110		R. Smith, capital		510
DR	CR			DR	CR	
Aug 28 10,000					Aug 28 10,000	

Figure 2-7: The Bookkeeping Process

STEPS 5, 6, AND 7 *Preparing the trial balance, income statement and balance sheet.* Once the ledger is up-to-date from the journal, the next step—step 5—is to balance each title in the ledger, that is, summarize the left side and right side. For example, the cash account debit side is $12,500, and the credit side is $1,600. The difference between the two sides is a $10,900 debit, since the left side is larger.

	CASH		
(A)	10,000	(B)	500
(D)	2,000	(G)	600
(F)	500	(H)	400
	12,500	(I)	100
Bal.	10,900		1,600

After each title (Cash, Accounts Payable, Salary Expense, and so on) is summarized, a list of the ledger is made, which is called the *trial balance* (Figure 2-8). All the titles are listed down the left side, next to their

Step 3

Russell Smith, Attorney-at-Law
General Journal

Date		PR	Debit	Credit
19XX				
A. Aug. 28	Cash	110*	10,000	
	R. Smith Capital	510		10,000
B. 29	Equipment	171	500	
	Cash	110		500
C. 30	Equipment	171	100	
	Accounts Payable	310		100
D. Sept. 30	Cash	110	2,000	
	Legal Fees	710		2,000
E. 30	Accounts Receivable	141	1,000	
	Legal Fees	710		1,000
F. 30	Cash	110	500	
	Accounts Receivable	141		500
G. 30	Salaries Expense	910	600	
	Cash	110		600
H. 30	Rent Expense	960	400	
	Cash	110		400
I. 30	Supplies Expense	980	100	
	Cash	110		100

→ Posted to Ledger

Cash
110

(A) 10,000	500 (B)
(D) 2,000	600 (G)
(F) 500	400 (H)
12,500	100 (I)
10,900	1,600

Accounts Payable
310

	100 (C)

Salary Expense
910

(G) 600	

Accounts Receivable
141

(E) 1,000	500 (F)
500	

R. Smith Investment
510

	10,000 (A)

Rent Expense
960

(H) 400	

Equipment
171

(B) 500	
(C) 100	
600	

Legal Fees
710

	2,000 (D)
	1,000 (E)
	3,000

Supplies Expense
980

(I) 100	

Note how debits are put on left and credits on right. The hardest part was to analyze the transactions by debit and credit in Steps 1 & 2. Steps 3 & 4 will contain the same information as Steps 1 & 2 but in a different form.

*The "110" indicates that the information on this line has been transferred to Account No. 110 in the ledger.

Figure 2-8: Steps 3 and 4—Journalizing and Posting

corresponding debits and credits. The total of all the debits *should* equal the total of all the credits, in this case at $13,100. If they are not equal and if your addition is correct, your application of the debit-credit rules was probably wrong. You'd have to go back and check your analysis in steps 1 and 2. (This is the balancing-out we promised in those first steps.)

In step 6, all revenues and expenses from the trial balance are used to prepare the income statement for Russell. This report compares Russell's inward flows to his outward flows. It answers the question: What is the net income for the month? The answer is $1,900. Note that this statement lists only income or expense titles, that is, titles that involve the receiving or paying out of cash. It does not account for titles that are assets, liabilities, or equity. Observe the arrows in Figure 2-9.

The balance sheet, prepared in step 6, represents what the income statement does not—a listing of assets, liabilities, and the latest figure for the owner's capital. It shows how the business stands at the end of a given

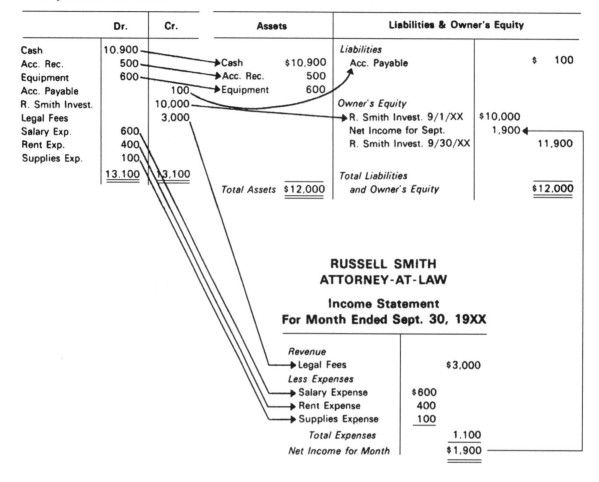

RUSSELL SMITH
ATTORNEY-AT-LAW

Trial Balance
September 30, 19XX

	Dr.	Cr.
Cash	10.900	
Acc. Rec.	500	
Equipment	600	
Acc. Payable		100
R. Smith Invest.		10,000
Legal Fees		3,000
Salary Exp.	600	
Rent Exp.	400	
Supplies Exp.	100	
	13.100	13,100

RUSSELL SMITH
ATTORNEY-AT-LAW

Balance Sheet
September 30, 19XX

Assets		Liabilities & Owner's Equity	
		Liabilities	
Cash	$10,900	Acc. Payable	$ 100
Acc. Rec.	500		
Equipment	600		
		Owner's Equity	
		R. Smith Invest. 9/1/XX	$10,000
		Net Income for Sept.	1,900
		R. Smith Invest. 9/30/XX	11,900
		Total Liabilities	
Total Assets	$12,000	*and Owner's Equity*	$12.000

RUSSELL SMITH
ATTORNEY-AT-LAW

Income Statement
For Month Ended Sept. 30, 19XX

Revenue		
Legal Fees		$3,000
Less Expenses		
Salary Expense	$600	
Rent Expense	400	
Supplies Expense	100	
Total Expenses		1.100
Net Income for Month		$1,900

Figure 2-9: Steps 5, 6 and 7—Trial Balance, Income Statement and Balance Sheet

period, September in this case. Note that the $1,900 of net income for September is added to Smith's investment of $10,000 to give him his new figure of $11,900.

Don't try to memorize all these forms. The purpose of showing them is to acquaint you with how the two financial reports are built. Keep in mind that this chapter is only an overview. The Russell Smith case is merely an attempt to show you the basic relationships of the puzzle.

A SINGLE-ENTRY OR DOUBLE ENTRY BOOKKEEPING SYSTEM?

JEN: Anne, one question: What is the difference between single-entry and double-entry bookkeeping systems? My relatives tell me there is no real difference.

ANNE: What we have been talking about is a double-entry system. The concept of debits and credits has allowed us to build our financial reports by putting information into the ledger by "left" sides and "right" sides. Remember, we prepared the trial balance, which helped to prove our accuracy. A single-entry system doesn't have this luxury. As a matter of fact, with the background material we've given you, here is a small excerpt from the business government publication 583: *Recordkeeping for Small Business*, 1979. The new version of *Recordkeeping for Small Business* no longer contains this information.

Another recordkeeping option open to the businessperson is the decision whether to use single- or double-entry bookkeeping.

The single-entry system of bookkeeping is the simplest bookkeeping system to maintain; however, it may not be satisfactory for every taxpayer. Some taxpayers may find that the double-entry system is more advantageous because it has built-in checks and balances which assure accuracy and control.

Single-entry bookkeeping is a partially complete system of accounts in that it usually concentrates only on the profit and loss statement and not the balance sheet. While this system has its limitations, it may be used effectively by one starting out in a small business. A single-entry system can be a relatively simple one which records the flow of income and expense. Through the use of a daily summary of cash receipts, a monthly summary of receipts, and a monthly disbursements journal, this system can be used to record income and expenses adequately for tax purposes.

Double-entry bookkeeping makes use of journals and ledgers. Transactions are entered first in a journal. Then summary totals are posted to ledger accounts (generally monthly) to show income, expenses, assets, liabilities, and net worth. Income and expense accounts are closed at the end of each accounting period, whereas asset, liability, and net worth accounts are kept open and maintained on a permanent basis.

A major feature of the double-entry system is that it is self-balancing. Since all business transactions consist of an exchange of one thing for another, double-entry bookkeeping is used to show this twofold effect by recording every transaction as a debit entry in one account and as a credit entry in another. Thus, under this system, after the journal entries are posted to the ledger accounts, the total of the amounts entered as debits must equal the total of the amounts entered as credits. If the accounts do not balance it is evident that an error has been made and steps can be taken to bring the accounts into balance. At the end of each accounting period, after the accounts are in balance, financial statements may be prepared. These statements normally consist of the profit and loss statement and the balance sheet. The profit and loss statement reflects current operations for the year, and the balance sheet shows the financial position of the business in terms of assets, liabilities, and net worth at an exact point in time.

Keep in mind that each business has its own unique "pieces of the puzzle." Chapter 3 will continue to look at specific recordkeeping tips to help keep the score of your business. You can't be an expert in this material overnight: the more you work with it, the more comfortable you will feel. It's like learning to type. Remember how you never thought you could learn to do it without looking at the keyboard? So let's continue down the road, looking at specific recordkeeping problems in your business.

This is a good time to talk a little bit about computers and computerized bookkeeping. The fact that you own a computer or are planning to purchase a computer in and of itself will not solve your recordkeeping problems. I have worked with many software packages ranging in price from $150 to $2000 and they all have one thing in common, they need someone who has a working understanding of bookkeeping procedures and terms to properly enter the information. As a matter of fact some software packages now come with a chapter or two devoted strictly to explaining bookkeeping basics (although not as well as we do). Obviously, the message has passed through to the developers that no matter how good or easy or comprehensive the software is, the person entering the information is the key to success.

Let me tell about a few situations I have encountered over the years. I have one client who started a business with a friend that absolutely took off in its first year of operation. I did not pick up the account until its third year of operation. This is what I found. One of the first things they did was to buy a computer. However, they were so busy taking care of their day-to-day operations they didn't have time to investigate software. Then they thought they would hire someone to investigate and recommend a couple of good packages for accounting and word processing. Another expenditure was made and the software was loaded onto the computer. Since they had no knowledge of bookkeeping, that software went untouched. At least they were able to get through the word processing manuals and begin to use the computer for those clerical functions. But what happened over that two-year period in the computer industry was incredible. For one thing the computer they purchased, although a good machine was now considered slow. To make matters worse the prices went down considerably. They could have purchased the same machine for 40 percent less or a faster version with more memory for the same money. They couldn't change the fact that they had very little time, but they could have changed their approach to the purchase, which in the long run would have been more cost effective. You wouldn't buy a car before you had your license or before you took driving lessons. Learn, investigate, then buy, in the long run it will save you money and it will save that very precious commodity for a business owner, time. Appendix 5 contains a special section, How To Get Started With A Small Business Computer.

SUMMARY OF KEY POINTS

1. Bookkeeping is the recording process of accounting. Other accounting functions include analyzing, classifying, sorting, reporting, and interpreting.

2. Don't throw out records until you are sure they are no longer

needed—better to put them down in the basement. When in doubt, keep them.

3. Steps of the accounting cycle include:
   - the business transaction itself;
   - its analysis by rules of debit and credit;
   - journalizing;
   - posting to the ledger;
   - preparing a trial balance;
   - preparing an income statement; and
   - preparing a balance sheet.

4. Double-entry is a self-balancing system based on the income statement and balance sheet. Single-entry is not self-balancing and is slanted toward the income statement. Double-entry provides many more "checks and balances."

		True	False	
1.	Bookkeeping is the interpreting part of accounting.	____	____	**CHECK YOUR PULSE**
2.	Recordkeeping systems need only to be accurate.	____	____	
3.	A recordkeeping system can be simple to use as long as it provides reliable, accurate information on a timely basis.	____	____	
4.	Some business records might have to be retained indefinitely.	____	____	
5.	Assets may include cash, accounts payable, supplies, buildings, and land.	____	____	
6.	The difference between assets and liabilities is owner equity.	____	____	
7.	Revenues represent an inward flow of cash and/or accounts receivable.	____	____	
8.	Information is posted from the journal to the ledger.	____	____	
9.	A trial balance is prepared directly from the journal.	____	____	
10.	An increase in an expense is a debit.	____	____	
11.	Revenues and assets go on the income statement.	____	____	
12.	The trial balance is a list of the ledger.	____	____	
13.	The financial report prepared as of a specific date is called a balance sheet.	____	____	
14.	An increase in supplies is a credit.	____	____	
15.	Posting to the ledger is done before journalizing.	____	____	
16.	On the trial balance, cash could have both a debit and credit balance.	____	____	
17.	Debits and credits are used strictly in single-entry bookkeeping.	____	____	
18.	In the single-entry system the income statement is most important.	____	____	
19.	A double-entry system is self-balancing.	____	____	
20.	The balance sheet shows the financial position of a firm.	____	____	

1. False	11. False
2. False	12. True
3. True	13. True
4. True	14. False
5. False	15. False
6. True	16. False
7. True	17. False
8. True	18. True
9. False	19. True
10. True	20. True

MATCHING

Column A

_____ 1. Rules of debit and credit
_____ 2. Single-entry
_____ 3. Recording system

_____ 4. Bookkeeping
_____ 5. A – L=
_____ 6. Retention of records
_____ 7. Trial balance
_____ 8. In asset
_____ 9. Double-entry
_____ 10. Asset
_____ 11. in liability
_____ 12. Ledger

_____ 13. Accumulates information
_____ 14. Posting
_____ 15. Accounting equation
_____ 16. Accounts payable
_____ 17. Income statement
_____ 18. Book of original entry
_____ 19. Balance sheet
_____ 20. Journal

Column B

A. Chronological order
B. Cash, accounts receivable
C. Concentrates on income statement
D. A=L +OE
E. As of a particular date
F. Book of final entry
G. Transferring
H. Credit
I. Recording part of accounting
J. Debit
K. Owner Equity
L. Minimum of six years; longer with some
M. Liability
N. Arbitrary
0. Ledger
P. Simple, accurate, timely
Q. Period of time
R. Journal
S. List of the ledger
T. Self-balancing

Answers

1.	N	11.	H
2.	C	12.	F
3.	P	13.	0
4.	I	14.	G
5.	K	15.	D
6.	L	16.	M
7.	S	17.	Q
8.	J	18.	R
9.	T	19.	E
10.	B	20.	A

3

THE ACCOUNTING PUZZLE: ADDING NEW PIECES

1. Define Merchandising Companies.
2. Define Cost of Goods Sold.
3. Examine an Income Statement for a merchandising business.
4. Define petty cash and change fund.
5. Prepare a petty cash voucher.
6. Prepare a daily summary of sales and cash receipts.
7. Identify and list the possible causes of cash "short" or "over."
8. Define:
   - accounts payable
   - accounts payable subsidiary ledger
   - accounts receivable
   - accounts receivable subsidiary ledger
   - cash payments, expense, and purchase journal
   - cash payments journal
   - cash receipts journal
   - posting
   - purchases journal
   - sales journal
   - sales and cash receipts journal
   - special journals
9. Journalize as well as explain a sales and cash receipts journal.
10. Explain the importance of giving sales discounts.
11. Journalize as well as explain cash payments, purchases, and expense journals.
12. Explain how to post special journals.

13. Explain the importance of taking purchase discounts.
14. Prepare a bank reconciliation.
15. Define:
    - checks outstanding
    - deposits in transit
    - NSF
16. Compare and contrast the cash receipts journal and the cash payments journal in the bank reconciliation process.
17. List the steps in the bank reconciliation process.
18. Define depreciation and accumulated depreciation.
19. Record depreciation of an asset and complete a depreciation record.

JEN: I have another question. What if I decide to sell musical instruments in my studio as well as give lessons? Will that cause a problem?

ANNE: It won't cause a problem, but it will open the door to a whole new section of our Income Statement because now you must account for merchandise for resale.

Did you notice the gap in the numbering system in our chart of accounts on page 20?

JEN: Yes, I did notice Revenue Accounts were given the #4 and then expenses jumped to the #6. I didn't think much of it.

ANNE: Nothing in accounting is random: At that point we were discussing service businesses and there was no need to include information that relates only to merchandising businesses. The #5 is assigned to all Cost of Goods Sold Accounts which are part of the Income Statement of Merchandising Business.

    #1 Assets
    #2 Liabilities
    #3 Equity
    #4 Revenue
    #5 Cost of Goods Sold
    #6 Expenses

I'm starting to toss terms around so we better begin the explanation of this new area right from the beginning.

Merchandise Companies: Merchandise is the goods brought into a store by a business for resale to its customers. Merchandise companies may be either wholesalers or retailers. For the service companies we have been talking about, net income equals revenue from services minus operating expenses. For a merchandising company much more is involved in figuring net income. Let's compare income statements for a service company and a merchandising company.

Service Company
(1) Revenue from Services
(2) – Operating Expenses
(3) = Net Income

Merchandise Company
(1) Gross Sales
(2) – Sales Returns & Allowances
(3) – Sales Discounts
(4) = Net Sales

Service Company	Merchandise Company
	(5) – Cost of Goods Sold
	(6) = Gross Profit
	(7) – Operating Expenses
	(8) = Net Income

ANNE: In your case, Jen, where you are primarily a service business, which also plans to sell musical instruments, your financial statement will resemble those of a merchandising business. Most of your income may come from giving music lessons, a service, but once you start selling musical instruments (merchandise), we must change the format of your income statement. As you can see there's a lot more going on here than we had looked at in a service company. To begin with let's define some of the new accounts and concepts we will be dealing with for a merchandising company. We'll take them one by one, as numbered in the chart on page 36. As you can see from our chart, cost of goods sold is subtracted from Net Sales to arrive at Gross Profit. But arriving at cost of goods sold involves a process in and of itself.

JEN: This is getting very complicated. Maybe I should just stick to giving music lessons.

ANNE: Never give up the opportunity to make more money. If you think you will be able to sell musical instruments you must pursue that avenue. Along with the instruments come musical cases and mouth pieces and cleaning apparatus and many other products. These extra sales will provide you with more profits. Remember, I just want you to be aware of what's going on in your business by having you become familiar with the accounting process. Let's proceed with Cost of Goods Sold, and don't worry, we're not preparing you to become an accountant; only to have a working understanding of what the accountant will be doing.

Cost of Goods Sold: (Formula)

    (1)   Beginning Inventory January 1
    (2) + Purchases
    (3) – Purchase Returns and Allowances
    (4) – Purchase Discounts
    (5) = Goods Available for Sale
    (6) – Ending Inventory December 31
    (7) = Cost of Goods Sold

Let's define these Costs of Goods Sold items as they are numbered in the chart.

(1) Beginning Inventory—Cost of inventory in the store that was for sale to customers at the beginning of the year.

(2) Purchases—Cost of additional merchandise brought into the store for resale to customers during the year.

(3) Purchase Returns and Allowances—Cost of merchandise returned to the store due to damage, defects, errors and so on.

(4) Purchase Discounts—Savings received by the buyer for paying for merchandise before a certain date.

(5) Goods Available for Sale—Sum of beginning inventory plus net purchases.

(6) Ending Inventory December 31—The cost of inventory remaining in the store to be sold on the last day of the year.

(7) Cost of Goods Sold—Beginning inventory plus net purchases less ending inventory.

The following are examples of Income Statements for a Service Business and a Merchandising Business.

Income Statements

Service Business			Merchandising Business			
Revenue:			Revenue:			
Service Fees		50,000	Sales			100,000
			Less: Sales Returns		2,000	
Operating Expenses:			Sales Discounts		1,000	3,000
Rent Expense	12,000		Net Sales			97,000
Wages Expense	15,000		Cost of Goods Sold:			
Advertising Expenses	1,000		Beginning Inventory		15,000	
Utilities Expenses	3,000		Purchases	30,000		
Payroll Tax Expenses	1,000		Less: Purchase Returns	2,000		
Depreciation	1,000		Net Purchases		28,000	
Total Operating Expenses		33,000	Goods Available for Sale		43,000	
Net Profit		17,000	Less: Ending Inventory		18,000	
			Cost of Goods Sold			25,000
			Gross Profit			72,000
			Operating Expenses:			
			Rent		12,000	
			Wages		20,000	
			Advertising		2,000	
			Office		3,000	
			Depreciation		3,000	
			Utilities		2,000	
			Payroll Taxes		2,000	
			Total Operating Expense			44,000
			Net Profit			28,000

ANNE: Here is my file on the George Marcus Company, a small convenience retail store. I'm also giving you some samples of the kinds of records he keeps.

JEN: Great! This'll save me lots of time. I'll use his set-up.

ANNE: Okay, but don't cast these records in *concrete*. The Marcus Company records may be great for them but could be a "disaster" for you. Each company has unique needs and time constraints. Think of a business as a person having a certain "frame" and of the recordkeeping system as "tailored" to fit the frame. The recordkeeping system developed provides information that is (1) simple to use, (2) easy to understand, (3) reliable, (4) accurate, (5) consistent, and (6) designed to provide information on a timely basis. Remember, we don't want to recreate the wheel, we just want to "smooth it."

George came to me and expressed his concern about "what records should be kept." With all the advice he was getting from family and friends, he wasn't really sure which way to go. So George and I talked about the needs of the business as well as about George's specific personal concerns. From this I developed, with George, a recordkeeping system that would best fit his "framework" of needs.

Concern #1: What Sort of Records Are Good for My Business?

ANNE: George needed a fixed amount of change for the cash register. He had many small items to pay for and wanted to minimize checkwriting. So we set up a *petty cash and change fund*. This fund let George set aside so much to keep a certain amount of change in the cash register, as well as a sum of money available to pay for "small" items. We decided that the fund should have a total of $30. Petty cash would be $18, and the change would be $12. Each time money is needed for a small item (that is, whenever the amount is so small that writing a check is not necessary), a petty cash voucher slip is filled out (Figure 3-1). This slip is kept in the petty cash fund. The total of the petty cash slips plus the cash not spent should equal the original amount of petty cash that was first established. At some

Concern #2: The Petty Cash Fund

```
Petty Cash Voucher No. 1

   Date: _____      Amount: _____

   Paid To: _____

   For: _____
                                Approved By: _____

              Payment Received By: _____

     Debit Account No.: _____
```

Figure 3-1: Petty Cash Voucher

point the slips, which show what the money was spent for, are summarized and updated in the ledger account of Marcus Company. The slips are stamped as processed, receipts are attached if possible, and the slips are removed from the fund. A new check, payable to the petty cash fund (run by a petty cash custodian), is then cashed and placed in the fund. The end result is the ledger now reflects the expenses that used up some of the petty cash, and the fund is replenished. If at some time the fund is not sufficient, the standard amount can be raised to a higher level. Keep in mind in this situation that the Marcus Company set aside $30 for the petty cash and change fund. Many businesses set up two distinct funds. But the end result is the same.

Concern #3: The Daily Summary Form

JEN: How would I set up a system of recording a daily summary of sales and cash receipts to make sure my cash is not short?

ANNE: In George's business they have cash as well as charge sales. There is a 5 percent sales tax on sales. The following is a *daily summary form*, as well as the actual figures, for December 2, 19xx. *Caution!* I told George that each day he should make a deposit at the bank as soon as possible and keep receipts of the deposit slips. Let's go over this daily summary form (Figure 3-2). First let's see how much George took in that day.

- *Line 1:* Took in $50 from cash sales; this amount is taken from cash register tape.
- *Line 2:* Collected $16.45 from past sales to customers on account.
- *Line 3:* $50 of new sales x 0.05 = $2.50. Note that sales tax is not taken on line 2, since it was recorded at time of the sale. You'll see how this is done when we get to the last three lines of the summary.
- *Line 4:* On December 2, Marcus Company took in $68.95 that had to be accounted for ($50.00 + 16.45 + 2.50).

The next step is to "prove" the $68.95. That is, we have to determine whether that total accurately reflects how much was taken in.

- *Line 5:* At the end of the day, there was $88.95 in the cash register, which *included* any of the petty cash fund not spent.
- *Line 6:* There was $10 worth of petty cash slips, which indicates the amount spent from petty cash.
- *Line 7:* The cash on hand, $88.95, plus the $10 worth of slips represents $98.95, or the amount we have *before* subtracting the total of the petty cash and change fund of $30.
- *Line 8:* The total amount $98.95 minus the total of petty cash and change fund (which is a fixed amount), $30.

Figure 3-2:[1]

[1] Robert C. Ragan, *Financial Recordkeeping for Small Stores*, Publication 583 (Washington, D.C.: Small Business Administration, 1976). This publication is no longer in print.

George Marcus Company:
Daily Summary of Sales
and Cash Receipts

DATE: 12/2/xx

1.	Cash sales	$50.00
2.	Collections from past sales	16.45
3.	Sales tax	2.50
4.	Total cash receipts to be accounted for	$68.95

Verification of Cash on Hand
(which includes petty cash not spent)
Register

5.	Coins	$15.25		
	Dollars	61.00		
	Checks	12.70		
	Total amount in register			$88.95
6.	Petty cash vouchers			10.00
7.	Total amount to be accounted for			98.95
8.	Minus: (1) Petty cash vouchers		$10	
	(2) Petty cash and change fund		20	30.00
9.	Total cash receipts to be accounted for			68.95
	Total sales breakdown			
10.	Cash sales	$50		
11.	Charge sales	28*		
12.	Total Sales			$78.00

*Sales tax is $1.40 ($28.00 × 0.05).
(charge sales 28.00 + sales tax 1.40 = 29.40, the total amount due from customers)

- *Line 9:* By step 8 we have proven that $68.95 was in fact accurate. If the figure was less, we would have had a cash shortage. If the figure was high, we would have a cash overage.

JEN: What are some of the reasons for having too much or too little cash?

ANNE: Well, if the total amount to be deposited is *more* than the total receipts recorded for the day, the overage could be caused by:

- neglecting to record or ring up a transaction;
- recording or ringing up a transaction for too small an amount; or
- giving a customer too little change.

If the amount to be deposited is less than the total receipts recorded for the day, the shortage could be caused by:

- recording or ringing up too large an amount for a transaction;
- giving a customer too much change; or
- taking money from the cash register or till without recording it.

JEN: But cash sales aren't the only sales they make, are they? What about charged purchases?

ANNE: The summary form shows these transactions, too:

- *Lines 10, 11, 12:* This section keeps track of total sales. Note in Line 11 the charge sale of $28 is not found anywhere else on the form. This figure is needed when we put sales information into the journal.

Concern #4: Keeping Journals

JEN: I don't want one general journal to record information, yet I don't want to keep separate journals for sales, cash receipts, purchases, expenses, as well as cash payments.

ANNE: Jen, before I show you what we developed for George, let me first go over some accounting terms. Some will be new, but much of it will be review. After this "primer," the books that I set up for George will then have more meaning to you.

The rest of this section consists of the workshop Anne gave Jen on Marcus's journalizing system.

ACCOUNTING TERMS FOR THE NONACCOUNTANT

Readers: Note that there is another more detailed glossary of terms at the end of this book. For enhancement of your present understanding, the following terms are important. Other terms can be looked up in the Glossary as you need them.

Accounts payable   A liability representing the amount owed to creditors.

Accounts payable subsidiary ledger   Not found in a journal or general ledger, a book or file that contains in alphabetical order the *individual* creditors and amounts owed them. This subsidiary ledger should be updated as often as possible to reflect current balances owed. It becomes important for a firm to take advantage of purchase discounts by paying within certain discount dates.

Accounts receivable   An asset representing the amounts that customers owe.

Accounts receivable Subsidiary ledger   Not found in a journal or general ledger, a book or file that contains in alphabetical order the *individual* records of amounts owed by various customers to a business. This subsidiary ledger should be updated as often as possible to reflect current balances.

A combination special journal that combines the features of the cash payments and purchase journal.	*Cash payments, expense, and purchase journal*
A special journal that records the outward flow of money.	*Cash payments journal*
A special journal that records only the receipt of cash.	*Cash receipts journal*
The book of original entry that records business transactions in terms of debits and credits.	*General journal*
Book of final entry that accumulates information from the journals and aids in preparing financial reports.	*General ledger*
Basically the process of transferring information from the journals to the ledger.	*Posting*
A special journal that records the purchase of merchandise or other items on account (buy now, pay later).	*Purchase journal*
A special journal recording only charge sales.	*Sales journal*
A combination special journal that combines the features of a sales journal and cash receipts journal into one. Instead of two books, we have one.	*Sales and cash receipts journal*
Books of original entry that record similar transactions. For example: 1. a cash receipts journal records all the money coming in; 2. a sales journal records only sales on account. These special journals fill much of the need for greater journals.	*Special journals*

THE SALES AND CASH RECEIPTS JOURNAL

The first special journal Anne designed for George is the sales and cash receipts journal (Figure 3-3). Remember that the headings in this special journal are not absolute; they are tailored to the needs of George's company. Keep in mind, as stated before, that nothing is cast in concrete. If changes are needed, always reserve the right to be flexible in responding to the recordkeeping process. For example, if the Marcus Company gave few sales discounts, there would be no need for the sales discount column. We could then put the information in the cash sales column. Now look at the explanation for each column in the journal in Figure 3-3.

What is very important is that the information in this journal accumulates basically in two places:

1. During the month, the Marcus Company wants to continually update the accounts receivable subsidiary ledger. (Remember, this subsidiary ledger is not in the general ledger; it is a separate book or file that lists what customers owe us, arranged in alphabetical order.) The continual update is quite important to Marcus in looking at their credit policy as well as in monitoring bad debts and "cash crisis" problems.

Figure 3-3

George Marcus Company:
Sales and Cash Receipts Journal

DATE	EXPLANATION	PR	ACCOUNTS RECEIVABLE		CASH SALES	CHARGE SALES	SALES TAX PAYABLE	PR	OTHER		SALES DISCOUNT	CASH DEPOSIT IN BANK
			Dr.	Cr.	Cr.	Cr.	Cr.		Dr.	Cr.	Dr.	Dr.
			A	B	C	D	E			F	G	H

A Records amounts that customers owe the company (sales tax would be added on: sale plus the tax is what the customer owes).

B Records amount customers are paying the company from previous sales on account, thus they owe less.

C Records inflow of cash sales.

D Records inflow of charge sales.

E Records owner's liability for sales tax owed to appropriate governmental agency.

F Records miscellaneous items that cause an increase in cash or sales. Examples include bank loans, cash overages, supplier refunds, interest income, exchanges, and the like.

G Records amount of price break offered to customers by paying bill within a specific period of time.

H Records inward flow of cash which is to be deposited in bank.

2. Since the information in this journal is accumulated in the general ledger at the end of the month, it contains debit and credit headings. These headings tell you which side to put the information into the specific ledger account. Keep in mind we still have, in the general ledger, an accounts receivable account; this controlling account summarizes the *total* amount customers owe us. At the *end of the month* the sum of the subsidiary ledger should equal the *one figure* in the controlling account. Also keep in mind that the controlling account doesn't tell us *who* owes us the money.

Now let's look at several transactions of the Marcus Company and then how they are recorded in the sales and cash receipts journal. First, let's look at the transactions and analyze them before we journalize.

Analysis of a Few Actual Transactions

Transaction #1

12/1/xx	Marcus Co. received a bank loan for $500 to be repaid in five years.
Analysis	Cash, which is an asset, is increasing. An increase in cash, by the rule of debit and credit, is a debit.
	Notes payable, which is a liability, is increasing. An increase in liability is a credit.

Transaction #2

12/2/xx	Recorded information from the daily summary form to the sales and cash receipts journal. (Refer to the Daily Summary Form we prepared on page 39 for amounts.)
Analysis	Cash, an asset, is increasing, and an increase in cash is a debit.
	Sales tax, a liability, is increasing. An increase in a liability is a credit.
	Cash sales, revenue, is increasing. An increase in revenue is a credit.
	Accounts receivable, an asset, is going up and down. This behavior results from customers buying more (⌂ to accounts receivable) as well as customers paying previous amounts (⌂ to accounts receivable). An increase is a debit, and a decrease is a credit.

Transaction #3

12/3/xx	Received $250 in rent income from space rented out to a food concession.
Analysis	Cash, an asset, is increasing. An increase in cash is a debit.
	Rental income, a source of other revenue, is increasing by a credit.

Journalizing the Transactions

Now let's see how these transactions are journalized in Figure 3-4 on p. 45.

COLUMN HEADINGS If George needed more specific information—such as for installment sales, tax-exempt sales, or even sales by department or category (food, drugs, and so on)—column headings could have been set up.

HOW IMPORTANT IS IT TO GIVE SALES DISCOUNTS? Why give a discount when you could get full price? Keep in mind that it might be well worth your while to get the money ten, twenty, or thirty days earlier even if it is less, because it can aid in your cash crises. Also, if competitors in your area give discounts, you must compete. The key is that you don't want your customers taking the discount *even* if they pay their bills late. (The truth is you might not have too much control over such customers if you want their business. We will talk more about this situation in the chapter on cash flows. For now the point is simply that the journal, which is recording the information, aids us in our decision making "down the road.")

POSTING At the end of the month the totals of all the columns are added up; this process, called "balancing" or "footing," is posted to the specific accounts in the ledger. Note the (√) on 12/2 in the PR column, which indicates that the accounts receivable ledger has been updated. The total for the "other" column is not posted since it is made up of miscellaneous items. The individual amounts are posted; the 210 means that the $500 has been posted to account 210 in the general ledger. If we assume that no other transactions occurred during the month of December except the three transactions we recorded in Figure 3-4, totals would be taken and these totals would be posted to the individual accounts in our ledger (Figure 3-5). Before you begin the posting process, always make sure your journal is in balance. This means you must have equality of Debits and Credits.

Debits		Credits	
Accounts Receivable	29.40	Accounts Receivable	16.45
Cash	818.95	Cash Sales	50.00
Total	848.35	Charge Sales	28.00
		Sales Tax Payable	3.90
		Other	750.00
		Total	848.35

WHAT'S DOWN THE ROAD Keep in mind once the information in the journal is accumulated in the ledger, we will then have the framework to prepare financial reports. If the information in the journal is inaccurate, you can be sure your financial reports will not give an accurate picture of the business.

Figure 3-4

George Marcus Company:
Sales and Cash Receipts Journal, Illustrated

DATE	EXPLANATION	PR	ACCOUNTS RECEIVABLE Dr.	ACCOUNTS RECEIVABLE Cr.	CASH SALES Cr.	CHARGE SALES Cr.	SALES TAX PAYABLE Cr.	PR	OTHER Dr.	OTHER Cr.	SALES DISCOUNT Dr.	CASH DEPOSIT IN BANK Dr.
19XX												
12/1	Notes Payable							210		500.00		500.00
12/2	Daily Summary	✓	29.40	16.45	50.00	28.00	1.40 2.50					68.95
12/3	Rental Income							430		250.00		250.00

Figure 3-5

George Marcus Company:
Sales and Cash Receipts Journal, Illustrated

DATE	EXPLANATION	PR	ACCOUNTS RECEIVABLE Dr.	ACCOUNTS RECEIVABLE Cr.	CASH SALES Cr.	CHARGE SALES Cr.	SALES TAX PAYABLE Cr.	PR	OTHER Dr.	OTHER Cr.	SALES DISCOUNT Dr.	CASH DEPOSIT IN BANK Dr.
19XX												
12/1	Notes Payable							210		500.00		500.00
12/2	Daily Summary	√	29.40	16.45	50.00	28.00	1.40 2.50					68.95
12/3	Rental Income							430		250.00		250.00
12/31	Totals	***	29.40 (120)	16.45 (120)	50.00 (410)	28.00 (420)	3.90 (220)	**430		750.00		818.95 (110)

```
            CASH                    110
12/31   818.95 |

     Accounts Receivable   120
12/31  29.40 | 12/31  16.45
```

```
Cash Sales          410
             | 12/31   50.00

Charge Sales        420
             | 12/31   28.00

Rental Income       430
             | 12/3   250.00**
```

```
Notes Payable       210
             | 12/1   500.00*

Sales Tax Payable   220
12/31  29.40 | 12/31   3.90
```

*** The account number under each total column indicates that the amounts have been posted and to which account. The (√) under the total of the "other" column indicates that this total is not posted as each item in this column is posted individually.

The second major journal developed for Marcus Company is the cash payments, purchase, and expense journal (Figure 3-6 on p. 48). Let's look at its structure, and then we will see how it "keeps the score."

While the sales and cash receipts journal looks at the inward flow, the cash payments, purchase, and expense journal centers on the outward or potential outward flow. In the previous section we looked at accounts receivable; this second journal deals with accounts payable. Yet the procedure doesn't change. Even the accounts payable subsidiary ledger parallels the accounts receivable subsidiary ledger.

Let's now look at five different business transactions of the Marcus Company and how they are recorded. As in the past, the analysis comes first.

Analyzing Transactions

Transaction #1
12/2/xx   Marcus Company paid $100 for insurance in advance. Prepaid insurance, an asset, increases by a debit; while cash, an asset, decreases by a credit. (When you buy insurance and pay for it in advance you won the insurance, therefore, it is classified as an asset. However, as the months pass and the insurance is used up, the used up portion becomes an expense. Your accountant will make the necessary update by preparing what's called an adjusting entry.)

Transaction #2
12/3/xx   Bought merchandise from Jones Company for $140 in cash, which will be resold to Marcus' customers. Merchandise, a cost of selling goods, increases, and an increase is a debit. Cash, an asset, decreases by a credit.

Transaction #3
12/4/xx   Bought additional merchandise for $50 on account from Jones Company.
                   Merchandise, a cost of selling goods, increases by a debit; and Marcus Company's liability, accounts payable, increases by a credit.

Transaction #4
12/4/xx   Payroll $73 - Deductions: FICA $4.00
                                                    FWT   6.00
                                                    SWT   3.00

Figure 3-6

George Marcus Company:
Cash Payments, Purchase, and Expense Journal

DATE	PAID TO ON ACCOUNT TERMS	CHECK NO.	CHECK AMOUNT	MERCHANDISE FOR RESALE (PURCHASES)	MERCHANDISE DISCOUNT	GROSS PAYROLL	FICA	FWT	SWT	DRAWINGS	ACCOUNTS PAYABLE		PR	OTHER	
			CASH Cr.	Dr.	Cr.	Dr.	Cr.	Cr.	Cr.	Dr.	Dr.	Cr.		Dr.	Cr.
			A	B	C	D	E	F	G	H	I	J		K	

A Records outward flow of cash. (By the way, checks should be prenumbered to aid internal control.)

B Records merchandise that George plans to resell. If it is paid in cash, column A is affected. If charged, column J is affected.

C Taking advantage of paying bills early George receives a purchase discount. (The savings can be substantial—don't miss Purchase Discounts!)

D Total of the payroll. (Deductions plus net pay should equal column D.)

E Social Security deductions (FICA).

F Federal withholding tax (FWT).

G State withholding tax (SWT).

H Owners' personal withdrawal from business. If the business is a proprietorship or partnership, the owners' salaries are treated as drawings and not as employee salaries.

I Reducing what the company owes creditors.

J Increasing what the company owes creditors.

K Miscellaneous items such as repairs, utilities, insurance, advertising, and so on. If a transaction is repetitive enough, new columns can be added.

Payroll check written is for $60 since the owner takes the deduction out of gross payroll. Deductions plus net pay equals gross pay. These deductions represent a *liability* to the boss. In effect, the payroll expense increases by a debit ($73). The deductions (liabilities) increase by credits, and cash, an asset, decreases by a credit.

Transaction #5
12/5/xx

Paid Jones the amount owed less a ten percent discount. Accounts payable, a liability, decreases by a debit.
Cash, an asset, is reduced by a credit.
Purchase discount, a savings or a *reduction to costs*, is increased by a credit. Remember that additions to costs are debits.

Now let's see how the journal would look with this information recorded (Figure 3 -7).

Journalizing the Transactions

COLUMN HEADINGS Once again, if deemed important, columns could have been set up for rent, advertising, utilities, and other items. "Flexibility" is the word. If certain transactions repeat often enough, the need to set up a new heading might be obvious.

THE PURCHASE DISCOUNT How important is the purchase discount? And how can you keep track of them? To maximize your profit, never miss a purchase discount. Missing one is not only poor planning, but it can also be extremely *expensive* to the business. Many businesses set up files by due dates so that purchase discounts are not missed. Many set up the file up by day or month. *The key point is that taking discounts should be a "priority."* Make time for doing so. Not taking discounts should raise the "red flag" that the recordkeeping system is not functioning as it should.

POSTING At the end of the month the column totals are updated into the ledger. The (√) indicates that the accounts payable subsidiary ledger is updated. The total of the "other" column, since it contains miscellaneous items, is not posted. The individual summary of each account is posted; so "114" is placed in the PR column. (Figure 3-8 on p. 51 shows Journal Totals and how they were posted to the individual accounts; don't forget to test for equality of debits and credits.)

Remember, as I have mentioned, flexibility in Journal design is of key importance. A tailor-made set of journals will simplify your recordkeeping and enhance your management capabilities. For the Marcus Company, I set up two journals in addition to the General Journal, Sales and Cash Receipts and Cash Payments, Purchases and Expenses. It should be noted that many companies break down these two journals into four separate

Figure 3-7

George Marcus Company:
Cash Payments, Purchase, and Expense Journal, Illustrated

DATE	PAID TO/ON ACCT./TERMS	CK NO	CK AMOUNT CASH Cr.	MERCHANDISE FOR RESALE (PURCHASES) Dr.	MERCHANDISE DISCOUNT Cr.	GROSS PAYROLL Dr.	FICA Cr.	FWT Cr.	SWT Cr.	DRAWINGS Dr.	ACCOUNTS PAYABLE Dr.	ACCOUNTS PAYABLE Cr.	PR	OTHER Dr.	OTHER Cr.
12/2	Prepaid Insurance	14	100										114	100	
12/3	Jones Company	15	140	140											
12/4	Jones Company			50								50	✓		
12/5	Payroll	16	60			73	4	6	3						
12/6	Jones Company	17	45		5						50		✓		

Figure 3-8

George Marcus Company:
Cash Payments, Purchase, and Expense Journal, Illustrated

DATE	PAID TO/ON ACCT./TERMS	CK NO	CK AMOUNT CASH Cr.	MERCHANDISE FOR RESALE (PURCHASES) Dr.	MERCHANDISE DISCOUNT Cr.	GROSS PAYROLL Dr.	FICA Cr.	FWT Cr.	SWT Cr.	DRAWINGS Dr.	ACCOUNTS PAYABLE Dr.	ACCOUNTS PAYABLE Cr.	PR	OTHER Dr.	OTHER Cr.
12/2	Prepaid Insurance	14	100										114	100	
12/3	Jones Company	15	140	140											
12/4	Jones Company			50								50	✓		
12/5	Payroll	16	60			73	4	6	3						
12/6	Jones Company	17	45		5						50		✓		
12/31	Totals		345 (110)	190 (510)	5 (511)	73 (610)	4 (230)	6 (240)	3 (250)		50 (200)	50 (200)	(✓)	100	

```
        CASH            110              Purchases        510           Accounts Payable   200
                 | 12/31   345.        12/31  190 |                  12/31  50 | 12/31   50.

     Prepaid Insurance                  Purchase Discounts  511         FICA Payable     230
 *12/31   100 |                                | 12/31    5.                     | 12/31    4.

                                                                        FWT Payable      240
                                                                                 | 12/31    6.

                                                                        SWT Payable      250
                                                                                 | 12/31    3.

     Salaries & Wages Exp   610
      12/31   73 |
```

journals (1) Sales Journal (2) Cash Receipts Journal (3) Purchases Journal and (4) Cash Disbursements Journal, combined with the General Journal, a total of five journals. Most computer accounting software packages utilize five journals. Special journals save posting and labor time by dividing transactions into similar groups. The General Journal is usually then used only for miscellaneous transactions that cannot be recorded in one of the special journals and for adjusting, closing and correcting entries. Most accounting software packages come with five or six standard Charts of Accounts. You would first select the chart that best reflects your needs and then edit that chart so that it exactly fits your requirements. In the past couple of years, accounting software has become much more user friendly and much more sophisticated in terms of options within the package. A tip to remember is that many of the lower priced packages (between $100 and $300) are in many ways as good if not better than some of the high priced ($600 to $1000) packages. This recent development is due to price wars within the industry and advancements in technology—a true exception to the rule you get what you pay for, and a real bonus for the small business person.

RECONCILIATION

JEN: How do these special journals relate to the company's checkbook? I can never seem to balance my own personal checkbook.

ANNE: Okay! Let's look at what the Marcus Company does with its business checkbook even before they reconcile their checkbook to the bank's. Here are the steps they take *before* the bank reconciliation:

Concern #5: Getting Your Checkbook and Bank Statement to Agree

1. They prenumber all checks for internal control.
2. They utilize a petty cash fund for small expenses.
3. They pay all other expenses by check.
4. Any checks payable to George himself for cash to pay for a business expense include receipts to verify they were not for personal reasons.

CHECKING YOUR CHECKBOOK AGAINST YOUR RECORDS   First George has to verify that his checkbook balance accurately represents the entries in his journals. To do so, he must take the following steps:

1. Take the balance shown in the checkbook at the end of the preceding month.
2. *Add* the total cash deposited for the month; this amount comes from a summary of the cash receipts (Figure 3-5).
3. *Subtract* all cash payments; this amount comes from the cash payments journal (Figure 3-8).
4. Compare this total with the actual checkbook balance at the end of the current month.

If the journal tally doesn't match the balance shown in the checkbook, George takes the following steps:

1. He compares checkstubs from the checkbook with amounts in the "check" column in the cash payments journal (Figure 3-8).
2. He adds the deposits in the checkbook and compares the total to the total of daily receipts shown in the monthly summary of cash receipts (Figure 3-5).
3. He then checks his addition and subtraction of the running balance in the checkbook.
4. If still in trouble, he gets a cup of coffee and repeats the process, making sure he clears the adding machine!

CHECKING THE BANK STATEMENT   After making certain that the checkbook accurately reflects the inward and outward flow of cash for the month, George's next step is to make sure that the bank statement is correct. Here's what George does with his statement each month:

1. He compares all the canceled checks enclosed with the statement and other debits (such as service charges) that are either in the checks or in the debits column of the statement. He makes sure that all the checks were properly issued by him and that the proper amounts were charged against his accounts.
2. He compares the deposits listed on the bank statement with the deposit amounts shown in his checkbook, accounting for all differences. As he goes through the deposits, he keeps a list of any "in-transit" deposits—deposits that are entered in the checkbook but that do not appear on this month's bank statement. Normally these are deposits made toward the end of the month.
3. He puts all the canceled checks into numerical order.
4. He then compares both the number and the dollar amount of each canceled check with the corresponding entry on each checkbook stub. If the check is correct, he marks (√) that number on the checkbook as having cleared the bank. After accounting for all the checks returned by the bank, he knows that those not checked on the checkbook are his outstanding checks. He has to then make a list of them.
5. Any errors in amounts discovered while carrying out any of the preceding steps are also noted—listed if there are many.

You should now have several pieces of information from this examination of your statement and checks:

1. A total of service charges and other debit charges from step 1.
2. A list of all "in-transit" deposits not recognized by the bank at the time of issuing the statement, from step 2.
3. A list of all outstanding checks that were not cleared by the bank at the time of issuing the statement, from step 4.
4. A list of any miscellaneous errors noted in the addition, subtraction, or recording of checks, from step 5.

RECONCILING THE CHECKBOOK AND BANK STATEMENT George has now verified that his checkbook agrees with his books and that his statement has recorded his checking activity accurately. The next question—the big one—is whether the balance in his checkbook is the same as the balance on the statement. This matching up is the whole point of the reconciliation process. Let's see how George goes about this part of the task. Figure 3-9 shows George's reconciliation calculations. The circled numbers are *not* part of his figuring; they are rather numbers that relate to the items of explanation that follow:

Figure 3-9

George Marcus Company:
Bank Reconciliation as of November 30, 19xx

① Checkbook balance of cash $6,642   ⑦ Bank statement balance $7,578
②   ADD: Note collected   ⑧ ADD:
             by bank   1,494   Deposit in transit   957
                              $8,136 $8,535
     DEDUCT: ⑨ DEDUCT:
③ Error of check No. 2 $27   Check Nos. 18 $279
④ NSF check   720   24   387
⑤ Bank service charge   9   756   36   489   1,155
⑥ Reconciled balance $7,380 ⑩ $7,380

1. The checkbook shows a beginning balance of $6,642.
2. When the bank sent the statement, it indicated that it collected money (from one of Marcus's customers) for $1,494. Since the bank knew about it, not Marcus, Marcus must add this amount to the balance in the checkbook.
3. Marcus wrote a check for $77 but recorded it as $50. When he reviewed the canceled check, Marcus realized the mistake and lowered his checkbook balance by $27. As far as the bank is concerned, the check was $77 so their records are okay.
4. Marcus deposited a check for $720 from Pete's Wholesale. The check bounced, and the bank lowered Marcus's balance by the $720. Actually Marcus didn't know about the bounced check until he received the bank statement. In actuality, Marcus must make good on the money until it can be collected from Pete's Wholesale.
5. The bank charged Marcus $9 for processing the checks, so Marcus lowers his checkbook balance by $9.
6. The end result is a balance of $7,380, which he hopes balances with the bank balance at the end of the reconciliation process.
7. The bank statement sent to Marcus indicates a balance of $7,578.
8. Marcus notices an "in-transit" deposit of $957 that he made but that did not reach the bank before this statement was prepared. Although Marcus knows about the deposit, the bank has no idea it is coming. So Marcus adds the $957 to the bank balance.

9. The bank did *not* process certain outstanding checks at the time of its statement preparation. Marcus knows about the checks, but the bank has no idea that they were written. These outstanding checks (checks 18, 24, and 36) are subtracted from the bank balance.
10. The end result is that the bank balance matches the book balance: $7,380.
11. All corrections made on the Marcus books must be (a) recorded in the journal and (b) updated in the ledger.
12. If George still has discrepancies, he checks back over the preceding steps for errors.

Even in a simple recordkeeping system, other records should keep track of the value of all equipment, buildings, vehicles, and other depreciable assets. Depreciation is an estimate that allocates the cost of an asset over its period of usefulness. When you take depreciation, it is a business expense, and the history of the accumulated depreciation is found in a contra account called accumulated depreciation. Remember: As the depreciation expense increases, a company's profit decreases, resulting in lower taxes. *Depreciation is an indirect tax savings.* Since we will get into various depreciation calculations in Chapter 6, suffice it to say for now that using depreciation can lower or even postpone payments on tax obligations. Be aware of the need to plan the depreciation of assets. Figure 3-10 is an example of the type of depreciation record you need to plan.

DEPRECIATION

ASSET AND DEPRECIATION RECORD No. 101

Item Computer-101
Serial No. A4321
Estimated Life 5 years
Depreciation per year $400.00

General Ledger Account Office Equipment
Bought from Marvy Co.
Salvage Value $110.00
per month $33.33

DATE	EXPLANATION	ASSET RECORD			DEPRECIATION RECORD		
		DEBIT	CREDIT	BALANCE	DEBIT	CREDIT	BALANCE
June 1, 1992		2110		2110			
June 1, 1993						400*	400

*Cost of computer — Salvage value
Number of estimated years

$\dfrac{2110-110}{5}$

$\dfrac{2000}{5}$ = 400 Depreciation per year

or

$\dfrac{400}{12}$ = $33.33 Depreciation per month

2110

Figure 3-10: Asset and Depreciation Record

1. Petty cash helps you to lessen the number of checks that you have to write. You are really shifting one asset, cash, into another asset, petty cash.

2. Petty cash vouchers and cash in the petty cash box must always equal the originally established amount of the fund. Periodically the slips in the box are updated in the general ledger to show what the money was used for.

3. Cash overage or shortage can easily result from human error—sometimes an "intentional" one and other times an honest mistake. *Remember: One of the worst problems owners complain about is "labor."* Good employees are hard to find.

4. The subsidiary ledgers are arranged in alphabetical order and are not found in the general ledger where the controlling account is found. The subsidiary ledgers aid a business in monitoring accounts receivable and accounts payable.

5. Special journals can take many forms. In this chapter, we looked specifically at (1) the sales and cash receipts journal and (2) the cash payments, purchase, and expense journal. Headings can change due to the new needs of a business. Think of these special journals as flexible.

6. Missing a purchase discount is an "expensive mistake." The discount lost shows "inefficiency" in the office or poor management planning. Taking discounts should be a *priority*. Missing them should be inexcusable.

7. Offering sales discounts might aid the overall cash flow of the business. A dollar today is worth more today than it will be in the future.

8. Comparing the company's bank balance to that reported on the bank statement constitutes the bank reconciliation process, which is done once a month.

9. NSF, service charges, and notes collected by the bank are items affecting the book balance.

10. In-transit deposits and outstanding checks affect the bank balance.

11. Check the bottom right of each check returned. The coded ink should be the amount of the check written. If not, either the bank or you are in error. Remember that the data entry person who types this amount at the bottom of thousands of checks daily can easily commit an error. The computer's information is only as good as what's put into it.

12. Depreciation is the allocating of the original cost of an asset over its period of "estimated" usefulness. Estimates of depreciation are by various formulas or guidelines developed by IRS.

	True	False	CHECK YOUR PULSE
1. All recordkeeping systems are quite rigid.	____	____	
2. Petty cash is a fixed amount.	____	____	
3. A change fund is never in the same place as petty cash.	____	____	
4. Deposits of cash to the bank should be made as soon as possible.	____	____	
5. The daily summary of sales and cash receipts doesn't involve petty cash.	____	____	
6. A cash shortage could result from giving a customer too much change.	____	____	
7. Not ringing up a sale can cause a cash shortage.	____	____	
8. The general journal is the same as a special journal.	____	____	
9. The sales and cash receipts journal deals with the outward flow of assets.	____	____	
10. The accounts payable subsidiary ledger is in numerical order.	____	____	
11. A subsidiary ledger needs to be updated monthly.	____	____	
12. A (√) indicates the subsidiary ledger has been updated.	____	____	
13. Sales discounts always have a negative impact on the seller.	____	____	
14. Merchandise represents items for resale.			
15. A purchase discount should always be taken.	____	____	
16. NSF checks are subtracted from the bank balance.	____	____	
17. Checks outstanding have been processed by the bank.	____	____	
18. In the bank reconciliation, checks are arranged alphabetically.	____	____	
19. Depreciation may provide some tax advantage.	____	____	
20. Deposits not received by the bank are in transit.	____	____	

Solutions

1. False
2. True
3. False
4. True
5. False
6. True
7. False
8. False
9. False
10. False
11. False
12. True
13. False
14. True
15. True
16. False
17. False
18. False
19. True
20. True

MATCHING

Column A		Column B
_____	1. NSF	A. Cash overage
_____	2. Deposits in transit	B. Numerical order
_____	3. Petty cash	C. Records receipt of money
_____	4. Straight-line	D. Trade-in
_____	5. ⌂ in drawings	E. Helps prove cash
_____	6. Headings of special journal	F. For resale
_____	7. Payroll deductions	G. Liability for owner
_____	8. Accumulated depreciation	H. Checks not processed by bank
_____	9. Daily summary	I. Not fixed
_____	10. Canceled checks arranged	J. Lessens check writing
_____	11. Salvage	K. Can be part of petty cash
_____	12. Sales tax	L. Accounts payable subsidiary ledger
_____	13. Merchandise	M. Aids cash flow
_____	14. Ringing up sale too small	N. Bounced check
_____	15. Change fund	O. Subsidiary updated
_____	16. Change fund	P. Debit
_____	17. Not located in general ledger	Q. Formula to calculate depreciation
_____	18. √	R. Added to bank balance
_____	19. Checks outstanding	S. Contra asset
_____	20. Sale discount	T. Liabilities

Answers

1.	N	11.	D
2.	R	12.	G
3.	J	13.	F
4.	Q	14.	A
5.	P	15.	K
6.	I	16.	C
7.	T	17.	L
8.	S	18.	0
9.	E	19.	H
10.	B	20.	M

4

PREPARING FINANCIAL REPORTS AND ANALYZING THEIR MEANING

1. Prepare a classified balance sheet.
2. Prepare a classified income statement.
3. Define:
   - current assets
   - fixed assets
   - current liabilities
   - long-term liabilities
   - stockholder's equity
   - retained earnings
4. Compare and contrast retained earnings to cash.
5. Define:
   - net sales
   - cost of goods sold
   - gross profit
6. Prepare ratio analyses on income statements and balance sheets.
7. Calculate and explain managerial implications for:
   - current ratio
   - quick ratio (acid test)
   - inventory turnover
   - fixed asset turnover
   - asset turnover
   - debt/total assets
   - profit margin on sales
   - return on investment
   - return on equity

8. Explain the purpose of industrial ratios.

9. List five sources that can be utilized in interpreting financial reports.

10. Define what is meant by specialized industry sources.

11. Calculate percentages from financial reports.

12. List steps to increase gross margin.

WHAT FINANCIAL STATEMENTS DO FOR YOUR BUSINESS

ANNE: I'd like to spend more time looking at the income statement and balance sheet.

JEN: What for? You told me these reports were prepared from the ledger. All revenues and expenses were recorded on the income statement; and all assets, liabilities, and equity go on the balance sheet. What else is there to say? Once these are prepared, what possible impact could they have on my future planning and record-keeping activities?

ANNE: Slow down. Over the past years we have seen the cost of home heating zooming up.

JEN: What does energy have to do with income statements and balance sheets?

ANNE: Let me explain. Many people have decided to insulate, weather-strip, or install electric heaters. Others have chosen alternatives such as wood-burning stoves, solar energy, and other energy-saving devices. Drivers compare the number of gallons that their cars consume, as well as the percentage of increase in the cost of fuel. Just think of the prices of gasoline for your car! More and more people are checking fuel gauges to monitor their car's performance. They devise plans for minimizing gas utilization but maximizing one's satisfaction.

JEN: Get to the point.

ANNE: In each situation, the homeowner has to take a hard look at how the present heating system is performing (just as business owners inspect their income statements) in relation to the overall structure of the house (or, in the case of a business, in relation to the balance sheet). The homeowner or business owner asks what kind of improvements can be made in light of my financial position? When could I pay back a loan? Factors such as past as well as present records become an important part of the analysis.

You should not think of the income statement or balance sheet as end products that are prepared and "filed away." They're like the odometer and fuel gauge on your car—monitoring devices. Consider these reports as reflections of the "life blood" of your company. We need to develop ways to monitor how well the "blood" is flowing—as well as how "healthy" the blood is. Like the blood pressure gauge, gasoline gauge, or thermostat in your home, accountants utilize specific techniques for analyzing financial reports by making comparisons and calculating percentages. These techniques help answer questions such as:

- Could the company pay its bills if business conditions tightened up temporarily?
- Is the money I have invested in the business bringing me as much profit as it could?
- If not, where are the problem areas?
- What percentage of profit could I promise investors if they put some money into the business?
- Are my inventories working hard enough?
- Does the record show that the business is strong enough and stable enough to qualify for a long-term loan?[1]

THE JONES COMPANY'S "FINANCIALS"

Figure 4-1 shows the Jones Company balance sheet. Keep in mind that this report gives a "financial picture" of a company's assets, liabilities, and equities. This balance sheet has more classifications than you've seen before. Before reading on, go over the report section by section in Figure 4-2. This review will help you understand what you're doing when we prepare an analysis of the Jones financial reports. After going over the balance sheet, turn your attention next to the Jones income statement (Figure 4-3), and examine it closely also. Remember, this report shows how well the business is performing for a specific period of time.

Bear in mind that these two reports try to reflect an accurate picture. Given the perplexities of the "real world," they might be drawn up under conditions of uncertainty, and many of the transactions involved might be incomplete at the end of the accounting period. Some of the figures might be based on the judgment of an accountant, who tries to "mesh" judgments with generally accepted accounting principles.[2] So always keep the "red flag" close at hand when reviewing financials.

RATIO ANALYSIS

Jones was very concerned about how he could use these two reports to aid in his planning for future activities. He knew how to read the reports, but now he wanted specific tools to identify weaknesses, to spot trends, as well as to improve upon areas of strength. As his accountant, Anne indicated that he needed to make comparisons between figures; hence the need to develop business ratios in analyzing his financial reports. Ratios are not difficult to do, but they represent meaningful relationships between figures.

Caution! Ratios are only one technique in the accountant's tool chest. Analyzing financial reports by business ratios should not be regarded as the ultimate solution to planning the future as well as to evaluating the past. Each ratio should not be treated as absolute. At the end of this section you will find a "roadmap" of sources used to evaluate financial ratios for different lines of businesses. Remember: The ratio is only a tool. *Calculating too many detailed ratios can become a meaningless exercise.*

---

[1] *Handbook of Small Business Finance,* Small Business Management Series, No. 15 (Washington, DC: Small Business Administration, 1975). Issue is no longer in print.

[2] *Handbook of Small Business Finance.*

Figure 4-1

**Jones Company
Balance Sheet,
December 31, 19xx
(Illustrated)**

Assets

Current Assets:

Cash on hand	$ 5,000	
Accounts receivable	25,000	
Inventories	22,000	
Total current assets		$52,000

Fixed Assets:

Land and building		$13,000
Equipment	$20,000	
Less: Accumulated Depreciation	6,000	14,000
Total fixed assets		$27,000

Total assets	$79,000

Liabilities and Stockholders' Equity

Liabilities

Current Liabilities:

Accounts payable	$10,000	
Salaries payable	10,000	
Total current liabilities		$20,000

Long-Term Liabilities:

Notes payable	$ 5,000	
Mortgage payable	10,000	
Total long-term liabilities		$15,000
Total liabilities		$35,000

Stockholders' Equity

Common Stock (12,500 Shares @ $1 par)	$12,500	
Retained earnings	31,500	
Total stockholders' equity		$44,000
Total liabilities and stockholders' equity		$79,000

Figure 4-2: Jones Company Balance Sheet, Broken Down

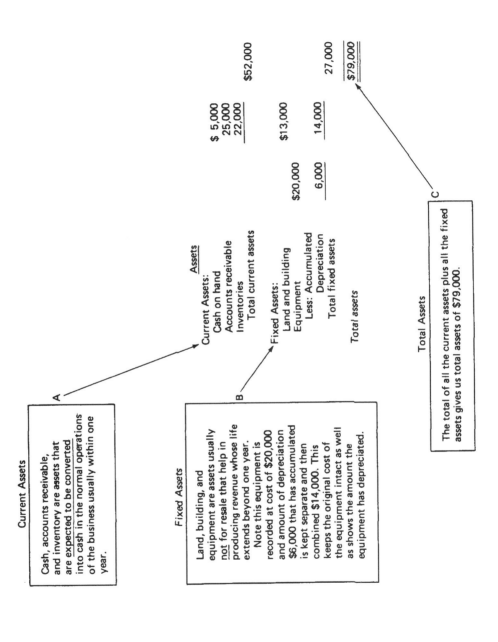

Current Assets

Cash, accounts receivable, and inventory are assets that are expected to be converted into cash in the normal operations of the business usually within one year.

Fixed Assets

Land, building, and equipment are assets usually not for resale that help in producing revenue whose life extends beyond one year. Note this equipment is recorded at cost of $20,000 and amount of depreciation $6,000 that has accumulated is kept separate and then combined $14,000. This keeps the original cost of the equipment intact as well as shows the amount the equipment has depreciated.

Total Assets

The total of all the current assets plus all the fixed assets gives us total assets of $79,000.

A

B

C

Assets

Current Assets:		
Cash on hand		$ 5,000
Accounts receivable		25,000
Inventories		22,000
Total current assets		$52,000
Fixed Assets:		
Land and building		$13,000
Equipment	$20,000	
Less: Accumulated Depreciation	6,000	14,000
Total fixed assets		27,000
Total assets		$79,000

Figure 4-2: (continued)

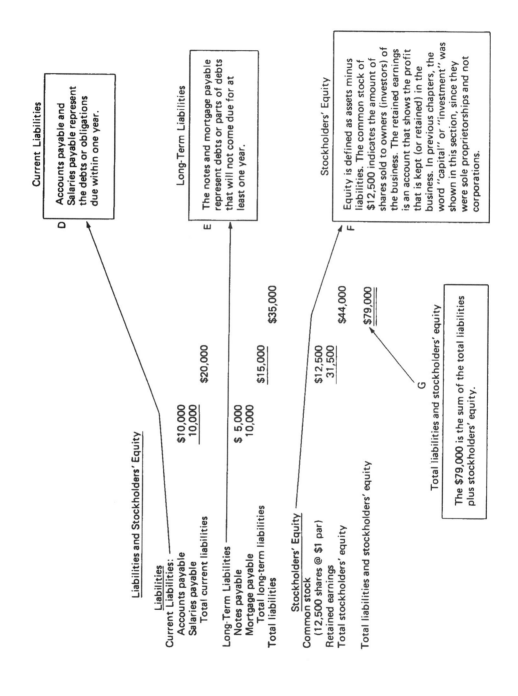

Current Liabilities

D   Accounts payable and Salaries payable represent the debts or obligations due within one year.

Long-Term Liabilities

E   The notes and mortgage payable represent debts or parts of debts that will not come due for at least one year.

Stockholders' Equity

F   Equity is defined as assets minus liabilities. The common stock of $12,500 indicates the amount of shares sold to owners (investors) of the business. The retained earnings is an account that shows the profit that is kept (or retained) in the business. In previous chapters, the word "capital" or "investment" was shown in this section, since they were sole proprietorships and not corporations.

G   The $79,000 is the sum of the total liabilities plus stockholders' equity.

Liabilities and Stockholders' Equity

Liabilities		
Current Liabilities:		
Accounts payable	$10,000	
Salaries payable	10,000	
Total current liabilities		$20,000
Long-Term Liabilities		
Notes payable	$ 5,000	
Mortgage payable	10,000	
Total long-term liabilities		$15,000
Total liabilities		$35,000
Stockholders' Equity		
Common stock		
(12,500 shares @ $1 par)	$12,500	
Retained earnings	31,500	
Total stockholders' equity		$44,000
Total liabilities and stockholders' equity		$79,000

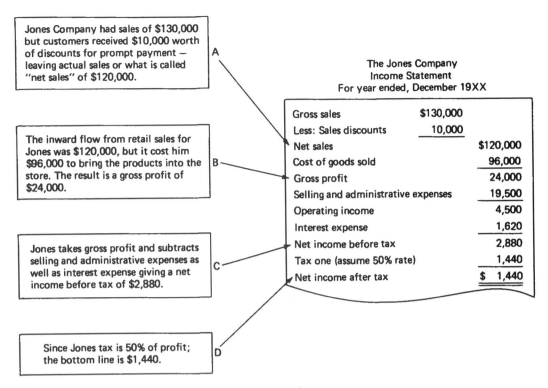

Figure 4-3: Jones Company Income Statement, Illustrated

The boxes in the figure read:

A. Jones Company had sales of $130,000 but customers received $10,000 worth of discounts for prompt payment — leaving actual sales or what is called "net sales" of $120,000.

B. The inward flow from retail sales for Jones was $120,000, but it cost him $96,000 to bring the products into the store. The result is a gross profit of $24,000.

C. Jones takes gross profit and subtracts selling and administrative expenses as well as interest expense giving a net income before tax of $2,880.

D. Since Jones tax is 50% of profit; the bottom line is $1,440.

The main questions facing Jones were:

1. How well were his assets managed?
2. What did the debt situation look like?
3. What was the profitability picture?

Several kinds of ratios were used to analyze Jones's concerns. *Don't memorize them:* The key is to know how to calculate them and then interpret what they really say, along with any implications.

Asset Management

CURRENT RATIO As you can see in Figure 4-4, current ratio is nothing more than a comparison of current assets over current liabilities. In this case it comes out to 2.6. If Jones decides his current ratio is too low, he could possibly raise it by:

1. paying back some debts;
2. obtaining loans (not due for at least a year) to increase his current assets;
3. converting some fixed assets into current assets; and/or
4. retaining more profit within the business.

Jones should be warned that if the ratio is high, it still does not tell us if the mix of cash to receivables and inventory is at the appropriate level.

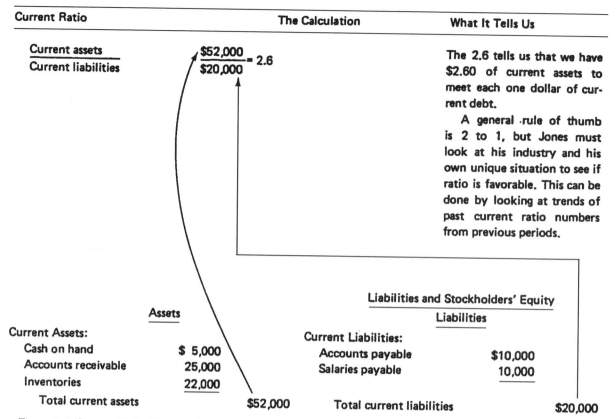

Current Ratio	The Calculation	What It Tells Us
$\dfrac{\text{Current assets}}{\text{Current liabilities}}$	$\dfrac{\$52,000}{\$20,000} = 2.6$	The 2.6 tells us that we have $2.60 of current assets to meet each one dollar of current debt. A general ·rule of thumb is 2 to 1, but Jones must look at his industry and his own unique situation to see if ratio is favorable. This can be done by looking at trends of past current ratio numbers from previous periods.

Assets

Current Assets:
Cash on hand $ 5,000
Accounts receivable   25,000
Inventories   22,000
    Total current assets $52,000

Liabilities and Stockholders' Equity

Liabilities

Current Liabilities:
Accounts payable $10,000
Salaries payable   10,000
    Total current liabilities $20,000

Figure 4-4: Current Ratio, Illustrated

ACID TEST RATIO Figure 4-5 shows that the acid test ratio is very much like current ratio, but you subtract the value of your inventory from current assets.

Acid Test Ratio	The Calculation	What It Tells Us
$\dfrac{\text{Current assets} - \text{Inventory}}{\text{Current liabilities}}$	$\dfrac{\$52,000 - \$22,000}{\$20,000} = 1.5$	This ratio is very similar to current ratio, except *inventory* is subtracted. Sometimes it is difficult to sell inventory quickly. This ratio reveals only $1.50 of current assets to meet each $1 of current debt.

Figure 4-5: Acid Test Ratio, Illustrated

Jones's acid test ratio is 1.5. If other companies in this industry have a ratio of 2 or 3, then Jones might be concerned about not being "liquid." If on the other hand, previous acid test ratios were less than 1, perhaps Jones has improved his debt-paying ability.

INVENTORY TURNOVER If you divide your net sales by inventory, you get your inventory turnover. In Figure 4-6, Jones' turnover is 5.5.

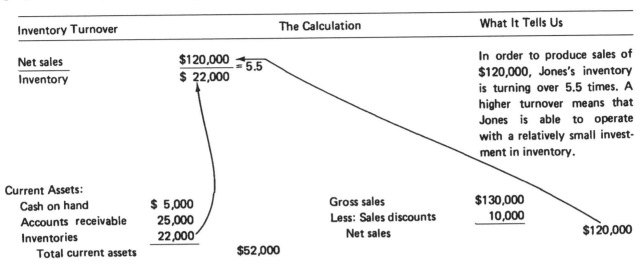

Inventory Turnover	The Calculation	What It Tells Us
$\dfrac{\text{Net sales}}{\text{Inventory}}$	$\dfrac{\$120,000}{\$\ 22,000} = 5.5$	In order to produce sales of $120,000, Jones's inventory is turning over 5.5 times. A higher turnover means that Jones is able to operate with a relatively small investment in inventory.
Current Assets:		
Cash on hand $5,000	Gross sales $130,000	
Accounts receivable 25,000	Less: Sales discounts 10,000	
Inventories 22,000	Net sales $120,000	
Total current assets $52,000		

Figure 4-6: Inventory Turnover, Illustrated

Striving for a higher turnover could possibly lead to inventory shortages and to potential customer dissatisfaction. If this condition presently exists, maybe the turnover is now too high. Since no business owners in their right minds would consider reducing sales, most managers reduce their turnover by increasing their inventory. (Do a little arithmetic to see what happens to the 5.5 when the inventory is increased to, say, $40,000.)

Figure 4-7: Inventory Trouble

COLLECTION PERIOD In Figure 4-8, Jones sees that it is taking him 75 days on the average to collect on credit accounts. Jones realizes that as the

Average Days Collection Period for Accounts Receivable	The Calculation	What It Tells Us
$\dfrac{\text{Accounts Receivable}}{\text{Sales/360 days}}$	$\dfrac{\$\ 25,000}{\$120,000/360}$ $= \dfrac{\$\ 25,000}{333.33}$ $= 75 \text{ days}$	It is taking Jones Company on the average 75 days to collect its accounts receivable.

Figure 4-8: Average Days Collection, Illustrated

number of days increases (if the number was less in previous periods), there is more chance that the clients will turn into bad debts. Also extending credit to customers can result in a "cash crisis." In general, a rule of thumb is that the average collection period should not exceed one-and-one-third times the credit terms.[3]

FIXED ASSET TURNOVER How hard are Jones' assets working for him? Figure 4-9 shows that, by dividing net sales by fixed assets, he calculates that each dollar's worth of assets generates $4.44 of net sales.

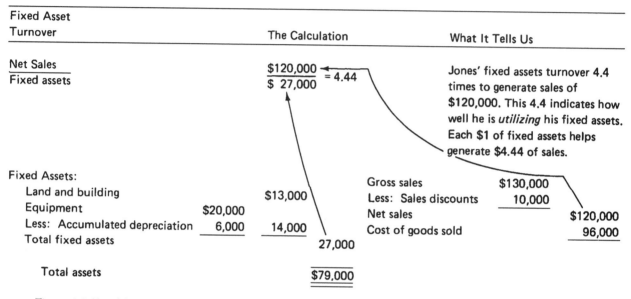

Figure 4-9: Fixed Asset Turnover, Illustrated

Let's see how Jones keeps an edge on this relationship of fixed assets to sales. If ratio is not in line with what similar businesses are doing, Jones might consider either adding or selling some fixed assets. This ratio helps Jones answer the question, "Am I making the best use of my fixed assets to aid me in the operation of the business?"

Figure 4-10: Excessive Fixed Assets

ASSETS TURNOVER In Figure 4-11 you can see this is basically the same ratio as fixed assets turnover, only you throw in all your assets. When Jones's total assets are divided into his net sales, the ratio drops to $1.52.

---

[3] *Handbook of Small Business Finance.*

Asset Turnover	The Calculation	What It Tells Us
Net sales / Total assets	$\dfrac{\$120,000}{\$79,000} = 1.52$	For Jones, each $1 invested in assets returns $1.52 in sales; or in other words, assets turn over 1½ times as fast as sales.

Figure 4-11: Asset Turnover, Illustrated

Now if the industrial average is 1.1, Jones seems to be utilizing his assets more effectively than most. On the other hand, if other companies are at 2.1, perhaps Jones's assets are not being utilized efficiently.

Debt Consideration

DEBT/TOTAL ASSETS Perhaps the most basic ratio, this comparison divides total liabilities by total assets, as shown in Figure 4-12. Jones's ratio is 0.44. If the average ratio for the industry was 0.32, Jones might think he has too much total debt. With inflation, this conclusion might not be true; in inflationary times, it is cheaper to pay debt in later years with "cheaper dollars."

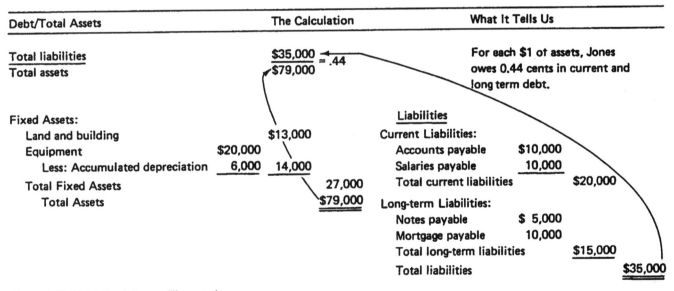

Figure 4-12: Debt/Total Assets, Illustrated

Performance Picture

NET PROFIT MARGIN OR SALES Sales are up, but what kind of profit is Jones making? The calculation in Figure 4-13 shows that he keeps 1.3 cents on each after-tax sales dollar.

If Jones feels that 1.3 cents is not in line with industry standards, he might consider lowering prices in hope of stimulating a greater volume of sales.

RETURN ON INVESTMENT Figure 4-13 shows the calculation that tells Jones how much after-tax income his total assets are earning—1.8 percent. If Jones believes his percentage to be too low a return, he could consider:

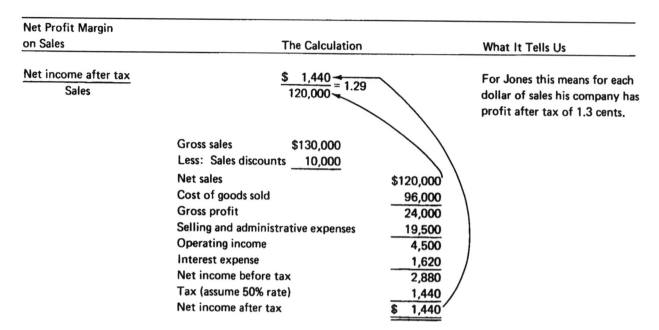

Net Profit Margin on Sales	The Calculation	What It Tells Us
$\dfrac{\text{Net income after tax}}{\text{Sales}}$	$\dfrac{\$\ 1{,}440}{120{,}000} = 1.29$	For Jones this means for each dollar of sales his company has profit after tax of 1.3 cents.

Gross sales	$130,000
Less: Sales discounts	10,000
Net sales	$120,000
Cost of goods sold	96,000
Gross profit	24,000
Selling and administrative expenses	19,500
Operating income	4,500
Interest expense	1,620
Net income before tax	2,880
Tax (assume 50% rate)	1,440
Net income after tax	$ 1,440

Figure 4-13: Net Profit Margin on Sales, Illustrated

1. trying to improve the profit margin (that is, to make more on each sale);
2. using the assets more effectively (quicker turnover) to generate increased sales of goods or services;
3. reducing costs as much as possible without hurting sales.

Return on Investment	The Calculation	What It Tells Us
$\dfrac{\text{Net income after tax}}{\text{Total assets}}$	$\dfrac{\$\ 1{,}440}{\$79{,}000} = 1.8\%$	For each $1 invested in assets, the Jones Company is earning $1.08 (or a 1.8% return).

Figure 4-14: Return on Investment, Illustrated

RETURN ON EQUITY In Figure 4-15, the calculation helps Jones answer the question as to whether the return on the equity is worthwhile. The stockholders' investment in this company results in an "opportunity lost" to earn a possibly higher rate of return from another investment. With inflation rates of 15 to 20 percent, rates like this are not uncommon.

SOURCES OF INFORMATION FOR FINANCIAL REPORTS INTERPRETATION

With each of these ratios, Jones had to compare his company's figures with some type of industry standard. All business owners therefore need a roadmap to sources of ratios by industry or product line.

Each year Dun and Bradstreet publishes key business ratios. Figure 4-16 contains key ratios for retailers. It is reproduced by special permission from Dun and Bradstreet, Inc. For a list of publications write to Dun and Bradstreet, 99 Church Street, New York, New York 10007.

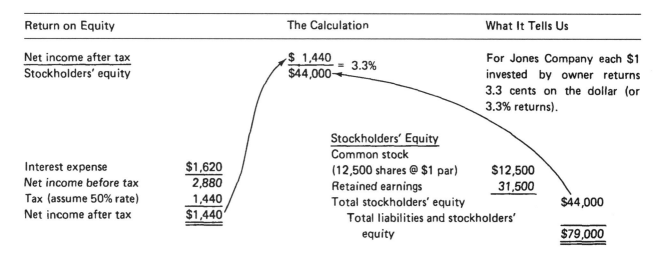

Return on Equity	The Calculation	What It Tells Us
Net income after tax / Stockholders' equity	$\dfrac{\$ 1{,}440}{\$44{,}000} = 3.3\%$	For Jones Company each $1 invested by owner returns 3.3 cents on the dollar (or 3.3% returns).

Interest expense	$1,620
Net income before tax	2,880
Tax (assume 50% rate)	1,440
Net income after tax	$1,440

Stockholders' Equity
Common stock (12,500 shares @ $1 par)	$12,500
Retained earnings	31,500
Total stockholders' equity	$44,000
Total liabilities and stockholders' equity	$79,000

Figure 4-15: Return on Equity, Illustrated

Line of Business (and number of concerns reporting)	Current assets to current debt	Net profits on net sales	Net profits on tangible net worth	Net profits on net working capital	Net sales to tangible net worth	Net sales to net working capital	Collection period	Net sales to inventory	Fixed assets to tangible net worth	Current debt to tangible net worth	Total debt to tangible net worth	Inventory to net working capital	Current debt to inventory	Funded debts to net working capital
	Times	Per cent	Per cent	Per cent	Times	Times	Days	Times	Per cent	Per cent	Per cent	Per cent	Per cent	Per cent
5531 Auto & Home Supply Stores (54)	3.81	3.33	13.73	18.62	8.76	9.22	—	5.9	9.2	49.5	75.0	59.9	49.4	18.4
	2.24	1.58	7.29	8.66	3.84	5.39	—	4.5	32.8	75.0	124.7	93.3	81.2	34.3
	1.66	(0.17)	0.00	2.03	2.39	2.76	—	3.2	49.1	192.4	413.6	140.9	116.7	77.7
5641 Children's & Infants' Wear Stores (39)	4.30	11.11	23.33	34.29	5.45	6.15	—	5.5	8.7	30.0	47.1	75.1	27.8	23.8
	2.93	3.95	10.71	13.51	4.26	4.51	—	3.8	17.2	50.0	128.9	105.9	46.7	63.7
	2.26	0.43	0.48	1.44	1.77	2.29	—	2.5	27.9	148.1	251.4	124.7	66.7	83.8
5611 Clothing & Furnishings, Men's & Boys' (220)	5.52	6.02	20.67	23.11	5.12	5.35	—	5.4	5.9	22.7	61.2	61.6	30.4	9.9
	2.87	2.76	7.89	10.14	3.45	3.76	—	3.8	16.5	52.1	111.4	94.9	54.8	33.2
	1.94	0.80	0.85	3.13	2.15	2.67	—	3.1	42.9	108.9	236.3	129.2	85.7	69.3
5311 Department Stores (333)	5.36	3.91	15.37	19.53	6.01	7.12	—	7.0	11.3	19.5	49.2	57.5	35.4	16.2
	3.06	2.12	8.18	10.97	4.03	4.59	—	5.5	27.3	45.0	96.7	77.8	60.6	38.2
	2.02	0.86	2.87	4.21	2.65	3.20	—	4.0	51.5	88.0	165.0	115.6	87.2	68.3
Discount Stores (98)	2.97	2.33	18.52	22.31	9.62	11.75	—	7.8	16.6	46.7	73.4	98.5	42.1	21.9
	2.21	1.26	11.22	12.88	7.03	8.53	—	5.2	35.5	72.1	122.2	135.3	65.3	40.0
	1.71	0.59	3.46	6.08	4.21	5.63	—	4.1	64.6	119.1	183.8	190.0	90.7	74.8
Discount Stores, Leased Depts. (27)	3.69	4.00	19.21	34.07	7.98	9.07	—	6.4	15.3	30.0	67.6	90.1	35.9	9.8
	2.90	2.72	13.68	14.49	5.43	6.20	—	5.1	22.6	52.3	129.8	115.7	51.8	25.2
	1.70	1.02	4.36	4.74	4.22	4.87	—	4.0	41.1	144.9	173.6	185.8	83.8	42.0
5651 Family Clothing Stores (97)	10.43	10.21	16.45	25.78	3.39	4.31	—	5.2	6.7	11.1	65.8	54.7	16.1	17.2
	3.86	3.27	8.26	12.79	2.59	2.99	—	3.7	16.4	43.2	100.0	78.0	40.8	29.9
	2.41	0.50	0.87	2.96	1.69	2.18	—	2.6	42.1	86.1	252.4	122.4	66.6	78.9
5712 Furniture Stores (158)	5.94	5.88	13.78	16.67	4.83	5.81	28	6.5	4.7	22.5	42.7	32.6	43.0	13.7
	3.70	2.80	6.50	8.33	2.59	2.70	76	4.6	12.7	59.9	102.2	67.1	76.2	26.2
	2.01	1.00	1.77	3.42	1.48	1.72	159	3.5	40.8	121.2	202.6	119.8	119.7	62.1
5541 Gasoline Service Stations (79)	4.11	6.11	19.72	59.62	8.94	18.92	—	35.6	20.9	22.3	38.7	30.6	70.0	19.2
	2.00	1.72	8.99	25.31	4.90	10.95	—	16.9	40.1	44.0	70.8	64.9	124.7	61.4
	1.31	0.54	2.61	6.98	2.68	6.51	—	10.3	82.1	83.1	142.2	118.8	238.5	137.3
5411 Grocery Stores (138)	2.20	1.77	16.78	44.95	15.56	40.24	—	23.3	43.9	44.1	78.7	84.6	72.9	44.3
	1.70	1.12	12.35	29.48	12.25	25.12	—	16.7	76.5	69.1	124.8	147.5	93.3	85.4
	1.36	0.57	8.04	17.77	8.41	16.25	—	12.7	114.6	123.1	225.2	226.2	127.0	177.5
5251 Hardware Stores (92)	6.46	6.80	17.90	21.33	3.89	5.17	—	5.3	5.8	16.9	47.4	71.4	20.7	11.2
	3.79	3.56	8.63	14.18	2.97	3.30	—	3.9	14.3	35.0	96.8	89.3	46.3	38.2
	2.21	1.25	2.03	4.80	1.74	2.21	—	2.6	35.6	84.1	242.0	107.9	66.9	69.9

— Not computed. Necessary information as to the division between cash sales was available in too few cases to obtain an average collection period usable as a broad guide.
( ) Indicates loss

Figure 4-16: Key Ratios for Retailers

Other sources you might consider writing to include:

Robert Morris Associates
Philadelphia National Bank Building
Philadelphia, PA 19107

Small Business Reporter
Department 3120
P.O. Box 37000
San Francisco, CA 94137

Editor, Journal of Small Business
Bureau of Business Research
West Virginia University
Morgantown, WV 26505

U.S. Small Business Administration
P.O. Box 30
Denver, CO 80201-0030
(800) 827-5722 (SBA Small Business Answer Desk)

Superintendent of Documents
U.S. Government Printing Office
Washington, DC 20402

Your local **Chamber of Commerce**
might be your best source.

The following is a list of reference books that can put you in touch with specific organizations and associations. They may be found at your local library.

Encyclopedia of Associations, reference book published by Gale Research, Detroit, MI. Lists trade and professional associations throughout the U.S.

National Trade and Professional Associations of the U.S., reference book published by Columbia Books, Washington, D.C. Trade and professional associations are indexed by association, geographic region, subject and budget.

ANALYZING REPORTS BY THE PERCENTAGES

Analyzing and interpreting financial reports by means of ratios is one way to go. Another way is simply to translate the dollar amounts for entries on the reports into percentages. On an income statement, net sales is considered

Figure 4-17

Jones Company
Income Statement
For Year Ended December 19xx

		Percentage Breakdown
Gross sales	$130,000	
Less: Sales discounts	10,000	
Net sales	$120,000	100%
Cost of goods sold	96,000	80%*
Gross profit	24,000	20%
Selling and administrative expenses	19,500	16.25%**
Operating income	4,500	3.75%
Interest expense	1,620	1.35%
Net income before tax	2,880	2.40%
Tax (assume 50% rate)	1,440	1.20%
Net income after tax	$ 1,440	1.20%

$$ * \frac{\$96,000}{\$120,000} = 0.8 $$

$$ ** \frac{\$19,500}{\$120,000} = 0.1625 $$

Figure 4-18

Jones Company
Balance Sheet
December 31, 19xx

Assets

Current Assets:				Percentage	Percentage
Cash on hand		$ 5,000		6.33%*	
Accounts receivable		25,000		31.65%	
Inventories		22,000		27.85%	
Total current assets			$52,000	65.82%	
Fixed Assets:					
Land and building		$13,000		16.46%	
Equipment	$20,000				
Less: Accumulated depreciation	6,000	14,000		17.72%	
Total Fixed assets			27,000	34.18%	
Total assets			$79,000		

* $ 5,000 ** $10,000
  $79,000 $79,000

Liabilities and Stockholders' Equity

Liabilities

Current Liabilities			Percentage	Percentage
Accounts Payable	$10,000		12.67%	
Salaries Payable	10,000		12.66%**	
Total Current Liabilities		$20,000	25.32%	
Long-term Liabilities:				
Notes Payable	$ 5,000		6.33%	
Mortgage Payable	10,000		12.66%	
Total Long-term Liabilities		$15,000	18.99%	
Total Liabilities		$35,000		

Stockholders' Equity

Common Stock				
(12,500 shares @ $1 par)	$12,500		15.82%	
Retained Earnings	31,500		39.87%	
Total Stockholders' Equity		$44,000	55.69%	
Total Liabilities and Stockholders' Equity		$79,000		

the "100 percent" against which all other entries are compared. In Figure 4-17, for example, the net sales for The Jones Company is $120,000 (100 percent). The cost of goods sold is $96,000, or 80 percent of net sales. Note in the right-hand column, each entry is represented by a percentage of net sales. On a balance sheet, the total assets is taken as "100 percent." In Figure 4-18, the cash on hand, $5,000, represents 6.33 percent of The Jones Company's total assets of $79,000. On the liabilities and owner equity side of the balance sheet, the total there (also $79,000) is used as the "100-percent" figure.

From Balance Sheet

Jones Percentage of total			Hypothetical Industry Standard
Cash	6.3%		2.5%
Accounts receivable	31.6%		25.0%
Current liabilities	25.3%	(12.6 + 12.6)	18.0%
Long-term liabilities	18.99%	(6.3 + 12.6)	32.5%
Cost of goods sold	80.00%		65 %

From Income Sheet

Figure 4-19: Comparison of Jones Company Percentages to Industrial Standards

These percentage breakdowns bear interesting meaning for Jones. It *could* be that Jones

1. holds too much cash;
2. has slow collection procedures;
3. has too much short-term debt;
4. does not have enough long-term financing; or
5. allows costs to be too high in proportion to the retail sales price.

On the other hand, Jones might have improved his situation, or in fact he might be quite satisfied with results.

Previous records can be compared with this report, that is, Jones can compare percentages from year to year. For example, last year on the balance sheet, accounts receivable were 38 percent of assets. This year's balance sheet shows 31.6 percent—a definite improvement.

USING COMMON SENSE

Jones realizes that industry standards are important, but he also feels that his business is unique. So he does not rely solely on ratios and percentages to make his decisions. Maximizing his profit requires a variety of management tools. He weighs the percentage calculations (for past and current reports), industry standards, financial ratios, and many other factors. But his *most important tool is common sense*. When the "red flag" is raised by financial tools, he then takes a step-by-step procedure in monitoring as well as solving the financial problems. The next chapter looks at some of these other tools—such as budgeting and cash flow—that keeps the business "in tune" and out of cash crises.

Following is a checklist for improving the profitability of your business:[4]

I. Increasing your markon
    A. Buying for less
        1. Do you take advantage of all discount opportunities?
        2. Do you watch purchases under seasonal rebate agreements so that they will not fall below limits?
        3. Do you keep your transportation costs to a minimum by using the most economical common carrier, packing methods, and consolidations?
        4. Do you concentrate your purchases with key suppliers?
        5. Do you actually use the facilities of a resident buying office to obtain better values?
        6. Could you realize savings by placing orders further ahead?
        7. Could you realize savings by placing blanket orders?
        8. Have you an undeveloped opportunity to use private brands to compete with national brands?
        9. Do you resist special quantity price concessions for merchandise that will not turn over for a long period of time?

    B. Selling for more
        1. Do you take every opportunity to buy exclusive merchandise?
        2. Do you price every item on its merits (rather than applying at an average markup on most goods)?
        3. Are goods costing the same put into stock at different prices when there is a difference in value in the customers' eyes?
        4. Could you raise price line endings slightly without detracting from your sales volume?

    C. Promoting higher markup goods
        1. Do you know the markup of each price line and in each classification?
        2. Do you make an adequate effort to feature in your advertising those price lines and items that bear a long markup?
        3. Is your long-markup merchandise adequately displayed in the store?
        4. Are your salespeople trained to give special attention to the higher-markup goods in stock?
        5. Do you give rewards for selling high-markup goods?
        6. Do you avoid giving valuable space to slow sellers?

II. Curtailing your reductions
    A. Buying:
        1. Will your markdowns be reduced by rising wholesale prices?
        2. Do your buyers make careful buying plans before they go to market?

[4] From *Small Store Planning for Growth*, Small Business Management Series, No. 32, 2nd. ed. (Washington, DC: Small Business Administration, 1977).

3. Do your buyers frequently overbuy promotional merchandise, later forcing you to take heavy markdowns on remainders?
4. Are your stocks peaked well in advance of the sales peak?
5. Do you curtail reorders at the peak of the selling season?
6. Are you developing classic lines with a long life?
7. Are merchandise shortcomings leading to customer returns and markdowns? (If so, demand higher quality standards.)
8. Do you place your orders on time so that they will have the proper merchandise in your store when the demand is great?
9. Do you concentrate your buying on what you know will sell instead of experimenting with fringe sizes, colors, fabrics and types of merchandise?
10. Do you "test" new merchandise in small quantities before the beginning of a season and then concentrate heavily on the items that were successful?
11. Do you buy "items," where possible, instead of full lines?
12. Do you follow up your orders carefully to check for better deliveries?
13. Do you refuse to accept past due merchandise when the demand falls off?
14. Do you receive merchandise at regular staggered intervals as opposed to receiving it "when ready"?

B. Selling
1. Are your salespeople adequately presenting the older goods in your stock?
2. Do you have a good followup system to insure that goods don't become slow sellers?
3. Do you carefully instruct your salespeople in the selling points of merchandise that is slow moving?
4. Are your salespeople using forced selling methods that lead to returns and eventual markdowns?
5. Do you provide your salespeople with proper rewards for selling slow-moving merchandise?

C. Control
1. Do you have any opportunities to increase your stock turn and reduce the length of time goods are on hand before being sold?
2. Do you take your markdowns early enough?
3. Do you take them too soon?
4. Do you set the first markdown low enough to move most of the goods marked down?
5. Have you established special markdown prices?
6. Do you have a system of good physical control of stock that avoids shortages?
7. Do you reorder well enough in advance to avoid being out of best sellers?

8. Do you avoid unnecessary markdowns on staple merchandise that can be carried over to next year?
9. Do you keep a record of markdowns by sizes, to avoid errors in future ordering?

III. Increasing your cash discounts
    A. Are you getting the largest possible cash discounts from your cash suppliers?
    B. Do you pay all your bills on time so as to obtain the discounts offered?
    C. Are you taking advantage of anticipation opportunities?

IV. Lowering your workroom and alteration costs
    A. Are charges to your customers desirable, and are they adequate?
    B. Is your workroom being run as economically as possible?
    C. Would it be feasible to eliminate your workroom operation?

1. A classified balance sheet categorizes assets according to whether they are current or fixed. A current asset turns into cash or is used up within one year. A fixed asset lasts for more than one year.
2. The classified balance sheet for a corporation has a stockholders' equity section made up of (a) stock and (b) retained earnings. Retained earnings consist of the profit retained in the business.
3. Sales less the cost of goods sold equals gross profit. Gross profit less operating expenses equals net income. Remember that the cost of goods sold is matched against your inward flow of revenue.
4. Ratio analysis is not absolute. Industrial averages provide reasonable comparisons for the individual company ratios. We looked at the following ratios:

Assets

a. Current ratio	$\dfrac{\text{Current assets}}{\text{Current liabilities}}$	$\dfrac{CA}{CL}$
b. Acid test (quick ratio)	$\dfrac{\text{Current assets} - \text{Inventory}}{\text{Current liabilities}}$	$\dfrac{CA - I}{CL}$
c. Inventory turnover	$\dfrac{\text{Net sales}}{\text{Inventory}}$	$\dfrac{NS}{I}$
d. Average days collections	$\dfrac{A/R}{\text{Sales}/360 \text{ days } S} \div 360$	
e. Fixed asset turnover	$\dfrac{\text{Net sales}}{\text{Fixed assets}}$	$\dfrac{NS}{FA}$
f. Asset turnover	$\dfrac{\text{Net sales}}{\text{Total assets}}$	$\dfrac{NS}{TA}$

Debit Situation

g. Debt/total assets	$\dfrac{\text{Total liabilities}}{\text{Total assets}}$	$\dfrac{\text{TL}}{\text{TA}}$

Profitability

h. Net profit margin	$\dfrac{\text{Net income after taxes}}{\text{Sales}}$	$\dfrac{\text{NIAT}}{\text{S}}$
i. Return on investment (Assets)	$\dfrac{\text{Net income after taxes}}{\text{Total assets}}$	$\dfrac{\text{NIAT}}{\text{TA}}$
j. Return on equity (Investment)	$\dfrac{\text{Net income after taxes}}{\text{Stockholders' equity}}$	$\dfrac{\text{NIAT}}{\text{SE}}$

5. Statements can also be broken down into percentages. Trends can be seen over a period of time. For example, maybe our cost of goods sold has gone from 40 to 60 percent while competitors have a 50-percent cost of goods sold. The more data we look at, the clearer the implications will be.

CHECK YOUR PULSE

	True	False
1. Financial ratios are used only on the income statement.	____	____
2. Land, building, and accounts receivable are examples of fixed assets.	____	____
3. Fixed assets help produce revenue.	____	____
4. Current liabilities are obligations that will not be due for at least one year.	____	____
5. Retained earnings is an account that reflects profits kept in the business.	____	____
6. Sales less cost of goods sold equals gross profit.	____	____
7. A current ratio of 3.5 means we have $3.50 of assets to cover each $1 of current liabilities.	____	____
8. Inventory is included in the acid test ratio.	____	____
9. Too high an inventory turnover could lead to a "glut" of inventory.	____	____
10. Usually all accounts receivable are collected within 30 days.	____	____
11. Asset turnover is a measure of debt performance.	____	____
12. Industry average ratios are always the final word in where your company stands.	____	____
13. Cost of goods sold should be at most 65 percent of sales.	____	____
14. Ratios should be calculated weekly.	____	____

15. Many special industry sources supply ratios to small businesses. ____ ____
16. The balance sheet lists all revenues and expenses. ____ ____
17. Sales discounts increase total sales. ____ ____
18. Too many calculations of financial ratios could possibly do more harm than good. ____ ____
19. Financial ratios are only one tool in trying to interpret financial reports. ____ ____
20. Stockholders' equity is made up of stock and retained earnings. ____ ____

1. False	11. False
2. False	12. False
3. True	13. False
4. False	14. False
5. True	15. True
6. True	16. False
7. True	17. False
8. False	18. True
9. False	19. True
10. False	20. True

Column A	Column B
____ 1. Current assets	A. A – L
____ 2. Common sense	B. Not for resale
____ 3. Gross profit	C. Part of stockholders' equity
____ 4. Industrial ratio averages	D. Inventory turnover
____ 5. Current ratio	E. Due within a year
____ 6. Current liabilities	F. Net sales/Total assets
____ 7. Net profit margin	G. Cash, accounts receivable, inventory
____ 8. Sales less sales	H. The guide used in analyzing ratios
____ 9. Acid test	I. CA/CL
____ 10. Income statement	J. Where cost of goods sold is found
____ 11. Stockholders' equity	K. Sales less cost of goods sold
____ 12. Balance sheet	L. Only one type of tool
____ 13. Asset turnover	M. Memorized
____ 14. Financial ratios	N. Inventory not part of calculation
____ 15. Dun and Bradstreet	O. Net sales/Fixed assets
____ 16. Fixed assets	P. Supplies industrial ratios
____ 17. Ratios should not be __	Q. Performance picture
____ 18. Retained earnings	R. Assets, liabilities, owner equity
____ 19. Fixed asset turnover	S. Net sales
____ 20. Net sales/Inventory	T. Should only be used wisely

Answers

1.	G	11.	A
2.	H	12.	R
3.	K	13.	F
4.	T	14.	L
5.	I	15.	P
6.	E	16.	B
7.	Q	17.	M
8.	S	18.	C
9.	N	19.	0
10.	J	20.	D

5

CASH MANAGEMENT: HOW TO AVOID A CASH CRISIS

OBJECTIVES

1. Explain the survival checklist.
2. Explain the need to budget.
3. Define and illustrate the cash cycle.
4. Define and illustrate the purpose of a cash budget.
5. Prepare a cash budget.
6. Define:
   - break-even analysis
   - fixed costs
   - variable costs
   - unit contribution
   - break-even point in units
   - target profit
7. Prepare a break-even chart.
8. Discuss the advantages and disadvantages of utilizing break-even analysis.
9. Define what is meant by projected financial reports.
10. Prepare a projected income statement and balance sheet.

ANNE: So far we have looked at the recordkeeping process, as well as how to read and interpret financial reports. Now I'd like to go back to the survival checklist, which I'm showing you again for your convenience, and spend some time on how to plan the future so as to avoid a cash crisis:

THE SURVIVAL CHECKLIST REVISITED

1. lots of unsold inventory
2. customers aren't paying bills on time
3. not meeting tax obligations on time
4. writing business checks for personal expenses
5. bank loan is overdue
6. not paying suppliers on time—paper backlogged
7. theft unusually high
8. making lots of money but not enough food on table
9. paying bills too early
10. seasonal slump creating a cash crisis
11. buying trucks instead of leasing
12. bank balance and checkbook reconciled once a year
13. missing many purchase discounts
14. interest costs draining the business—sales falling
15. expense rising dramatically from previous years
16. financial reports prepared once a year
17. bad debts increasing substantially

By now, Jen, you should have a better handle on items 2, 4, 6, 12, 15, 16, and 17. So let's zero in on items 1, 5, 8, 9, 10, 11, 13, and 14.

JEN: These are areas I'm most interested in. But my relative told me that if I plan, I run a greater risk of "failure." He felt planning tends to "lock" a business in, so it can't adapt to changing times.

ANNE: Hold on! As I said before, relatives mean well but . . . For example, let's look at the Jim Moore Company. Jim makes daily deposits in the bank. Some days the deposits are in excess of $10,000. His problem was that no matter how much money the company deposited, there was a continuous shortage of cash. Every day was a new brush fire to put out. Loans were coming due. Purchase discounts were missed. Suppliers would deliver goods only COD. Payrolls were not met. Legal obligations were overdue.

THE NEED TO BUDGET

I encouraged Jim to set up a plan that would force him to think ahead. This plan, called a *budget*, became a tool that aided him in setting benchmarks, as well as allowing him to measure his performance. Budgeting is not new. In your own family you estimate what your financial condition will be. Think of Christmas time. Did you charge too much? Did you develop a repayment schedule? Did you build in a plan that was reasonable to see if you reached your goals? Did you *discipline* yourself? You have to think of budgeting as a positive tool. Before looking at a sample cash budget for Jim, let's look at how cash tends to flow in a company.

Cash Flow

As shown in Figure 5-1, cash is decreased by the acquisition of materials and services to produce the finished goods. It is also reduced by paying off the amounts owed to suppliers, that is, by accounts payable. When inventory is sold, these sales generate cash and/or accounts receivable, that is, money owed from customers. As customers pay up on their accounts, accounts receivable are reduced, and the cash account increases. Yet cash flows from accounts receivable are not necessarily related to the sales in the same period because customers must pay in the next period.[1] *So if accounts receivable are collected too slowly, they impact on the cash cycle.*

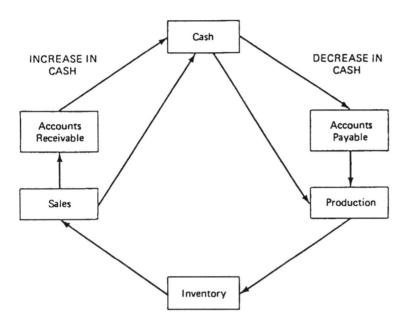

Figure 5-1: The Cash Cycle

Other factors affect the cash cycle also. If you pay your bills too quickly, maybe you're creating a greater outward flow of cash than in fact you have to. Theft can play a big part in this cycle. By lowering your sales, it brings about less of a cash inflow, which means that you have to borrow more to replenish the stock of goods for sale. Of course, the more a company owes, the greater the interest charges—like the old domino theory. Sales that are down influence the inward or potential inward flow of cash, which in turn affects the amount of loans needed to produce the desired inventory level. On the favorable side of the cash cycle, an excess of cash can be invested in outside sources—marketable securities—to produce a greater return.

Take a moment now to look back at our survival checklist and see how a slowdown in the cash cycle can affect its seventeen items.

The Moore Company Cash Budget

Now let's look specifically at how Moore budgets his cash flow. Keep in mind that, although there are many varieties of budgets for sales, cash, inventory, and other items, our attention is now on the Moore Company's cash budget, which was developed to satisfy the follow objectives:

1. to identify cash deficiency periods;
2. to monitor bank repayment schedules;

[1] This section is reproduced from SBA *Management Aid No. 277* (Washington, DC: Small Business Administration, 1975).

3. to identify times when cash is available to invest;
4. to detect trends to minimize the strain in the cash position for possible cash expansion or during an unusual "crisis."

The key to developing a good cash budget is first to make a *realistic and not-too-optimistic estimate of sales*. Predicting the future isn't easy, but, in building a cash budget, you have to do your best because the sales estimate is crucial. Let's build Moore Company's cash budget (Figure 5-2) step-by-step. For Moore there are seven basic steps, which are represented by the circled numbers in Figure 5-2.

STEP 1 As shown in Figure 5-2, Moore Company managers estimated sales from August to the end of December—quite conservatively in their opinion. They didn't want their budget based just on "hope." Note that the receipt section in Figure 5-2 is a *cash* inflow, which at $69,300 is heaviest in December.

STEPS 2 AND 3 Moore anticipated the heaviest outward flow of cash in August, to the extent that Moore showed a cash deficiency of $24,860 in August. The outward flow of $46,860 was much greater than the inward flow of $22,000. Hence the cash deficiency of $24,860.

STEP 4 The Moore Company indicated they wanted to keep a $5,000 minimum cash balance.

STEP 5 Since the payments in August are $24,860 more than the receipts, the company needs a loan of $29,860 (which includes the $5,000 minimum balance). Notice that the borrowing increases by another $12,780 (from line 3 in cash budget) in September to make total borrowing of $42,640.

STEP 6 The balance owed the bank hits a peak of $42,640 in September. Moore is able to begin paying off the bank loan in October and repays the entire loan by December. So their need to borrow doesn't mean that they're in trouble—only that they're organized enough to identify a temporary cash shortage.

STEP 7 Moore will not have excess cash ($16,840) until December. Moore realizes that this cash should be put to use. Bear in mind that keeping cash idle, especially in these inflationary times, make it of less real value in the future.

BREAK-EVEN ANALYSIS

ANNE: Moore Company has shown us the need to stay on top of cash flow and how important it can be controlling in a cash crisis.

JEN: I think I've seen enough!

ANNE: Not yet. Let's go on to another tool for controlling, as well as analyzing, expense levels in relation to the selling price and to the volume of the units sold. This tool is commonly referred to as

Figure 5-2

Jim Moore Company
Cash Budget, Steps 1-7

	August	September	October	November	December
Planned Receipts					
Cash sales	$ 1,600	$ 1,200	$ 1,400	$ 2,400	$ 5,600
Charge sales	20,000	20,400	31,600	40,000	63,200
Miscellaneous	400	800	400	960	500
① Total estimated receipts	$22,000	$22,400	$33,400	$43,360	$69,300
Planned Payments					
Accounts payable	$34,000	$22,000	$16,400	$ 5,400	$ 4,400
Salaries	5,200	8,400	8,400	15,800	11,600
Operating expenses	2,400	3,600	4,000	5,400	1,200
Interest expense	260	260	260	260	260
Fixed assets	5,000	920	1,200	1,600	200f
Reserve for taxes				7,600	7,600
② Total estimated payments	$46,860	$35,180	$30,260	$36,060	$25,260
③ Planned receipts versus planned payments (Step 1 versus 2)	($24,860)	($12,780)	$ 3,140	$ 7,300	$44,040
④ Desired cash balance	5,000	5,000	5,000	5,000	5,000
⑤ Borrowing needed	29,860 (5,000 + 24,860)	42,640 (29,860 + 12,780)	–0–	–0–	–0–
⑥ Balance of loan	29,860	42,640	39,500 (42,640 – 3,140)	32,200 (39,500 – 7,300)	–0–
⑦ Actual cash balance	$ 5,000	$ 5,000	$ 5,000	$ 5,000	$16,840

"break-even analysis." Break-even analysis can be of tremendous value in monitoring various expense levels in relation to sales. Remember, just as increased sales can result in additional cash flow, the expenses paid or incurred to get those extra sales can also affect cash flow. You don't have to be an expert on break-even, but it is a sound tool in profit planning and control.

One word of caution: *Break-even analysis doesn't replace judgment.* It doesn't tell you if your costs are out of "whack" in relation to sales volume. In other words, this tool tells you what your costs will be at a certain level of sales, but it is up to you to decide if those costs are reasonable. I will show you some basic key terms used in break-even analysis, along with an insight or two into specific calculations. Before looking at the technique of preparing a break-even chart, let's first go over the key terms. Don't memorize them. Just refer back to them.

Fixed costs Costs that remain constant throughout a volume of sales activity. Examples include insurance, rent, salaried workers, property tax, and interest costs.

Variable costs Costs that vary with the volume of sales activity. Examples include sales commissions, payroll taxes, and advertising expenses. A variable cost of, say, 80 percent of sales means that, for each $1 of sales, 80 cents covers variable cost.

Unit contribution (contribution margin) The excess of sales revenue over variable costs. For example:

Cost of product	$250
Variable cost	180
Contribution margin	$70

Break-even point The level of sales in dollars in which the total revenue equals the total cost. At this point a business owner is neither making money nor losing it. He or she is able only to cover variable and fixed costs. The formula for calculating a break-even point per sales is:

Sales = Fixed costs + Variable costs (as a percentage of sales)
$$S = FC + VC$$

Let's assume:

$$FC = \$100,000$$
$$VC = 60\% \text{ (60 cents of each dollar covers variable cost)}$$
$$S = ?$$
$$S = \$100,000 + 0.6S$$
$$S - 0.6S = \$100,000$$
$$0.4S = \$100,000$$
$$S = \frac{\$100,000}{0.4}$$
$$S = \$250,000$$

Let's see if it balances:

$250,000=$100,000 + 0.6 ($250,000)
$250,000=$100,000 + $150,000
$250,000=$250,000

So: At a sales level of $250,000, the fixed cost of $100,000 and the variable cost of $150,000 result in no profit and no loss. That sales level is the break-even point.

The number of units sold (instead of sales dollars) at which the business *Break-even point in units* breaks even. The formula for calculating a break-even point in units is:

$$\frac{\text{Units of sales}}{\text{to Break-Even}} = \frac{\text{Fixed Cost}}{\text{Unit Sales Price} - \text{Unit Variable Cost}}$$

$$\text{B/E} = \frac{\text{FC}}{\text{USP} - \text{UVC}}$$

Let's assume:

$$
\begin{aligned}
\text{FC} &= \$100,000 \\
\text{USP} &= \$18 \\
\text{UVC} &= \$14 \\
\text{B/E} &= ? \\
\text{B/E} &= \frac{\$100,000}{\$18 - \$14} \\
\text{B/E} &= \frac{\$100,000}{\$4} \\
\text{B/E} &= 25,000 \text{ units}
\end{aligned}
$$

Let's see if it works:

Units x Selling price = Fixed costs = Units x Variable cost statement:
B/E x SP = FC + B/E = x VC
25,000 x $18 = $100,000 + 25,000 x $14
$450,000 = $100,000 + $350,000
$450,000 = $450,000

Income Statement

Sales 25,000 @ 18 =	450,000
– Variable Costs 25,000 @ 14	350,000
= Contribution Margin	100,000
– Fixed Costs	100,000
N/I (L)	0

Indeed, at a volume of 25,000 we are at the point of no profit and no loss—the break-even point.

Target profit (in units)   Basically, the profit of the company that is desired beyond the break-even point. All we need to do is to insert the desired target profit into the break-even formula.

$$\begin{array}{c}\text{Unit Sales}\\\text{To Achieve}\\\text{Target Profit}\end{array} = \frac{\text{Fixed Cost} + \text{Target Profit}}{\text{Unit Selling Price} - \text{Unit VariableCost}}$$

$$= \frac{FC + TP}{USP - UVC}$$

Using the same figures as in the break-even calculation, let's see what happens if the company wanted to calculate the number of units that must be sold in order to achieve a profit of $40,000.

$$FC = \$100,000$$
$$USP = 18$$
$$UVC = 14$$

$$\begin{array}{c}\text{Units to}\\\text{Achieve Target}\\\text{Profit}\end{array} = \frac{100,000 + 40,000}{18 - 14}$$

$$= \frac{140,000}{4}$$

$$= 35,000 \text{ units}$$

We can prove that this formula works by preparing an Income Statement:

Sales 35,000 with units x 18	=	630,000
Variable Costs 35,000 Units x 14	=	$490,000
Contribution Margin 35,000 x 4	=	140,000
Fixed Costs		100,000
Net Income		40,000

So at 35,000 units the company shows a net income of $40,000.

BEN'S TV: APPLICATION OF BREAK-EVEN ANALYSIS

With this background let's look at Ben's TV and how we can apply break-even analysis.

Concern #1: Unit Break-Even Point

How many TV sets must Ben sell to break even? Given:

Selling price of a TV =	$	500
Variable cost	= $	300
Fixed cost	=	$70,000
Break Even (BE)	=	?

Let's apply the formula:

$$\text{Break Even} = \frac{\text{Fixed cost}}{\text{Unit sale price} - \text{Unit variable cost}}$$

$$BE = \frac{FC}{USP - UVC}$$

$$BE = \frac{70{,}000}{500 - 300}$$

$$BE = \frac{70{,}000}{200}$$

$$BE = 350 \text{ Units}$$

Let's check it:

Income Statement at Break Even

Sales 350 TVs @ 500	=	$175,000
– Variable Cost 350 TVs @ 300	=	105,000
= Contribution Margin 350 @ 200		$70,000
– Fixed Costs		70,000
Net Income		0

If Ben wants to make $30,000, how many TVs must he sell?

$$\begin{array}{l}\text{Unit Sales} \\ \text{To Achieve} \\ \text{Target Profit}\end{array} = \frac{\text{Fixed Costs} + \text{Target Profit}}{\text{Unit Selling Price} - \text{Unit Variable Cost}}$$

$$= \frac{70{,}000 + 30{,}000}{500 - 300}$$

$$= \frac{100{,}000}{200}$$

$$= 500$$

Let's see if it works:

Sales 500 TVs @ 500	=	$250,000
Variable Costs 500 TVs @ 300	=	150,000
Contribution Margin 500 TVs @ 150 (S/B <u>200</u>?) =		100,000
Fixed Costs	=	70,000
Net Income	=	30,000

So, yes, with sales of 500 TVs, Ben reaches a profit of $30,000. This break-even calculation is put into graph form in Figure 5-3.

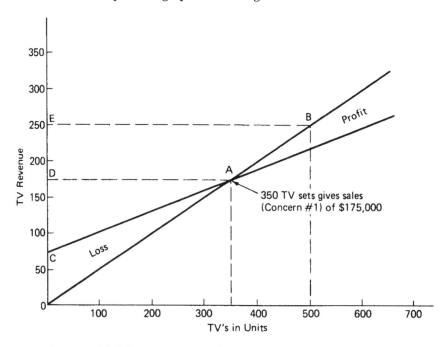

A at sales of 350 TVs, there is no profit or loss.
B at sales of 500 TVs, there is a profit of $30,000.
C Note fixed cost is at $70,000.
D Represents $175,000.
E Represents $250,000.

Figure 5-3: Break-Even Analysis, Illustrated

Advantages and Limitations of Break-Even Analysis

Break-even analysis is not a panacea that solves all of a business's problems. Following is a list of advantages and disadvantages of break-even analysis:

Advantages	Disadvantages
Inexpensive tool—good yardstick to evaluate target profit goals.	No project or decision can be made in isolation—too many assumptions. For example, the fixed cost might not be constant.
Aids analysis of fixed versus variable costs.	Does not take in time value of money.
Aids in estimating unknowns—a way of attacking business uncertainty.	Tool might be too static. Relationship of variable and fixed costs continually changing.
Allows you to make comparisons among various projects.	Might be too simple a tool for analyzing complex problems.
Shows how different selling prices could affect profit picture.	Too many assumptions between cost and revenue relationships.
Highlights contribution margin—forces management to monitor margin of	People think it replaces judgment.

Advantages *(cont.)*	Disadvantages *(cont.)*
profit versus volume—for instance, should plant be expanded or do we have ideal capacity?	
Break-even point can be shown in a simple graphic presentation.	Doesn't judge competitors and strategies.
Aids in the analysis and development of budgets. Gets you to look closer at sales.	Assumes selling price is held constant.
	Doesn't compare your product mix. Cost of inventories and accounts receivable are not analyzed.

PROJECTED REPORTS

Another type of planning involves estimating or "projecting" what your income statement and balance sheet might look like in the future. They are invaluable tools in seeking financing. The projected reports (often referred to as "pro forma" reports) try to get you to think ahead. Remember, these reports are *estimates*. Don't cast them as concrete.

These projected reports should be prepared every three months or, if necessary, for shorter periods of time. These reports can be built many ways, based on estimates and assumptions. Think of them as rough sketches. After the actual results, your trouble spots are identified and unrealistic estimates revealed.[2]

The Projected Income Statement

The projected income statement (Figure 5-4) of the German Company is an estimate of future inward and outward flows. Many of the *estimates are based on past experience, customer trends, economic forecasts, and the like.* You don't

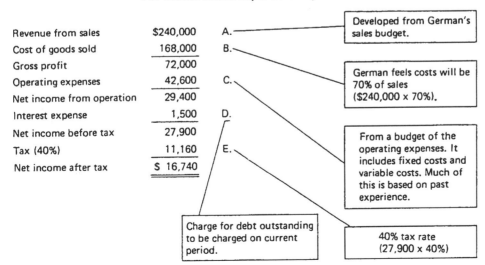

Figure 5-4

The German Company
Projected Income Statement
For Month Ended September 30, 19xx

Revenue from sales	$240,000	A.
Cost of goods sold	168,000	B.
Gross profit	72,000	
Operating expenses	42,600	C.
Net income from operation	29,400	
Interest expense	1,500	D.
Net income before tax	27,900	
Tax (40%)	11,160	E.
Net income after tax	$ 16,740	

Developed from German's sales budget.

German feels costs will be 70% of sales ($240,000 x 70%).

From a budget of the operating expenses. It includes fixed costs and variable costs. Much of this is based on past experience.

Charge for debt outstanding to be charged on current period.

40% tax rate (27,900 x 40%)

[2] *Handbook of Small Business Finance*, SBA series No. 15 (Washington, D.C.: Small Business Administration, 1975). Publication is no longer in print.

see the beauty of this report until you compare it to actual results. Then you see, in fact, how accurate you were in planning for the future. Once again, the sales estimate is all-important; if this is wrong, your troubles have begun.

The Projected Balance Sheet

The Projected Balance Sheet (Figure 5-5) is an attempt to estimate assets, liabilities, and owner equity. It is a reflection of the various budgets, estimates of sales, timing of collections, as well as terms of payment to creditors. Many of the estimates are based on past experience, trends, and reasonable projections. Don't memorize the sample projected balance sheet in Figure 5-5. Keep in mind that this report is also only an estimate, which is eventually compared against actuality.

Figure 5-5

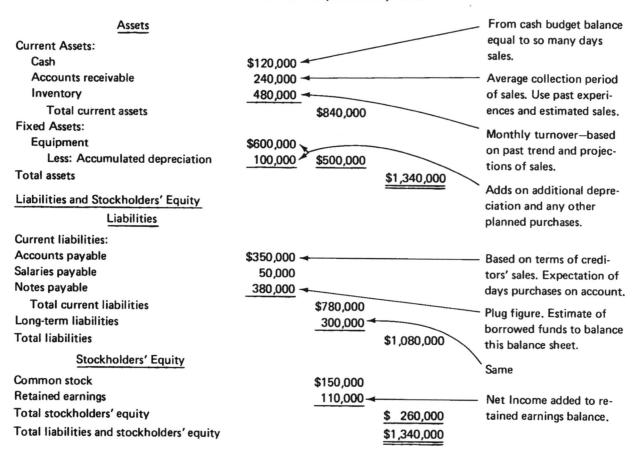

The German Company
Projected Balance Sheet
For Month Ended September 30, 19xx

Assets

Current Assets:			
Cash	$120,000		From cash budget balance equal to so many days sales.
Accounts receivable	240,000		Average collection period of sales. Use past experiences and estimated sales.
Inventory	480,000		
Total current assets		$840,000	
Fixed Assets:			Monthly turnover—based on past trend and projections of sales.
Equipment	$600,000		
Less: Accumulated depreciation	100,000	$500,000	
Total assets		$1,340,000	Adds on additional depreciation and any other planned purchases.

Liabilities and Stockholders' Equity
Liabilities

Current liabilities:			
Accounts payable	$350,000		Based on terms of creditors' sales. Expectation of days purchases on account.
Salaries payable	50,000		
Notes payable	380,000		
Total current liabilities		$780,000	
Long-term liabilities		300,000	Plug figure. Estimate of borrowed funds to balance this balance sheet.
Total liabilities		$1,080,000	

Stockholders' Equity

			Same
Common stock	$150,000		
Retained earnings	110,000		Net Income added to retained earnings balance.
Total stockholders' equity		$ 260,000	
Total liabilities and stockholders' equity		$1,340,000	

1. The process of budgeting *must* be looked upon as a positive process. It really helps you "hedge" on the future. Your time will not be wasted.

2. Budgeting is really a tool that prepares a plan to set benchmarks so performance can be measured. Be realistic. Don't indulge in pipe dreams.

3. Discipline yourself to make budgeting a priority. Doing so allows you to reach specific goals and objectives. Be organized. Be a "thinker" as well as a "doer."

4. The cash cycle reinforces the need for careful budgeting. Watch collections! Are they slow coming in? Are you taking advantage of purchase discounts?

5. The cash budget:
   • identifies cash deficiencies;
   • aids in monitoring bank repayments;
   • draws a lead on cash surpluses; and
   • minimizes the strain of a cash crisis.
   With inflation, you cannot avoid the cash budget. It is a necessity in the lifeblood of your business.

6. Budgeting centers around the estimate for sales. Sales estimates can be based on trends, industrial forecasts, expectations, and the like.

7. Break-even analysis is a tool that analyzes various expense levels in relation to sales.

8. Costs that are constant are called "fixed." Costs that fluctuate are called "variable."

9. Contribution margin equals total costs minus variable costs.

10. The break-even point in sales volume equals:

Break-even point = Fixed costs + Variable costs (as a percentage of sales)

$$BEP = FC + VC (\%)$$

11. The BEP for units equals:

$$B/E = \frac{\text{Fixed costs}}{\text{Unit sales price} - \text{Unit variable cost}}$$

$$B/E = \frac{FC}{USP - UVC}$$

12. Target profit equals:

$$\text{Units to Achieve Target Profit} = \frac{\text{Fixed Costs} + \text{Target Profit}}{\text{Unit Selling Price} - \text{Unit Variable Cost}}$$

13. As good a tool as break-even is, there are many pros and cons, as we noted in our list of pluses and minuses. Break-even can't do it all. It is only one piece of the planning "pie."

		True	False
1.	Budgeting looks only at the past.	___	___
2.	Disciplining yourself always makes for a successful budget.	___	___
3.	Budgeting identifies cash deficiency periods.	___	___
4.	Sales estimates are crucial in budget development.	___	___
5.	Borrowing is a sign that a business is definitely in financial trouble.	___	___
6.	Fixed costs always change with volume.	___	___
7.	Payroll taxes are a fixed cost.		
8.	A contribution margin of 20 cents aids in covering fixed costs.	___	___
9.	Sales are satisfactory at the break-even point.	___	___
10.	Break-even shows how different selling prices could affect the profit picture.	___	___
11.	Judgment can always take the place of break-even analysis.	___	___
12.	Break-even assumes that the selling price remains constant.	___	___
13.	Projected income statements are perfectly accurate.	___	___
14.	Projected balance sheets contain revenue and expenses.	___	___
15.	Projected financial reports are supposed to be compared to actual performance.	___	___
16.	Experience should not be considered a factor in planning.	___	___
17.	Projected financial reports should be prepared at least quarterly.	___	___
18.	Break-even can replace the budget.	___	___
19.	Target profit in sales = Variable cost + Fixed costs + Net income.	___	___
20.	A variable cost fluctuates in the same proportion as fixed costs.	___	___

Solutions

1. False
2. False
3. True
4. True
5. False
6. False
7. False
8. True
9. False
10. True

11. False
12. True
13. False
14. False
15. True
16. False
17. True
18. False
19. True
20. False

_____ 1. Fixed cost

_____ 2. Positive tool

_____ 3. Cost of inventories

_____ 4. Break-even

_____ 5. Disadvantage of break-even

_____ 6. Budget

_____ 7. Discipline

_____ 8. Total fixed cost/Unit contribution

_____ 9. Part of the cash cycle

_____ 10. Aids in estimating unknowns

_____ 11. Insurance, property tax interest

_____ 12. Cash deficiency

_____ 13. Total cost less variable cost

_____ 14. No profit or loss

_____ 15. Key to budgeting

_____ 16. Advice from relatives

_____ 17. Fixed cost/Unit sales price – Unit variable

_____ 18. S = VC + FC + NI

_____ 19. Paying bills early

_____ 20. Cash budget

A. A plan

B. Examples of fixed cost

C. Seasonal business

D. Relieve the cash crisis

E. S = FC + VC

F. Break-even point

G. Cost remains constant

H. Not analyzed in break-even

I. Advantage of break-even

J. Taking the time to plan

K. Estimating sales

L. Potential danger signal

M. Target profit

N. Break-even point in units

0. Tool that compares costs to sales

P. Listen cautiously

Q. Assumes selling price constant

R. Contribution margin

S. Accounts receivable

T. Budget

1.	G	11.	B
2.	T	12.	C
3.	H	13.	R
4.	0	14.	E
5.	Q	15.	K
6.	A	16.	P
7.	J	17.	N
8.	F	18.	M
9.	S	19.	L
10.	I	20.	D

6

TAX OBLIGATIONS: THE RULES OF THE GAME

1. Explain the difference between tax evasion and tax avoidance.
2. List specific kinds of federal taxes.
3. List specific kinds of state taxes.
4. List specific kinds of local taxes.
5. Explain the purpose of the small business tax workshop.
6. Explain the purpose of preparing a worksheet for meeting tax obligations.
7. Explain the need for Form SS-4.
8. Prepare Form W-4.
9. Complete federal withholding tax (FWT) deductions by utilizing a wage bracket table.
10. Explain the difference between FICA and FWT.
11. Explain the time table for paying FWT and FICA.
12. Explain what a "quarter" is.
13. Prepare an employer's quarterly federal tax return.
14. Explain exempt wages.
15. List the specific deposit requirements for Form 941.
16. Define and explain the relationship between the payroll register, weekly payroll, individual earnings record, and general ledger.
17. Prepare a payroll register.
18. Complete an individual earnings record.
19. Complete the W-2, and explain where the information comes from.
20. Explain FUTA.
21. Prepare Form 940.
22. Prepare a tax calendar for your company.

JEN: I really enjoyed the area of cash management, break-even, and projected financial reports. But to be honest, I'm really concerned about how I will meet my tax obligations. I don't want to be "caught" for tax evasion.

ANNE: The words "tax evasion" bother me. Let's get one thing straight: There is a definite difference between tax evasion and tax avoidance. As an accountant, my job is to *minimize* your tax liability; that's tax *avoidance*. This is not to say I will be doing anything illegal. My goal is to pay only the taxes that are legally required. The IRS issues the game rules, and we "play the game" based on their rules. Tax avoidance to me is the minimizing of your tax liability, as well as paying only what is "due" to the Internal Revenue Service. No more, no less. On the other hand, tax *evasion* means we would *not* pay taxes that are due. This is a different ballgame altogether.

JEN: Truthfully, are taxes really as complicated as you accountants make them out to be? How much do I really have to get into all this tax business?

ANNE: As with all the areas of planning we have discussed, the tax area is no exception. You as the owner *must* know the following:

1. How much tax is owed?
2. Are you paying *all* the taxes required by law? If so, are you paying them on time or being charged with penalties?
3. Do you have the cash (remember our discussion on cash flow) to pay the taxes?
4. Are you up-to-date with all the changes in tax regulations? (This is why an accountant and lawyer can be so valuable to you.)

JEN: Just what kinds of business taxes are we talking about?

ANNE: Before getting into specifics, here is a generalized sample of taxes that a business might run into (Figure 6-1).

JEN: How am I going to keep track of all these tax responsibilities?

ANNE: Step one is to get a good accountant (like me) whom you can trust. It is also important for you to have a basic understanding so we can work together to set up your tax strategy. First of all, you should attend the Small Business Tax Workshop. Here is a brochure on how to register (Figure 6-2, page 99).

Meeting tax obligations is no different from the planning needed in your recordkeeping. For example, this worksheet (Figure 6-3, page 100) is used to remind owners which taxes are due. We'll go over each type of tax and their specific requirements in a few minutes.

Keep in mind that, although tax regulations are continually changing, many tax obligations stay the same in general. The rates, the taxable bases, or the forms might change, but the basic theory remains. Tax regulations should not be memorized. The key is to know where to *find* the information. At the end of our discussion, I'll show you a sample tax calendar that tries to put it all together. Now let's turn our attention to specific tax obligations and their implications for your business. Let's first look at federal taxes.

```
FEDERAL          Individual income taxes
                 Corporate income taxes
                 Excise taxes—manufacturers, retailers
                 Employment taxes
                 Social Security taxes
                 Death taxes
                 Stamp taxes
                 Occupational taxes
                 Customs

STATE            Individual income taxes
(specific taxes  Corporate income taxes
vary in          Gross receipts and sales taxes
each state)      Business real and personal property taxes
                 Capital stock taxes
                 Business automobile and truck licenses, inspection fees
                 Death taxes
                 Foreign-state business taxes
                 Workmen's compensation insurance premiums
                 Incorporation fees
                 Employment taxes
                 Meal tax
                 Excise tax

LOCAL            Individual income taxes
                 Sales taxes
                 City, school district, and county real and personal
                     property taxes
                 Business licenses
                 Business real and personal property taxes
```

Figure 6-1: Kinds of Business Taxes

FEDERAL TAXES

Since as an employer you are obliged to collect and pay certain taxes, you need an employer identification number. To obtain one, you must fill out Form SS-4 (Figure 6-4, page 101) and turn it in to the Internal Revenue Center where you file your federal return.[1]

The owner's income tax is dealt with as an appendix at the end of this text and will show samples from *The Tax Guide for Small Business*. The taxes you have to collect or pay are:

1. federal withholding tax (FWT)
2. Social Security taxes (FICA), (Medicare Taxes);
3. federal unemployment taxes (FUTA); and
4. federal excise taxes.

Federal Withholding Tax (FWT)

When you hire workers in your business, you must have them complete Form W-4, Employee's Withholding Allowance Certificate (Figure 6-5). This form enables you or your bookkeeper to calculate the amount of

---

[1] There may be slight variations from year to year in the forms in this chapter and in the appendixes. For the most up-to-date information, consult the Internal Revenue Service for printed instructions for current forms.

Take a STEP in the right direction for your small business!

a cooperative effort to provide business tax education. . .

Department of the Treasury
Internal Revenue Service
Publication 1057 (Rev. 8-92)
Catalog Number 46913E

What is the First STEP for Your Small Business?

The Internal Revenue Service's Small Business Tax Education Program (STEP) is a cooperative effort with local organizations to provide business tax education to the small business owner.

Why Should I Be Interested in the Small Business Tax Education Program?

If you are self-employed, a small business owner, office manager or bookkeeper, you need to know how to handle tax transactions. Do you know what business organization system is best for you from a tax perspective? Do you know which taxes you are responsible for and which you are not? Do you know how to fill out the business or employment tax forms correctly? Do you know when you must withhold tax money from employees and when you don't? Do you know the most efficient recordkeeping process so you keep the information that's required, but don't spend your time or money gathering or tracking information you don't really need?

What Will I Learn?

Instructors will teach you:
- The tax advantages and disadvantages of the various forms of business organizations
- What records to keep and how to keep them
- How to use Federal Tax Deposit Coupons and how to fill out other business and employment tax forms
- The role of the IRS and how to deal effectively with various offices in the IRS
- What other help is available from the IRS and other federal, state or local agencies and how to get it when you need it
- Technical information on a series of selected tax topics pertinent to a small business

How Much Does It Cost?

The costs for this program vary. Some courses are offered free as a community service. Courses offered through an educational facility may include costs for course materials in addition to tuition. Still others are offered at a nominal fee to offset administrative costs of sponsoring organizations. If you would like your name forwarded to one of these sponsoring organizations, please check the box on the interest form.

How Do I find Out What Is Available Locally?

Turn this over and complete the Small Business Tax Education Program Interest Form. Mail it to the IRS Taxpayer Education Coordinator nearest you, listed on the other side of this brochure. Send any other questions or inquiries to the same address or call the number listed for your area. The IRS will provide you with information about locally scheduled programs, workshops or business tax seminars.

What Other Services Does the IRS Offer the Business Community?

The IRS will send you Publication 15, Circular E, Employer's Tax Guide and some of the forms you will be required to file automatically, when you apply for your employer identification number (EIN). Other assistance is only a phone call away. Just check the telephone number of the IRS office closest to you or call 1-800-829-1040.

Check into the IRS
Small Business Tax Education Program
In Your Area and
Take the First STEP to
Make Your Taxes Less Taxing!

Small Business Tax Education Program Interest Form

Please Type or Print

Check One:

☐ Sole Proprietorship ☐ Partnership ☐ Corporation ☐ S Corporation

☐ I would like my name forwarded to a STEP sponsoring organization.

Name

Street

City   State   Zip Code

Daytime telephone number (include area code)

Complete both sides and mail to the nearest IRS office listed on this brochure.

Figure 6-2: Small Business Tax Education Program

Kind of Tax	Due Date	Amount Due	Pay to	Date for Writing the Check
FEDERAL TAXES				
Employee income tax and Social Security tax	____	____	____	____
	____	____	____	____
	____	____	____	____
	____	____	____	____
	____	____	____	____
Excise tax Owner-manager's and/or corporation's income tax	____	____	____	____
	____	____	____	____
	____	____	____	____
Unemployment tax	____	____	____	____
	____	____	____	____
STATE TAXES				
Unemployment tax	____	____	____	____
Income taxes	____	____	____	____
Sales taxes	____	____	____	____
	____	____	____	____
Franchise tax	____	____	____	____
Other	____	____	____	____
	____	____	____	____
LOCAL TAXES				
Sales tax	____	____	____	____
	____	____	____	____
	____	____	____	____
Real estate tax	____	____	____	____
Personal property tax	____	____	____	____
	____	____	____	____
Licenses (retail, vending machine, etc.)	____	____	____	____
	____	____	____	____
Other	____	____	____	____
	____	____	____	____

Figure 6-3: Worksheet for Meeting Tax Obligations.[2]

federal withholding tax (FWT) to deduct from the worker's gross pay. These taxes are forwarded periodically to a depository bank or to the Internal Revenue Service.

[2] *Steps in Meeting Your Tax Obligation*, Small Marketers Aid No. 142 (Washington, DC: Small Business Administration). No longer in print.

Form SS-4
(Rev. April 1991)
Department of the Treasury
Internal Revenue Service

Application for Employer Identification Number

(For use by employers and others. Please read the attached instructions before completing this form.)

EIN

OMB No. 1545-0003
Expires 4-30-94

Please type or print clearly.

1 Name of applicant (True legal name) (See instructions.)

2 Trade name of business, if different from name in line 1

3 Executor, trustee, "care of" name

4a Mailing address (street address) (room, apt., or suite no.)

5a Address of business (See instructions.)

4b City, state, and ZIP code

5b City, state, and ZIP code

6 County and state where principal business is located

7 Name of principal officer, grantor, or general partner (See instructions.) ▶

8a Type of entity (Check only one box.) (See instructions.)
- ☐ Individual SSN _____
- ☐ REMIC
- ☐ Personal service corp.
- ☐ State/local government
- ☐ National guard
- ☐ Other nonprofit organization (specify) _____ If nonprofit organization enter GEN (if applicable) _____
- ☐ Other (specify) ▶ _____
- ☐ Estate
- ☐ Plan administrator SSN _____
- ☐ Other corporation (specify) _____
- ☐ Federal government/military
- ☐ Church or church controlled organization
- ☐ Trust
- ☐ Partnership
- ☐ Farmers' cooperative

8b If a corporation, give name of foreign country (if applicable) or state in the U.S. where incorporated ▶ | Foreign country | State

9 Reason for applying (Check only one box.)
- ☐ Started new business
- ☐ Hired employees
- ☐ Created a pension plan (specify type) ▶ _____
- ☐ Banking purpose (specify) ▶
- ☐ Changed type of organization (specify) ▶ _____
- ☐ Purchased going business
- ☐ Created a trust (specify) ▶ _____
- ☐ Other (specify) ▶

10 Date business started or acquired (Mo., day, year) (See instructions.)

11 Enter closing month of accounting year. (See instructions.)

12 First date wages or annuities were paid or will be paid (Mo., day, year). **Note:** *If applicant is a withholding agent, enter date income will first be paid to nonresident alien. (Mo., day, year)* ▶

13 Enter highest number of employees expected in the next 12 months. **Note:** *If the applicant does not expect to have any employees during the period, enter "0."* ▶ | Nonagricultural | Agricultural | Household

14 Principal activity (See instructions.) ▶

15 Is the principal business activity manufacturing? ☐ Yes ☐ No
If "Yes," principal product and raw material used ▶

16 To whom are most of the products or services sold? Please check the appropriate box. ☐ Business (wholesale)
- ☐ Public (retail)
- ☐ Other (specify) ▶
- ☐ N/A

17a Has the applicant ever applied for an identification number for this or any other business? . . . . ☐ Yes ☐ No
Note: *If "Yes," please complete lines 17b and 17c.*

17b If you checked the "Yes" box in line 17a, give applicant's true name and trade name, if different than name shown on prior application.

True name ▶ | Trade name ▶

17c Enter approximate date, city, and state where the application was filed and the previous employer identification number if known.
Approximate date when filed (Mo., day, year) | City and state where filed | Previous EIN

Under penalties of perjury, I declare that I have examined this application, and to the best of my knowledge and belief, it is true, correct, and complete. | Telephone number (include area code)

Name and title (Please type or print clearly.) ▶

Signature ▶ | Date ▶

Note: *Do not write below this line.   For official use only.*

Please leave blank ▶ | Geo. | Ind. | Class | Size | Reason for applying

For Paperwork Reduction Act Notice, see attached instructions.   Cat. No. 16055N   Form **SS-4** (Rev. 4-91)

Figure 6-4: Application for Employer Identification Number (Form SS-4)

EXAMPLE: Let's see how John Sullivan's federal income tax is calculated. There are three basic ingredients to the calculation:

1. how much John earns for each payroll period, in this case $410;
2. the payroll period, in this case weekly; and
3. the number of exemptions that John claims on his W-4, in this case one.

To find out how much to withhold, you have to use the Wage Bracket Withholding Table (Figure 6-6, page 104) in the *Employer's Tax Guide Circular E*. In this case, you have to use the table for single persons since John is unmarried. Looking down the left-most column to $410 and then over to the right to the "1" allowance column, you see that $48 has been deducted from John Sullivan's pay. Note: If he had claimed a 0, his tax would be $55. So the higher the exemption claimed, the less tax you take out. Later we will discuss when the employer must remit these deductions to the appropriate agency.

Social Security (FICA)

The FICA *(Federal Insurance Contributions Act)* tax is paid by both the employee and the employer. The employer must match the amount contributed by workers. Unlike income taxes, the FICA tax is calculated without regard for exemptions or marital status. Also, the rates and bases are subject to change by Congress at any time. The following are the current and projected rates in the future:

EXAMPLE: In 1993 Jim Smith, an employee of John's Sweater Mills, earns $1,500 in the fifth week of the year. The amount of FICA deducted from his paycheck for that week is calculated as follows: $1,500 x 0.0765 = $114.75. This amount is contributed and matched by Jim's employer. At this point Jim's cumulative earnings are $6,800. If his cumulative earnings exceed $57,600 in a calendar year, no more tax is taken out for Social Security, however the medicare portion continues up to $135,000. If, say, Jim earns $1,500 in the fifth week and had cumulative earnings of $29,000 before this payroll, the calculations are as follows:

Payroll $1,500
FICA $1,500 x .0765 = $114.75
FICA is made up of Social Security Tax .062 (6.2%)
Medicare Tax .0145 (1.45%)
Total .0765 (7.65%)

The $114.75 represents Jim's FICA tax this week and is withheld from his pay. Jim's employer must match this amount.

Employer's Quarterly Federal Tax Return: Form 941

When do you pay FWT and FICA? Federal regulations require each business (that has employees) to file a quarterly report (Form 941, Employer's Quarterly Federal Tax Return). This form summarizes any FWT or FICA

19**93** Form W-4

Department of the Treasury
Internal Revenue Service

Purpose. Complete Form W-4 so that your employer can withhold the correct amount of Federal income tax from your pay.

Exemption From Withholding. Read line 7 of the certificate below to see if you can claim exempt status. *If exempt, complete line 7; but do not complete lines 5 and 6.* No Federal income tax will be withheld from your pay. Your exemption is good for one year only. It expires February 15, 1994.

Basic Instructions. Employees who are not exempt should complete the Personal Allowances Worksheet. Additional worksheets are provided on page 2 for employees to adjust their withholding allowances based on itemized deductions, adjustments to income, or two-earner/two-job situations. Complete all worksheets that apply to your situation. The worksheets will help you figure

the number of withholding allowances you are entitled to claim. However, you may claim fewer allowances than this.

Head of Household. Generally, you may claim head of household filing status on your tax return only if you are unmarried and pay more than 50% of the costs of keeping up a home for yourself and your dependent(s) or other qualifying individuals.

Nonwage Income. If you have a large amount of nonwage income, such as interest or dividends, you should consider making estimated tax payments using Form 1040-ES. Otherwise, you may find that you owe additional tax at the end of the year.

Two-Earner/Two-Jobs. If you have a working spouse or more than one job, figure the total number of allowances you are entitled to claim on

all jobs using worksheets from only one Form W-4. This total should be divided among all jobs. Your withholding will usually be most accurate when all allowances are claimed on the W-4 filed for the highest paying job and zero allowances are claimed for the others.

Advance Earned Income Credit. If you are eligible for this credit, you can receive it added to your paycheck throughout the year. For details, get Form W-5 from your employer.

Check Your Withholding. After your W-4 takes effect, you can use **Pub. 919,** Is My Withholding Correct for 1993?, to see how the dollar amount you are having withheld compares to your estimated total annual tax. Call 1-800-829-3676 to order this publication. Check your local telephone directory for the IRS assistance number if you need further help.

Personal Allowances Worksheet

For 1993, the value of your personal exemption(s) is reduced if your income is over $108,450 ($162,700 if married filing jointly, $135,600 if head of household, or $81,350 if married filing separately). Get Pub. 919 for details.

A   Enter "1" for **yourself** if no one else can claim you as a dependent . . . . **A** _____

B   Enter "1" if:
- You are single and have only one job; or
- You are married, have only one job, and your spouse does not work; or
- Your wages from a second job or your spouse's wages (or the total of both) are $1,000 or less.

. . **B** _____

C   Enter "1" for your **spouse.** But, you may choose to enter -0- if you are married and have either a working spouse or more than one job (this may help you avoid having too little tax withheld) . . . . **C** _____

D   Enter number of **dependents** (other than your spouse or yourself) whom you will claim on your tax return . . . . . **D** _____

E   Enter "1" if you will file as **head of household** on your tax return (see conditions under **Head of Household,** above) . **E** _____

F   Enter "1" if you have at least $1,500 of **child or dependent care expenses** for which you plan to claim a credit . . **F** _____

G   Add lines A through F and enter total here. **Note:** *This amount may be different from the number of exemptions you claim on your return* ▶ **G** _____

For accuracy, do all worksheets that apply.
- If you plan to **itemize or claim adjustments to income** and want to reduce your withholding, see the Deductions and Adjustments Worksheet on page 2.
- If you are **single** and have **more than one job** and your combined earnings from all jobs exceed $30,000 OR if you are **married** and have a **working spouse or more than one job,** and the combined earnings from all jobs exceed $50,000, see the Two-Earner/Two-Job Worksheet on page 2 if you want to avoid having too little tax withheld.
- If **neither** of the above situations applies, **stop here** and enter the number from line G on line 5 of Form W-4 below.

- - - - - - - - - - - - - - - - **Cut here and give the certificate to your employer. Keep the top portion for your records.** - - - - - - - - - - - - - - - -

Form **W-4** Department of the Treasury Internal Revenue Service	**Employee's Withholding Allowance Certificate** ▶ **For Privacy Act and Paperwork Reduction Act Notice, see reverse.**	OMB No. 1545-0010 19**93**

1   Type or print your first name and middle initial   *John   L.*   Last name   *Sullivan*   **2** Your social security number   *021 36 9494*

Home address (number and street or rural route)   *2 Roundy Rd.*

3 ☒ Single ☐ Married ☐ Married, but withhold at higher Single rate.
Note: *If married, but legally separated, or spouse is a nonresident alien, check the Single box.*

City or town, state, and ZIP code   *Marblehead   MA   02169*

4   If your last name differs from that on your social security card, check here and call 1-800-772-1213 for more information · · · · ▶ ☐

5   Total number of allowances you are claiming (from line G above or from the worksheets on page 2 if they apply) .   **5** */*

6   Additional amount, if any, you want withheld from each paycheck . . . .   **6** $

7   I claim exemption from withholding for 1993 and I certify that I meet **ALL** of the following conditions for exemption:
- Last year I had a right to a refund of **ALL** Federal income tax withheld because I had **NO** tax liability; **AND**
- This year I expect a refund of **ALL** Federal income tax withheld because I expect to have **NO** tax liability; **AND**
- This year if my income exceeds $600 and includes nonwage income, another person cannot claim me as a dependent.

If you meet all of the above conditions, enter "EXEMPT" here . . . . ▶ | **7** |

Under penalties of perjury, I certify that I am entitled to the number of withholding allowances claimed on this certificate or entitled to claim exempt status.

Employee's signature ▶ *John L. Sullivan*   Date ▶ *3/15*   , 19 *93*

8   Employer's name and address (Employer: Complete 8 and 10 only if sending to the IRS)   **9** Office code (optional)   **10** Employer identification number

Cat. No. 10220Q

21

Figure 6-5: Employees Witholding Allowance Certificate (Form W-4)

SINGLE Persons—WEEKLY Payroll Period
(For Wages Paid in 1993)

| If the wages are— | | And the number of withholding allowances claimed is— | | | | | | | | | | |
At least	But less than	0	1	2	3	4	5	6	7	8	9	10
		The amount of income tax to be withheld is—										
$0	$50	$0	$0	$0	$0	$0	$0	$0	$0	$0	$0	$0
50	55	1	0	0	0	0	0	0	0	0	0	0
55	60	1	0	0	0	0	0	0	0	0	0	0
60	65	2	0	0	0	0	0	0	0	0	0	0
65	70	3	0	0	0	0	0	0	0	0	0	0
70	75	4	0	0	0	0	0	0	0	0	0	0
75	80	4	0	0	0	0	0	0	0	0	0	0
80	85	5	0	0	0	0	0	0	0	0	0	0
85	90	6	0	0	0	0	0	0	0	0	0	0
90	95	7	0	0	0	0	0	0	0	0	0	0
95	100	7	1	0	0	0	0	0	0	0	0	0
100	105	8	1	0	0	0	0	0	0	0	0	0
105	110	9	2	0	0	0	0	0	0	0	0	0
110	115	10	3	0	0	0	0	0	0	0	0	0
115	120	10	4	0	0	0	0	0	0	0	0	0
120	125	11	4	0	0	0	0	0	0	0	0	0
125	130	12	5	0	0	0	0	0	0	0	0	0
130	135	13	6	0	0	0	0	0	0	0	0	0
135	140	13	7	0	0	0	0	0	0	0	0	0
140	145	14	7	1	0	0	0	0	0	0	0	0
145	150	15	8	1	0	0	0	0	0	0	0	0
150	155	16	9	2	0	0	0	0	0	0	0	0
155	160	16	10	3	0	0	0	0	0	0	0	0
160	165	17	10	4	0	0	0	0	0	0	0	0
165	170	18	11	4	0	0	0	0	0	0	0	0
170	175	19	12	5	0	0	0	0	0	0	0	0
175	180	19	13	6	0	0	0	0	0	0	0	0
180	185	20	13	7	0	0	0	0	0	0	0	0
185	190	21	14	7	1	0	0	0	0	0	0	0
190	195	22	15	8	1	0	0	0	0	0	0	0
195	200	22	16	9	2	0	0	0	0	0	0	0
200	210	23	17	10	3	0	0	0	0	0	0	0
210	220	25	18	11	5	0	0	0	0	0	0	0
220	230	26	20	13	6	0	0	0	0	0	0	0
230	240	28	21	14	8	1	0	0	0	0	0	0
240	250	29	23	16	9	2	0	0	0	0	0	0
250	260	31	24	17	11	4	0	0	0	0	0	0
260	270	32	26	19	12	5	0	0	0	0	0	0
270	280	34	27	20	14	7	0	0	0	0	0	0
280	290	35	29	22	15	8	2	0	0	0	0	0
290	300	37	30	23	17	10	3	0	0	0	0	0
300	310	38	32	25	18	11	5	0	0	0	0	0
310	320	40	33	26	20	13	6	0	0	0	0	0
320	330	41	35	28	21	14	8	1	0	0	0	0
330	340	43	36	29	23	16	9	2	0	0	0	0
340	350	44	38	31	24	17	11	4	0	0	0	0
350	360	46	39	32	26	19	12	5	0	0	0	0
360	370	47	41	34	27	20	14	7	0	0	0	0
370	380	49	42	35	29	22	15	8	2	0	0	0
380	390	50	44	37	30	23	17	10	3	0	0	0
390	400	52	45	38	32	25	18	11	5	0	0	0
400	410	53	47	40	33	26	20	13	6	0	0	0
410	420	55	48	41	35	28	21	14	8	1	0	0
420	430	56	50	43	36	29	23	16	9	2	0	0
430	440	58	51	44	38	31	24	17	11	4	0	0
440	450	59	53	46	39	32	26	19	12	5	0	0
450	460	61	54	47	41	34	27	20	14	7	0	0
460	470	64	56	49	42	35	29	22	15	8	1	0
470	480	67	57	50	44	37	30	23	17	10	3	0
480	490	70	59	52	45	38	32	25	18	11	4	0
490	500	73	60	53	47	40	33	26	20	13	6	0
500	510	75	63	55	48	41	35	28	21	14	7	1
510	520	78	66	56	50	43	36	29	23	16	9	2
520	530	81	68	58	51	44	38	31	24	17	10	4
530	540	84	71	59	53	46	39	32	26	19	12	5
540	550	87	74	61	54	47	41	34	27	20	13	7
550	560	89	77	64	56	49	42	35	29	22	15	8
560	570	92	80	67	57	50	44	37	30	23	16	10
570	580	95	82	70	59	52	45	38	32	25	18	11
580	590	98	85	73	60	53	47	40	33	26	19	13

Figure 6-6: Wage Bracket Withholding Table

amounts deposited, along with any obligations due. The due dates for filing this form for each quarter are as follows:

Quarter Ends	Filing Due Dates
March 31	April 30
June 30	July 31
September 30	October 31
December 31	January 31

Keep in mind that this form is made out for only four taxes:

1. the employee's FWT;
2. the employee's Social Security contributions;
3. the employer's Social Security contributions;
4. the employee's medicare contributions; and
5. the employer's medicare contributions.

Form **941**		**Employer's Quarterly Federal Tax Return**		
(Rev. January 1993) Department of the Treasury Internal Revenue Service	4141	► See separate instructions for information on completing this form. **Please type or print.**		

Enter state code for state in which deposits made . (see page 2 of instructions).

Name (as distinguished from trade name) Joseph Wells	Date quarter ended 3/11/XX
Trade name, if any Wells Shoes	Employer identification number 01-111888
Address (number and street) 9 Long Drive Atlanta, GA. 30328	City, state, and ZIP code

OMB No. 1545-0029
Expires 1-31-96

T
FF
FD
FP
I
T

If address is different from prior return, check here ►

IRS Use

```
1 1 1 1 1 1 1 1 1 1    2    3 3 3 3 3    4 4 4
5 5 5    6    7    8 8 8 8 8    9 9    10 10 10 10 10 10 10 10 10 10
```

If you do not have to file returns in the future, check here . ► ☐   Date final wages paid . . ►

If you are a seasonal employer, see **Seasonal employers** on page 1 and check here ► ☐

1	Number of employees (except household) employed in the pay period that includes March 12th ►		Four	
2	Total wages and tips subject to withholding, plus other compensation	2	18000	
3	Total income tax withheld from wages, tips, pensions, annuities, sick pay, gambling, etc. .	3	2100	—
4	Adjustment of withheld income tax for preceding quarters of calendar year (see instructions) . .	4		
5	Adjusted total of income tax withheld (line 3 as adjusted by line 4—see instructions) . . .	5	2100	—
6a	Taxable social security wages . . . . . $ 18000 — × 12.4% (.124) =	6a	2232	—
b	Taxable social security tips . . . . . . $ × 12.4% (.124) =	6b		
7	Taxable Medicare wages and tips . . . $ 18000 — × 2.9% (.029) =	7	522	—
8	Total social security and Medicare taxes (add lines 6a, 6b, and 7)	8	2754	—
9	Adjustment of social security and Medicare taxes (see instructions for required explanation) .	9		
10	Adjusted total of social security and Medicare taxes (line 8 as adjusted by line 9—see instructions)	10	2754	—
11	Backup withholding (see instructions)	11		
12	Adjustment of backup withholding tax for preceding quarters of calendar year	12		
13	Adjusted total of backup withholding (line 11 as adjusted by line 12)	13		
14	**Total taxes** (add lines 5, 10, and 13)	14	4854	—
15	Advance earned income credit (EIC) payments made to employees, if any	15		
16	Net taxes (subtract line 15 from line 14). **This should equal line 20, col. (d), below or line D of Schedule B** (plus line D of Schedule A if you treated backup withholding as a separate liability)	16	4854	—
17	**Total deposits for quarter,** including overpayment applied from a prior quarter, from your records	17	4854	—
18	**Balance due** (subtract line 17 from line 16). This should be less than $500. Pay to the Internal Revenue Service	18	O	
19	**Overpayment,** if line 17 is more than line 16, enter excess here ► $ _____ and check if to be: ☐ Applied to next return **OR** ☐ Refunded.			

20 **Monthly Summary of Federal Tax Liability. If line 16 is less than $500, you need not complete line 20.** If you are a monthly depositor, summarize your monthly tax liability below. If you are a semiweekly depositor or have accumulated a tax liability of $100,000 or more on any day, attach Schedule B (Form 941) and check here (see instructions) . . . . ► ☐

	(a) First month	(b) Second month	(c) Third month	(d) Total for quarter
Liability for month	1618 —	1618 —	1618 —	4854 —

Sign Here Under penalties of perjury, I declare that I have examined this return, including accompanying schedules and statements, and to the best of my knowledge and belief, it is true, correct, and complete.

Signature ► Joseph Wells   Print Your Name and Title ► Joseph Wells, Owner   Date ► 4/15/XX

For Paperwork Reduction Act Notice, see page 1 of separate instructions.   Cat. No. 17001Z   Form **941** (Rev. 1-93)

Figure 6-7: Employer's Quarterly Federal Tax Return (Form 941)

Department of the Treasury
Internal Revenue Service

Notice 931 (November 1992)

New Deposit Requirements for 1993

New rules for determining when you deposit Federal employment and withholding taxes (other than FUTA taxes) take effect January 1, 1993. Under the new rules, you will be either a monthly or a semiweekly depositor. The IRS will notify you each November, starting in 1992, what your deposit status is for the coming calendar year.

Your deposit schedule for a calendar year is determined from the total taxes reported on your Form 941 (or Form 941E) in a four-quarter lookback period—July 1 through June 30—as shown in the chart below. If you reported $50,000 or less of employment taxes for the lookback period, you are a monthly depositor; if you reported more than $50,000, you are a semiweekly depositor. Two special exception rules—the $500 rule and the $100,000 rule—carry over from the old deposit rules. The deposit rules and exceptions are discussed in the following sections.

Lookback Period For Calendar Year 1993

Calendar Year 1993

Jan–Mar	Apr–June	Jul–Sep	Oct–Dec

Lookback Period

1991		1992	
Jul–Sep	Oct–Dec	Jan–Mar	Apr–June

Transition Rule for 1993.—While you are converting your deposit system to the new rules, you will not be penalized for continuing to use the old deposit rules. Your conversion to the new rules, however, must be completed by December 31, 1993. The instructions for Form 941 will explain how to report your tax liabilities while you are in this transition period.

Monthly Rule

Under the **monthly rule,** employment and other taxes withheld on payments made during a calendar month must be deposited by the 15th day of the following month. An employer is a monthly depositor for a calendar year if the total employment taxes for the four quarters in the lookback period was $50,000 or less.

New Employers.—During the first calendar year of your business, your tax liability for each quarter in the lookback period is considered to be zero. Therefore, you generally will be a monthly depositor for the first year of your business (but see the **$100,000 One-Day Rule** exception below).

Semiweekly Rule

An employer is a semiweekly depositor for a calendar year if the total employment taxes during its lookback period was more than $50,000. Under the **semiweekly rule,** amounts accumulated on payments made on Wednesday, Thursday, and/or Friday must be deposited by the following Wednesday. Amounts accumulated on payments made on Saturday, Sunday, Monday, and/or Tuesday must be deposited by the following Friday.

If a quarterly return period ends on a day other than Tuesday or Friday, employment taxes accumulated on the days covered by the return period just ending are subject to one deposit obligation, and employment taxes accumulated on the days covered by the new return period are subject to a separate deposit obligation. For example, if one quarterly return period ends on Thursday and a new quarter begins on Friday, employment taxes accumulated on Wednesday and Thursday are subject to one deposit obligation and taxes accumulated on Friday are subject to a separate obligation. Separate Federal Tax Deposit (FTD) coupons are required for each deposit obligation.

Example of Monthly and Semiweekly Rules

Employer A reported employment tax liability as follows:

3rd Quarter 1991 - $12,000	3rd Quarter 1992 - $15,000
4th Quarter 1991 - $12,000	4th Quarter 1992 - $15,000
1st Quarter 1992 - $12,000	1st Quarter 1993 - $15,000
2nd Quarter 1992 - $12,000	2nd Quarter 1993 - $15,000

Employer A is a monthly depositor for 1993 because its tax liability for the four quarters in its lookback period (3rd quarter 1991 through 2nd quarter 1992) was not more than $50,000. However, for 1994, Employer A must follow the semiweekly rule described above because A's liability exceeded $50,000 for the four quarters in its lookback period (3rd quarter 1992 through 2nd quarter 1993).

Deposits on Banking Days Only

If a deposit is required to be made on a day that is not a banking day, the deposit is considered to have been made timely if it is made by the close of the next banking day. For example, if a deposit is required to be made on a Friday and Friday is not a banking day, the deposit will be considered timely if it is made by the following Monday.

A special rule is provided for **semiweekly depositors** which allows these depositors at least 3 banking days to make a deposit. For example, if a semiweekly depositor has employment taxes accumulated for payments made on Friday and the following Monday is not a banking day, deposits made by the following Thursday would be considered timely (allowing 3 banking days to make the deposit).

Cat. No. 14736T

Figure 6-8: IRS Notice 931

$500 Rule

If an employer accumulates less than $500 tax liability during a quarter, no deposits are required and this liability may be paid with the tax return for the quarter. However, if you are unsure that you will accumulate less than $500, it would be prudent to deposit in accordance with the monthly depositor rules. If you were to accumulate a liability of $500 or more by the end of the quarter and failed to make your monthly deposits, you would be subject to deposit penalties.

$100,000 One-Day Rule

If the total accumulated tax reaches $100,000 or more on any day during a deposit period, it must be deposited by the next banking day, whether an employer is a monthly or semiweekly depositor. For monthly depositors, the deposit period is a calendar month. The deposit periods for a semiweekly depositor are Wednesday through Friday and Saturday through Tuesday. For purposes of the $100,000 rule, do not continue accumulating employment tax liability after the end of a deposit period. For example, if a semiweekly depositor has accumulated a liability of $95,000 on a Tuesday (of a Saturday-through-Tuesday accumulation period) and accumulated a $10,000 liability on Wednesday, the $100,000 one-day rule does not apply.

If a monthly depositor accumulates a $100,000 employment tax liability on any day, it becomes a semiweekly depositor on the next day and remains so for at least the remainder of the calendar year and for the following calendar year.

Example of $100,000 One-Day Rule.—Employer B started its business on February 1, 1993. On February 10, it paid wages for the first time and accumulated a tax liability of $60,000. On February 11, Employer B paid wages and accumulated a liability of $40,000, bringing its accumulated employment tax liability to $100,000. Because this was the first year of its business, the tax liability for its lookback period is considered to be zero, and it would be a monthly depositor based on the lookback rules. However, since Employer B accumulated $100,000 on February 11, it became a semiweekly depositor on February 12. It will be a semiweekly depositor for the remainder of 1993

and for 1994 (which has the 1st quarter of 1993 in its lookback period). Employer B is required to deposit the $100,000 by February 12, the next banking day.

Adjustments and the Lookback Rule

Determine your tax liability for the quarters in the lookback period based on the tax liability as *originally* reported. If you made adjustments to correct errors on previously filed employment tax returns, these adjustments do not affect the amount of tax liability for purposes of the lookback rule. If you report adjustments on your current employment tax return to correct errors on prior period returns, include these adjustments as part of your tax liability for the current quarter. If you filed Form 843 to claim a refund for a prior period overpayment, your tax liability does not change for either the prior period or the current period quarter for purposes of the lookback rule.

Example of Adjustments and the Lookback Rule.—An employer originally reported a tax liability of $45,000 for the four quarters in the lookback period ending June 30, 1992. The employer discovered during January 1993 that the tax during one of the lookback period quarters was understated by $10,000 and corrected this error with an adjustment on the 1993 first quarter return. This employer would be a monthly depositor for 1993 since the lookback period tax liabilities are based on the amounts originally reported and were less than $50,000. The $10,000 adjustment would be treated as part of the 1993 first quarter tax liability.

Accuracy of Deposits (98% Rule)

You will be considered to have satisfied the above deposit requirements if you deposit timely at least 98% of your tax liability or if any deposit shortfall does not exceed $100. No deposit penalties will be applied if the above shortfall is deposited by the shortfall make-up date. The shortfall make-up date for monthly depositors is the due date for the return period in which the shortfall occurs. The make-up date for semiweekly or one-day rule depositors is the first Wednesday or Friday, whichever is earlier, falling on or after the 15th day of the month following the month in which the shortfall occurred.

*U.S. Government Printing Office: 1992 — 343-034/60160

Notice 931
(November 1992)

Figure 6-8: IRS Notice 931, **continued**

Let's look at the Wells Shoe Company to see how its owner, Joseph Wells, handles his company's tax responsibilities. To keep the illustration simple, we'll look at only one quarter—January to March. (Take note that each of these quarters is actually a thirteen-week period.) Figure 6-7 is the completed 941, as submitted by Joe Wells on April 30. Let's look at the individual lines of this quarterly report:

LINES 1 THROUGH 5 Joe, who has four workers, paid $18,000 of salaries that are subject to federal withholding taxes. Using the wage bracket tables in conjunction with the employees' W-4s, Joe withholds $2,100 in income tax from his employees' paychecks.

LINES 6-11 Since no worker comes close to breaking the maximum taxable base, all wages are subject to the Social Security Tax and Medicare Tax.

In Figure 6-7, the 12.4 percent represents the owner's as well as the employees' share of Social Security tax and 2.9 percent represents owner's and employee's share of Medicare Tax. This rate times $18,000 of wages indicates that Joe owes $2232 for Social Security and $522 of Medicare Tax. All together, Joe is responsible to pay a total of $4854 in this first quarter; this is the total of FICA (for both employee and employer) and income tax withheld from the worker.

RECORD OF FEDERAL TAX DEPOSITS This bottom section of the form deals with the question as to how all this money is to be paid. Is it all due at the end of the quarter? Or must Joe follow certain regulations? Note in the middle of this form that Joe, in fact, made three deposits before this form was completed. Why? In respect to deposit regulations, the law states the following:

In Joe's case, the IRS supplies him with monthly deposit tickets. Joe receives these tickets with his identification number printed on them since the sum of his FICA and FWT is below 50,000. Because Joe makes these deposits periodically, you'll notice at the bottom of the quarterly reports that he owes no additional money for the quarter. See figure 6-8, p. 106.

WHERE TO FILE The quarterly deposit is then filed according to the following instructions:

If your legal residence, principal place of business, office, or agency is in	File with the Internal Revenue Service Center at
New Jersey, New York City and counties of Nassau, Rockland, Suffolk, and Westchester	Holtsville, NY 00501
New York (all other counties), Connecticut, Maine, Massachusetts, New Hampshire, Rhode Island, Vermont	Andover, MA 05501

If your legal residence, principal place of business, office, or agency is in	File with the Internal Revenue Service Center at
District of Columbia, Delaware Maryland, Pennsylvania	Philadelphia, PA 19255
Alabama, Florida, Georgia Mississippi, South Carolina	Atlanta, GA 31101
Michigan, Ohio	Cincinnati, OH 45999
Arkansas, Kansas, Louisiana, New Mexico, Oklahoma, Texas	Austin, TX 73301
Alaska, Arizona, Colorado, Idaho, Minnesota, Montana, Nebraska, Nevada, North Dakota, Oregon, South Dakota, Utah, Washington, Wyoming	Ogden, UT 84201
California, Hawaii	Fresno, CA 93888
Indiana, Kentucky, North Carolina, Tennessee, Virginia, West Virginia	Memphis, TN 37501
If you have no legal residence or principal place of business in any state	Philadelphia, PA 19255
Illinois, Iowa, Missouri, Wisconsin	Kansas City, MO 64999[3]

Payroll Records

Where do you get the information for Form 941? The information is accumulated each pay period in the payroll records. Joe handles the recordkeeping for his payroll as shown in Figure 6-9. (Bear in mind that this is not the only way to keep payroll; in Appendix 5 of this book is a sample payroll register and individual earning record based on the "one-write" system, a method that saves journalizing and posting time.) Joe's payroll register (Figure 6-10) records the data for payroll. The law requires employers to keep adequate payroll records for each employee so as to verify that they are complying with payroll regulations. Joe's employee's individual earnings record (Figure 6-11 on p. 111) shows a card that eventually will contain records for all four quarters of 13 weeks each.

[3] Form 941, 1/92, U.S. Government Printing Office.

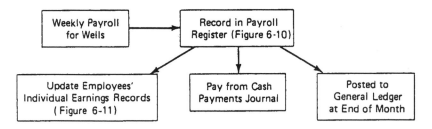

Figure 6-9: Wells Shoe Company—Payroll Register

Week Ended	Employee Name	Withholding Exemption	Salary	Deductions				Net Ck. Pay	No.
				FWT	FICA		SWT		
					Social Security	Medicare			
19XX Jan. 6									
	Bill Flynn	4	500.00	32.00	31.00	7.25	46.62	383.13	18
	Ron Tagney	2	410.00	31.00	25.42	5.95	24.22	323.41	19
	Joe Smooth	4	800.00	77.00	49.60	11.60	58.60	603.20	20
	Bill Robin	3	680.00	65.00	42.16	9.86	43.74	519.24	21
	Robyn Hartman	3	600.00	53.00	37.20	8.70	40.28	460.82	22
	Jim Moore	2	500.00	32.00	31.00	7.25	46.62	383.13	23
			3,490.00	290.00	216.38	50.61	250.08	2,672.93	

Figure 6-10: Wells Shoe Company—Payroll Register

The records consist of:

1. employees' names;
2. their Social Security numbers;
3. their addresses / phone numbers;
4. data as to when employed and date of birth;
5. sex and marital status;
6. exemptions claimed and pay dates;
7. earnings (and possibly cumulative earnings);
8. deductions for FWT, FICA, SWT (and perhaps for union, medical, or other items); and
9. net pay.

At the end of each quarter, you use the cumulative total on the individual earnings record to complete Form 941.

Wage and Tax Statement: Form W-2

The individual earning record also enables you to fill out still another form required by the federal government at year's end. After the end of the year, you have to total up the earnings and tax deductions for the four quarters and complete Form W-2, the Wage and Tax Statement (Figure 6-12). You have to give a W-2 to each employee by January 31 of the following year. The employee uses this form to complete his or her annual tax return. You

Name of Employee: <u>Jim Moore</u>

Address: <u>2 Bounty Terrace</u>

Date of Birth: <u>9/6/47</u>   Married
                      or Single

Position: <u>Store Manager</u>

Social Sec. # <u>021-36-9449</u>

City or Town: <u>Marblehead, MA 01945</u>

Number   Phone # <u>631-0288</u>
of   3
exemptions   Date Started <u>1/8/XX</u>
                    Date Terminated

		First Quarter							Second Quarter			
Week	Earnings	Cum. Earn.	FICA*	FWT	SWT	Net Pay	Week	Earnings	Cum. Earn.	FICA	FWT	SWT	Net Pay
1	500.00	500.00	38.25	32.00	46.62	383.13	14						
2	500.00	1,000.00	38.25	32.00	46.62	383.13	15						
3	500.00	1,500.00	38.25	32.00	46.62	383.13	16						
4	500.00	2,000.00	38.25	32.00	46.62	383.13	17						
5	500.00	2,500.00	38.25	32.00	46.62	383.13	18						
6	500.00	3,000.00	38.25	32.00	46.62	383.13	19						
7	500.00	3,500.00	38.25	32.00	46.62	383.13	20						
8	500.00	4,000.00	38.25	32.00	46.62	383.13	21						
9	500.00	4,500.00	38.25	32.00	46.62	383.13	22						
10	500.00	5,000.00	38.25	32.00	46.62	383.13	23						
11	500.00	5,500.00	38.25	32.00	46.62	383.13	24						
12	500.00	6,000.00	38.25	32.00	46.62	383.13	25						
13	500.00	6,500.00	38.25	32.00	46.62	383.13	26						
Cumulative Totals	6,500.00	6,500.00	497.25	416.00	606.06	4980.69						

		Third Quarter							Fourth Quarter			
Week	Earnings	Cum. Earn.	FICA	FWT	SWT	Net Pay	Week	Earnings	Cum. Earn.	FICA	FWT	SWT	Net Pay
27							40						
28							41						
29							42						
30							43						
31							44						
32							45						
33							46						
34							47						
35							48						
36							49						
37							50						
38							51						
39							52						

* The $38.25 includes Medicare tax.

Figure 6-11: Wells Shoe Company—Individual Earnings Record

also have to send Copy A of this form to the Social Security Administration, who then forwards it to the Internal Revenue Service.

Federal Unemployment Tax (FUTA): Form 940

Levied only on employers, the federal unemployment tax is a co-operative federal-state system to provide wages for the unemployed. As an employer, you must file a Form 940 (Employer's Annual Federal Unemployment Tax Return) if:

1. you paid wages of $1,500 or more in any calendar quarter, or
2. you had one or more employees in any (not necessarily consecutive) twenty weeks out of the calendar year.

a Control number		Void ☐		

b Employer's identification number	1 Wages, tips, other compensation	2 Federal income tax withheld
04 – 123456	26,000.00	2422.00

c Employer's name, address, and ZIP code	3 Social security wages	4 Social security tax withheld
ACE HARDWARE	26,000.00	1612.00
22 RIVER RD.	5 Medicare wages and tips	6 Medicare tax withheld
MARBLEHEAD MA 01945	26,000.00	377.00
	7 Social security tips	8 Allocated tips

d Employee's social security number	9 Advance EIC payment	10 Dependent care benefits
001 – 01 – 0001		

e Employee's name, address, and ZIP code	11 Nonqualified plans	12 Benefits included in Box 1
JOHN DUDLY	13 See Instrs. for Box 13	14 Other
15 PRISCILLA CIRCLE		
LYNN MA 01907		

15 Statutory employee ☐	Deceased ☐	Pension plan ☐	Legal rep. ☐	942 emp. ☐	Subtotal ☐	Deferred compensation ☐

16 State	Employer's state I.D. No.	17 State wages, tips, etc.	18 State income tax	19 Locality name	20 Local wages, tips, etc.	21 Local income tax
MA	04-123456	26,000.00	1300.00			

Department of the Treasury—Internal Revenue Service

Form **W-2** Wage and Tax Statement **1993**

This information is being furnished to the Internal Revenue Service.

Copy B To Be Filed With Employee's FEDERAL Tax Return

OMB No. 1545-0008

Figure 6-12: Wage and Tax Statement (W-2)

In 1992, the federal rate was .8 percent on the first $7,000 of an employees' earnings,

On Form 940 for Moore Shoes (Figure 6-13), the total FUTA is $144 ($18,000 x 0.008). If the total tax obligation for the year is less than $100, it may be paid by the end of January of the following year, when the 940 is filed. If the tax obligation is more than $100 per year, a Federal Tax deposit (Form 508) must be made during the year.

Excise Tax

Federal excise taxes are imposed on the sale or use of some items, on certain transactions, and on certain occupations. For example, there is an occupational tax on retail dealers in adulterated butter, retail dealers in beer, retail liquor dealers, and wholesale beer and liquor dealers. Diesel fuel and certain special motor fuels carry a retailers' excise tax.

An owner-manager who is in doubt about the excise tax liability of his business should check with the nearest Internal Revenue Service office. If you are liable for any excise taxes, you must file a quarterly return on Form 720. When you owe more than $100 per month in excise taxes, you must make monthly deposits of that tax in a Federal Reserve Bank or other authorized depositories in the same manner as federal income taxes.

Form **940-EZ**	**Employer's Annual Federal Unemployment (FUTA) Tax Return**	OMB No. 1545-1110

Department of the Treasury
Internal Revenue Service

19**93**

		T	
		FF	
		FD	
		FP	
		I	
		T	

If incorrect, make any necessary changes. ▶

Name (as distinguished from trade name)
James Moore

Trade name, if any
Moore Shoes

Address and ZIP code
10 Salem St.
Salem, MA 01970

Calendar year

Employer identification number
04 : 123456

*Follow the chart under **Who May Use Form 940-EZ** on page 2. If you cannot use Form 940-EZ, you must use Form 940 instead.*

A Enter the amount of contributions paid to your state unemployment fund. (See instructions for line A on page 4.) ▶ $ .... *540.—*

B (1) Enter the name of the state where you have to pay contributions . . . . ▶ *MASSACHUSETTS*

(2) Enter your state reporting number as shown on state unemployment tax return. ▶ *80-12345*

If you will not have to file returns in the future, check here (see **Who Must File**, on page 2) complete, and sign the return . . . . . ▶ ☐

If this is an Amended Return check here . . . . ▶ ☐

Part I   Taxable Wages and FUTA Tax

			Amount paid		
1	Total payments (including payments shown on lines 2 and 3) during the calendar year for services of employees	1			*42000 —*
2	Exempt payments. (Explain all exempt payments, attaching additional sheets if necessary.) ▶	2			
3	Payments for services of more than $7,000. Enter only amounts over the first $7,000 paid to each employee. Do not include any exempt payments from line 2. Do not use your state wage limitation. The $7,000 amount is the Federal wage base. Your state wage base may be different	3	*24,000*		
4	Total exempt payments (add lines 2 and 3)			4	*24000 —*
5	**Total taxable wages** (subtract line 4 from line 1) . . . . ▶			5	*18000 —*
6	**FUTA tax.** Multiply the wages on line 5 by .008 and enter here. (If the result is over $100, also complete Part II) .			6	*144 —*
7	Total FUTA tax deposited for the year, including any overpayment applied from a prior year (from your records)			7	*100 —*
8	**Amount you owe** (subtract line 7 from line 6). This should be $100 or less. Pay to "Internal Revenue Service" . ▶			8	*44 —*
9	**Overpayment** (subtract line 6 from line 7). Check if it is to be: ☐ **Applied to next return,** or ☐ **Refunded** ▶			9	

Part II   Record of Quarterly Federal Unemployment Tax Liability (Do not include state liability.) Complete only if line 6 is over $100.

Quarter	First (Jan. 1 – Mar. 31)	Second (Apr. 1 – June 30)	Third (July 1 – Sept. 30)	Fourth (Oct. 1 – Dec. 31)	Total for year
Liability for quarter					

Under penalties of perjury, I declare that I have examined this return, including accompanying schedules and statements, and, to the best of my knowledge and belief, it is true, correct, and complete, and that no part of any payment made to a state unemployment fund claimed as a credit was, or is to be, deducted from the payments to employees.

Signature ▶ *James Moore*   Title (Owner, etc.) ▶ *Owner*   Date ▶ *1/31/xx*

Cat. No. 10983G

Form **940-EZ** (1993)

Figure 6-13: Employer's Annual Federal Unemployment Tax Return (Form 940EZ)

Semimonthly, rather than monthly, deposits of excise taxes are required if you were liable for more than $2,000 on all excise taxes reportable on Form 720 for any month during the previous quarter.

If you own and operate trucks in your business, you have to pay federal highway-use tax. This tax is described in detail in a free IRS publication, *Federal Highway Use Tax* (IRS Publication No. 349).

If an owner-manager is engaged in occupations involving gaming devices, liquor, narcotics, gambling, or firearms, he must pay occupational (excise) tax. Details are available at the nearest IRS office.[4]

STATE AND LOCAL TAXES

Some states impose an income tax (state withholding taxes, or SWT). When they do, owner-managers are required to deduct this tax from their employees' wages.

State Income Taxes

In some cases, the state tax returns are similar to those used by the federal government. Other areas use a different approach. Many states require you to file an information return.

You should contact the state authorities in your area and find out what requirements apply to your business. If the requirements differ from those for federal income tax returns, make sure that your records give you the necessary information for state income taxes.[5]

Sales Tax

Many states have sales taxes. In meeting this tax obligation, the owner-manager acts as though he were an agent. He collects the tax and passes it on to the appropriate state agency.

The owner-manager is required to use a system which the taxing jurisdiction has set up. The owner-manager who has a doubt about his system of collecting, reporting, and paying sales taxes should describe his system to the taxing authorities and ask them whether it complies with their requirements.[6]

Local Taxes

Counties, towns, and cities impose various kinds of taxes. Among them are real-estate taxes, personal-property taxes, taxes of gross receipts of businesses, and unincorporated business taxes. A license to do business is also a tax even though some owner-managers don't think of it as such. And some localities (most large cities) have an income tax.

You should check with the authorities in your locality to be sure your business is paying the various taxes to which it is subject.[7]

THE TAX CALENDAR CHECKLIST

The tax calendar checklist in Figure 6-14 is reproduced from the *Businessman's Tax Kit*. To be honest, you might need a good accountant to help you interpret all the details. The key point of this calendar is to make you aware of what you might be liable for, which forms are utilized, and which payments are due. In Figure 6-15 is a list of free publications and information related to business.

---

[4] Reproduced from *Steps in Meeting Your Tax Obligations*, Small Marketers Aid No. 142 (Washington, DC: Small Business Administration). This issue is no longer in print.
[5] *Steps in Meeting Your Tax Obligations*.
[6] *Steps in Meeting Your Tax Obligations*.
[7] *Steps in Meeting Your Tax Obligations*.

TAX CALENDAR	Form	Due Dates[1]			
U.S. Individual Income Tax Return	1040	April 15			
Declaration of Estimated Tax for Individuals	1040-ES	April 15			
Estimated Tax Declaration—Voucher for Individuals	1040-Es	4th voucher Jan 15	1st voucher April 15	2nd voucher June 15	3rd voucher Sept 15
U.S. Corporation Income Tax Return	1120	March 15 for calendar year taxpayers. Return for fiscal year taxpayers is due on the 15th day of the third month following the close of the fiscal year.			
U.S. Small Business Corporation Income Tax Return	1120S	March 15 for calendar-year-electing small business corporations. Fiscal year returns are due on the 15th day of the third month following the close of the fiscal year.			
U.S. Partnership Return of Income	1065	April 15 for partnerships operating on a calendar year. Return for fiscal year partnerships is due on the 15th day of the fourth month following the close of the fiscal year.			
Employer's Annual Federal Unemployment Tax Return	940	January 31.			
Federal Tax Deposit, Unemployment Taxes	508	4th quarter Jan. 31	1st quarter April 30	2nd quarter July 31	3rd quarter Oct. 31
Employer's Quarterly Federal Tax Return	941	4th quarter Jan. 31	1st quarter April 30	2nd quarter July 31	3rd quarter Oct. 31
Employer's Quarterly Tax Return for Household Employees	942	4th quarter Jan. 31	1st quarter April 30	2nd quarter July 31	3rd quarter Oct. 31
Federal Tax Deposit, Withheld Income and FICA Taxes	501	If your liability for the quarter is less than $200,[2] make your payment with Form 941 on the dates shown above.			
Quarterly Federal Excise Tax Return	720 [2]	4th quarter Jan. 31	1st quarter April 30	2d quarter July 31	3d quarter Oct. 31
Federal Tax Deposit, Excise Taxes	504	If you are liable for more than $100 of excise taxes in any calendar quarter,[3] you are required to make semi-monthly, monthly, or quarterly deposits on Form 504 in accordance with instructions in Form 702, Quarterly Federal Excise Tax Return.			
Wage and Tax Statement	W—2	You must complete and give this form to the employee on or before January 31; if his or her employment ended before December 31, within 30 days after his or her last wage payment.			
Statement for Recipients of Income	1099 (Series)	Generally, these statements should be given to recipients on or before January 31.			

[1]Due dates that fall on a Saturday, Sunday, or legal holiday are postponed until the next day that is not a Saturday, Sunday, or legal holiday.

[2]The due dates for filing Form 720 to report excise taxes for transportation and communications are:

4th quarter	1st quarter	2nd quarter	3rd quarter
Feb. 28	May 31	Aug. 31	Nov. 30

[3]For special deposit rules that apply to large liabilities for employment and excise taxes see Publication 509, Tax Calendar and Check List for 1974.

Note: This list is not all-inclusive. Due dates for returns filed less frequently, such as Forms 11, 2290, and 4638, are covered in Publication 509.

Figure 6-14: Tax Calendar for 1993. Publication 509, Department of the Treasury

Schedules E&R (Form 1040)
Supplemental Income Schedule
and Retirement Income Credit
Computation

Schedule F (Form 1040)
Farm Income and Expenses

Schedule SE (Form 1040)
Computation of Social Security
Self-Employment Tax

Form 1040-ES
Declaration of Estimated Tax
for Individuals

Circular E (Publication 15)
Employer's Tax Guide

Circular A (Publication 51)
Agricultural Employer's Tax
Guide

Notice 109
Information about Depositing
Employment and Excise Taxes

Publication 349
Federal Highway Use Tax on
Trucks, Truck-Tractors and Buses

Publication 510
Information on Excise Taxes

Publication 539
Withholding Taxes From Your
Employee's Wages

Form 941
Employer's Quarterly Federal
Tax Return

Form 941a
Continuation Sheet for
Schedule A of Form 941

Form 942c
Statement to Correct
Information

Form W-2
Wage and Tax Statement

Form W-3
Transmittal of Income and
Tax Statements
(Contains instructions for
preparation of Form W-2)

Form W-4
Employee's Withholding
Allowance certificate

Form W-4E
Exemption from Withholding

Form SS-5
Application for a Social Security
Number

Form 940
Employer's Annual Federal
Unemployment Tax Return

Form 942
Employer's Quarterly Tax Return
for Household Employees

Form 943
Employer's Annual Tax Return
for Agricultural Employees

Form 720
Quarterly Federal Excise Tax
Return

Form 11
Special Tax Return

Form 2290
Federal Use Tax Return on
Highway Motor Vehicles

Form 1096
Annual Summary and Transmittal
of U.S. Information Returns
(Instructions contain specific
information about preparation
of Form 1099 series)

Not all of the forms listed above are applicable to all employers. You need file only
those forms that apply to your business. Contact the Internal Revenue Service in your local area.

Figure 6-15: Listing of Free Publications and Information Related to Business

SUMMARY OF KEY POINTS

1. Tax avoidance and tax evasion have two distinct meanings.
2. Tax law continually changes. This is where your accountant can save you tax money that you "legally" don't owe.
3. Going to the small business tax workshop is a must for those just beginning a business. Your specific concerns can be addressed there.
4. Developing a worksheet for meeting tax obligations is crucial. You have to be organized to meet tax obligations.
5. Form SS-4 should be completed to obtain an employer's identification number.
6. The W-4 indicates allowances claimed by an employee. This form aids in deducting FWT from the wage bracket table found in circu-

lar E. There are many tables for married, single, weekly, monthly, and other situations.

7. The employer and employee both contribute equally to Social Security. If you own your own business, check into Social Security for the self-employed. The rate is not the same as for the employee.

8. The quarterly report (941) involves only FICA and FWT. Failure to report on time leads to penalties.

9. Each quarter in the calendar year is thirteen weeks.

10. The deposit requirements for the quarterly report (941) can be found on the backside of the form. Basically, the higher amounts withheld result in earlier deposits (501) in the quarter.

11. The employer should have an individual earnings record set up for each worker.

12. The W-2 reflects earnings of a worker for a calendar year. This form aids the completion of a worker's tax return for the year. The form is to be sent to each employee by January 31 of the following calendar year.

13. The employer pays a federal unemployment tax; the employee does not. If federal unemployment tax is less than $100 for the year, no quarterly payments are due, and a simple payment is due by January 31 of the following calendar year. In most states, state unemployment is paid for only by the employer.

14. In your business, it is important to check with local, state and federal agencies to keep up-to-date with specific tax requirements (which are always subject to change.)

	True	False	**CHECK YOUR PULSE**
1. Tax evasion and tax avoidance are basically the same.	___	___	
2. Business licenses come under federal regulations.	___	___	
3. Only the employee pays FICA.	___	___	
4. Form SS-4 is completed only when applying for an employer identification number.	___	___	
5. The wage bracket table is used only to calculate Social Security.	___	___	
6. Social Security taxes have to be reported only once a year by the employer.	___	___	
7. If your wage is "exempt" from a tax, it basically means you owe more taxes.	___	___	
8. The end of the third quarter is September 30.	___	___	
9. Federal unemployment tax is levied solely on the employee.	___	___	
10. The employer's quarterly federal tax return records only information about federal withholding taxes and Social Security.	___	___	
11. The law does not require owners to keep individual earnings records of their employees.	___	___	
12. Net pay plus deductions equals gross pay.	___	___	

13. Form W-2 Wage and Tax Statement gets much of the information from the employee's individual earnings record.

14. In a calendar year, tax of greater than $100 results in quarterly deposits for federal unemployment.

15. State unemployment tax is usually paid quarterly.

16. All states require a sales tax.

17. A person earning $100,000 and another worker earning $50,000 both pay the same amount of Social Security.

18. Deposit tickets are never used for FWT and Social Security.

19. Social Security rates are fixed.

20. The higher the withholding exemption, the less taken out in tax.

Solutions

1. False		11. False
2. False		12. True
3. False		13. True
4. True		14. True
5. False		15. True
6. False		16. False
7. False		17. True
8. True		18. False
9. False		19. False
10. True		20. True

MATCHING

Column A

_____ 1. Merit rating
_____ 2. Four quarters
_____ 3. W-4
_____ 4. Tax calendar
_____ 5. 941
_____ 6. Federal taxes
_____ 7. Excise tax
_____ 8. Payroll register
_____ 9. $200-$2,000 tax (FICA + FWT)
_____ 10. 940
_____ 11. Small Business Tax Workshop
_____
_____ 12. 940 due (less than $100)
_____ 13. Wage bracket
_____ 14. Social Security
_____ 15. Wage and tax statement
_____ 16. Penalties
_____ 17. Employer identification number

Column B

A. Beer
B. Not taxable
C. September 30
D. Paid only by employer
E. Monthly deposits
F. SS-4
G. FICA and FWT
H. Owner's collection from employee
I. State unemployment
J. State or local
K. Allowances claimed
L. Gross pay = Net pay + Deductions
M. By January 31 to employee
N. Paid by employer and employee
O. Individual earnings record
P. Aid in paying taxes
Q. By end of January of following year.
R. Free—contact IRS

_____18. End of third quarter   S.   Taxes paid late
_____19. Business licenses   T.   FWT deduction
_____20. Exempt

Answers

1.	I	11.	R
2.	0	12.	Q
3.	K	13.	T
4.	P	14.	N
5.	G	15.	M
6.	H	16.	S
7.	A	17.	F
8.	L	18.	C
9.	E	19.	J
10.	D	20.	B

APPENDIX 1: GET OFF THE FENCE AND TAKE A STAND

The instructional program in this appendix reviews and integrates the material found in the text. After you answer each question, you have a chance to check your answer, which is printed in the margin next to each question. Before reading the questions on each page, cover the answers with a blank sheet of paper. Once you have your answer, compare it to the correct response. If you're wrong and do not understand the correct answer, you can have the answer "explained" by looking it up in the index at the end of this book. Simply look up the answer to the side or, in its absence, the *italicized word or words* in the question.

1. In adequate planning and recordkeeping, poor management, fraud, neglect, managerial incompetence are key indicators of _____ _____.
2. _____ of failure may be worse than the failure itself.
3. Which of the following is a potential danger signal of financial trouble: (a) sold inventory, (b) reconciling the bank statement each month (c) writing business checks for personal expenses.
4. Self-discipline can be the key to sound _____.
5. Planning effectively might require setting aside one night a week. True or false?
6. The _____, in the eyes of the law, is considered a living person.
7. The _____ _____ has unlimited liability.
8. Double taxation results in a (a) sole proprietorship, (b) partnership, or (c) corporation.
9. The _____ _____ _____ *might* provide a tax benefit to an owner or owners of a proprietorship or partnership, but it retains the limited liability feature of a corporation.
10. Bookkeeping is the _____ phase of _____.

11. The law states that some records must not be permanent and accurate. True or false?
12. *Recordkeeping* should be (a) _____ _____ _____, (b) _____ _____ _____, (c) reliable, (d) _____, (e) consistent, and (f) designed to provide information on a timely basis.
13. Records of your business must be retained for two years. True or false?

1. business failures

2. Fear
3. C, see Survival checklist

4. planning
5. True

6. corporation
7. sole proprietorship
8. corporation

9. S-type corporation

10. recording, accounting

11. False

12. (a) simple to use (b) easy to understand (d) accurate
13. False, see Recordkeeping

14. b

15. d, see Ratios and Ratio analysis

16. ledger

17. cash, accounts receivable

18. credit

19. trial balance

20. income statement, given period of time

21. particular date

22. False

23. False, see Journal

24. c, see Rules of debit and credit

25. False

26. journals, ledgers

27. checks

28. c, see Cash, deficit

29. books, original

30. alphabetical, see Subsidiary, accounts receivable

31. True

32. False

33. b

34. True

35. merchandise, resale

36. True

37. deposits in transit

38. subtracted, checkbook

39. checks outstanding

40. True

41. b

42. True

43. Fixed assets

14. Which of the following is not part of a company's *assets?* (a) land, (b) accounts payable, (c) supplies, or (d) building.

15. Which of the following is correct? (a) Assets – Liabilities = Revenue; (b) Assets = Expenses – Liabilities; (c) Assets – Capital = Expenses; (d) Assets – Liabilities = Owner equity.

16. A book that accumulates information about business transactions is called the _____.

17. Revenue creates two possible inward flows: _____ and/or _____ _____.

18. An increase in a liability by the rules of debit and credit is a _____.

19. A list of the ledger is called a _____.

20. The _____ _____ is a financial report that compares revenues and expenses for a _____ _____ _____ _____.

21. The *balance sheet* is prepared as of a _____ _____.

22. The *balance sheet* is a list of assets and expenses. True or false?

23. Journalizing comes after posting. True or false?

24. Equipment bought on account results in (a) Dr. accounts payable, Cr. cash; (b) Cr. accounts payable, Dr. equipment; (c) Dr. equipment, Cr. accounts payable; or (d) Dr. equipment, Cr. cash.

25. *Single-entry bookkeeping* is never allowed in the recording process. True or false?

26. *Double-entry* makes use of _____ and _____.

27. *Petty cash* aids in writing fewer _____.

28. A cash shortage could result from (a) forgetting to ring up a sale, (b) giving customers too little change, or (c) ringing up a sale for too much.

29. A *general journal* and a *special journal* are _____ of _____ entry.

30. The accounts receivable subsidiary ledger is arranged in _____ order.

31. Missing a *purchase discount* can be quite costly to a business. True or false?

32. The column headings for a *special journal* are fixed. True or false?

33. *Sales tax* payable is (a) an asset, (b) a liability, or (c) an expense.

34. The *daily summary* is recorded in a sales and cash receipts journal. True or false?

35. *Purchases* are defined as _____ for _____.

36. Taking *discounts* in your business should be a priority. True or false ?

37. Deposits made but not shown on the *bank statement* are called _____ _____ _____.

38. *NSF* checks are _____ from the company's _____ balance.

39. Checks written by the company but not received by the bank are called _____ _____.

40. *Depreciation* is an indirect cash savings. True or false?

41. Which of the following is not part of a company's current assets? (a) cash, (b) land, (c) supplies, or (d) accounts receivable?

42. In general, *Stockholders' equity* = Stock + Retained earnings. True or false?

43. _____ _____ are usually not for resale, and they help in producing revenue. Their life is greater than one year.

44. Sales less cost of goods sold = _____ _____. 44. gross profit

45. Calculate the *current ratio* if current assets equal 8 and current liabilities equal 2. (a) not enough data given, (b) 4, (c) .25. 45. b

46. The *acid test ratio* deducts _____ from the current assets. 46. inventory

47. Net sales /
    Inventory = _____. 47. Inventory turnover

48. The *average collection period* in days for accounts receivable has no effect on cash flow. True or false? 48. False

49. Calculate the *asset turnover* if assets are $50 and sales are $100: _____. 49. 2

50. A *return on investment* of 22 percent means that, for each $2 of investment, you received 22 cents. True or false? 50. False

51. Each industry has only one set of ratios that are absolute for a minimum of ten years. True or false? 51. False, see Industrial ratios

52. Sources of business ratios could include (a) Dun and Bradstreet, (b) Robert Morris Associates, (c) your local chamber of commerce, or (d) all of the above. 52. d, see Sources of information for interpreting financial reports

53. *Ratio analysis* over a period of time should indicate specific _____. 53. trends

54. A _____ is a tool used to plan ahead. It allows us to set benchmarks and measure performance. 54. budget

55. The first key step in preparing a budget is to make a realistic estimate of _____. 55. sales, see Sales, projection (estimate)

56. The *cash budget* aids a company in planning its borrowing needs for seasonal inventory build-up. True or false? 56. True

57. *Break-even analysis* is a substitute for judgment. True or false? 57. False

58. If a desk retails for $300 and its *contribution margin* is $80, calculate the variable cost. _____ 58. $220

59. Assume fixed cost is $240,000 and variable costs are 60 percent. Calculate the *break-even point in sales*. _____

59. $600,000
$$S = \$240,000 + 0.6S$$
$$S - 0.6S = \$240,000$$
$$0.4S = \$240,000$$
$$S = \$600,000$$

60. Calculate the *break-even point in units* assuming fixed costs are $200,000, the unit sales price is $20, and the unit variable cost is $16. _____

60. 50,000 units
$$\frac{\$200,000}{\$20 - \$16} = 50,000$$

61. Bob Jones uses the *target profit* method to calculate the number of units (*u*) sold. He wishes to earn a net income of $80,000. The selling price is $400, the variable cost is $300, and the fixed cost is $240,000. Calculate the number of units Bob must sell to make the $80,000 profit.

61. 3,200
$$\$400u = \$300u + \$240,000 + \$80,000$$
$$\$100u = \$320,000$$
$$u = 3,200$$

62. Which of the following is not a disadvantage of *break-even analysis*? (a) People think it replaces judgment. (b) It does not take into account the time value of money. (c) It is a simple graphic presentation. (d) It assumes the selling price is held constant. 62. c

63. The *projected financial reports* cannot be modified. True or false? 63. False

64. Estimates are not allowed on *projected financial reports*. True or false? 64. False

65. False

66. False

67. federal withholding

68. Jill

69. *Employer's Tax Guide*

70. employee, employer

71. September 30, see Form 941

72. FICA, state unemployment, federal unemployment

73. FICA

74. January 31

75. 3

76. True

77. True, see Payroll deductions

78. 4

79. January 31

80. unemployment tax

81. quarterly deposits

---

65. *Tax avoidance* maximizes your liability. True or false?

66. Completion of *Form SS-4* indicates that the employer has contributed its share of Social Security. True or false?

67. *Form W-4* is used in conjunction with the wage bracket tables to deduct _____ _____ from the gross pay.

68. Jim claimed two allowances on *Form W-4*, while Jill claimed three allowances. Both have the same gross pay, and both are single. Who receives the larger net pay at time of payment? _____

69. The _____ _____ _____ (Circular E) contains the withholding table for FWT deductions.

70. The _____ and _____ both contribute to our *Social Security tax* system equally.

71. The third quarter ends on _____.

72. Employers have to contribute to the following taxes: _____, _____ _____, and _____ _____.

73. The employer's quarterly federal tax return involves _____ and FWT.

74. The fourth-quarter *Form 941* must be filed by _____.

75. In relation to *Form 941*, if at the end of a quarter-monthly period your total undeposited taxes for the quarter are $3,000 or more, you must deposit the taxes within _____ banking days.

76. The *payroll register* can help update information into the employee's earning record. True or false?

77. Net pay + Deductions = Gross pay. True or false?

78. The *individual earnings record* contains _____ quarters.

79. Employees should receive their *Form W-2s* by _____.

80. Federal _____ _____ is levied strictly on the employer.

81. If the employer owes more than $100 of *federal unemployment tax*, the employer must make _____ _____.

APPENDIX 2: RECORDKEEPING IN SMALL BUSINESS

Published by the U.S. Small Business Administration. Used by kind permission.

INTRODUCTION

An appropriate record-keeping system can determine the survival or failure of a new business. For those already in business, good record-keeping systems can increase the chances of staying in business and the opportunity to earn larger profits. Complete records will keep you in touch with your business's operations and obligations and help you see problems before they occur. This publication explains the characteristics of and procedure for establishing a good record-keeping system.

THE NEED FOR GOOD RECORDS

Accounting records furnish substantial information about your volume of business, such as how present and prior volumes compare, the amount of cash versus credit sales and the level and status of accounts receivable. In addition, good accounting records help to accomplish the following tasks.

Monitor Inventory While a large inventory allows goods to be delivered when they are ordered, too large an inventory represents an excess investment. If your inventory does not turn over quickly, your business may lose profits due to obsolescence, deterioration or excess investment.

Any items removed from inventory for personal use should be set aside in a special account for two reasons: first, they need to be recognized separately for tax purposes and, second, including these items in business gross profit calculations can be misleading.

Control Expenses Accounting records detail the amounts owed to suppliers and other creditors so that you can plan the availability of cash to meet your obligations. Such records also provide information regarding expenditures and allow you to establish controls over them. At all times, you must be aware of your individual expense requirements and how they relate to the overall picture.

Fulfill Payroll Requirements Payroll is one of the largest expenses in a small business. Adequate payroll records should meet the requirements of the

> Internal Revenue Service.
>
> State department of revenue.
>
> Local department of revenue.
>
> Workers' compensation laws.
>
> Wage and hour laws.
>
> Social security requirements.
>
> Unemployment insurance requirements.

For each of these categories you are required to provide annual reports and summaries. In addition, you must provide employees with the W-2 forms needed to file federal and other income tax returns. In order to provide this detailed information, it is essential for you to maintain good accounting records.

Determine Profit Margin Good accounting records will indicate a business's level of profit, and provide specific information on the profitability of certain departments or lines of goods within your business. Such analysis is important to avoid continuing product lines far beyond their profitability. In most cases, you can avoid losses if you maintain current records and analyze the information from your records on an ongoing basis.

Improve Cash Flow Good accounting records provide detailed reports of cash availability, both on hand and in the bank, and of cash shortages or the diversion of cash. Since cash is your most liquid asset, you must carefully account for it.

Use Supplier Discounts A cash budget will provide the business owner with a projection of the availability of cash that may be used to pay invoices as they become due. Discounts from suppliers for prompt payment can amount to substantial savings. A 2 percent discount is common if you pay the bill in full within 10 days; if not, full payment is due within 30 days. In business, this is commonly referred to as 2/10, n/30 where n = the net sum due. It means you pay 2 percent less if you pay within 10 days or you pay full price within 30 days. Take into account that this discount is cumulative. If you make timely payments for each month of the year you will gain a 24 percent benefit (2 percent 12 months).

Measure Performance Finally, good business records help you measure your business's performance by comparing your actual results with the figures in your budget and those of other similar businesses.

REQUIREMENTS OF A GOOD SYSTEM

The following criteria are essential to a good record-keeping system:

Simplicity

Accuracy

Timeliness

Consistency

Understandability

Reliability and completeness

There are several copyrighted accounting systems that can be purchased and adapted to the individual business, or you may find it is better to use a system specifically designed for your business and one that meets the above-mentioned criteria.

Commercial Record-Keeping Systems Record-keeping systems are currently available from various sources in the marketplace: stationery stores, publishers and business advisory services. These systems either are specifically designed for a cer-

tain type of business or are general enough to be used by many different types of businesses. Systems are available for cash basis recording, accrual basis recording and for both single and double entry.

Computerized Record-Keeping Consider using a computer for your business operations. Compare different software systems and make sure that the system you choose provides accurate and timely information and offers more than adequate presentation of accounting information for small businesses.

Low-cost computer programs are available that can handle many of the book entries that are necessary in a system that is maintained by hand. Appropriate hardware and a good general ledger software program can offer you substantial assistance in recording business transactions and summarizing the information into appropriate accounting presentations.

Currently available software allows you to enter transactions individually; these transactions are posted directly to the general ledger. A printout at the end of a given period shows the individual account activity, and also includes a balance and total of the accounts and provides a trial balance presentation. If the software is designed properly, it will provide appropriately prepared financial statements (balance sheet, income statements).

METHODS OF ACCOUNTING

There are two basic methods of accounting: cash basis and accrual basis. The method you choose will depend on your type of business. Cash basis is the simpler method. It is mainly used by service businesses that do not maintain inventory or startup businesses that do not offer credit. The accrual method is used by businesses that provide for credit sales or maintain an inventory.

Cash Basis Method In cash basis accounting, you record sales when cash is received and expenses when they are actually paid. Using the cash basis method is like maintaining a checkbook.

Under this method, accounts receivable are not recorded as sales until they are collected. Accounts payable are not recorded as expenses until the account is paid. Bad debt, accruals and deferrals are not appropriately recorded under cash basis because they are examples of outstanding credit (business notes). The cash basis method is not appropriate for businesses that extend credit.

Accrual Basis Method In accrual basis accounting, you report income or expenses as they are earned or incurred rather than when they are collected or paid. Record credit sales as accounts receivable that have not yet been collected.

The accrual basis also provides a method for recording expenditures paid in a single installment but covering more than one period. For example, interest may be paid semiannually or annually, but it is recorded on a monthly basis.

The accrual method satisfies the matching concept, i.e., matching income with related expenditures. Consequently, it can provide a clear and accurate view of business operations for a given period.

THE ACCOUNTING CYCLE

The accounting cycle can be described as follows:

1. A business transaction occurs, giving rise to an original document that is recorded in a book of original entries called a journal.
2. The totals from the journal are summarized and reported in a book of accounts, known as a general ledger.
3. The general ledger contains the individual accounts maintained by the business.
4. The individual accounts are listed in the form of debits and credits, known as the trial balance of the general ledger.
5. From this trial balance, after making certain adjustments, you prepare the business's financial statements.

Journals You derive the information for each journal entry from original source documents, such as, sales slips, cash register tapes, check stubs, purchase invoices and other items that record your business transactions. You may need to create subsidiary journals for specific, frequently occurring types of transactions, such as sales and expenses.

General Ledgers The summary and totals from all journals are entered into the general ledger. A general ledger is a summary book that records transactions and balances of individual accounts, and is organized into five classes of individual accounts, as follows:

1. Assets A record of all items that the business owns.
2. Liabilities A record of all debts the business owes.
3. Capital A record of all ownership or equity.
4. Sales A record of all income earned for a specific period.
5. Expenses A record of all expenditures incurred during a given period.

When the trial balance is prepared, these classifications are easily recognized.

Trial Balance At the end of the fiscal year or accounting period, the individual accounts in the general ledger are totaled and closed.

The balances of the individual accounts are summarized in the financial statements.

Financial Statements The main types of financial statements are the balance sheet and the income statement, also known as the profit and loss statement. The balance sheet is a report of a business's financial condition (assets, liabilities and capital) at a specific moment in time (see Example 1) and the income statement is a summary of profit and loss for a specific period of time, generally a month, quarter or year (see Example 2).

Other statements may be prepared. For example, a cash flow statement identifies the sources and applications of cash. Statements may also be prepared to indicate manufacturing expenses or other special areas that are of interest to you.

Percentages   Percentages are used in financial statements to show the part of each sales dollar used by the various expenses. Percentages are especially helpful for comparing current year financial statements with those of prior years to determine business trends. Percentages are also helpful for comparing your figures with those of other firms in the same line of business (see Example 3).

HOW TO ANALYZE YOUR RECORDS

To chart the progress of your business, you should become familiar with various forms of financial statements analysis and measurement.

Financial statements indicate which items need more attention. For example, profits may be too low or rent unnecessarily high. Perhaps there is a way to use the business vehicles more efficiently, to increase inventory turnover or to reduce long distance telephone bills.

In analyzing financial statements, carefully examine all items that do not seem realistic. Answer the following questions:

Why are certain expenses at a particular level?

Are there any ways to reduce or avoid certain expenses?

Should you incur all of your expenses?

Does the level of profit justify your investment, time and effort?

Financially significant items should be analyzed regularly. For example, examine payroll as a percentage of total administrative expenses. Keep in mind that, if your business is a proprietorship, your salary is not a payroll expense; however, if your business is a corporation, your salary should be a payroll expense.

Analyzing Payroll Expenses   In justifying payroll and other expenses, answer the following questions:

Are accurate records maintained for time spent on various jobs and functions?

Is the eight-hour day of each employee accounted for appropriately?

When employees are paid overtime, is the additional expense reflected in charges to the customer?

Is the level of payroll expense appropriate for your type of business?

Are you billing on a guaranteed price basis or on an hourly basis?

When using guaranteed price basis for billing, does actual time spent exceed time estimated for the job?

Do employees work with a minimum of wasted effort and time?

Are you operating at maximum efficiency? What strategies can be implemented to maximize efficiency?

Ratios   Accountants use various ratios to evaluate financial statements, such as ratios that assess liquidity, solvency and profitability.

Liquidity   These ratios indicate the availability of cash and the firm's ability to pay liabilities.

Current ratio:	Current assets
	Current liabilities
Acid test (liquidity ratio):	Cash, cash equivalents and receivables
	Current liabilities
Day's sales in receivables:	Accounts receivable
	Credit sales divided by 360
Inventory turnover:	Cost of sales
	Average inventory

Capital and Long-term Solvency   These ratios indicate the firm's ability to meet debts when due.

Equity/debt ratio:	Total equity
	Total debt
Total equity to fixed assets:	Total equity
	Net fixed assets

Profitability   These ratios indicate your firm's performance.

Gross profit margin:	Gross profit
	Sales

Net income to sales:	Net income
	Sales
Operating income to sales:	Income before income taxes
	Total assets
Return on total assets:	Net income and interest expenses
	Total assets
Return on total:	Net income
	Total equity

OTHER IMPORTANT RECORDS

In addition to accounting records, you will need to keep separate records for accounts receivable, payroll and taxes, petty cash, insurance, business equipment and perhaps other items.

Accounts Receivable A good record-keeping system should provide you with a detailed report of accounts receivable, including current information on customers and a running balance of their accounts. To maintain a good accounts receivable system, record credit charges on a regular basis. It is essential that you follow up on all late paying and delinquent customers.

Accounts receivable should be aged at the end of each month. This means organizing the accounts into those that are current; 30-, 60-, and 90-days old and older. This arrangement helps you to take appropriate, timely actions.

One example of a timely action is to transfer delinquent accounts to a notes receivable account. Notes receivable are loans the business makes to others, either inside or outside the business.

Each note receivable should contain specific terms of credit and interest and should be signed by the customer. An additional timely action to decrease the number of bad accounts and avoid the effort of collecting payments from slow-paying customers is to issue a formal complaint with your local credit bureau.

Payroll and Taxes Current Internal Revenue Service (IRS) regulations require that you withhold federal income tax and social security (FICA) from each employee. You must remit the amount for taxes to the IRS on a quarterly, monthly or more frequent basis. A detailed reporting system for payroll will help you make timely tax payments.

Gather specific information about each employee on individual employee record cards. All employees should fill out federal Form W-4, which indicates their filing status and the number of exemptions they claim. Use this information to compute the federal withholding and social security (FICA) deductions for each payroll check.

Prepare Employees Quarterly Federal Tax Return (Form 941) by totaling each employee's withholding for federal taxes and social security. File Form 941 with the IRS.

Each payroll period, total the accumulated withholdings of both federal taxes and social security for all employees. If this total exceeds $500 for any month, you must deposit this amount by the 15th day of the following month in a depository bank (an authorized financial institution or a federal reserve bank).

Generally, when the total exceeds $3,000, you must deposit this amount within three business days. Any overpayment in taxes is paid back to you quarterly.

At the year's end, you are required to prepare not only the information normally required for that quarter, but also summaries of each employee's total earnings and withholdings for the year (Form W-2). Provide this form to each employee and the IRS.

A Word of Caution It is very easy to fall behind in making tax payments. If you find yourself short of cash, do not be tempted to delay payment of taxes. The IRS will not bill your business for taxes due nor will it notify you of late payments. Delayed payments can easily add up to a large sum; the debt may impede the growth of your business and may even force you to close your business, to say nothing of the federal penalties incurred for late payments.

With a good record-keeping system, you can simplify the process of filing taxes to the point where the information needed to complete the forms is automatically generated. Setting up such a system is a rather technical task and you may need to seek guidance.

Petty Cash Sometimes a petty cash fund is needed to purchase small items required on a day-to-day basis. If this is necessary, draw a check to petty cash for a nominal amount.

Problems often arise when cash is easily available; therefore, if possible, avoid a petty cash fund. However, very often the convenience of having a small amount of cash available will facilitate the smooth operation of your business. Be sure to balance this fund monthly, based on the cash balance plus receipts for all expenditures.

Insurance   Most businesses have several types of insurance. For each policy, you should have the following information:

Clear statement of the type of coverage.

Names of individuals covered.

Effective dates and expiration date.

Annual premium.

Review your insurance policies on a regular basis. In addition, annually consult an insurance specialist, who will review the total insurance package to determine what coverage is appropriate and ensure that premiums remain in line with prior quotations.

Business Equipment   Keep an accurate list of permanent business equipment used on both a regular and stand-by basis. The list should describe the equipment and provide serial numbers, date of purchase and original cost. Keep the list available for insurance or other purposes. You will also need this information to prepare accurate depreciation schedules.

ACCOUNTING SERVICES

You have several choices in who should maintain your accounting system. You can

Maintain the books yourself.

Hire a bookkeeper on a full-time or part-time basis.

Hire the accountant who set up your books.

Set up a hybrid system in which you

maintain the day-to-day reports, while an accountant does the period-end record preparation, summaries and reconciliations and the returns for sales tax, excise tax and payroll taxes.

In making the choice, you must decide whether you have the ability and time to set up and maintain good records or if you should engage an outside accounting service. It is usually suggested that you hire an accountant to do the final year-end preparations and to advise you. No matter what you choose, you should remain familiar with your books and participate in the record-keeping process. This will maximize the services provided by the accountant and allow you to keep track of your business.

Selecting the Accounting Service   If you decide to hire an outside service, find an accounting firm that will work closely with your business and provide you with the information necessary to develop a successful operation. Interview several accounting professionals and compare their level of accounting knowledge, computer literacy, knowledge of and experience with small business accounting and any specialized knowledge required in your business.

There are many types of professionals you may consider, such as a certified public accountant, an enrolled agent or an accredited accountant.

Certified Public Accountant (CPA) A person who has passed the American Institute of CPAs' national examination, which tests an individual's ability in accounting, auditing, law and related areas.

Enrolled Agent (EA) An individual who has passed a two-day exam prepared by the IRS, covering many areas of federal taxation. This person is generally considered a tax specialist.

Accredited Accountant An individual who has passed a rigorous examination prepared by the Accreditation Council of Accountancy and Taxation, a national accounting accreditation board affiliated with the National Society of Public Accountants and the College for Financial

Planning in Denver, Colorado. Accredited accountants specialize in small business accounting.

Other accountants in public practice perform various levels of accounting and write-up services.

When selecting an accountant, the cost of the accountant's fees must be weighed against the benefits received. Frequently, the accountant's professional advice can increase profits to more than cover the expense. Monthly services by an accounting firm will provide you with complete and timely information and also will allow the accountant to develop knowledge of your business and be in a more comfortable position to render professional advice as the business grows.

Advice and Assistance In addition to bookkeeping, an accountant can advise you on financial management. He or she can assist with cash flow requirements and budget forecasts, business borrowing, choosing a legal structure for your business and preparation and advice on tax matters.

Cash Flow Requirements An accountant can help you work out the amount of cash needed to operate the business during a certain period, for example, a three-month, six-month or one-year projection. The accountant considers how much cash you will need to carry your accounts receivable, to increase inventory, to cover current invoices, to acquire needed equipment and to retire outstanding debts.

Additionally, the accountant can determine how much cash will come from collection of accounts receivable and how much will have to be borrowed or provided from other sources. In determining cash requirements, the accountant may notice and call attention to danger spots, such as accounts that are in arrears or delinquent areas or areas of excess expenditure.

Business Borrowing An accountant can assist you in compiling the information necessary to secure a loan: the assets the business will offer for collateral, the present debt obligations, a summary of how the money will be used and re-

payment schedules. Such data show the lender the financial condition of the business and your ability to repay the loan. Remember, lenders have two very definite requirements: (1) that the business have adequate collateral to secure the loan and (2) that the business will be able to repay the loan. An accountant can advise on whether you need a short- or long-term loan. In addition, your accountant may introduce you to a banker who knows and respects his or her financial judgment.

Legal Structure It is wise to discuss the type of business organization that best fits your needs with an accountant and an attorney. They can point out the advantages and disadvantages of the various forms of business organization, such as a

Proprietorship	An extension of individual ownership.
Partnership	Multiple proprietors.
Corporation	A completely separate legal entity.

In addition, they can advise you on immediate plans regarding management, financing, long-range plans to bring others into the business and estate planning, all of which affect the type of business you choose.

Tax Considerations This is an area in which an accountant can provide much advice and assistance. Your accountant can suggest methods to record and document the various types of information necessary for taxes.

APPENDIX A: FINANCIAL STATUS CHECKLIST

What You Should Know
Daily
1. The balance of cash on hand.
2. The bank balance.
3. Daily summaries of sales and cash receipts.
4. Any errors or problems that have occurred in collections.

5. A record of monies paid out, both by cash and by check.

Weekly

1. Accounts receivable (particularly those accounts that appear to be slow paying).
2. Accounts payable (be aware of the discount period mentioned above).
3. Payroll (be aware of the accumulation of hours and the development of the payroll liability).
4. Taxes (be aware of any tax items that are due and reports that might be required by government agencies).

Monthly

1. If you engage an outside accounting service, provide records of receipts, disbursements, bank accounts and journals to the accounting firm. This will allow the firm to maintain good records and present them to you for review, consideration and support in decision making.
2. Make sure that income statements are available on a monthly basis, and certainly within 15 days of the close of the month.
3. Review a balance sheet that indicates the balance of business assets and the total current liability.
4. Reconcile your bank account each month so that any variations are recognized and necessary adjustments made.
5. Balance the petty cash account on a monthly basis. If you allow this account to extend for a longer period, it may create substantial problems.
6. Review federal tax requirements and make deposits.
7. Review and age accounts receivable so that slow and bad accounts are recognized and handled.

APPENDIX B: INFORMATION RESOURCES

U.S. Small Business Administration (SBA)

The SBA offers an extensive selection of information on most business management topics, from how to start a business to exporting your products.

This information is listed in The Small Business Directory. For a free copy write to: SBA Publications, P.O. Box 1000, Fort Worth, TX 76119.

SBA has offices throughout the country. Consult the U.S. Government section in your telephone directory for the office nearest you. SBA offers a number of programs and services, including training and educational programs, counseling services, financial programs and contract assistance. Ask about Service Corps of Retired Executives (SCORE), a national organization sponsored by SBA of over 13,000 volunteer business executives who provide free counseling, workshops and seminars to prospective and existing small business people.

Small Business Development Centers (SBDCs), sponsored by the SBA in partnership with state and local governments, the educational community and the private sector. They provide assistance, counseling and training to prospective and existing business people.

Small Business Institutes (SBIs), organized through SBA on more than 500 college campuses nationwide. The institutes provide counseling by students and faculty to small business clients. For more information about SBA business development programs and services call the Small Business Answer Desk at 1-800-U-ASK-SBA (827-5722).

Other U.S. Government Resources Many publications on business management and other related topics are available from the Government Printing Office (GPO). GPO bookstores are located in 24 major cities and are listed in the Yellow Pages under the bookstore heading. You can request a Subject Bibliography by writing to Government Printing Office, Superintendent of Documents, Washington, DC 20402-9328.

Many federal agencies offer publications of interest to small businesses. There is a nominal fee for some, but most are free.

Below is a selected list of government agencies that provide publications and other services targeted to small businesses. To get their publications, contact the regional offices listed in the telephone directory or write to the addresses below:

Consumer Information Center (CIC)
P.O. Box 100
Pueblo, CO 81002
The CIC offers a consumer information catalog of federal publications.

Consumer Product Safety Commission (CPSC)
Publications Request
Washington, DC 20207
The CPSC offers guidelines for product safety requirements.

U.S. Department of Agriculture (USDA)
12th Street and Independence Avenue, SW
Washington, DC 20250
The USDA offers publications on selling to the USDA. Publications and programs on entrepreneurship are also available through county extension offices nationwide.

U.S. Department of Commerce (DOC)
Office of Business Liaison
14th Street and Constitution Avenue, NW
Room 5898C
Washington, DC 20230
DOC's Business Assistance Center provides listings of business opportunities available in the federal government. This service also will refer businesses to different programs and services in the DOC and other federal agencies.

**U.S. Department of Health
and Human Services (HHS)**
Public Health Service
Alcohol, Drug Abuse and Mental Health Administration
5600 Fishers Lane
Rockville, MD 20857
Drug Free Workplace Helpline:
1-800-843-4971.
Provides information on Employee Assistance Programs.

National Institute for Drug Abuse Hotline:
1-800-662-4357.
Provides information on preventing substance abuse in the workplace.

**The National Clearinghouse for
Alcohol and Drug Information:**
1-800-729-6686 toll-free.
Provides pamphlets and resource materials on substance abuse.

**U.S. Department of Labor (DOL)
Employment Standards Administration**
200 Constitution Avenue, NW
Washington, DC 20210
The DOL offers publications on compliance with labor laws.

**U.S. Department of Treasury
Internal Revenue Service (IRS)**
P.O. Box 25866
Richmond, VA 23260
1-800-424-3676
The IRS offers information on tax requirements for small businesses.

**U.S. Environmental Protection Agency
(EPA)**
Small Business Ombudsman
401 M Street, SW (A-149C)
Washington, DC 20460
1-800-368-5888 except DC and VA
703-557-1938 in DC and VA
The EPA offers more than 100 publications designed to help small businesses understand how they can comply with EPA regulations.

**U.S. Food and Drug Administration
(FDA)**
FDA Center for Food Safety and Applied Nutrition
200 Charles Street, SW
Washington, DC 20402
The FDA offers information on packaging and labeling requirements for food and food-related products.

For More Information   A librarian can help you locate the specific information you need in reference books. Most libraries have a variety of directories, indexes and encyclopedias that cover many business topics. They also have other resources, such as:

Trade association information   Ask the librarian to show you a directory of trade associations. Associations provide a valuable network of resources to their members through publications and services such as newsletters, conferences and seminars.

Books   Many guidebooks, textbooks and manuals on small business are published annually. To find the names of books not in your local library check *Books In Print*, a directory of books currently available from publishers.

Magazine and newspaper articles   Business and professional magazines provide information that is more current than that found in books and textbooks. There are a number of indexes to help you find specific articles in periodicals.

In addition to books and magazines, many libraries offer free workshops, lend skill-building tapes and have catalogues and brochures describing continuing education opportunities.

Example 1
ABC SALES CO.
BALANCE SHEET
December 31,199

Assets	Current assets	Liabilities	Current liabilities
Cash	$23,590	Accounts Payable	$22,420
Notes receivable	10,000	Mortgage note payable	
Accounts receivable	20,880	(current portion)	5,000
Merchandise receivable	62,150	Salaries payable	1,152
Store supplies	960	**Total Current Liabilities**	**$28,572**
Office supplies	480		
Prepaid insurance	1,650	*Long-term liabilities*	
Total Current Assets	**$119,710**	Mortgage note payable	20,000
		Total liabilities	$48,572
Plant assets		Stockholders' Equity	
Land	$20,000	Capital Stock	$100,000
Building	$140,000	Retained earnings	115,488
Less accumulated depreciation		Total stockholder's equity	$215,488
33,900	106,100	**Total Liabilities and**	
Office equipment	15,570	**Stockholders' Equity**	**$264,060**
Less accumulated depreciation			
8,720	6,850		
Store equipment	27,100		
Less accumulated depreciation			
15,700	11,400		
Assets	*Current assets*		
Total plant assets	144,350		
Total Assets	**$264,060**		

Example 2
ABC SALES CO.
INCOME STATEMENT
December 31,199X

Revenue from Sales

Sales	$732,163	
Less: Sales returns and allowances	$6,140	
Less: Sales discount		
5,822	11,962	
Net Sales	**$720,201**	

Cost of merchandise

Merchandise inventory		
January 1 purchases	530,280	
Less purchases discount	2,525	
Net purchases	527,755	
Merchandise available for sale	587,455	
Less merchandise inventory		
December 31	62,150	
Cost of merchandise sold	$525,305	

Gross Profit	**$194,896**	

Operating Expenses

Selling expenses

Sales salaries	$60,044	
Advertising	10,460	
Depreciation store equipment	3,100	
Insurance selling	2,080	
Store supplies	2,010	
Miscellaneous (selling)	630	
Total Selling Expenses	**$78,324**	

General expenses

Office salaries	$21,032	
Heating and lighting	8,100	
Taxes	6,810	
Depreciationbuilding	4,500	
Depreciationoffice equipment	1,490	
Insurancegeneral	830	
Office supplies	610	
Miscellaneous	760	
Total General Expenses	**$44,132**	

Total Operating Expenses	**$122,456**	
Net income from operations	$72,440	
Other Income		
interest income	3,600	
Other Expense		
interest expense	2,440	
Net Income	**$73,600**	

Example 3
APPLIANCE REPAIR COMPANY
INCOME STATEMENT SHOWING
EXPENSES AS PERCENTAGE OF SALES
Total Parts Service

	Amount	Percent	Amount	Percent	Amount	Percent
Gross Sales	$70,000	100.00	$25,000	100.00	$45,000	100.00
Cost of sales						
Opening inventory	13,000		13,000			
Purchases	25,000		25,000			
Total	38,000		38,000			
Ending inventory	14,000		14,000			
Total cost of sales	24,000	34.29	24,000	96.00		
Gross Profit	46,000	65.71	1,000	4.00		
Operating expenses						
Payroll	26,000	37.14	26,000	57.78		
Rent	3,000	4.29	1,500	6.00	1,500	3.33
Payroll taxes	1,500	2.14	1,500	3.33		
Interest	600	.86	300	1.20	300	.67
Depreciation	1,400	2.00	1,400	3.11		
Truck expense	5,500	7.86	5,500	12.22		
Telephone	2,400	3.43	1,200	4.80	1,200	2.67
Insurance	1,000	1.43	400	1.60	600	1.33
Miscellaneous	1,000	1.43	500	2.00	500	1.11
Total Expenses	42,400	60.58	3,900	15.60	38,500	85.55
Net Profit (Loss)						
(Exclusive of owner's salary)	$ 3,600	5.14	($2,900)	(11.60)	$ 6,500	14.44

APPENDIX 3: THE STRESS-RELIEVER CROSSWORD PUZZLE

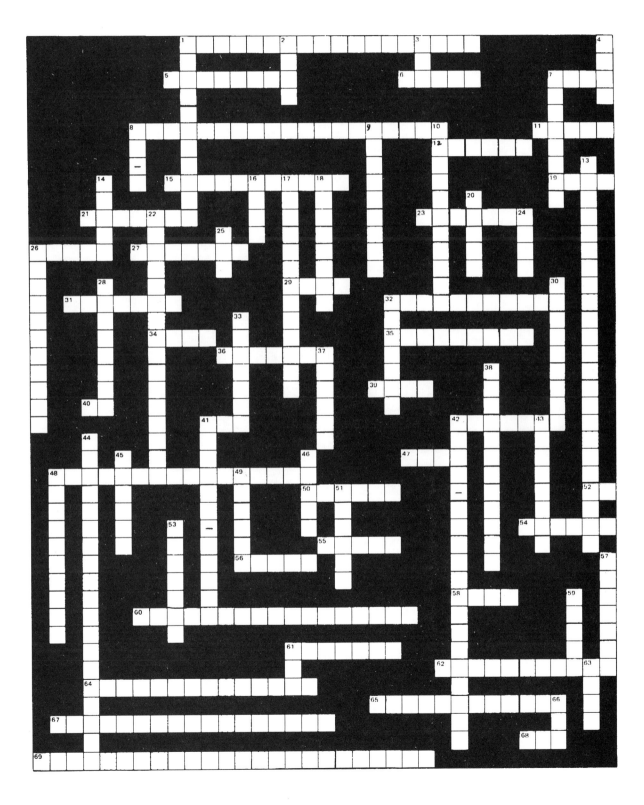

Across

1. _____ _____ is the process of verifying our checkbook balances to the bank statements.
5. Entries in _____ are recorded in chronological order.
6. Business owners must "make" _____ time for planning and record-keeping.
7. There are many pros and _____ in how long records should be kept.
8. A _____ _____ is owned by one person.
11. In the eyes of the law, the corporation is a _____ entity.
12. _____ = Liabilities + Owner equity.
15. Assets − _____ = Owner equity.
19. The abbreviation for "account."
21. The process of transferring information from the journals to the ledger.
23. _____ consists of the inward flow of cash and/or accounts receivable.
26. Exempt _____ are not taxed.
27. The ledger consists of many an _____.
29. Equipment − Accumulated depreciation = _____ value.
31. The petty cash _____ helps owners write fewer checks.
32. The owners of a _____ are stockholders.
34. The _____ proprietorship results in unlimited liability for the owner.
35. A _____ financial report requires an estimate of future sales so you can plan the present.
36. The _____ sheet lists permanent accounts.
39. The _____ flow aids projecting our borrowing needs.
40. The abbreviation for "credit."
41. The abbreviation for "state withholding taxes."
42. Owners of a corporation have _____ liability.
47. The budget is a tool to _____ for the future.
48. The _____ _____ is a system of steps to accurately record a company's transactions.
50. The _____ profit results in net income added onto the break-even point.
52. The abbreviation for "debit."
54. A trial balance is prepared from the _____.
55. The credit is defined as the _____ side of the account.
56. The _____ of the accounts receivable ledger should equal the one figure in accounts receivable in the ledger at the end of the month.
58. The debit is defined as the _____ side of the account.
60. Double-_____ _____ is based on both the income statement and the balance sheet.
61. Balancing or _____ is a way of summarizing an account or verifying the totals of journal columns.
62. Rents are a good example of _____ _____.
64. _____ _____ are costs that are subject to change with the volume of business activity.
65. Retail price − Variable cost = _____ margin.

67. The accounts receivable _____ _____ is a book or file, in alphabetical order, of what individual customers owe a company.
68. _____ income results when earned income exceeds incurred expenses.
69. The _____ _____ _____ _____ _____ aid in accumulating information in the ledger.

1. _____ is the recording part of accounting.
2. The _____ crisis happens often, especially in seasonal businesses.
3. The _____ calendar is an aid for completing tax obligations on time.
4. A net _____ occurs when incurred expenses are greater than earned revenues.
7. The tax _____ is an optional tool.
8. The owners of a new business should complete Form _____ _____.
10. A _____ has unlimited liability.
13. The _____ _____ _____ is not found in the general ledger.
14. _____ pay = Net pay + Deductions.
16. Sales _____ sales discounts equals net sales.
17. A _____ _____ is a list of the ledger.
18. The accounting _____ is: Assets = Liabilities + Owner equity.
20. An increase in an asset is a _____.
22. Revenues and expenses are found on the _____ _____.
24. Break-_____ ascertains the sales point at which no profit or no loss is realized.
25. The abbreviation for "inventory."
26. "FWT" stands for federal _____ tax.
28. Asset turnover indicates how well assets are being managed.
30. _____ liability is found in the corporate structure.
32. Assets – Liabilities = _____.
33. FWT can be read from the wage _____ table.
37. A corporation is a legal _____ in the eyes of the law.
38. Federal _____ tax is paid only by the employer.
41. _____ - _____ bookkeeping is not a self-balancing system.
42. Mortgage payable is classified as a _____ - _____ _____.
43. _____ cause an owner's investment to increase.
44. _____ _____ is an asset indicating the amount owed to the company.
45. The _____ is a tool used to plan by setting benchmarks.
46. A _____ cash fund helps owners to write fewer checks.
48. The _____ cycle is completed at least once a year.
49. An increase in accounts payable is a _____.
51. A merit _____ is related to state unemployment.
53. Owners, whether they realize it or not, have the _____ to plan because planning is only common sense.
57. Financial _____ are prepared from information accumulated in the ledger.

59. Revenue is matched against the _____ incurred to produce the revenue.
61. The abbreviation for "federal withholding tax."
63. The _____ dilemma requires owners to plan and to set priorities.
66. Sales – Sales discounts = _____ sales.

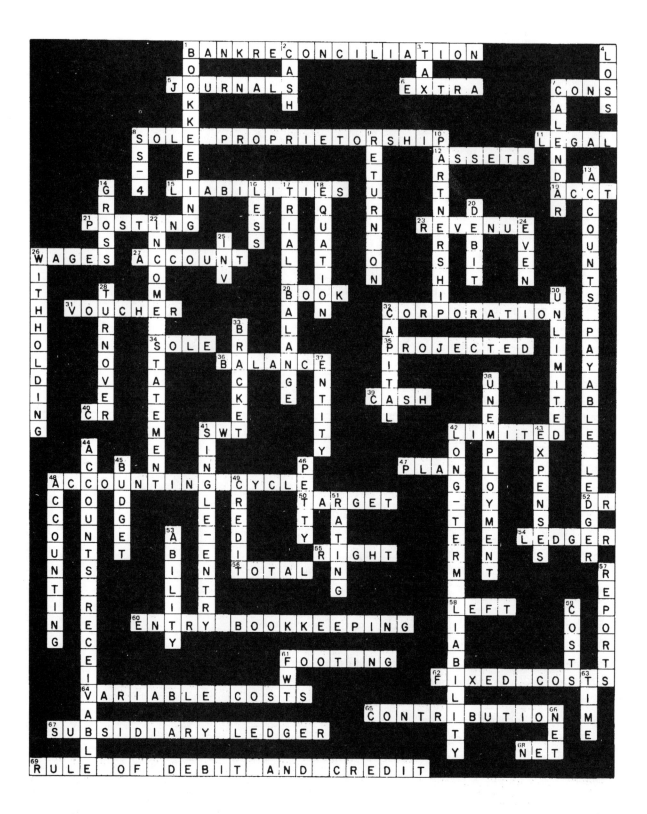

APPENDIX 4: CHECKLIST FOR GOING INTO BUSINESS

Published by the U.S. Small Business Administration. Used by kind permission.

INTRODUCTION

Owning a business is the dream of many Americans . . . starting that business converts your dream into reality. But there is a gap between your dream and reality that can only be filled with careful planning. As a business owner, you will need a plan to avoid pitfalls, to achieve your goals and to build a profitable business.

The "Checklist for Going into Business" is a guide to help you prepare a comprehensive business plan and determine if your idea is feasible, to identify questions and problems you will face in converting your idea into reality and to prepare for starting your business.

Operating a successful small business will depend on a practical plan with a solid foundation; dedication and willingness to sacrifice to reach your goal; technical skills; and basic knowledge of management, finance, record keeping and market analysis.

As a new owner, you will need to master these skills and techniques if your business is to be successful.

As a first and often overlooked step, ask yourself why you want to own your own business. Check the reasons that apply to you.

	YES
1. Freedom from the 9-5 daily work routine.	___
2. Being your own boss.	___
3. Doing what you want when you want to do it.	___
4. Improving your standard of living.	___
5. Boredom with your present job.	___
6. Having a product or service for which you feel there is a demand.	___

Some reasons are better than others, none are wrong; however, be aware that there are trade-offs. For example, you can escape the 9–5 daily routine, but you may replace it with a 6 a.m. to 8 p.m. routine.

A SELF-ANALYSIS

Going into business requires certain personal characteristics. This portion of the checklist deals with you, the individual. These questions require serious thought. Try to be objective. Remember, it is your future that is at stake!

Personal Characteristics

	YES	NO
1. Are you a leader?	___	___
2. Do you like to make your own decisions?	___	___
3. Do others turn to you for help in making decisions?	___	___
4. Do you enjoy competition?	___	___
5. Do you have will power and self discipline?	___	___
6. Do you plan ahead?	___	___
7. Do you like people?	___	___
8. Do you get along well with others?	___	___

Personal Conditions

This next group of questions though brief is vitally important to the success of your plan. It covers the physical, emotional, and financial strains you will encounter in starting a new business.

	YES	NO
1. Are you aware that running your own business may require working 12–16 hours a day six days a week and maybe even Sundays and holidays?	___	___

2. Do you have the physical stamina to handle the workload and schedule?   ____ ____

3. Do you have the emotional strength to withstand the strain?   ____ ____

4. Are you prepared if needed to temporarily lower your standard of living until your business is firmly established?   ____ ____

5. Is your family prepared to go along with the strains they too must bear?   ____ ____

6. Are you prepared to lose your savings?   ____ ____

PERSONAL SKILLS AND EXPERIENCE

Certain skills and experience are critical to the success of a business. Since it is unlikely that you possess all the skills and experience needed you'll need to hire personnel to supply those you lack. There are some basic and special skills you will need for your particular business.

By answering the following questions you can identify the skills you possess and those you lack (your strengths and weaknesses).

YES   NO

1. Do you know what basic skills you will need in order to have a successful business?   ____ ____

2. Do you possess those skills?   ____ ____

3. When hiring personnel will you be able to determine if the applicants' skills meet the requirements for the positions you are filling?   ____ ____

4. Have you ever worked in a managerial or supervisory capacity?   ____ ____

5. Have you ever worked in a business similar to the one you want to start?   ____ ____

6. Have you had any business training in school?   ____ ____

7. If you discover you don't have the basic skills needed for your business will you be willing to delay your plans until you've acquired the necessary skills?   ____ ____

FINDING A NICHE

Small businesses range in size from a manufacturer with many employees and millions of dollars in equipment to the lone window washer with a bucket and a sponge. Obviously the knowledge and skills required for these two extremes are far apart but for success they have one thing in common: each has found a business niche and is filling it.

The most critical problems you will face in your early planning will be to find your niche and determine the feasibility of your idea. Get into the right business at the right time is very good advice but following that advice may be difficult. Many entrepreneurs plunge into a business venture so blinded by the dream that they fail to thoroughly evaluate its potential.

Before you invest time, effort, and money the following exercise will help you separate sound ideas from those bearing a high potential for failure.

IS YOUR IDEA FEASIBLE?

1. Identify and briefly describe the business you plan to start.

   _____
   _____
   _____
   _____

2. Identify the product or service you plan to sell.

   _____

3. Does your product or service satisfy an unfilled need?   Yes ___ No ___

4. Will your product or service serve an existing market in which demand exceeds supply?

Yes ___ No ___

5. Will your product or service be competitive based on its quality, selection, price, or location?

Yes ___ No ___

Answering yes to any of these questions means you are on the right track; a negative answer means the road ahead could be rough.

MARKET ANALYSIS

For a small business to be successful the owner must know the market. To learn the market you must analyze it—a process that takes time and effort. You don't have to be a trained statistician to analyze the marketplace nor does the analysis have to be costly.

Analyzing the market is a way to gather facts about potential customers and to determine the demand for your product or service. The more information you gather the greater your chances of capturing a segment of the market. Know the market before investing your time and money in any business venture.

These questions will help you collect the information necessary to analyze your market and determine if your product or service will sell.

	YES	NO
1. Do you know who your customers will be?	___	___
2. Do you understand their needs and desires?	___	___
3. Do you know where they live?	___	___
4. Will you be offering the kind of products or services that they will buy?	___	___
5. Will your prices be competitive in quality and value?	___	___
6. Will your promotional program be effective?	___	___
7. Do you understand how your business compares with your competitors?	___	___
8. Will your business be conveniently located for the people you plan to serve?	___	___
9. Will there be adequate parking facilities for the people you plan to serve?	___	___

This brief exercise will give you a good idea of the kind of market planning you need to do. An answer of no indicates a weakness in your plan so do your research until you can answer each question with a yes.

PLANNING YOUR START-UP

So far this checklist has helped you identify questions and problems you will face converting your idea into reality and determining if your idea is feasible. Through self-analysis you have learned of your personal qualifications and deficiencies and through market analysis you have learned if there is a demand for your product or service.

The following questions are grouped according to function. They are designed to help you prepare for Opening Day.

Name and Legal Structure

	YES	NO
1. Have you chosen a name for your business?	___	___
2. Have you chosen to operate as sole proprietorship partnership or corporation?	___	___

Your Business and the Law

A person in business is not expected to be a lawyer but each business owner should have a basic knowledge of laws affecting the business. Here are some of the legal matters you should be acquainted with:

	YES	NO
1. Do you know which licenses and permits you may need to operate your business?	___	___
2. Do you know the business laws you will have to obey?	___	___
3. Do you have a lawyer who can advise you and help you with legal papers?	___	___
4. Are you aware of Occupational Safety and Health Administration (OSHA) requirements?	___	___
___ Regulations covering hazardous material?	___	___
___ Local ordinances covering signs, snow removal, etc.?	___	___
___ Federal Tax Code provisions pertaining to small business?	___	___
___ Federal regulations on withholding taxes and Social Security?	___	___
___ State Workmen's Compensation laws?	___	___

Protecting Your Business

It is becoming increasingly important that attention be given to security and insurance protection for your business. There are several areas that should be covered. Have you examined the following categories of risk protection?

	YES	NO
___ Fire	___	___
___ Theft	___	___
___ Robbery	___	___
___ Vandalism	___	___
___ Accident liability	___	___

Discuss the types of coverage you will need and make a careful comparison of the rates and coverage with several insurance agents before making a final decision.

Business Premises and Location

	YES	NO
1. Have you found a suitable building in a location convenient for your customers?	___	___
2. Can the building be modified for your needs at a reasonable cost?	___	___
3. Have you considered renting or leasing with an option to buy?	___	___
4. Will you have a lawyer check the zoning regulations and lease?	___	___

Merchandise

	YES	NO
1. Have you decided what items you will sell or produce or what service(s) you will provide?	___	___
2. Have you made a merchandise plan based upon estimated sales to determine the amount of inventory you will need to control purchases?	___	___
3. Have you found reliable suppliers who will assist you in the start-up?	___	___
4. Have you compared the prices, quality, and credit terms of suppliers?	___	___

Business Records

	YES	NO
1. Are you prepared to maintain complete records of sales income and expenses accounts payable and receivables?	___	___
2. Have you determined how to handle payroll records, tax reports, and payments?	___	___
3. Do you know what financial reports should be prepared and how to prepare them?	___	___

FINANCES

A large number of small businesses fail each year. There are a number of reasons for these failures but one of the main reasons is insufficient funds. Too many entrepreneurs try to start and operate a business without sufficient capital (money). To avoid this dilemma you can review your situation by analyzing these three questions:

1. How much money do you have?
2. How much money will you need to start your business?
3. How much money will you need to stay in business?

Use Chart 1 to answer the first question: Chart 2 will help you answer the second question: How much money will you need to start your business? The chart is for a retail business; items will vary for service construction and manufacturing firms. The answer to the third question (How much money will you need to stay in business?) must be divided into two parts: immediate costs and future costs. From the moment the door to your new business opens a certain amount of income will undoubtedly come in. However this income should not be projected in your operating expenses. You will need enough money available to cover costs for at least the first three months of operation. Chart 3 will help you project your operating expenses on a monthly basis. Now multiply the total of Chart 3 by three. This is the amount of cash you will need to cover operating expenses for three months. Deposit this amount in a savings account before opening your business. Use it only for those purposes listed in the above chart because this money will ensure that you will be able to continue in business during the crucial early stages. By adding the total start-up costs (Chart 2) to the total expenses for three months (three times the total cost on Chart 3) you can learn what the estimated costs will be to start and operate your business for three months. By subtracting the totals of Charts 2 and 3 from the cash available (Chart 1) you can determine the amount of additional financing you may need if any. Now you will need to esti-mate your operating expenses for the first year after start-up. Use the Income Projection Statement (Appendix A) for this estimate. The first step in determining your annual expenses is to estimate your sales volume month by month. Be sure to consider seasonal trends that may affect your business. Information on seasonal sales patterns and typical operating ratios can be secured from your trade associations.

(NOTE: The relationships among amounts of capital that you invest levels of sales each of the cost categories the number of times that you will sell your inventory (turnover) and many other items form financial ratios. These ratios provide you with extremely valuable checkpoints before it's too late to make adjustments. In the reference section of your local library are publications such as *The Almanac of Business and Industrial Financial Ratios* to compare your performance with that of other similar businesses. For thorough explanations of these ratios and how to use them follow up on the sources of help and information mentioned at the end of this publication.) Next determine the cost of sales. The cost of sales is expressed in dollars. Fill out each month's column in dollars, total them in the annual total column and then divide each item into the total net sales to produce the annual percentages. Examples of operating ratios include cost of sales to sales and rent to sales.

AFTER START-UP

The primary source of revenue in your business will be from sales but your sales will vary from month to month because of seasonal patterns and other factors. It is important to determine if your monthly sales will produce enough income to pay each month's bills. An estimated cash flow projection (Chart 4) will show if the monthly cash balance is going to be subject to such factors as Failure to recognize seasonal trends; Excessive cash taken from the business for living expenses; Too rapid expansion; and Slow collection of accounts if credit is extended to customers.

Use Chart 4 to build a worksheet to help you with this problem. In this example all sales are made for cash.

CHART 1 — PERSONAL FINANCIAL STATEMENT

_____ , 19 _____

ASSETS		LIABILITIES	
Cash on hand	____	Accounts payable	____
Savings account	____	Notes payable	____
Stocks, bonds, securities	____	Contracts payable	____
Accounts/notes receivable	____	Taxes	
Real estate	____	Real estate loans	____
Life insurance (cash value)	____	Other liabilities	____
Automobile/other vehicles	____		
Other liquid assets	____		
TOTAL ASSETS	____	TOTAL LIABILITIES	____

NET WORTH
(ASSETS MINUS LIABILITIES) ____

CHART 2 — START-UP COST ESTIMATES

Decorating, remodeling	_____
Fixtures, equipment	_____
Installing fixtures, equipment	_____
Services, supplies	_____
Beginning inventory cost	_____
Legal, professional fees	_____
Licenses, permits	_____
Telephone utility deposits	_____
Insurance	_____
Signs	_____
Advertising for opening	_____
Unanticipated expenses	_____
TOTAL START-UP COSTS	_____

CHART 1 — EXPENSES FOR ONE MONTH

Your living costs	_____
Employee wages	_____
Rent	_____
Advertising	_____
Supplies	_____
Utilities	_____
Insurance	_____
Taxes	_____
Maintenance	_____
Delivery/transportation	_____
Miscellaneous	_____
TOTAL EXPENSES	_____

CHART 4 — ESTIMATED CASH FLOW FORECAST

	June	Feb.	Mar.	Apr.	May	Jun.	(etc.)
Cash in bank (1st of month)	____	____	____	____	____	____	____
Petty cash (1st of month)	____	____	____	____	____	____	____
Total cash (1st of month)	____	____	____	____	____	____	____
Anticipated cash sales	____	____	____	____	____	____	____
Total receipts	____	____	____	____	____	____	____
Total cash & receipts	____	____	____	____	____	____	____
Disbursements for month (rent, loan payments, utilities, wages, etc.)	____	____	____	____	____	____	____
Cash balance (end of month)	____	____	____	____	____	____	____

INSTRUCTIONS FOR INCOME PROJECTION STATEMENT

The income projection (profit and loss) statement is valuable as both a planning tool and a key management tool to help control business operations. It enables the owner-manager to develop a preview of the amount of income generated each month and for the business year, based on reasonable predictions of monthly levels of sales, costs and expenses.

As monthly projections are developed and entered into the income projection statement, they can serve as definite goals for controlling the business operation. As actual operating results become known each month, they should be recorded for comparison with the monthly projections. A completed income statement allows the owner-manager to compare actual figures with monthly projections and to take steps to correct any problems.

Industry Percentage

In the industry percentage column, enter the percentages of total sales (revenues) that are standard for your industry, which are derived by dividing

$$\frac{\text{cost/expense items}}{\text{total net sales}} \times 100\%$$

These percentages can be obtained from various sources, such as trade associations, accountants or banks. The reference librarian in your nearest public library can refer you to documents that contain the percentage figures, for example, Robert Morris Associates' Annual Statement Studies (One Liberty Place, Philadelphia, PA 19103).

Industry figures serve as a useful benchmark against which to compare cost and expense estimates that you develop for your firm. Compare the figures in the industry percentage column to those in the annual percentage column.

Total Net Sales (Revenues)

Determine the total number of units of products or services you realistically expect to sell each month in each department at the prices you expect to get. Use this step to create the projection to review your pricing practices.

- What returns, allowances and markdowns can be expected?
- Exclude any revenue that is not strictly related to the business.

Cost of Sales

The key to calculating your cost of sales is that you do not overlook any costs that you have incurred. Calculate cost of sales for all products and services used to determine total net sales. Where inventory is involved, do not overlook transportation costs. Also include any direct labor.

Gross Profit

Subtract the total cost of sales from the total net sales to obtain gross profit.

Gross Profit Margin

The gross profit margin is expressed as a percentage of total sales (revenues). It is calculated by dividing

$$\frac{\text{gross profits}}{\text{total net sales}}$$

Controllable Expenses

- *Salary expenses*—Base pay plus overtime.
- *Payroll expenses*—Include paid vacations, sick leave, health insurance, unemployment insurance and social security taxes.
- *Outside services*—Include costs of subcontracts, overflow work and special one-time services.

- *Supplies*—Service and items purchased for use in the business.
- *Repairs and maintenance*—Regular maintenance and repair, including periodic large expenditures such as painting.
- *Advertising*—Include desired sales volume and classified directory advertising expenses.
- *Car, delivery and travel*—Include charges if personal car is used in business, including parking, tolls, buying trips, etc.
- *Accounting and legal*—Outside professional services.

Fixed Expenses

- *Rent*—List only real estate used in the business.
- *Depreciation*—Amortization of capital assets.
- *Utilities*—Water, heat, light, etc.
- *Insurance*—Fire or liability on property or products. Include workers' compensation.
- *Loan repayments*—Interest on outstanding loans.
- *Miscellaneous*—Unspecified; small expenditures without separate accounts.

Net Profit (loss) (before taxes)	• Subtract total expenses from gross profit.
Taxes	• Include inventory and sales taxes, excise tax, real estate tax, etc.
Net Profit (loss) (after taxes)	• Subtract taxes from net profit (before taxes).

Annual Total	• For each of the sales and expense items in your income projection statement, add all the monthly figures across the table and put the result in the annual total column.
Annual Percentage	• Calculate the annual percentage by dividing $$\frac{\text{annual total}}{\text{total net sales}} \times 100\%$$
	• Compare this figure to the industry percentage in the first column.

CONCLUSION

Beyond a doubt preparing an adequate business plan is the most important step in starting a new business. A comprehensive business plan will be your guide to managing a successful business. The business plan is paramount to your success. It must contain all the pertinent information about your business; it must be well written factual and organized in a logical sequence. Moreover it should not contain any statements that cannot be supported. If you have carefully answered all the questions on this checklist and completed all the worksheets you have seriously thought about your goal. But . . . there may be some things you may feel you need to know more about. Owning and running a business is a continuous learning process. Research your idea and do as much as you can yourself but don't hesitate to seek help from people who can tell you what you need to know.

Income Projection Statement

	Industry %	J	F	M	A	M	J	J	A	S	O	N	D	Annual total	Annual %
Total net sales (revenues)															
Cost of sales															
Gross profit															
Gross profit margin															
Controllable expenses															
Salaries/wages															
Payroll expenses															
Legal/accounting															
Advertising															
Automobile															
Office supplies															
Dues/subscriptions															
Utilities															
Miscellaneous															
Total controllable expenses															
Fixed expenses															
Rent															
Depreciation															
Utilities															
Insurance															
Licenses/permits															
Loan payments															
Miscellaneous															
Total fixed expenses															
Total expenses															
Net profit (loss) before taxes															
Taxes															
Net profit (loss) after taxes															

APPENDIX 5: HOW TO GET STARTED WITH A SMALL BUSINESS COMPUTER

Published by the U.S. Small Business Administration. Used by kind permission.

INTRODUCTION

The purpose of this publication is to help you forecast your computer needs, evaluate the alternatives, and select the right computer system for your business.

Micro- or personal computers (PCs) make it economically possible for small businesses to acquire electronic data processing equipment. With its business applications, a microcomputer system provides professional management planning and control capabilities that can help you reach your goals for growth and profit. To take advantage of this opportunity, you must use your best analysis and judgment when choosing a computer for your small business.

WHAT CAN COMPUTERIZATION DO FOR YOU?

To answer this question, you must have a clear understanding of your firm's long- and short-range goals, the advantages and disadvantages of all of the alternatives to a computer and, specifically, what you want to accomplish with a computer.

Compare the best manual (noncomputerized) system you can develop with the computer system you hope to get. It may be possible to improve your existing manual system enough to accomplish your goals. In any event, one cannot automate a business without first creating and improving manual systems.

Business Applications

A computer's multiple capabilities can solve many business problems. Some of the most common applications are keeping transaction records (such as a cash receipts journal, receivables ledger, and general journal) and preparing statements and reports (such as a balance sheet, income statement or inventory status report). Other equally important tasks include maintaining customer and lead lists, creating brochures and paying your staff.

A business that handles large volumes of detailed or repetitive information in short periods of time will benefit from computerization. A complete computer system can:

1. Organize and store many similarly structured pieces of information (i.e., addresses including name, street, city, state and zip code).

2. Retrieve a single piece of information from many stored records (i.e., the address of John Smith).

3. Perform complicated mathematical computations quickly and accurately (i.e., the terms of a loan amortized over many years).

4. Print information quickly and accurately (i.e., a sales report).

5. Perform the same activity almost indefinitely, in precisely the same way each time (i.e., print a hundred copies of the same form letter).

6. Facilitate communications among individuals, departments and branches (i.e., quickly transmit messages and/or documents that require review or editing).

7. Link the office to many sources of data available through larger networks.

Improving Business Operations

Consider the following manual operations that can be streamlined by computerization.

Accounts Receivable—Even if properly organized and maintained, a large volume of active accounts can require many hours of posting sales and receipts and, especially, of preparing statements. Unfortunately, as the volume of information to be handled increases, the number of errors often also increases. Don't forget, too, that if your customer isn't billed on time, you'll wait longer to be paid.

Advertising—Using only manual systems, it is costly and complicated to have special sales programs directed toward particular customers. Manually prepared mass mailings are time consuming and expensive.

Inventory—A large number of items or high-volume turnover can cause major errors in tracking inventory. Errors in inventory control can result in lost sales and in the maintenance of unnecessarily high quantities of slow-moving products.

Payroll—Calculating and writing checks are tedious operations in payroll administration. It can also be difficult to effectively implement an employee incentive plan using manual procedures.

Planning—Manual systems or procedures make planning for the future time consuming and difficult. What if situations such as If sales increase, to what extent will expenses increase?are not easy to simulate with a manual system.

Computer Business Applications

Computers also can perform more complicated operations, such as the following:

Financial modeling programs prepare and analyze financial statements.

Spreadsheet and accounting programs compile statistics, plot trends and markets and do market analysis, modeling, graphs and forms. They can combine all these functions and can interchange and evaluate data from four programs simultaneously.

Word processing programs produce typewritten documents and provide text editing functions. Many offer options such as a thesaurus, a speller, and punctuation and style checkers.

Desktop publishing programs enable you to create good quality print materials on your computer.

Critical path analysis programs divide large projects into smaller, more easily managed segments or steps. This helps to target goals and set dates for completion.

Legal programs track cases and tap information from data bases.

Payroll system programs keep all payroll records; calculate pay, benefits and taxes; and prepare paychecks.

File management programs enable you to create and design forms, then store and retrieve the forms and the information on them.

The business applications for PCs are available in packaged software programs that enable you to interact with the computer through entering, manipulating and processing complex evaluations and computations of voluminous quantities of data.

Realistic Expectations

After analyzing your application needs, consider (1) the investment decision (pay-back period, depreciation, tax impact, etc.) and (2) the potential increase in your management capability.

There are, however, some things you should not expect your computer to do.

Don't expect a computer to clean up a mess in the office. The mess must be organized before you can attempt to computerize, or you will wind up with a computerized mess.

Don't install a computer because you don't have the right people to do the jobs in your organization. Initially, at least, the computer will make more, not fewer, demands on your organization.

Don't install a computer with the idea that any information you want will be instantly available. Computers require structured, formal processing that may not produce some information as fast as an informal system could.

Don't expect the installation of a computer to help define the jobs that must be done. The computer is a tool to get those jobs done, but the jobs must first be well-defined.

Don't expect computer installation to occur like magic. Computer selection and installation will be successful only through methodical work.

Don't expect any computer system to exactly fit your present methods of completing jobs. If you are not willing to listen to new ideas for solving problems, you will not be able to install a computer successfully or at a reasonable cost.

Don't acquire a computer to generate information you will not use. Growing companies may benefit from structured management information systems, but many owner-managers of small companies already have their fingers on the pulse of their businesses and do not need a formal, electronic system.

SELECTING A SUITABLE COMPUTER SYSTEM

Two options for your own in-house computer system are the minicomputer and the microcomputer.

A minicomputer is a general purpose computer that links a number of dumb terminals, i.e., display units that can only function if connected to the minicomputer. It can be programmed to do a variety of tasks and is generally designed so data can be inputted directly into the system. For example, data on a sales order are put into the computer at the same time the order is written. A minicomputer can be operated by users who don't have special computer knowledge. Minicomputers cost ten or more times as much as micro (or personal) computers; sophisticated systems may cost well over a hundred times more. The computer power/cost ratio is relative, however, and may be readily justified by the application required. Don't forget to include monthly costs for system administration and maintenance of both hardware and software. Minicomputer costs are decreasing rapidly, so inquire for the latest estimates.

The microcomputer or personal computer is a household word, if not quite yet a universal household item. It can operate independently of a network, is relatively inexpensive, and is compact enough to sit on a desk. These computers run programs that do an astonishing variety of tasks and can be operated without special computer knowledge. Microcomputers can satisfy the needs of many small business owners. They usually handle one task at a time, although some may have modest capabilities for multitasking and multiuser applications (more than one program and terminal at one time). Personal computers are easily affordable by virtually any business, although prices may vary widely depending upon the manufacturer. There are supermicros equipped with multitasking operating systems and networking capabilities. These may cost five times as much as a personal computer, or more, but they can be used by multidepartmented companies, sharing and using the same data on a daily basis.

CHOOSING THE RIGHT COMPUTER

To computerize your business you will have to choose the right programs, select the right equipment and implement the various applications. This involves training personnel, establishing and maintaining security procedures, and maintaining equipment, supplies and day-to-day operations. If you follow a well-laid plan and make well-informed choices, your computer system should provide the information and control intended.

Computer Components

Component and Function

Hardware

Central processing unit (CPU) — The CPU performs logic calculations, manages the flow of data within the computer and executes the program instructions. CPUs are either XT (8088), AT (80286) or 80386. The AT is a good choice for businesses looking to link their PCs in a LAN (local area network).

Main memory — Memory is measured in the K you'll often hear mentioned for example, 32K (or 32 1,024 bits). It is simply a storage area readily accessible to the CPU.

Mass storage — This storage is simply permanent. There are a number of mass storage devices available, such as disk, diskette and magnetic tape. Input device(s), These units are used to enter data into the system for processing. One type of input device is a keyboard.

Scanners are a new way to input data.

Output device(s) — These display the data. The most common output device is a printer.

Software

Operating system software — This is software that tells the hardware how to run. MS-DOS is a common operating system for PCs.

Applications programs — These are programs written to perform a particular function such as word processing accounts receiv-able payroll or inventory control applications.

Compilers and interpreters — This type of special software translates programs into machine language that the CPU can execute. As a user of PCs you won't be required to work much with this type of software.

CHOOSING THE RIGHT PROGRAMS (SOFTWARE)

A program, usually referred to as software, is a set of instructions that tells the computer to do a particular task. Programs are written in a computer language (such as FORTRAN, COBOL, BASIC). The software determines what information is to be entered into the computer and what output or report is to be returned by the computer after it has performed as instructed by the program. The act of entering information into a computer is called inputting the data.

Generally, there are three types of software:

1. Compilers and interpreters   This is special software that translates programs written in programming language that people can use (such as FORTRAN, COBOL, BASIC) into machine language that the CPU can execute.

2. Operating system software   These are the programs that control all the separate components of the computer, such as the printer and disk drives, and how they work together. System software generally comes with the computer and must be present (or loaded into memory) before the application software can work.

3. Application software   This is software composed of programs that make the computer perform particular functions, such as payroll check writing, accounts receivable posting or inventory reporting. Application software programs, particularly the more specialized ones, are normally purchased separately from

the computer hardware. Before beginning your search for the application software that is right for you, identify what the software must accomplish. Your time will be well spent if you research and write down your requirements before visiting your software vendor.

Determine Your Requirements

To determine your requirements, prepare a list of all functions in your business in which speed and accuracy are needed for handling volumes of information. These are called applications. For each of these applications make a list of all reports that are currently (or will need to be) produced. You should also include any preprinted forms such as checks, billing statements or vouchers. If such forms don't exist, develop a good idea of what you want-a hand-drawn version will help. For each report list the frequency with which it is to be generated, who will generate it and the number of copies needed.

In addition to printed matter, make a list of information you want displayed on the computer video screen (CRT). Again, design a hand-drawn version. List the circumstances under which you want this information displayed.

For each application make a list of all materials used as input into your manual system. These may include items such as time cards, work orders, receipts, etc. Describe the time period in which these items are created, who creates them and how they get into the system. Also, describe the maximum and average expected number of these items generated in the appropriate time period.

As with the reports, include copies of the input items or drawn drafts.

For all files you are keeping manually or expect to computerize (such as customer files or employee files), list the maximum and average expected number of entries in a specific time period, such as 10 employees per year, 680 cus-

tomers per year. Normally, a file, manual or otherwise, is cleaned out after a specified time and the inactive entries are removed.

Identify how you retrieve a particular entry. Do you use account numbers or are they organized alphabetically by name? What other methods would you like to use to retrieve a particular entry? Zip code? Product purchased?

Note which of your requirements are a must and those on which you can compromise. The more detailed you are, the better your chance of finding programs compatible with your business. It is also true that the more detailed you are, the more time it will take to research and evaluate each alternative application software package.

Evaluate Your Choices

If, after compiling all of your information, you find your needs are fairly complex, you may wish to engage the services of a small business consultant to help evaluate your software requirements. Or you can submit your requirements to software retailers, custom software vendors or mail order software houses. They will propose software packages that meet as many of your requirements as possible.

At this point you should review and compare the software packages and verify the extent to which each meets your needs. Ask yourself these questions: Does it cover all of my musts? How many of my other requirements does it fulfill? Does it provide additional features I had not thought of earlier but now believe to be important?
After you have identified one or more software packages fitting your needs, examine other general features of the software.

- Does it come with effective documentation?

- Do you understand it?

- Is the operating manual written for the novice?

- Is the information organized so you can use it effectively after you gain experience?

- How easy is the software to use? Does the information displayed on the computer screen make sense?

- Is there a help facility?

- How flexible is the software package?

- Can you change data that have already been processed?

- Can you change the program instructions, such as payroll withholding rates, or will you have to pay the vendor to change these for you?

- If you must pay a vendor, what will it cost?

- Will you be required to change any of your business practices? If so, are these changes you should make anyway?

- Will the software provide the accounting and management information you need?

- How well is the software documented? You should be able to understand the general flow of information, i.e., which program does what and when.

- Does the software have security features, such as passwords or user identification codes? Can it prevent unauthorized access to private information?

- Is it easy to increase the size of files?

- Will the software vendor support the software? Does the vendor have a good track record? Will the vendor make changes and, if so, how much will the changes cost?

- How long has the vendor been in business? What are the vendor's prospects for staying in business?

Ready-Made Software

If you find a ready-made software package that fits your business's needs and price range, take it. You may still have to do a lot of work adapting your procedure, but generally you will be better off than if you design your own software system. Although different brands of software and hardware can be adapted to work together compati-

bly, such standardization is not yet prevalent. For this reason, it is important that you first find the right software and then select the hardware that can handle it.

Preparing a Request for Proposal

If you are unable to find a software package that fits your needs, send a request for proposal (RFP) to selected hardware vendors and turnkey systems houses. (The latter are companies that put together complete, ready-to-use hardware and software systems.) The form of your RFP depends on the kind of proposals you are soliciting: a turnkey system with customized software, a turnkey system with packaged software, or hardware and/or software in separate packages. Because most first time users get turnkey systems, the following guidelines apply to RFPs for this method:

1. Give a brief description of your company.

2. Describe the business operation to be computerized.

3. Submit the materials you designed and accumulated earlier.

4. Describe the criteria that will be used to evaluate proposals and request a response to each criterion (i.e., maintenance, technical support, training, etc.).

5. Specify which of your requirements must be met exactly and which must be met only in substance. This is important when dealing with software packages.

6. Request a detailed price quotation that includes all charges to meet your needs, including one-time charges, such as for equipment, training, applications and systems software, and ongoing charges, such as maintenance and technical support. Request financing alternatives such as lease-purchase and direct or third-party lease.

CHOOSING THE RIGHT EQUIPMENT HARDWARE

Choosing the software is by far the most difficult part of deciding on the computer system that is right for you. Because most software is written for one or more specific computers, you will probably have narrowed your equipment choices down considerably by the time you have selected your software.

Review the choices and ask the same questions about potential computer hardware vendors that you asked when evaluating software vendors. Don't forget to check the cost of shipping, installation and equipment maintenance.

The computer and associated equipment known as hardware consist of a number of components that do different jobs. They include

Processor—The thinking part of the computer is known as the processor or central processing unit (CPU) and is designed to execute software instructions, perform calculations, control the flow of data to and from the memory and control other hardware components. The faster the CPU, the quicker you can work with your data.

Computer memory—Computer memory usually is measured in bytes (which is a grouping of binary digits or bits). Roughly speaking, each byte of memory holds one character of data, either a letter or a number. A 2K (2,048 bytes) memory in practical terms holds about one double-spaced, typed page. There are two kinds of memory: ROM (read-only memory) and RAM (random access memory). We are only concerned with RAM.

ROM—Read-only memory is a program stored in the computer memory that cannot be changed by the user or an externally entered program.

RAM—Random access memory is located in the CPU and is normally measured in Ks or 1024s (64K = approximately 65,536 characters or

about 32 pages of information). RAM is used to store all the information necessary for the CPU to do its job: the program running the portion of data that is currently being processed and some portion of the system software. Information stored in RAM lasts only as long as the power is on. Once the power is turned off, all RAM information is erased. Store your RAM-based data on more permanent storage media, such as diskettes.

DOS—The disk operating system (DOS) is software that controls the interactions among the CPU, disk drive, keyboard, video monitor and printer. ROM, RAM, DOS and the applications program may need about 55K, depending upon your version of DOS.

Storage—Just as a company retains its relatively permanent records in a file cabinet, a computer most commonly retains relatively permanent information on disks. These resemble small phonograph records and may be floppy or hard. A floppy disk is made of soft, thin plastic encased in a stiff paper envelope and comes in 3-, 5-, and 8-inch diameters. Hard disks are encased in metal and have faster access and more storage capacity than floppy disks. Hard disks are also much more expensive than floppies, but their greater storage capacity and speed usually make up for the difference in cost. Information on a disk is recorded, retrieved and erased through a disk drive, which is controlled by the system and application software.

Terminal—In order for a computer to perform useful work, you must be able to communicate with it. Most often this two-way communication is carried out through a keyboard, used to enter data into the computer, and a display monitor. The monitor (screen) should be able to display 24 lines of 80 characters at one time. Some monitors can handle color and graphics. Color graphics quality is determined by pixels or picture elements. If a display is 280 by 192 pixels, the screen is divided into 280 rows and 192 columns. The larger the number of pixels, the finer or more precise the picture display will be. EGA or

VGA monitors are your best choice for color monitors.

Printer—The main output of a computer system is usually printed material: reports, checks, invoices, etc. As with all other hardware choices you make, choose a printer that can accomplish your specific jobs. The print quality of various printers ranges from dot matrix to letter quality. Laser printers have surged in use because of their high quality print and speed and because of lowering prices and increasing interest in desktop publishing.

Drives—Disk drives are single- or double-sided. Diskettes, either 3 inch or 5 inch, are loaded into these drives. You store and retrieve data from diskettes. You may find it helpful to configure your PC with both size diskette drives. Diskettes are also high and low density, referring to the quantity of data that can be stored on them. A high-density diskette, although it costs more, will store more data than a low-density diskette.

Warmware—Warmware are the critical services and support you will require after your purchase. If you choose wisely, the combined software and hardware packages can become an invaluable tool to enable you to better manage your business. However, without qualified people to train your staff, install the system and be available to answer questions, your system may never get off the ground. Once your computer system is up and running, you will need support to help you solve any problems that may arise.

Evaluating the Computer System

The most important sources of feedback in judging a computer system are companies using the computer system you think you will buy. Try to find companies with configurations and applications as close to yours as possible and visit them, without the computer sales representative.

Use the following criteria, listed in order of importance, to evaluate a computer system.

1. *Software developer's past performance record*— Software developer should have prior experience with similar applications for the same equipment configuration as the one you are considering.

2. *Commitment of hardware vendor*—Where will your commission sales representative be after the contract is signed? How many systems engineers does the vendor have in your area?

3. *Hardware capacity*—Does the hardware have adequate processing capability to meet your requirements within acceptable time frames?

4. *Quality of systems software*—The quality of the system software (operating systems and utilities) dramatically affects how difficult the system is to program and use.

5. *Systems documentation*—What kind of systems documentation does the vendor provide and how is it updated? Can it be understood at some basic level by the user? Is it designed so other experts can understand how things were done and change them when necessary?

6. *Service and maintenance support*—When your system breaks down, how long will it take to get it fixed? Who will do it? Will it be subcontracted? Are there any provisions for backup during downtime?

7. *Expandability and compatibilities*—What are the technical limits of your system and how close to those limits is your current configuration? Is there software compatibility among the vendor's product lines?

8. *Security*—What security features will your system have to prevent unauthorized use of the system or unauthorized program modifications?

9. *Financial stability of vendors*—Satisfy yourself about the financial stability of your vendor.

10. *Environmental Requirements*—Mini and microcomputers do not usually require special environments such as raised floors, special wiring or special air-conditioning. Some may, however, and it pays to find out in advance. Local area networks (LANs) require cabling.

11. *Price*—With computers, as with anything else, you generally get what you pay for. Low price alone should not be a prime evaluation criterion.

CONTRACTING FOR A TURNKEY SYSTEM

If you decide to purchase a complete hardware and software system (turnkey system) rather than buying the software and hardware separately, you should have a contract or agreement. Examine the standard contract supplied by the vendor. Be aware it may not protect your interests. If you have any questions, have your lawyer review the contract and suggest changes to help you implement the system.

An important part of the contract is the payment schedule. Do you pay before or after installation? Will you pay for the installation periodically on a draw schedule? The more money held back until the installation is complete, the more power you will have to ensure that the vendor satisfactorily completes all that has been promised and contracted.

The contract should include detailed references to the following:

Description of equipment and software.

Installation responsibilities.

Provisions for additional equipment.

Performance guarantees.

Responsibility for training.

Software rights.

Provisions for default, bankruptcy of vendor or termination of contract.

Software documentation.

Systems documentation.

Responsibility for hardware freight charges and sales tax.

Acceptance testing.

Conversion responsibilities (from manual system to computer).

Upgrading privileges and trade-in rights.

Restart (what is required to restart system from failure).

If the contract is for software developed especially for you, the contract should specifically refer to your RFP and the vendor's responding proposal. A good contract will help you prepare for the system's installation and ensure a more satisfactory business transaction.

Points to consider when selecting your computer system include

- *Reliability*—How qualified are the manufacturer and the vendor? What is their reputation? What is the incidence of repair on the system equipment?

- *Resources*—How long have the manufacturer and vendor been in business? How strong are their financial positions and credit ratings?

- *Services*—Are ongoing consulting, training, supply and repair available?

- *Rates*—Are charges competitive? What terms are offered?

- *Backup*—What happens if your system fails?

IMPLEMENTATION

Immediate Concerns—As was suggested before, successful computer applications for your business depend heavily on the implementation process. Problems are inevitable but proper planning can help avoid some of them and mitigate the effects of others.

Employee Involvement—The success of a new computer system will depend on the cooperation of your employees; therefore, it is important to involve them as early as possible in the implementation. Explain to each affected employee how his or her position will change. To those unaffected, explain why their jobs will remain unchanged.

Schedule for implementation—Set target dates for key phases of the implementation, especially the last date for format changes.

Installation site—Prepare the installation site. Check the hardware manual to be sure the location for your new computer meets the system's requirements for temperature, humidity and electrical power.

Converting applications—Prepare a prioritized list of applications to be converted from manual to computer systems. It is important to convert them one at a time, not all at once. Prepare a list of all business procedures that will be changed so the computer system will fit into the regular work flow. Develop new manual procedures to interface with the computer system.

Training—Train, or have the vendors train, everyone who will be using the system.

When these steps are complete, the computer system can be installed. Each application on the conversion list should be entered (files set up, historical data entered and the system prepared for new transactions) and run parallel with the preexisting, corresponding manual system for a number of processing periods. This means that two complete systems will be running, placing a great deal of pressure on your employees and on

you. However, until you have verified that the new system works, it will be worth the effort.

Be sure to insist on progress reports from everyone involved in the changeover.

Long-Term Concerns

At the same time you are converting each application, you must begin dealing with the long term issues that will keep your computer operation successful.

System security—If you will have confidential information in your system, you will want safeguards to keep unauthorized users from stealing, modifying or destroying the data. You can simply lock up the equipment, or you can install user identification and password software. You can also

☐ Control access to your computer, disks and reports. Label all disks to identify their contents and verify correct labeling.

☐ Initiate original accounting transactions, adjustments or corrections yourself.

☐ Rotate computer employees or schedule their vacations to expose possible unauthorized practices. Require dual signature authorizations to control software modifications.

Data Safety—Data, confidential or otherwise, can be destroyed by unexpected disasters (fire, water, power fluctuations, magnetic fields, etc.) or through employee tampering, resulting in high replacement costs. The best and cheapest insurance against lost data is to back-up information on each diskette regularly. Copies should be kept in a safe place away from the business site. Also, it is useful to

☐ Have and test a disaster recovery plan.

☐ Identify all data, programs and documents needed for essential tasks during recovery from a disaster.

- *Employee cross-training* Just as with a manual system, it is important to have more than one employee who knows how to operate the system. Once your business relies on the computer system, the absence (sickness, termination, etc.) of a computer operator can be devastating unless another person is prepared to fill in.

- *Management controls* Although computer systems allow small businesses to process more data more accurately than ever before, there is a chance that the same system can cause greater problems if left unsupervised. All systems, manual or otherwise, must be continually monitored to ensure the quality of the input and output data.

SUMMARY

If all this seems like a lot of work, it is. The computer, like any tool, requires learned skills in order to fulfill its purpose. If you believe that you and your business need a computer, plan to spend the time and the money it takes to make its installation and operation of the system successful.

With no prior knowledge of computers, you can buy a personal computer with applications for your business. With some guidance, study and experience, you can develop computer-based management planning and control expertise. By taking advantage of the speed and complex capabilities of a computer, you can tap the potential for growth and profit in yourself and your business.

APPENDIX 6: SAMPLINGS FROM THE NEBS SYSTEMS CATALOG

This appendix is reproduced from *NEBS Business & Checks Supplies* (Groton, MA: NEBS, Inc., 1993), with the kind permission of NEBS, Inc. Information on *One-Write Plus*® accounting software was provided by NEBS Software, Inc., Nashua, NH. For further information on these systems and software, call 800-882-5254 or fax 800-234-4324.

ACCOUNTS PAYABLE

Write checks as always—One-Write Systems take care of your recordkeeping. Just write a check and your One-Write System records the information directly onto your ledgers and/or journals.

- Cuts bookkeeping time by 60 to 75 percent.
- Eliminates copying errors and duplication of effort.
- Standardizes recordkeeping procedures—automatically.
- Keeps your accounting records up-to-date . . . to the second.
- Offers "fail-safe" protection against missing checks.

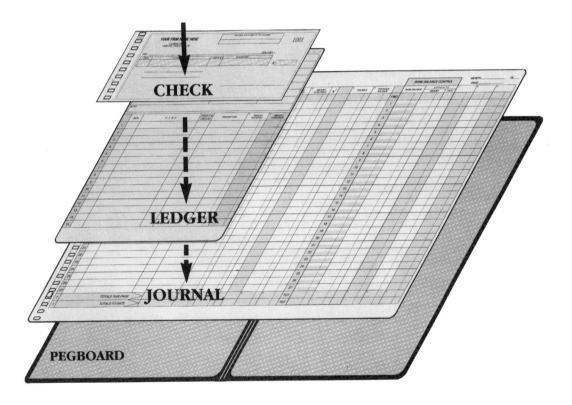

CASH DISBURSEMENTS SYSTEM

Paying bills is easier than ever before with this Cash Disbursement System.

- Pay bills in one simple step.
- Eliminate transcription errors—carbonless strip copies data from your check right to the register.
- Balance your checkbook in one quick step.
- Make tax time less of a hassle—column headings help you classify expenses.
- Get up-to-the-minute account information at a glance.

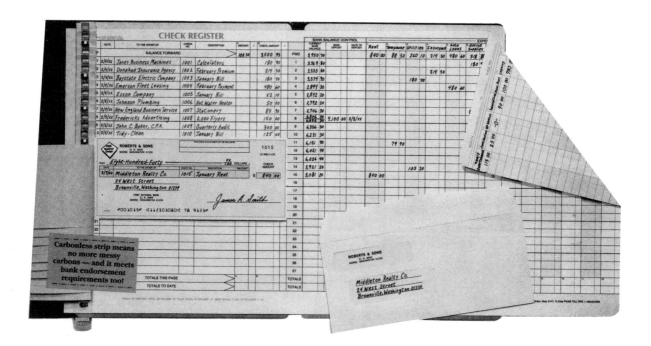

PAYROLL DISBURSEMENT SYSTEM

Make quick work of bills and payroll with a Payroll/Disbursement System.

- Complete bill paying and payroll in just one simple step.
- Cut out repetitive entries—plus balance you records with the easy proof formulas on the journal.
- Eliminate transcription errors—carbonless strip updates employee earnings record and the journal at the same time.
- Make tax reporting easy with quarterly and year-to-date totals.

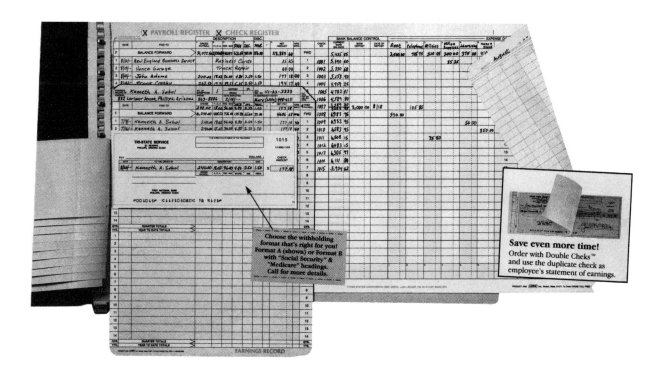

ACCOUNTING SOFTWARE

NEBS Software, Inc.'s *One-Write Plus*® accounting and payroll software is easy to understand and use. This program will automatically set up a Chart of Accounts or let you design your own. It customizes your ledgers and journals and lets you tailor the program to track inventory, job costs, property management, commissions and more. *One-Write Plus* also lets you keep detailed records and quickly generates invoices and statements.

One-Write Plus does all this:

- Checkwriting
- Billing/Invoicing
- Automatic Bank Reconciliation
- General Ledger
- Accounts Receivable
- Accounts Payable
- Payroll

- Inventory Tracking
- Job Cost Tracking
- Sales Analysis
- Financial Reports
- Budget vs. Actual
- Budgeting

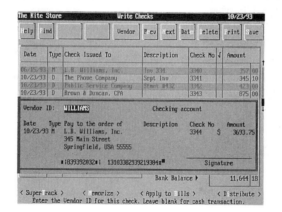 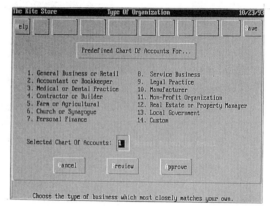

Pop-up cards, menus and screens that look familiar help guide you through the program effortlessly.

DO YOUR BANKING LIGHTNING FAST

One-Write Plus® keeps track of all the checks and bank deposits you have entered so you can easily reconcile your accounts. Track checking, savings, payroll accounts and more. Instantly updates balances.

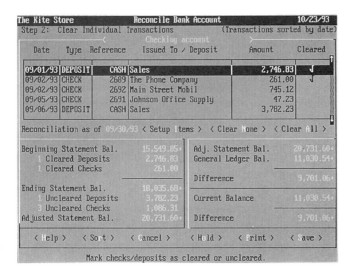

WRITE CHECKS AND PAY BILLS IN RECORD TIME

Easily enter all your bills into *One-Write Plus*. Write checks and pay bills unbelievably fast. All the things you do often are on one menu.

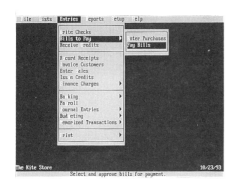

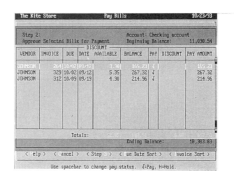

Accounting *Features*   Checkwriting
- Handles up to 15 individual checking accounts
- Calculates new balance after each check
- Easily enter manual checks

Billing/Invoicing
- Automatically transfers information from customer card to invoice.
- Prints three types of invoice formats: service, professional, inventory

General Ledger
- Detail General Ledger
- Offers customizable Chart of Accounts
- Handles up to 99 companies and departments
- Handles up to 15 bank and credit card accounts
- Handles prior-period adjustments
- Recurring Journal entries
- Add Customer, Vendor and General Ledger accounts on the fly
- Variable monthly budgeting

Accounts Receivable
- Accommodates up to 5000 customers
- Stores detail customer history
- Tracks customer receipts and deposits
- Pop-up customer list
- Prints detailed Sales/Customer Analysis Reports
- Prints customer Aging Report
- Calculates sales tax
- Automatically calculates discounts and finance charges
- Allows flexible aging and payment terms

Accounts Payable
- Accommodates up to 5,000 vendors
- Stores detail vendor history
- Includes pop-up vendor lists and cards
- Automatically selects invoices due for payment and allows you to choose the ones you want to pay, in whole or in part
- Prints Pre-Checkwriting Reports
- Tracks bills and generates automatic payments for approval
- Prints Vendor Aging Reports

Banking
- Bank deposit slip
- Balances checkbook
- Generates Bank Reconciliation Worksheet and Report

Inventory Tracking
- Tracks individual items by weight, size, color, etc.
- Tracks reorder plans
- Prints inventory list
- Handles up to 5,000 items

FINANCIAL REPORTS
- Balance Sheet
- Comparative Income Statement
- Trial Balance

- General Ledger Reports
- Open Invoice Report
- Disbursements and Receipts Analysis
- Inventory, Job Cost and other SuperTrack™ Reports

One-Write Plus® makes it easy to automate your company's payroll. No accounting experience is required. You can cut payroll preparation time and costs and eliminate errors. Just enter employee data once and this powerful, yet easy-to-use program automatically calculates all taxes and deduction. This program can also help you plan better by generating timely reports. This software gives you instant access to: *Payroll Analysis, Employee Histories, FUTA, SUTA and 941 Quarterly Tax Reports*, plus powerful SuperTrack™ to customize your financial data.

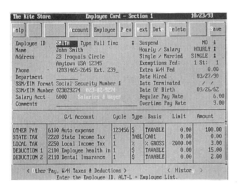
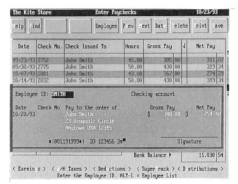

One-Write Plus Payroll *Features*
FLEXIBLE—PAYROLL MATCHES THE WAY YOU DO BUSINESS
- Flexible pay periods: daily, weekly, biweekly, monthly, semi-monthly, annually
- Salary, hourly, tipped and commissioned employees
- Full or part-time employees and subcontractors
- Tracks commissions, bonuses, vacation and sick time
- Automatically calculates FICA, federal, state and local taxes
- W-2s and 1099s
- FUTA and SUTA
- Monthly Tax Liability Reports
- 941 Quarterly Information

Other features of the *One-Write Plus®* system is the collections capabilities, which offer word processing, mail merging and business letters. The accounting features include: links to and compatibility with Lotus 1-2-3®, Quatro®, Quatro Pro®, Microsoft® Excel, to name a few; cash flow analysis; budgets and forecasts; charts and graphs; trends and financial ratios; loan analysis; and trial balance. The datasave features a prompt to remind you to backup last company changed and the ability to compress the material so it requires half as many disks as a regular backup. To find out more about these programs contact NEBS at 800-752-5266.

APPENDIX 7: CHOOSING A RETAIL LOCATION

Published by the U.S. Small Business Administration. Used by kind permission.

"Selecting A Business Location" is a merger of former SBA publications, "Locating or Relocating Your Business" and " Choosing a Retail Location." Segments of this publication were written by Fred I. Weber, Jr., Manager, Economic Development and Research, Portland General Electric Company; Jeffrey P. Davidson, Management Consultant, The EMAY Corporation; James R. Lowry, Head, Department of Marketing, College of Business, Ball State College; and J. Ross McKeever and Frank H. Spink, Jr., Urban Land Institute.

INTRODUCTION

The choice of a business location has a profound effect on the entire business life of an operation. A bad choice may all but guarantee failure, a good choice, success.

The first step in choosing a business location takes place in your head. Before you do anything else, define your type of business in the broadest terms and determine your long-term objectives. Write them down. This exercise will help you greatly in choosing a location later.

There are six basic criterion an owner or manager should consider when evaluating business locations: market, labor force, transportation, suppliers, suitable site, and to buy or lease. Each of these is described, in detail, in the following sections.

MARKET

Perhaps the most important consideration in any location is being able to satisfy the market. This means studying the market and determining who is interested in your product or service. The business must be located with convenient access to all of your customers, present and potential, and the customers must have convenient access to you.

If you are a small retailer, one item that needs to be given heavy consideration is the type of goods sold. Consumers tend to group products into three major categories: convenience, shopping, and specialty goods.

Convenience goods are characterized by a low unit price, frequent purchases, little selling effort, habit purchases and sold in numerous outlets. Examples include candy bars, cigarettes and milk.

For stores carrying convenience goods, the quantity of traffic is very important. The corner of the intersection which offers two distinct traffic streams and a large window display area is usually a better site than the middle of the block. Downtown convenience goods stores, such as low-priced, ready-to-wear stores and drugstores, have a limited ability to generate their own traffic.

If consumers must make a special trip to purchase such convenience staple goods as food and drug items, they want the store to be close to home. One study of foodstore purchases in the central city area revealed that nearly seventy percent of the people patronized stores within one to five blocks of their homes. Another study indicated that for suburban locations, the majority of customers lived within three miles of the stores, while the maximum trading area was five miles. For rural locations, the majority of consumers lived within a ten minute drive of the store, with the maximum trading area within a twenty minute drive.

Shopping goods normally have a high unit price, are purchased infrequently, require a more intensive selling effort, and are sold in selectively franchised outlets. Examples include men's suits, automobiles and furniture.

For stores carrying shopping goods, the quality of traffic is most important. While convenience goods are purchased by nearly everyone, certain kinds of shopping goods are purchased by only particular segments of shoppers. Moreover, it is sometimes the character of the retail establishment rather than its type of goods that governs the selection of a site.

In many cases, buyers of shopping goods like to compare the items in several stores by traveling only a minimum distance. As a result, stores offering complementary items tend to locate close to one another. An excellent site for a shopping goods store is next to a department store or between two large department stores where traffic flows. Another good site is one between a major parking area and a department store.

A small business specializing in shopping goods can have a wide trading area because it can generate its own traffic. A location with low traffic density but easy accessibility from a residential area is a satisfactory site. The consumer buys these goods infrequently and plans these purchases.

If you offer shopping goods, however, do not locate too far away from your potential customers. One study of a discount department store showed that nearly eighty percent of the shoppers lived within five miles of the store and another sixteen percent lived within a ten-mile radius. The relative distance your customers travel can be determined by a customer survey, automobile license check, sales slips, charge account records, store deliveries, and local newspaper circulation.

Specialty goods have a high unit price, are bought infrequently, require a special effort on the part of the customer to make the purchase, are seldom compared and generally sold in exclusively franchised outlets. Examples include specific brands jewelry, expensive perfume, and fine furs.

Specialty goods are often sought by consumers who are already "sold" on the product. Stores catering to this type of consumer may use isolated locations because they generate their own consumer traffic.

Stores carrying specialty goods that are complementary to certain other kinds of shopping goods may desire to locate close to the shopping goods stores. In general, the specialty goods retailer should locate in the type of neighborhood where the adjacent stores are compatible with his or her operation.

Each type of good—convenience, shopping and specialty—depends on traffic at the business location. To understand traffic and methods for measuring it, look at the section entitled, "How to Make a Traffic Count," located in Appendix A.

LABOR FORCE

Your next consideration is where your labor force will come from. Although labor is more mobile today than it was twenty years ago, some areas do not always have an adequate group to draw on. One rule of thumb is that the ideal site is in an area that can provide ten persons for consideration for each one hired. Furthermore, prevailing wage rates must be in line with your competitors'.

If you find the present supply of labor inadequate, consider whether or not the living conditions of the area are conducive to attracting new people. Certain climates have constant appeal. In other areas, the climate makes it difficult for employers to attract people whom their companies need. Unskilled people, in general, will move more readily than skilled people.

A number of firms considering relocating to another city have tested the labor market by advertising for prospective help in the local paper to determine the number of respondents. These people are interviewed and ideas usually develop from the interviews. Firms have found in many cases the labor supply was different than what the population and employment figures indicated.

During times of high inflation, the cost of living can vary greatly between areas. Obviously, this has a bearing on the wages you must pay. Look at the cost-of-living data as an indicator of your costs.

SUITABLE SITE

Is a suitable site available in the general area in which you want to locate? You have to consider whether or not the terrain is suitable and the foundations are adequate. Zoning is another aspect that cannot be overlooked. The city zoning commission has "mappings" of the areas you are considering. There are questions about zoning that need to be considered:

- Are there restrictions that will limit or hamper the business operations?

- Will construction or changes in traffic or new highways present barriers to the business?

- Will any competitive advantages at the potential location be erased by zoning changes that will be advantageous for competitors or that will even allow new competitors to enter the trade area?

In recent years, problems in securing proper zoning have been more intense. Delays can be long and, in more than a few instances, zone changes have been granted. As a result, most firms are no longer even considering a site that is not already been cleared for construction.

Many retailers would rather occupy an existing building, specifically, a shopping center.

Shopping centers are distinctly different than the other two major locations—downtown and local business strips. The shopping center building is pre-planned as a merchandising unit for interplay among tenants. Its site is deliberately selected by the developer for easy access to pull customers from a trade area. It has on-site parking as a common feature of the layout.

Besides the items that should be considered in selecting any location, there are a few special ones for shopping centers worth pointing out.

LEASING SPACE

In finding tenants whose line of goods will meet the needs of the desired market, the developer/owner first signs on a prestige merchant as the lead tenant. Then, the developer selects other types of stores that will complement each other. In this way, a "tenant mix" offers a varied array of merchandise. Thus, the center's competitive strength is bolstered against other centers as well as supplying the market area's needs.

To finance a center, the developer needs major leases from companies with strong credit ratings. The developer's own lenders favor tenant rosters that include the triple-A ratings of national chains. However, local merchants with good business records and a proven understanding of the local markets have a good chance of being considered by a shopping center developer.

If you are considering a shopping center for a first-store venture you may have trouble. Your financial backing and merchandising experience may be unproven to the developer/owner. In this situation, you must convince the developer that the new store has a reasonable chance of success and will help the "tenant mix."

TYPES OF SHOPPING CENTERS

Suppose that the developer/owner of a shopping center asks you to be a tenant. In considering the offer, you would need to make sure of what you can do in the center. What rules will there be on your operation? In exchange for the rules, what will the center do for you?

Choosing the proper type of shopping center is also a very important decision you will need to make.

In a **Neighborhood Shopping Center**, the leading tenant is a supermarket or drug store. The typical leasable space is 50,000 square feet but may range from 30,000 to 100,000 square feet. The typical site area is from 3 to 10 acres. The minimum trade population is 2,500 to 40,000.

The **Community Shopping Center's** leading tenant is a variety/junior department store or discount department store. The typical leasable space is 150,000 square feet but may range from 100,000 to 300,000 square feet. The typical site area is 10 to 30 acres. The minimum trade population is 40,000 to 150,000.

Finally, one or more full-line department stores are the leading tenants in a, **Regional Shopping Center.** The typical leasable space is 400,000 square feet with a range from 300,000 to more than 1,000,000 square feet. The typical site area is 30 to 50 acres. The minimum trade population is 150,000 or more. When the regional center exceeds 750,000 square feet and includes three or more department stores, it becomes a **Super-Regional Center.**

BUY OR LEASE

The fourth consideration in selecting a location is whether you should lease or buy the facility. Your decision should be based on the following factors.

1. Are your requirements going to change rapidly over the next few years? If they are, you should probably consider leasing.
2. Do you find yourself in a very short supply of capital? Can you use your available money better if it is not tied up in a building? What return can you expect from your funds if they are invested elsewhere? If your capital is tight, leasing may be preferable.

3. Can you secure a favorable lease from the owner of the building with an option to purchase? Because of tax considerations, a property owner may prefer to lease his property rather than sell it. In such a case, he or she is apt to make the lease price more attractive than the selling price. You should explore this possibility.

4. Your accountant can advise you on the financial aspects of how leasing or purchasing might affect your financial picture. If you can buy property at a favorable price and the purchase does not cause a shortage in your working capital, then purchasing may be indicated.

5. Consider resale. Is the building one that will be readily resold? If so, to purchase may be wise. On the other hand, leasing may be better if there is something about the building (for example, little or no adjacent land for parking or expansion) that would limit resale of the property.

6. Some states have revenue bonding programs, tax forgiveness, and other assistance. You might check your state and local economic development group to determine what help is available.

If you decide to lease, two additional items should be taken into consideration.

LEASE AGREEMENT

Is the lease flexible, so that you have an option to renew after a specified number of years? (On the other hand, is the lease of limited duration so, if needed, you can seek another location?) Does the agreement:

- Peg rent to sales volume (with a definite ceiling) or is rent merely fixed?
- Protect you as well as the property owner?

- Put in writing the promises the property owner has made about repairs, construction and reconstruction, decorating, alteration, and maintenance?

- Contain prohibitions against subleasing?

LANDLORD RESPONSIVENESS

By restricting the placement and size of signs, by foregoing or ignoring needed maintenance and repairs, by renting adjacent retail spaces to incompatible—or worse, directly competing—businesses, landlords may cripple a retailer's attempts to increase business.

Sometimes landlords lack the funds to maintain their properties. Rather than continuing to "invest" in their holdings by maintaining a proper appearance for their buildings and supporting their tenants, they try to "squeeze" the property for whatever they can get.

To find out if a landlord is responsive to the needs of the retail tenants, talk to the tenants before you commit to an agreement. Ask them: 1) Does the landlord return calls in a reasonable period and send service people quickly? 2) Is it necessary to nag the landlord just to get routine maintenance taken care of? 3) Does the landlord just collect the rent and disappear, or is he or she sympathetic to the needs of the tenant? 4) Does the landlord have any policies that hamper marketing innovations?

In addition to speaking with current tenants, talk to previous ones of the location you have in mind. You'll probably come up with a lot of helpful information. Find out what businesses they were in and why they left.

TRANSPORTATION

Transportation is another factor in choosing a location. Radical changes in the past twenty years make for greater flexibility when locating a business. The growth of air shipping makes sites near airports more attractive. Interstate highways have increased the popularity of trucks as a method of moving goods. More pipeline facilities are available. Railroads are indispensable for certain products.

Have a transportation expert furnish shipping rates and delivery times for your major customers via the various modes of transportation. You may discover the preferable method of shipment to be different than what you had expected.

In addition to determining what mode of transportation is important for your present needs, you should consider what will be vital in the next twenty years. Look at access to freeways, available rail service, barge and deep water transportation, and the possibilities of using or expanding upon air shipments.

Consider the *landed* (delivered) cost to your customer as a significant point. If you have a low-value, high-weight item such as concrete, then your location decision is weighted heavily by the transportation cost while for electronic parts transportation would not be so significant. Bear in mind also your customers' preferences for service. If your customers required 3-hour deliveries, that is important to your transportation plans.

SUPPLIERS

Closely related to transportation is the location of your suppliers in choosing your own location. It is important to know if all your supplies come from one general area or if they are spread out around you. If they come from one area, what advantages does a business have in locating adjacent to these sources or in a more remote section? Being closer to your suppliers may be more important than being close to your customers, or vice versa.

Some other considerations about suppliers include:

- Can you always be assured a supply regardless of the season?

- Are you assured of consistent service from this source in the foreseeable future?

- Should you consider an alternate source?

- Will prices from the present source change dramatically in the future?

- Are there facilities to bring in supplies rapidly and economically?

OTHER CONSIDERATIONS

A host of other considerations have varying importance in choosing a location, depending on your line of business. The following questions, may help you arrive at a decision.

- How much office, storage, or workroom space do you need?

- Is parking space available and adequate?

- Do you require special lighting, heating or cooling, or other installations?

- Is the area served by public transportation?

- Is there adequate fire and police protection?

- Will sanitation or utility supply be a problem?

- Is the facility easily accessible?

- Will crime insurance be prohibitively expensive?

- Is the trade area heavily dependent on seasonal business?

- Is the location convenient to where you live?

SCORE SHEET

As you consider the factors relevant to your location decision, you should have some type of scoresheet that you can use to evaluate sites. See Appendix B, the "Rating Sheet on Sites," at the end of this publication. This rating sheet, when completed for each site you are considering, will help you see its strengths and weaknesses. It also helps you eliminate the factors that may be equal in all the sites.

As you tally the sheet, some factors may be more important to you than to people in other businesses. For example, if you are in the apparel business, the availability of qualified labor may be far more important than any other factor. It would be wise to assign some weight to those factors that are abnormally important because of the nature of your business.

RELOCATING FOR GROWTH

Sometimes an owner/manager should consider relocating even though the need for it is not apparent because present space seems adequate and is serving customers without complaints.

However, what about technological improvements? Have you thought that if you move you could take advantage of the technological improvements that have come along in your industry since your present facility was built? If your facility has become a competitive liability because of such innovations, moving to another building may be the most economical way to become competitive again.

You should keep in mind the danger of putting off relocating because you "can't afford it now." Some owner/managers find that, as time goes by and their competitive position worsens, they can afford relocating even less. They learn the hard way that if a company stays too long in a location it can die in that location.

The company that prospers is the one in which the owner/manager chooses the best possible site and remains there only until the factors dictating that location no longer outweigh the advantages to be gained by moving. With ever changing technology and more efficient machinery and floor plan layouts, the most expensive cost in a business can be an obsolete facility.

APPENDIX A

HOW TO MAKE A TRAFFIC COUNT

First of all, be sure you need a traffic count. Although knowledge of the volume and character of passing traffic is always useful, in certain cases a traffic survey may not really make any difference. Other selection factors involved may be so significant that the outcome of a traffic study will have relatively little bearing on your decision. When the other selection factors, such as parking, operating costs, or location of competitors, become less important and data on traffic flow becomes dominant, then a count is indicated. Once you have determined that you really need a traffic count, the general objective is to count the passing traffic—both pedestrian and vehicular—that would constitute potential customers who would probably be attracted into your type of store. To evaluate the traffic available to competitors, you may desire to conduct traffic counts at their sites, too.

Data from a traffic count should not only show how many people pass by but generally indicate what kinds of people they are. Analysis of the characteristics of the passing traffic often reveals patterns and variations not readily apparent from casual observation.

For counting purposes, the passing traffic is divided into different classifications according to the characteristics of the customers who would patronize your type of business. Whereas, a drugstore is interested in the total volume of passing traffic, a men's clothing store is obviously more concerned with the amount of male traffic, especially men between the ages of sixteen and sixty-five.

It is also important to classify passing traffic by its reasons for passing. A woman on the way to a beauty salon is probably a poor prospect for a paint store, but she may be a good prospect for a drugstore. The hours at which individuals go by are often an indication of their purpose. In the early morning hours people are generally on their way to work. In the late afternoon these same people are usually going home from work. When one chain organization estimates the number of potential women customers, it considers women passing a site between 10 a.m. and 5 p.m. to be the serious shoppers.

Evaluation of the financial bracket of passersby is also significant. Out of 100 women passing a prospective location for an exclusive dress shop, only ten may appear to have the income to patronize the shop. Of course, the greater your experience in a particular retail trade, the more accurately you can estimate the number of your potential customers. To determine what proportion of the passing traffic represents your potential shoppers, some of the pedestrians should be interviewed about the origin of their trip, their destination, and the stores in which they plan to shop. This sort of information can provide you with a better estimate of the number of potential customers.

In summary, the qualitative information gathered about the passing traffic should include counting the individuals who seem to possess the characteristics appropriate to the desired clientele, judging their reasons for using that route, and calculating their ability to buy.

PEDESTRIAN TRAFFIC COUNT

In making a pedestrian count you must decide: who is to be counted; where the count should take place; and when the count should be made. In considering who is to be counted, determine what types of people should be included. For example, the study might count all men presumed to be between sixteen and sixty-five. The directions should be completely clear as to the individuals to be counted so the counters will be consistent and the total figure will reflect the traffic flow.

As previously indicated, it is frequently desirable to divide the pedestrian traffic into classes. Quite often separate counts of men and women and certain age categories are wanted. A trial run will indicate if there are any difficulties in identifying those to be counted or in placing them into various groupings.

You next determine the specific place where the count is to be taken. You decide whether all the traffic near the site should be counted or only the traffic passing directly in front of the site. Remember that if all the pedestrians passing through an area are counted, there is the possibility of double counting. Since a person must both enter and leave an area, it is important that each person be counted only once. Therefore, it is essential that the counter consistently counts at the same location.

When the count should be taken is influenced by the season, month, week, day and hour. For example, during the summer season there is generally an increased flow of traffic on the shady side of the street. During a holiday period such as the month before Christmas or the week before Easter, traffic is denser than it is regularly. The patronage of a store varies by day of the week, too. Store traffic usually increased during the latter part of the week. In some communities, on factory paydays and days when social security checks are received, certain locations experience heavier than normal traffic.

The day of the week and the time of day should represent a normal period for traffic flow. Pedestrian flow accelerates around noon as office workers go out for lunch. Generally, more customers enter a downtown store between 10 a.m. and noon and between 1 p.m. and 3 p.m. than at any other time. Local custom or other factors, however, may cause a variation in these expected traffic patterns.

After you choose the day that has normal traffic flow, the day should be divided into half-hour and hourly intervals. Traffic should be counted and recorded for each half-hour period of a store's customary operating hours. If it is not feasible to count the traffic for each half-hour interval, the traffic flow can be sampled. Traffic in representative half-hour periods in the morning, noon, afternoon, and evening can be counted.

ESTIMATE OF STORE SALES

Data from a pedestrian traffic survey can give you information on whether or not the site would generate a profitable volume for your store. A retailer with some past experience in the same merchandise line for which a store is planned can make a reasonable estimate of sales volume if the following information is available (in lieu of past personal experience, the trade association for your type of business may be of help):

- Characteristics of individuals who are most likely to be store customers (from pedestrian interviews);

- Number of such individuals passing the site during store hours (from traffic counts);

- Proportion of passersby who will enter the store (from pedestrian interviews);

- Proportion of those entering who will become purchasers (from pedestrian interviews); and

- Amount of the average transaction (from past experience, trade associations, and trade publications).

One retailer divides the people who pass a given site into three categories: those who enter a store; those who, after looking at the windows, may become customers; and those who pass without entering or looking. Owing to prior experience, this retailer is able to estimate from the percentage falling into each classification not only the number who will make purchases but also how much the average purchase will be. If, out of 1,000 passersby each day, five percent (fifty) enter and each spends an average of $8, a store at that site which operates 300 days a year will have an annual sales volume of $120,000.

AUTOMOBILE TRAFFIC COUNT

A growing number of retail firms depend on drive-in traffic for their sales. Both the quantity and quality of automotive traffic can be analyzed in the same way as pedestrian traffic. For the major streets in urban areas, either the city engineer, the planning commission, the state highway department, or an outdoor advertising company may be able to provide you with data on traffic flows. However, you may need to modify this information to suit your special needs. For example, you should supplement data relating to total count of vehicles passing the site with actual observation in order to evaluate such influences on traffic as commercial vehicles, changing of shifts at nearby factories, through highway traffic, and increased flow caused by special events or activities.

APPENDIX B

RATING SHEET ON SITES

Grade each factor: 1 (lowest) to 10 (highest)
Weigh each factor: 1 (least important) to 5 (most important)

1. Centrally located to reach my market.

2. Supplies readily available.

3. Quantity of available labor.

4. Transportation availability and rates.

5. Labor rates of pay/estimated productivity.

6. Adequacy of utilities (sewer, water, electricity, gas).

7. Local business climate.

8. Provision for future expansion.

9. Tax burden.

10. Topography of the site (slope and foundation).

11. Quality of police and fire protection.

12. Housing availability for workers and managers.

13. Environmental factors (schools, cultural, community atmosphere).

14. Estimate of quality of this site in years.

15. Estimate of this site in relation to my major competitor.

BIBLIOGRAPHY

How to Organize and Operate a Small Business. Clifford M. Baumback, Prentice Hall, New Jersey, 1988.

How to Select a Business Site. Jon E. Browning, McGraw-Hill, Inc., New York, 1980.

Locating & Layout Planning. W. Domschke and A. Drexel, Springer-Verlag, Inc., New York, 1985.

Making Business Location Decisions. Roger W. Schmenner, Prentice Hall, New Jersey, 1982.

Regional & Urban Location. Colin Clark, St. Martin Press, Inc., New York, 1982.

We hope this publication has met your business needs. For a free copy of the Directory of Business Development Publications, write to: Publications, P.O. Box 1000, Fort Worth, Texas 76119 or contact your local SBA office.

SBA has a number of other programs and services available. They include training and educational programs, advisory services, financial programs, and contract assistance. Our offices are located throughout the country. For the one nearest you, consult the telephone directory under U.S. Government or call the Small Business Answer Desk at 1-800-368-5855. In Washington, D.C., call 653-7561.

All of SBA's Programs and Services are extended to the public on a nondiscriminatory basis.

APPENDIX 8: SAMPLING OF TAX FORMS FROM *THE TAX GUIDE FOR SMALL BUSINESS*

Filled-in Forms: *The purpose of this Part is to illustrate the tax forms used to report business income or loss. The use of each form is illustrated by an example of a business and how that business would fill out its tax return.*

38. SCHEDULE C SOLE PROPRIETORSHIP

If you are the sole owner of an unincorporated business or a *statutory employee* (see Chapter 33), you must report business income and expenses on Schedule C or C–EZ (Form 1040). A sample Schedule C with Form 4562 and Schedule SE (Form 1040) for Susan J. Brown are illustrated on the following pages. She does not qualify to use Schedule C–EZ.

Preparing Schedule C

Susan J. Brown owns and operates Milady Fashions, a ladies ready-to-wear apparel shop. She uses the accrual method of accounting and files her return on a calendar year basis.

Five employees worked in her shop during 1992. She had filed all the necessary employment tax forms and made the required tax deposits. See Chapter 34.

First, Susan fills in the information required at the top of Schedule C. On line A, she enters "Retail, ladies' apparel" and on line B, she enters the 4-digit business code for a ladies apparel shop. These codes are found on page 2 of Schedule C. Susan locates the major business category that describes her business. She reads down the items under "Trade, Retail" to find the code that applies to her business. This is 3913—"Clothing, women's." Susan enters 3913 on line B. She then completes items C through L.

Part I — Income

Susan enters items of income in Part I.

Line 1. Susan had sales of $397,742 in 1992. She enters her total sales on line 1.

Line 2. On line 2, she enters the refunds she gave on merchandise her customers returned, as well as other adjustments she made to customers' purchases. They total $1,442.

Line 4. Susan uses *Part III* on page 2 of Schedule C to figure her cost of goods sold.

Part III, line 33. Her inventory at the beginning of 1992, $42,843, is the same as her inventory at the end of 1991. This figure matches the amount on Part III, line 39 of her 1991 Schedule C.

Part III, line 34. The total cost of goods she bought to sell to customers, minus the cost of the goods she returned to her suppliers, was $241,026. From this stock, she withdrew clothing and accessories for her own use that cost $774. She subtracts the cost of these items from her total purchases to figure net purchases of $240,252.

Part III, line 38. She then adds her net purchases to her beginning inventory. This sum is the total goods Susan had available for sale during the year.

Part III, line 39. Susan's inventory at the end of the year was $43,746.

Part III, line 40. Subtracting her inventory at the end of the year (line 39) from the goods that were available for sale (line 38) gives Susan the cost of goods sold during the year. For more information on inventories and cost of goods sold, see Chapters 4 and 8.

Line 5. Gross profit, $156,951, is the difference between Susan's net sales (line 3) and the cost of goods sold (line 4).

Line 7. Because Susan did not have any income to report on line 6, the gross income is the same as the gross profit (line 5).

Part II — Expenses

Susan enters her expense items in Part II.

Line 8. Susan paid $3,500 for ads.

Line 9. During 1992, Susan determined that she would not be able to collect $479 from bad checks and deducted this amount as bad debts. See Chapter 15.

Line 10. Susan deducts $2,250 for gas and oil for her van. She used the van 75% for business in 1992. She spent a total of $3,000 for gas and oil in 1992. She can deduct 75% of $3,000 or $2,250. Other van expenses include $712 (75% of $950) for insurance, $812 (75% of $1,083) for repairs and upkeep, and $75 (75% of $100) for tags. She enters the total, $3,849, on line 10.

Line 13. Susan figures her depreciation on Form 4562. She bought and placed in service in her business on March 20, 1992, a van. The van weighs over 6,000 pounds; therefore, it is not a passenger automobile for the special deduction limits. The van is 5-year property and the deduction is figured using the 200% declining balance method and applying the half-year convention under MACRS.

The van cost $8,667. Susan can depreciate 75% of $8,667, or $6,500. Susan did not choose to deduct any part of the cost of the van as a section 179 deduction. Since the van is listed property, Susan must complete Part V on page 2 of Form 4562. The depreciation for listed property from Part V is entered on line 19, Part IV of Form 4562.

Susan also bought and placed in service on May 19, 1992, a new adding machine and some clothing racks. The adding machine is 5-year property and the clothing racks are 7-year property. The adding machine cost $200 and the clothing racks cost $800.

Susan chooses to deduct the cost of the adding machine as a section 179 deduction. The deduction for the clothing racks is figured using the 200% declining balance method and applying the half-year convention under MACRS. Susan must complete Part I and Part II of Form 4562.

For items bought after 1980 and before 1987, she uses the regular Accelerated Cost Recovery System (ACRS) percentages. For items bought before 1981, she uses the straight-line method. The total depreciation for these items appears on line 18, Part III of Form 4562. See Chapter 13.

Susan has no deduction for amortization. However, if she had recently acquired or set up the business, she could choose to deduct amortization for certain business start-up expenses. See Chapter 14.

Line 15. Susan's $238 deduction is for insurance on her business property (van insurance included in line 10). The deduction is only for premiums that give her coverage for 1992. See Chapter 18.

Line 16b. Susan had borrowed money to use in her business. The interest on these loans was $2,633 for 1992.

Line 18. The $216 Susan paid for postage in 1992 is her only office expense.

Line 20b. Her rent for the store was $1,000 a month, or $12,000 for the year.

Line 21. She had her store counters refinished and other painting was done at a total cost of $964. See Chapter 20.

Line 22. She spent $1,203 on supplies.

Line 23. Susan renewed her business license and paid property tax on her store fixtures. She also paid the employer's share of social security and Medicare taxes for her employees, and paid state and federal unemployment taxes. She enters the total of all these taxes, $5,727, on this line. See Chapter 19.

Line 25. Susan's total expense for heat, light, and telephone for the year is $3,570.

Line 26. Susan paid her employees a total of $63,450 for the year. She does not include in wages any amounts she paid to herself or withdrew from the business for her own use.

Susan has two employees whose wages qualify for the jobs credit. She figures the jobs credit on Form 5884, *Jobs Credit*, and uses it to reduce her income tax on Form 1040. However, Susan must subtract the credit of $4,400 from her wage and salary expense for the year. She figures her deductible salary expense to be $59,050

($63,450 − $4,400) and enters this amount on line 26. See Chapter 32.

Since Susan has claimed only the jobs credit, she does not have to prepare Form 3800. The general business credit consists of the investment, jobs, research, low-income housing, alcohol fuel, disabled access and enhanced oil recovery credits. If you have more than one of these credits, or a carryforward or carryback of any of these credits, you must summarize them on Form 3800.

Line 27. Susan enters other business expenses here that are not listed separately on the schedule. See Chapter 20.

Completing Schedule C
Susan completes Schedule C to determine her net profit or (loss) for 1992.

Line 28. Susan adds all her deductions listed in Part II and enters the total on this line.

Line 29. She subtracts her total deductions (line 28) from her gross income (line 7). Susan has a tentative profit of $52,713.

Line 30. Susan did not use any part of her home for business, so does not make an entry here.

Line 31. Susan has a net profit of $52,713 (line 30 from line 29). She enters her net profit here, on line 12 of Form 1040, and on line 2, Section A of Schedule SE (Form 1040).

Line 32. Susan does not have a loss, so she skips this line. If she had a loss and she was not "at risk" for all of her investment in the business, the amount of loss she could enter on line 12 of Form 1040 might be limited. See Chapter 21 and the instructions for Schedule C for an explanation of an investment "at risk."

SCHEDULE C
(Form 1040)

Department of the Treasury
Internal Revenue Service (5)

Profit or Loss From Business
(Sole Proprietorship)

▶ Partnerships, joint ventures, etc., must file Form 1065.

▶ Attach to Form 1040 or Form 1041. ▶ See Instructions for Schedule C (Form 1040).

OMB No. 1545-0074

19**92**

Attachment
Sequence No. **09**

Name of proprietor **Susan J. Brown**

Social security number (SSN) **111 00 1111**

A Principal business or profession, including product or service (see page C-1) **Retail Ladies' Apparel**

B Enter principal business code (from page 2) ▶

C Business name **Milady Fashions**

D Employer ID number (Not SSN) **1 0 1 2 3 4 5 6 7**

E Business address (including suite or room no.) ▶ ....
City, town or post office, state, and ZIP code

F Accounting method: **(1)** ☐ Cash **(2)** ☑ Accrual **(3)** ☐ Other (specify) ▶ ....

G Method(s) used to value closing inventory: **(1)** ☑ Cost **(2)** ☐ Lower of cost or market **(3)** ☐ Other (attach explanation) **(4)** ☐ Does not apply (if checked, skip line H)

	Yes	No
		✓

H Was there any change in determining quantities, costs, or valuations between opening and closing inventory? If "Yes," attach explanation — ✓

I Did you "materially participate" in the operation of this business during 1992? If "No," see page C-2 for limitations on losses — ✓

J Was this business in operation at the end of 1992? ....

K How many months was this business in operation during 1992? ▶ **12**

L If this is the first Schedule C filed for this business, check here ▶ ☐

Part I   Income

1 Gross receipts or sales. **Caution:** If this income was reported to you on Form W-2 and the "Statutory employee" box on that form was checked, see page C-2 and check here ▶ ☐	1	397,742
2 Returns and allowances	2	1,442
3 Subtract line 2 from line 1	3	396,300
4 Cost of goods sold (from line 40 on page 2)	4	234,349
5 **Gross profit.** Subtract line 4 from line 3	5	156,951
6 Other income, including Federal and state gasoline or fuel tax credit or refund (see page C-2) ▶	6	
7 **Gross income.** Add lines 5 and 6	7	156,951

Part II   Expenses (Caution: *Do not* enter expenses for business use of your home on lines 8–27. Instead, see line 30.)

8 Advertising	8	3,500	21 Repairs and maintenance	21	964
9 Bad debts from sales or services (see page C-3)	9	479	22 Supplies (not included in Part III)	22	1,203
10 Car and truck expenses (see page C-3—also attach **Form 4562**)	10	3,849	23 Taxes and licenses	23	5,727
11 Commissions and fees	11		24 Travel, meals, and entertainment:		
12 Depletion	12		a Travel	24a	
13 Depreciation and section 179 expense deduction (not included in Part III) (see page C-3)	13	2,731	b Meals and entertainment		
14 Employee benefit programs (other than on line 19)	14		c Enter 20% of line 24b subject to limitations (see page C-4)		
15 Insurance (other than health)	15	238	d Subtract line 24c from line 24b	24d	
16 Interest:			25 Utilities	25	3,570
a Mortgage (paid to banks, etc.)	16a		26 Wages (less jobs credit)	26	59,050
b Other	16b	2,633	27a Other expenses (list type and amount):		
17 Legal and professional services	17		....		
18 Office expense	18	216	....		
19 Pension and profit-sharing plans	19		....		
20 Rent or lease (see page C-4):			....		
a Vehicles, machinery, and equipment	20a				
b Other business property	20b	12,000	27b Total other expenses	27b	8,078

28 **Total expenses** before expenses for business use of home. Add lines 8 through 27b in columns ▶	28	104,238
29 Tentative profit (loss). Subtract line 28 from line 7	29	52,713
30 Expenses for business use of your home. Attach **Form 8829**	30	
31 **Net profit or (loss).** Subtract line 30 from line 29. If a profit, enter here and on Form 1040, line 12. Also, enter the net profit on Schedule SE, line 2 (statutory employees, see page C-5). If a loss, you MUST go on to line 32 (fiduciaries, see page C-5)	31	52,713

32 If you have a loss, you MUST check the box that describes your investment in this activity (see page C-5)

If you checked 32a, enter the loss on Form 1040, line 12, and Schedule SE, line 2 (statutory employees, see page C-5). If you checked 32b, you MUST attach **Form 6198**.

32a ☐ All investment is at risk.
32b ☐ Some investment is not at risk.

For Paperwork Reduction Act Notice, see Form 1040 instructions.   Cat. No. 11334P   Schedule C (Form 1040) 1992

SAMPLING OF TAX FORMS AND INSTRUCTIONS FROM THE TAX GUIDE FOR SMALL BUSINESS 183

	Part III	**Cost of Goods Sold** (see page C-5)		
33	Inventory at beginning of year. If different from last year's closing inventory, attach explanation . .	33	*42,843*
34	Purchases less cost of items withdrawn for personal use	34	*240,252*
35	Cost of labor. Do not include salary paid to yourself	35	
36	Materials and supplies	36	
37	Other costs	37	
38	Add lines 33 through 37.	38	*283,095*
39	Inventory at end of year.	39	*43,746*
40	**Cost of goods sold.** Subtract line 39 from line 38. Enter the result here and on page 1, line 4 . .	40	*239,349*

Part IV   **Principal Business or Professional Activity Codes**

Locate the major category that best describes your activity. Within the major category, select the activity code that most closely identifies the business or profession that is the principal source of your sales or receipts. **Enter this 4-digit code on page 1, line B.** For example, real estate agent is under the major category of **"Real Estate,"** and the code is **"5520."** **Note:** *If your principal source of income is from farming activities, you should file* **Schedule F** *(Form 1040), Profit or Loss From Farming.*

Agricultural Services, Forestry, Fishing
Code
1990 Animal services, other than breeding
1933 Crop services
2113 Farm labor & management services
2246 Fishing, commercial
2238 Forestry, except logging
2212 Horticulture & landscaping
2469 Hunting & trapping
1974 Livestock breeding
0836 Logging
1958 Veterinary services, including pets

Construction
0018 Operative builders (for own account)
Building Trade Contractors, Including Repairs
0414 Carpentering & flooring
0455 Concrete work
0273 Electrical work
0299 Masonry, dry wall, stone, & tile
0257 Painting & paper hanging
0232 Plumbing, heating, & air conditioning
0430 Roofing, siding & sheet metal
0885 Other building trade contractors (excavation, glazing, etc.)
General Contractors
0075 Highway & street construction
0059 Nonresidential building
0034 Residential building
3889 Other heavy construction (pipe laying, bridge construction, etc.)

Finance, Insurance, & Related Services
6064 Brokers & dealers of securities
6080 Commodity contracts brokers & dealers; security & commodity exchanges
6148 Credit institutions & mortgage bankers
5702 Insurance agents or brokers
5744 Insurance services (appraisal, consulting, inspection, etc.)
6130 Investment advisors & services
5777 Other financial services

Manufacturing, Including Printing & Publishing
0679 Apparel & other textile products
1115 Electric & electronic equipment
1073 Fabricated metal products
0638 Food products & beverages
0810 Furniture & fixtures
0695 Leather footwear, handbags, etc.
0836 Lumber & other wood products
1099 Machinery & machine shops
0877 Paper & allied products
1057 Primary metal industries
0851 Printing & publishing
1032 Stone, clay, & glass products
0653 Textile mill products
1883 Other manufacturing industries

Mining & Mineral Extraction
1537 Coal mining
1511 Metal mining

1552 Oil & gas
1719 Quarrying & nonmetallic mining

Real Estate
5538 Operators & lessors of buildings, including residential
5553 Operators & lessors of other real property
5520 Real estate agents & brokers
5579 Real estate property managers
5710 Subdividers & developers, except cemeteries
6155 Title abstract offices

Services: Personal, Professional, & Business Services
Amusement & Recreational Services
9670 Bowling centers
9688 Motion picture & tape distribution & allied services
9597 Motion picture & video production
9639 Motion picture theaters
8557 Physical fitness facilities
9696 Professional sports & racing, including promoters & managers
9811 Theatrical performers (musicians, agents, producers & related services
9613 Video tape rental
9837 Other amusement & recreational services
Automotive Services
8813 Automotive rental or leasing, without driver
8953 Automotive repairs, general & specialized
8839 Parking, except valet
8896 Other automotive services (wash, towing, etc.)
Business & Personal Services
7658 Accounting & bookkeeping
7716 Advertising, except direct mail
7682 Architectural services
8318 Barber shop (or barber)
8110 Beauty shop (or beautician)
8714 Child day care
7872 Computer programming, processing, data preparation & related services
7922 Computer repair, maintenance, & leasing
7286 Consulting services
7799 Consumer credit reporting & collection services
8755 Counseling (except health practitioners)
7732 Employment agencies & personnel supply
7518 Engineering services
7773 Equipment rental & leasing (except computer or automotive)
8532 Funeral services & crematories
7633 Income tax preparation
7914 Investigative & protective services
7617 Legal services (or lawyer)
7856 Mailing, reproduction, commercial art, photography, & stenographic services
7245 Management services
8771 Ministers & chaplains
8334 Photographic studios
7260 Public relations
8733 Research services

7708 Surveying services
8730 Teaching or tutoring
7880 Other business services
6882 Other personal services

Hotels & Other Lodging Places
7237 Camps & camping parks
7096 Hotels, motels, & tourist homes
7211 Rooming & boarding houses

Laundry & Cleaning Services
7450 Carpet & upholstery cleaning
7419 Coin-operated laundries & dry cleaning
7435 Full-service laundry, dry cleaning, & garment service
7476 Janitorial & related services (building, house, & window cleaning)

Medical & Health Services
9274 Chiropractors
9233 Dentist's office or clinic
9217 Doctor's (M.D.) office or clinic
9456 Medical & dental laboratories
9472 Nursing & personal care facilities
9290 Optometrists
9258 Osteopathic physicians & surgeons
9241 Podiatrists
9415 Registered & practical nurses
9431 Offices & clinics of other health practitioners (dieticians, midwives, speech pathologists, etc.)
9886 Other health services

Miscellaneous Repair, Except Computers
9019 Audio equipment & TV repair
9035 Electrical & electronic equipment repair, except audio & TV
9050 Furniture repair & reupholstery
2881 Other equipment repair

Trade, Retail—Selling Goods to Individuals & Households
3038 Catalog or mail order
3012 Selling door to door, by telephone or party plan, or from mobile unit
3053 Vending machine selling

Selling From Showroom, Store, or Other Fixed Location
Apparel & Accessories
3921 Accessory & specialty stores & furriers for women
3939 Clothing, family
3772 Clothing, men's & boys'
3913 Clothing, women's
3756 Shoe stores
3954 Other apparel & accessory stores
Automotive & Service Stations
3558 Gasoline service stations
3319 New car dealers (franchised)
3533 Tires, accessories, & parts
3335 Used car dealers
3517 Other automotive dealers (motorcycles, recreational vehicles, etc.)
Building, Hardware, & Garden Supply
4416 Building materials dealers
4457 Hardware stores
4473 Nurseries & garden supply stores
4432 Paint, glass, & wallpaper stores

Food & Beverages
0612 Bakeries selling at retail
3086 Catering services
3095 Drinking places (bars, taverns, pubs, saloons, etc.)
3079 Eating places, meals & snacks
3210 Grocery stores (general line)
3251 Liquor stores
3236 Specialized food stores (meat, produce, candy, health food, etc.)
Furniture & General Merchandise
3988 Computer & software stores
3970 Furniture stores
4317 Home furnishings stores (china, floor coverings, drapes)
4119 Household appliance stores
4333 Music & record stores
3996 TV, audio & electronic stores
3715 Variety stores
3731 Other general merchandise stores
Miscellaneous Retail Stores
4812 Boat dealers
5017 Book stores, excluding newsstands
4853 Camera & photo supply stores
3277 Drug stores
5058 Fabric & needlework stores
4655 Florists
5090 Fuel dealers (except gasoline)
4630 Gift, novelty & souvenir shops
4838 Hobby, toy, & game shops
4671 Jewelry stores
4895 Luggage & leather goods stores
5074 Mobile home dealers
4879 Optical goods stores
4697 Sporting goods & bicycle shops
5033 Stationery stores
4614 Used merchandise & antique stores (except motor vehicle parts)
5884 Other retail stores

Trade, Wholesale—Selling Goods to Other Businesses, etc.
Durable Goods, Including Machinery Equipment, Wood, Metals, etc.
2634 Agent or broker for other firms—more than 50% of gross sales on commission
2618 Selling for your own account
Nondurable Goods, Including Food, Fiber, Chemicals, etc.
2675 Agent or broker for other firms—more than 50% of gross sales on commission
2659 Selling for your own account

Transportation, Communications, Public Utilities, & Related Services
6619 Air transportation
6312 Bus & limousine transportation
6676 Communication services
6395 Courier or package delivery
6361 Highway passenger transportation (except chartered service)
6536 Public warehousing
6114 Taxicabs
6510 Trash collection without own dump
6635 Travel agents & tour operators
6338 Trucking (except trash collection)
6692 Utilities (dumps, snow plowing, road cleaning, etc.)
6551 Water transportation
6650 Other transportation services
8888 **Unable to classify**

Form **4562**	**Depreciation and Amortization** **(Including Information on Listed Property)**	OMB No. 1545-0172 **1992**
Department of the Treasury Internal Revenue Service (10)	▶ See separate instructions. ▶ Attach this form to your return.	Attachment Sequence No. **67**

Name(s) shown on return
Susan J. Brown

Identifying number
111-00-1111

Business or activity to which this form relates
Milady Fashions / Retail Ladies' Apparel

Part I — Election To Expense Certain Tangible Property (Section 179) (Note: *If you have any "Listed Property," complete Part V before you complete Part I.*)

1	Maximum dollar limitation (see instructions)	1	$10,000
2	Total cost of section 179 property placed in service during the tax year (see instructions)	2	7,500
3	Threshold cost of section 179 property before reduction in limitation	3	$200,000
4	Reduction in limitation. Subtract line 3 from line 2, but do not enter less than -0-	4	
5	Dollar limitation for tax year. Subtract line 4 from line 1, but do not enter less than -0-	5	10,000

(a) Description of property	**(b)** Cost	**(c)** Elected cost	
6 Adding Machine	200	200	

7	Listed property. Enter amount from line 26.	7	
8	Total elected cost of section 179 property. Add amounts in column (c), lines 6 and 7	8	200
9	Tentative deduction. Enter the smaller of line 5 or line 8	9	200
10	Carryover of disallowed deduction from 1991 (see instructions)	10	
11	Taxable income limitation. Enter the smaller of taxable income or line 5 (see instructions)	11	10,000
12	Section 179 expense deduction. Add lines 9 and 10, but do not enter more than line 11	12	200
13	Carryover of disallowed deduction to 1993. Add lines 9 and 10, less line 12 ▶	13	

Note: *Do not use Part II or Part III below for automobiles, certain other vehicles, cellular telephones, computers, or property used for entertainment, recreation, or amusement (listed property). Instead, use Part V for listed property.*

Part II — MACRS Depreciation For Assets Placed in Service ONLY During Your 1992 Tax Year (Do Not Include Listed Property)

(a) Classification of property	**(b)** Month and year placed in service	**(c)** Basis for depreciation (business/investment use only—see instructions)	**(d)** Recovery period	**(e)** Convention	**(f)** Method	**(g)** Depreciation deduction
14 General Depreciation System (GDS) (see instructions):						
a 3-year property						
b 5-year property						
c 7-year property		800	7	HY	200 DB	114
d 10-year property						
e 15-year property						
f 20-year property						
g Residential rental property			27.5 yrs.	MM	S/L	
			27.5 yrs.	MM	S/L	
h Nonresidential real property			31.5 yrs.	MM	S/L	
			31.5 yrs.	MM	S/L	
15 Alternative Depreciation System (ADS) (see instructions):						
a Class life					S/L	
b 12-year			12 yrs.		S/L	
c 40-year			40 yrs.	MM	S/L	

Part III — Other Depreciation (Do Not Include Listed Property)

16	GDS and ADS deductions for assets placed in service in tax years beginning before 1992 (see instructions)	16	
17	Property subject to section 168(f)(1) election (see instructions)	17	
18	ACRS and other depreciation (see instructions)	18	1,117

Part IV — Summary

19	Listed property. Enter amount from line 25.	19	1,300
20	**Total.** Add deductions on line 12, lines 14 and 15 in column (g), and lines 16 through 19. Enter here and on the appropriate lines of your return. (Partnerships and S corporations—see instructions)	20	2,730
21	For assets shown above and placed in service during the current year, enter the portion of the basis attributable to section 263A costs (see instructions)	21	

For Paperwork Reduction Act Notice, see page 1 of the separate instructions.   Cat. No. 12906N   Form **4562** (1992)

| **Part V** | **Listed Property—Automobiles, Certain Other Vehicles, Cellular Telephones, Computers, and Property Used for Entertainment, Recreation, or Amusement** |

*For any vehicle for which you are using the standard mileage rate or deducting lease expense, complete **only** 22a, 22b, columns (a) through (c) of Section A, all of Section B, and Section C if applicable.*

Section A—Depreciation (Caution: *See instructions for limitations for automobiles.*)

22a Do you have evidence to support the business/investment use claimed? ☑ **Yes** ☐ **No** | **22b** If "Yes," is the evidence written? ☑ **Yes** ☐ **No**

(a) Type of property (list vehicles first)	(b) Date placed in service	(c) Business/ investment use percentage	(d) Cost or other basis	(e) Basis for depreciation (business/investment use only)	(f) Recovery period	(g) Method/ Convention	(h) Depreciation deduction	(i) Elected section 179 cost
23 Property used more than 50% in a qualified business use (see instructions):								
USA 280 S van	3/20/92	75 %	8,667	6,500	5 yrs.	200 DB/HY	1,300	0
		%						
		%						
24 Property used 50% or less in a qualified business use (see instructions):								
		%			S/L –			
		%			S/L –			
		%			S/L –			

25 Add amounts in column (h). Enter the total here and on line 19, page 1 . . . . . | **25** | 1,300 |

26 Add amounts in column (i). Enter the total here and on line 7, page 1 . . . . | **26** | |

Section B—Information Regarding Use of Vehicles—*If you deduct expenses for vehicles:*

- *Always complete this section for vehicles used by a sole proprietor, partner, or other "more than 5% owner," or related person.*
- *If you provided vehicles to your employees, first answer the questions in Section C to see if you meet an exception to completing this section for those vehicles.*

		(a) Vehicle 1		(b) Vehicle 2		(c) Vehicle 3		(d) Vehicle 4		(e) Vehicle 5		(f) Vehicle 6	
27	Total business/investment miles driven during the year (DO NOT include commuting miles)	7,500											
28	Total commuting miles driven during the year	2,025											
29	Total other personal (noncommuting) miles driven	475											
30	Total miles driven during the year. Add lines 27 through 29.	10,000											
		Yes	No	Yes	No	Yes	No	Yes	No	Yes	No	Yes	No
31	Was the vehicle available for personal use during off-duty hours?	✓											
32	Was the vehicle used primarily by a more than 5% owner or related person?	✓											
33	Is another vehicle available for personal use?	✓											

Section C—Questions for Employers Who Provide Vehicles for Use by Their Employees

*Answer these questions to determine if you meet an exception to completing Section B. **Note:** Section B must always be completed for vehicles used by sole proprietors, partners, or other more than 5% owners or related persons.*

		Yes	No
34	Do you maintain a written policy statement that prohibits all personal use of vehicles, including commuting, by your employees?		
35	Do you maintain a written policy statement that prohibits personal use of vehicles, except commuting, by your employees? (See instructions for vehicles used by corporate officers, directors, or 1% or more owners.)		
36	Do you treat all use of vehicles by employees as personal use?		
37	Do you provide more than five vehicles to your employees and retain the information received from your employees concerning the use of the vehicles?		
38	Do you meet the requirements concerning qualified automobile demonstration use (see instructions)? . .		

Note: *If your answer to 34, 35, 36, 37, or 38 is "Yes," you need not complete Section B for the covered vehicles.*

| **Part VI** | **Amortization** |

(a) Description of costs	(b) Date amortization begins	(c) Amortizable amount	(d) Code section	(e) Amortization period or percentage	(f) Amortization for this year
39 Amortization of costs that begins during your 1992 tax year:					
40 Amortization of costs that began before 1992			**40**		
41 Total. Enter here and on "Other Deductions" or "Other Expenses" line of your return . . .			**41**		

<table>
<tr><td>

SCHEDULE SE
(Form 1040)

Department of the Treasury
Internal Revenue Service (5)

</td><td>

Self-Employment Tax

▶ See Instructions for Schedule SE (Form 1040).

▶ **Attach to Form 1040.**

</td><td>

OMB No. 1545-0074

19**92**

Attachment
Sequence No. **17**

</td></tr>
</table>

Name of person with **self-employment** income (as shown on Form 1040)	Social security number of person with **self-employment** income ▶
Susan J. Brown	111 : 00 : 1111

Who Must File Schedule SE

You must file Schedule SE if:

- Your wages (and tips) subject to social security AND Medicare tax (or railroad retirement tax) were less than $130,200; **AND**
- Your *net earnings from self-employment from other than church employee income* (line 4 of Short Schedule SE or line 4c of Long Schedule SE) were $400 or more;
  OR
- You had church employee income (as defined on page SE-1) of $108.28 or more.

Exception. If your only self-employment income was from earnings as a minister, member of a religious order, or Christian Science practitioner, AND you filed **Form 4361** and received IRS approval not to be taxed on those earnings, DO NOT file Schedule SE. Instead, write "Exempt–Form 4361" on Form 1040, line 47.

May I Use Short Schedule SE or MUST I Use Long Schedule SE?

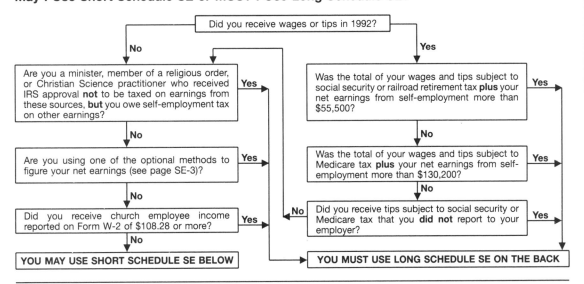

YOU MAY USE SHORT SCHEDULE SE BELOW	▶	**YOU MUST USE LONG SCHEDULE SE ON THE BACK**

Section A—Short Schedule SE. Caution: *Read above to see if you must use Long Schedule SE on the back (Section B).*

1	Net farm profit or (loss) from Schedule F, line 36, and farm partnerships, Schedule K-1 (Form 1065), line 15a	**1**	
2	Net profit or (loss) from Schedule C, line 31; Schedule C-EZ, line 3; and Schedule K-1 (Form 1065), line 15a (other than farming). See page SE-2 for other income to report	**2**	52,713
3	Combine lines 1 and 2	**3**	52,713
4	**Net earnings from self-employment.** Multiply line 3 by 92.35% (.9235). If less than $400, **do not** file this schedule; you do not owe self-employment tax . . . . ▶	**4**	48,680
5	**Self-employment tax.** If the amount on line 4 is: • $55,500 or less, multiply line 4 by 15.3% (.153) and enter the result. • More than $55,500 but less than $130,200, multiply the amount in excess of $55,500 by 2.9% (.029). Then, add $8,491.50 to the result and enter the total. • $130,200 or more, enter $10,657.80. Also, enter this amount on Form 1040, line 47	**5**	7,448

Note: Also, enter **one-half** of the amount from line 5 on **Form 1040, line 25.**

For Paperwork Reduction Act Notice, see Form 1040 instructions.	Cat. No. 11358Z	Schedule SE (Form 1040) 1992

Form 1065 Example

The filled-in Form 1065 is for the AbleBee Book Store, a partnership composed of Frank Able and Sami Bee. The partnership uses the accrual method of accounting and a calendar year for reporting income and loss. Mr. Able works fulltime in the business, while Ms. Bee works approximately 25% of her time in it. Both partners are general partners.

The partnership agreement states that Mr. Able will receive a yearly guaranteed payment of $20,000, and Ms. Bee will receive $5,000. Any profit or loss will be shared equally by the partners. The partners are personally liable for all partnership liabilities. Both partners materially participate in the operation of the business.

In addition to income and expense from partnership business operations, AbleBee received $50 tax-exempt interest from municipal bonds, $150 dividend income, and made a $650 charitable contribution.

Note that each partner's distributive share of specially allocated items should be shown on the appropriate line of the applicable partner's Schedule K–1, and the total amount on Schedule K instead of on page 1, Form 1065.

Page 1

The preaddressed label from the cover of the Form 1065 package that the partnership received in the mail is placed in the address area of the form. (However, a partnership should wait to do this until after completing the return, in case a mistake is made and the return has to be redone.) Make any necessary corrections on the label. If a partnership does not receive a Form 1065 package in the mail and does not have a preaddressed label, the partnership should enter its name and address in this area. All the information asked for at the top of page 1, Form 1065, is supplied in this example.

Income

The partnership's ordinary income (loss) is shown on lines 1a through 8.

Line 1. Gross sales of $409,465 are entered on line 1a. Returns and allowances of $3,365 are entered on line 1b, resulting in net sales of $406,100, entered on line 1c.

Line 2. Cost of goods sold, $267,641, from Schedule A, line 8 (discussed later), is entered here.

Line 3. Gross profit of $138,459 is shown on this line.

Line 7. Interest income on accounts receivable, $559, is entered on this line. The schedule that must be attached for this line is not shown.

Line 8. Total income, $139,018 (lines 3 through 7), is shown on line 8.

Deductions

The partnership's allowable deductions are shown next on lines 9 through 21.

Line 9. All salaries and wages are included on line 9a, *except* guaranteed payments to partners (shown on line 10). The AbleBee Book Store lists $29,350 on lines 9a and 9c. Be-

cause the partnership was not eligible for the jobs credit, no entry is made on line 9b. See Form 5884, *Jobs Credit*, for more information on the jobs credit.

Line 10. Guaranteed payments of $25,000 to partners Able ($20,000) and Bee ($5,000) are entered here. If a guaranteed payment is for interest paid to a partner, enter it here and not on line 15.

Line 11. Repairs of $1,125 made to partnership equipment are entered on this line. To qualify for the deduction, repairs must not add to the value or appreciably prolong the life of the property repaired.

LINE 12. During the year, $250 of amounts owed to the partnership was determined to be worthless. This amount is shown on line 12. If debts previously written off and deducted are collected in later years, the amount collected generally must be included in partnership gross income for the year in which the amount is collected. See Chapter 12 in Publication 535 for more information.

Line 13. Rent paid for the business premises, $20,000, is listed on this line.

Line 14. Deductible taxes of $3,295 are entered on this line.

Line 15. Interest paid to suppliers during the year totaled $1,451. This is business interest, so it is entered on line 15. Interest paid to a *partner* that is not a guaranteed payment is also included on this line. For more information, see Chapter 6 in Publication 535.

Lines 16a and 16c. Depreciation of $1,174 from Form 4562, *Depreciation and Amortization*, is entered here. Any amount on line 16b is also from Form 4562. The partnership must use Form 4562 to report the depreciation expense claimed on this line and elsewhere on the partnership return. A filled-in Form 4562 is not shown in this example.

Line 20. Other allowable deductions of $8,003 that are not claimed elsewhere on the return or for which a separate line is not provided on page 1 are included on this line. The partnership attaches a schedule that lists each deduction and its amount that is included on line 20. This schedule is not illustrated.

Line 21. The total of all deductions, $89,648 (lines 9c through 20), is entered on this line.

Line 22. The amount on line 21 is subtracted from the amount on line 8. The result, $49,370, is entered on line 22 of page 1 and is allocated to each partner on line 1 of Schedule K–1. The total is shown on line 1 of Schedule K.

Signatures

The return must be signed by a general partner. Also, any person, firm, or corporation that prepares the return for compensation, other than a full-time employee of the partnership, must sign it. The AbleBee Book Store did not have a paid preparer who was required to sign the return.

Page 2
Schedule A

Schedule A is the computation of cost of goods sold. Beginning inventory, $18,125 (en-

tered on line 1), is added to net purchases, $268,741, and is entered on line 2. The total, $286,866, is entered on line 6. Ending inventory, $19,225 (entered on line 7), is subtracted from the amount on line 6 to arrive at cost of goods sold, $267,641 (entered on line 8 and on page 1, line 2).

The partnership answered all applicable questions for item 9.

Schedule B

Schedule B contains 13 questions pertaining to the partnership. Answer questions 1 through 12 by marking the "yes" or "no" boxes.

Question 5 asks if the partnership meets all the requirements listed in items 5a, b, and c. If all three of these requirements are met, mark

the "yes" box to Question 5 and the partnership is not required to complete Schedules L, M–1, and M–2. For question 13, enter the number of months the partnership was in operation for the 1992 calendar year.

Page 3
Schedule K

Schedule K must be completed by all partnerships. It lists the total of all partners' shares of income, deductions, credits, etc. The partnership agreement can provide for the manner in which the partners will share each item of income, gain, loss, deduction, or credit, etc., of the partnership. If the main purpose of any provision in the partnership agreement, regarding a partner's share of any item, is to evade or avoid federal income tax, the provision will be disregarded.

Each partner is allocated his or her distributive share of any item from the partnership if a different income tax liability will result from the item being distributable to the partner separately, rather than being distributable to the partner as part of the partnership's income or loss (line 22, page 1).

Each partner's distributive share of income, deductions, credits, etc., should be reported on Schedule K–1. The line items for Schedule K are discussed in combination with the Schedule K–1 line items, later.

Page 4
Schedules L, M–1, and M–2

Partnerships do not have to complete Schedules L, M–1, or M–2 if all of the tests listed under Question 5 are met and Question 5 on page 2 is marked "Yes." The AbleBee Book Store does not meet all of the tests, so these schedules must be completed.

Schedule L

Schedule L contains the partnership's balance sheets at the beginning and end of the tax year. All information shown on the balance sheets for the AbleBee Book Store should agree with its books of account. Any differences should be reconciled and explained in a separate schedule attached to the return.

The entry for total assets at the end of the year, $45,391, is carried to Item F at the top of page 1 if Item F is required to be completed. See the instructions for Form 1065 for more information.

Schedule M–1

Schedule M–1 is the reconciliation of income per the partnership books with income per Form 1065.

Line 1. This line shows the net income per the books of $48,920. This amount is from the profit and loss account (not shown in this example).

Line 3. This line includes the guaranteed payments to partners.

Line 5. This is the total of lines 1 through 4 of $73,920.

Line 6. Included in line 6 is the $50 tax-exempt interest income from municipal bonds that is recorded on the books but is not included on Schedule K, lines 1 through 7. Each partner's share of this interest is reported on his or her Schedule K–1 on line 19.

Line 9. This line is the same as Schedule K, line 23a. It is also the same as line 5 less line 8, $73,870.

Schedule M–2

Schedule M–2 is an analysis of the partners' capital accounts. It shows the total equity of all partners in the partnership at the beginning and end of the tax year and shows the adjustments that caused any increase or decrease. The total of all the partners' capital accounts is the difference between the partnership's assets and liabilities shown on Schedule L. A partner's capital account will not necessarily represent the tax basis for an interest in the partnership.

Line 1. As of January 1, the total of the partners' capital accounts was $27,550 (Mr. Able—$14,050; Ms. Bee—$13,500). This amount should agree with the beginning balance shown on Schedule L for the partners' capital accounts.

Line 3. This is the net income per the books.

Line 5. This is the total of lines 1 through 4.

Line 6. Each partner withdrew $26,440 (totaling $52,880) from the partnership. The partners' guaranteed payments, which were actually paid, are not included in this column because they were deducted in arriving at the amount shown in line 3. Any other distributions to the partners, in cash or property other than cash, would also be included here.

Line 9. This shows the total equity of all partners as shown in the books of account as of December 31. This amount should agree with the year-end balance shown on Schedule L for the partners' capital accounts.

Item J on Schedule K–1 reflects each partner's share of the amounts shown in lines 1 through 9 of Schedule M–2.

Schedule K–1

Schedule K–1 lists each partner's share of income, deductions, credits, etc. It also shows where to report the items on the partner's individual income tax return. Illustrated is a copy of the Schedule K–1 for Frank W. Able. All information asked for at the top of Schedule K–1 must be supplied for each partner.

Since all line items on Schedule K–1 are not applicable to every partnership, a substitute Schedule K–1 may be used. See the instructions for Form 1065 for more information.

Allocation of Partnership Items

The partners' shares of income, deductions, etc., are shown next in lines 1 through 22, Schedule K, and lines 1 through 23, Schedule K–1.

Income (Loss)

Line 1. This line on Schedule K–1 shows Able's share, $24,685, of the income from the partnership shown on line 22, page 1. The total amount of income is shown on line 1, Schedule K.

Line 4b. Dividends are among the items that must be separately stated and not included in the income (loss) of the partnership on Form 1065, page 1, line 22. This line on Schedule K–1 shows Able's share, $75. This line on Schedule K shows the total dividends of $150.

Line 5. This line on Schedule K–1 should show only the guaranteed payments to Able of $20,000. This line on Schedule K shows the total guaranteed payments, to all partners, of $25,000.

Deductions

Line 8. During the year, the partnership made a $650 contribution to the American Lung Association. Each partner can deduct all or part of his or her share of the partnership's charitable contributions on his or her individual income tax return, if the partner itemizes deductions. Able's share of the contribution, $325, is entered on line 8, Schedule K–1. This line on Schedule K shows the total contribution. For more information, see Publication 526, *Charitable Contributions*.

Investment Interest

Lines 12a–12b. The partnership's total interest on investment debt, and items of investment income and expenses, are entered on the applicable lines of Schedule K, and each partner's share is entered on Schedule K–1. For more information, see Publication 550, *Investment Income and Expenses*, and the instructions for Form 1065. This partnership did not have any investment interest expense or other investment expenses. It did have investment income as shown on line 4b, Schedule K. The total of all portfolio income, lines 4a through 4f, is shown on line 12b(1), Schedule K, and the partner's share is shown on line 12b(1), Schedule K–1.

Self-Employment Tax

Line 15a. Net earnings (loss) from self-employment are entered on Schedule K, and each individual partner's share is shown on his or her Schedule K–1. Guaranteed payments are included in net earnings from self-employment. Each partner uses his or her share to figure his or her self-employment tax on Schedule SE (Form 1040), *Self-Employment Tax*.

Analysis

Lines 23a–23b (Schedule K only). An analysis must be made of the distributive items on Schedule K. This analysis is based on the type of partner. Since the AbleBee Book Store has two persons, both of whom are general partners, the entries are $73,870 on lines 23a and 23b(1), column (b)i.

Form **1065**		U.S. Partnership Return of Income		OMB No. 1545-0099

Form **1065**
Department of the Treasury
Internal Revenue Service

U.S. Partnership Return of Income

For calendar year 1992, or tax year beginning .... , 1992, and ending .... , 19 .... .
▶ **See separate instructions.**

OMB No. 1545-0099

1992

A Principal business activity
Retail

B Principal product or service
Books

C Business code number
5942

Use the IRS label. Otherwise, please print or type.

Name of partnership
ABLEBEE Book Store

Number, street, and room or suite no. (If a P.O. box, see page 9 of the instructions.)
334 West Main Street

City or town, state, and ZIP code
Orange, MD 20904

D Employer identification number
10-9876543

E Date business started
10/1/78

F Total assets (see Specific Instructions)
$ 45,391

G Check applicable boxes: **(1)** ☐ Initial return **(2)** ☐ Final return **(3)** ☐ Change in address **(4)** ☐ Amended return
H Check accounting method: **(1)** ☐ Cash **(2)** ☑ Accrual **(3)** ☐ Other (specify) ▶ ....
I Number of partners in this partnership . . . . ▶ 2

Caution: *Include **only** trade or business income and expenses on lines 1a through 22 below. See the instructions for more information.*

Income

1a Gross receipts or sales	**1a**	409,465		
b Less returns and allowances. . . .	**1b**	3,365	**1c**	406,100
2 Cost of goods sold (Schedule A, line 8) . . .			**2**	267,641
3 Gross profit. Subtract line 2 from line 1c. . .			**3**	138,459
4 Ordinary income (loss) from other partnerships and fiduciaries (attach schedule) .			**4**	
5 Net farm profit (loss) (attach Schedule F (Form 1040)) . . .			**5**	
6 Net gain (loss) from Form 4797, Part II, line 20. . .			**6**	
7 Other income (loss) (see instructions) (attach schedule) .			**7**	559
8 **Total income (loss).** Combine lines 3 through 7 . . .			**8**	139,018

Deductions (see instructions for limitations)

9a Salaries and wages (other than to partners). . .	**9a**	29,350		
b Less jobs credit	**9b**	0	**9c**	29,350
10 Guaranteed payments to partners . . .			**10**	25,000
11 Repairs			**11**	1,125
12 Bad debts			**12**	250
13 Rent			**13**	20,000
14 Taxes			**14**	3,295
15 Interest			**15**	1,451
16a Depreciation (see instructions) . . .	**16a**	1,174		
b Less depreciation reported on Schedule A and elsewhere on return	**16b**		**16c**	1,174
17 Depletion (**Do not deduct oil and gas depletion.**) . . .			**17**	
18 Retirement plans, etc. . . .			**18**	
19 Employee benefit programs . . .			**19**	
20 Other deductions (attach schedule) . . .			**20**	8,003
21 **Total deductions.** Add the amounts shown in the far right column for lines 9c through 20 .			**21**	89,648
22 **Ordinary income (loss)** from trade or business activities. Subtract line 21 from line 8 . .			**22**	49,370

Please Sign Here

Under penalties of perjury, I declare that I have examined this return, including accompanying schedules and statements, and to the best of my knowledge and belief, it is true, correct, and complete. Declaration of preparer (other than general partner) is based on all information of which preparer has any knowledge.

Signature of general partner: *Frank Able*
Date: 3-12-93

Paid Preparer's Use Only

Preparer's signature ▶		Date	Check if self-employed ▶ ☐	Preparer's social security no.
Firm's name (or yours if self-employed) and address ▶			E.I. No. ▶	
			ZIP code ▶	

For Paperwork Reduction Act Notice, see page 1 of separate instructions. Cat. No. 11390Z Form **1065** (1992)

Schedule A   **Cost of Goods Sold**

1	Inventory at beginning of year	1	18,125
2	Purchases less cost of items withdrawn for personal use	2	268,741
3	Cost of labor	3	0
4	Additional section 263A costs (see instructions) *(attach schedule)*	4	0
5	Other costs *(attach schedule)*.	5	0
6	**Total.** Add lines 1 through 5	6	286,866
7	Inventory at end of year	7	19,225
8	**Cost of goods sold.** Subtract line 7 from line 6. Enter here and on page 1, line 2	8	267,641

9a   Check all methods used for valuing closing inventory:

    (i) ☐ Cost

    (ii) ☑ Lower of cost or market as described in Regulations section 1.471-4

    (iii) ☐ Writedown of "subnormal" goods as described in Regulations section 1.471-2(c)

    (iv) ☐ Other (specify method used and attach explanation) ▶ ....

   b Check this box if the LIFO inventory method was adopted this tax year for any goods *(if checked, attach Form 970)*   ▶ ☐

   c Do the rules of section 263A (for property produced or acquired for resale) apply to the partnership? . . ☐ **Yes** ☑ **No**

   d Was there any change in determining quantities, cost, or valuations between opening and closing inventory? ☐ **Yes** ☑ **No**

     If "Yes," attach explanation.

Schedule B   **Other Information**

		Yes	No
1	Is this partnership a limited partnership?		✔
2	Are any partners in this partnership also partnerships?		✔
3	Is this partnership a partner in another partnership?		✔
4	Is this partnership subject to the consolidated audit procedures of sections 6221 through 6233? If "Yes," see **Designation of Tax Matters Partner** below	✔	
5	Does this partnership meet **ALL THREE** of the following requirements?		
a	The partnership's total receipts for the tax year were less than $250,000;		
b	The partnership's total assets at the end of the tax year were less than $250,000; **AND**		
c	Schedules K-1 are filed with the return and furnished to the partners on or before the due date (including extensions) for the partnership return.		
	If "Yes," the partnership is not required to complete Schedules L, M-1, and M-2; Item F on page 1 of Form 1065; or Item J on Schedule K-1		✔
6	Does this partnership have any foreign partners?		✔
7	Is this partnership a publicly traded partnership as defined in section 469(k)(2)?		✔
8	Has this partnership filed, or is it required to file, **Form 8264,** Application for Registration of a Tax Shelter? .		✔
9	At any time during calendar year 1992, did the partnership have an interest in or a signature or other authority over a financial account in a foreign country (such as a bank account, securities account, or other financial account)? (See the instructions for exceptions and filing requirements for form TD F 90-22.1.) If "Yes," enter the name of the foreign country. ▶		✔
10	Was the partnership the grantor of, or transferor to, a foreign trust that existed during the current tax year, whether or not the partnership or any partner has any beneficial interest in it? If "Yes," you may have to file Forms 3520, 3520-A, or 926		✔
11	Was there a distribution of property or a transfer (e.g., by sale or death) of a partnership interest during the tax year? If "Yes," you may elect to adjust the basis of the partnership's assets under section 754 by attaching the statement described under **Elections** on page 5 of the instructions		✔
12	Was this partnership in operation at the end of 1992?	✔	
13	How many months in 1992 was this partnership actively operated? ▶ _12_		

Designation of Tax Matters Partner (See instructions.)

Enter below the general partner designated as the tax matters partner (TMP) for the tax year of this return:

Name of designated TMP ▶	Identifying number of TMP ▶
Address of designated TMP ▶	

Schedule K	Partners' Shares of Income, Credits, Deductions, Etc.		
	(a) Distributive share items		**(b) Total amount**

Income (Loss)	**1** Ordinary income (loss) from trade or business activities (page 1, line 22)	**1**		49,370
	2 Net income (loss) from rental real estate activities (*attach Form 8825*)	**2**		
	3a Gross income from other rental activities	**3a**		
	b Expenses from other rental activities(*attach schedule*)	**3b**		
	c Net income (loss) from other rental activities. Subtract line 3b from line 3a	**3c**		
	4 Portfolio income (loss) (see instructions): **a** Interest income	**4a**		
	b Dividend income	**4b**		150
	c Royalty income	**4c**		
	d Net short-term capital gain (loss) (*attach Schedule D (Form 1065)*)	**4d**		
	e Net long-term capital gain (loss) (*attach Schedule D (Form 1065)*)	**4e**		
	f Other portfolio income (loss) (*attach schedule*)	**4f**		
	5 Guaranteed payments to partners	**5**		25,000
	6 Net gain (loss) under section 1231 (other than due to casualty or theft) (*attach Form 4797*)	**6**		
	7 Other income (loss) (*attach schedule*)	**7**		
Deductions	**8** Charitable contributions (see instructions) (*attach schedule*)	**8**		650
	9 Section 179 expense deduction (*attach Form 4562*)	**9**		
	10 Deductions related to portfolio income (see instructions) (itemize)	**10**		
	11 Other deductions (*attach schedule*)	**11**		
Investment Interest	**12a** Interest expense on investment debts	**12a**		
	b (1) Investment income included on lines 4a through 4f above	**12b(1)**		150
	(2) Investment expenses included on line 10 above	**12b(2)**		
Credits	**13a** Credit for income tax withheld	**13a**		
	b Low-income housing credit (see instructions):			
	(1) From partnerships to which section 42(j)(5) applies for property placed in service before 1990	**13b(1)**		
	(2) Other than on line 13b(1) for property placed in service before 1990	**13b(2)**		
	(3) From partnerships to which section 42(j)(5) applies for property placed in service after 1989	**13b(3)**		
	(4) Other than on line 13b(3) for property placed in service after 1989	**13b(4)**		
	c Qualified rehabilitation expenditures related to rental real estate activities (*attach Form 3468*)	**13c**		
	d Credits (other than credits shown on lines 13b and 13c) related to rental real estate activities (see instructions)	**13d**		
	e Credits related to other rental activities (see instructions)	**13e**		
	14 Other credits (see instructions)	**14**		
Self-Employment	**15a** Net earnings (loss) from self-employment	**15a**		74,370
	b Gross farming or fishing income	**15b**		
	c Gross nonfarm income	**15c**		
Adjustments and Tax Preference Items	**16a** Depreciation adjustment on property placed in service after 1986	**16a**		
	b Adjusted gain or loss	**16b**		
	c Depletion (other than oil and gas)	**16c**		
	d (1) Gross income from oil, gas, and geothermal properties	**16d(1)**		
	(2) Deductions allocable to oil, gas, and geothermal properties	**16d(2)**		
	e Other adjustments and tax preference items (*attach schedule*)	**16e**		
Foreign Taxes	**17a** Type of income ▶ .... **b** Foreign country or U.S. possession ▶			
	c Total gross income from sources outside the United States (*attach schedule*)	**17c**		
	d Total applicable deductions and losses (*attach schedule*)	**17d**		
	e Total foreign taxes (check one): ▶ ☐ Paid ☐ Accrued	**17e**		
	f Reduction in taxes available for credit (*attach schedule*)	**17f**		
	g Other foreign tax information (*attach schedule*)	**17g**		
Other	**18a** Total expenditures to which a section 59(e) election may apply	**18a**		
	b Type of expenditures ▶			
	19 Tax-exempt interest income	**19**		50
	20 Other tax-exempt income	**20**		
	21 Nondeductible expenses	**21**		
	22 Other items and amounts required to be reported separately to partners (see instructions) (*attach schedule*)			

Analysis	**23a** Income (loss). Combine lines 1 through 7 in column (b). From the result, subtract the sum of lines 8 through 12a, 17e, and 18a	**23a**	73,870

		(b) Individual				
b Analysis by type of partner:	**(a)** Corporate	i. Active	ii. Passive	**(c)** Partnership	**(d)** Exempt organization	**(e)** Nominee/Other
(1) General partners		73,870				
(2) Limited partners						

Caution: *If Question 5 of Schedule B is answered "Yes," the partnership is not required to complete Schedules L, M-1, and M-2.*

Schedule L　　Balance Sheets

Assets	Beginning of tax year (a)	(b)	End of tax year (c)	(d)
1 Cash		3,455		3,350
2a Trade notes and accounts receivable	7,150		10,990	
b Less allowance for bad debts		7,150		10,990
3 Inventories		18,125		19,225
4 U.S. government obligations				
5 Tax-exempt securities		1,000		1,000
6 Other current assets (attach schedule) . . .				
7 Mortgage and real estate loans				
8 Other investments (attach schedule)		1,000		1,000
9a Buildings and other depreciable assets . . .	15,000		15,000	
b Less accumulated depreciation	4,000	11,000	5,174	9,826
10a Depletable assets				
b Less accumulated depletion				
11 Land (net of any amortization)				
12a Intangible assets (amortizable only) . . .				
b Less accumulated amortization				
13 Other assets (attach schedule)				
14 **Total** assets		41,730		45,391
Liabilities and Capital				
15 Accounts payable		10,180		10,462
16 Mortgages, notes, bonds payable in less than 1 year .		4,000		3,600
17 Other current liabilities (attach schedule) . .				
18 All nonrecourse loans				
19 Mortgages, notes, bonds payable in 1 year or more .				7,739
20 Other liabilities (attach schedule)				
21 Partners' capital accounts		27,550		23,590
22 **Total** liabilities and capital		41,730		45,391

Schedule M-1　　Reconciliation of Income (Loss) per Books With Income (Loss) per Return (see instructions)

1 Net income (loss) per books	48,920	6 Income recorded on books this year not included on Schedule K, lines 1 through 7 (itemize):
2 Income included on Schedule K, lines 1 through 4, 6, and 7, not recorded on books this year (itemize):		a Tax-exempt interest $ 50
3 Guaranteed payments (other than health insurance)	25,000	7 Deductions included on Schedule K, lines 1 through 12a, 17e, and 18a, not charged against book income this year (itemize):
4 Expenses recorded on books this year not included on Schedule K, lines 1 through 12a, 17e, and 18a (itemize): a Depreciation $ .... b Travel and entertainment $		a Depreciation $ ....
		8 Total of lines 6 and 7 50
5 Total of lines 1 through 4	73,920	9 Income (loss) (Schedule K, line 23a). Subtract line 8 from line 5 73,870

Schedule M-2　　Analysis of Partners' Capital Accounts

1 Balance at beginning of year	27,550	6 Distributions: a Cash 52,880
2 Capital contributed during year		b Property . . . . .
3 Net income (loss) per books	48,920	7 Other decreases (itemize): ....
4 Other increases (itemize):		....
		8 Total of lines 6 and 7 52,880
5 Total of lines 1 through 4	76,470	9 Balance at end of year. Subtract line 8 from line 5 23,590

SCHEDULE K-1
(Form 1065)
Department of the Treasury
Internal Revenue Service

Partner's Share of Income, Credits, Deductions, Etc.

▶ See separate instructions.

For calendar year 1992 or tax year beginning ____ , 1992, and ending ____ , 19 ____

OMB No. 1545-0099

1992

Partner's identifying number ▶ 123-00-6789 | Partnership's identifying number ▶ 10-9876543

Partner's name, address, and ZIP code

Frank W. Able
10 Green St.
Orange, MD 20904

Partnership's name, address, and ZIP code

Able Bee Book Store
334 West Main St.
Orange, MD 20904

A Is this partner a general partner? . . . ☑ Yes ☐ No
B Partner's share of liabilities (see instructions):
Nonrecourse . . . . $ ____
Qualified nonrecourse financing . . $ ____
Other . . . . $ 10,900
C What type of entity is this partner? ▶ Individual
D Is this partner a ☑ domestic or a ☐ foreign partner?
E IRS Center where partnership filed return: Philadelphia

F Enter partner's percentage of:

	(i) Before change or termination	(ii) End of year
Profit sharing	____ %	50 %
Loss sharing	____ %	50 %
Ownership of capital . . .	____ %	50 %

G(1) Tax shelter registration number . ▶ N/A
(2) Type of tax shelter ▶ N/A
H Check here if this partnership is a publicly traded partnership as defined in section 469(k)(2) . . . . ☐
I Check applicable boxes: **(1)** ☐ Final K-1 **(2)** ☐ Amended K-1

J Analysis of partner's capital account:

(a) Capital account at beginning of year	(b) Capital contributed during year	(c) Partner's share of lines 3, 4, and 7, Form 1065, Schedule M-2	(d) Withdrawals and distributions	(e) Capital account at end of year (combine columns (a) through (d))
14,050		24,460	(26,440)	12,070

		(a) Distributive share item		(b) Amount	(c) 1040 filers enter the amount in column (b) on:
Income (Loss)	**1**	Ordinary income (loss) from trade or business activities . . .	**1**	24,685	⎱ See Partner's Instructions for Schedule K-1 (Form 1065).
	2	Net income (loss) from rental real estate activities	**2**		
	3	Net income (loss) from other rental activities	**3**		
	4	Portfolio income (loss):			
	a	Interest	**4a**		Sch. B, Part I, line 1
	b	Dividends	**4b**	75	Sch. B, Part II, line 5
	c	Royalties	**4c**		Sch. E, Part I, line 4
	d	Net short-term capital gain (loss)	**4d**		Sch. D, line 5, col. (f) or (g)
	e	Net long-term capital gain (loss)	**4e**		Sch. D, line 13, col. (f) or (g)
	f	Other portfolio income (loss) (attach schedule)	**4f**		(Enter on applicable line of your return.)
	5	Guaranteed payments to partner	**5**	20,000	⎱ See Partner's Instructions for Schedule K-1 (Form 1065).
	6	Net gain (loss) under section 1231 (other than due to casualty or theft)	**6**		
	7	Other income (loss) (attach schedule)	**7**		(Enter on applicable line of your return.)
Deductions	**8**	Charitable contributions (see instructions) (attach schedule) .	**8**	325	Sch. A, line 13 or 14
	9	Section 179 expense deduction	**9**		⎱ See Partner's Instructions for Schedule K-1 (Form 1065).
	10	Deductions related to portfolio income (attach schedule) . .	**10**		
	11	Other deductions (attach schedule)	**11**		
Investment Interest	**12a**	Interest expense on investment debts	**12a**		Form 4952, line 1
	b	**(1)** Investment income included on lines 4a through 4f above .	**b(1)**	75	⎱ See Partner's Instructions for Schedule K-1 (Form 1065).
		(2) Investment expenses included on line 10 above	**b(2)**		
Credits	**13a**	Credit for income tax withheld	**13a**		⎱ See Partner's Instructions for Schedule K-1 (Form 1065).
	b	Low-income housing credit:			
		(1) From section 42(j)(5) partnerships for property placed in service before 1990	**b(1)**		
		(2) Other than on line 13b(1) for property placed in service before 1990	**b(2)**		
		(3) From section 42(j)(5) partnerships for property placed in service after 1989	**b(3)**		Form 8586, line 5
		(4) Other than on line 13b(3) for property placed in service after 1989	**b(4)**		
	c	Qualified rehabilitation expenditures related to rental real estate activities (see instructions)	**13c**		
	d	Credits (other than credits shown on lines 13b and 13c) related to rental real estate activities (see instructions)	**13d**		⎱ See Partner's Instructions for Schedule K-1 (Form 1065).
	e	Credits related to other rental activities (see instructions) . .	**13e**		
	14	Other credits (see instructions)	**14**		

For Paperwork Reduction Act Notice, see Instructions for Form 1065. | Cat. No. 11394R | **Schedule K-1 (Form 1065) 1992**

(a) Distributive share item		(b) Amount	(c) 1040 filers enter the amount in column (b) on:
Self-employment	**15a** Net earnings (loss) from self-employment **15a**	44,685	Sch. SE, Section A or B
	b Gross farming or fishing income. **15b**		⎰ See Partner's Instructions for ⎱
	c Gross nonfarm income. **15c**		⎱ Schedule K-1 (Form 1065). ⎰
Adjustments and Tax Preference Items	**16a** Depreciation adjustment on property placed in service after 1986 **16a**		(See Partner's Instructions for Schedule K-1 (Form 1065) and Instructions for Form 6251.)
	b Adjusted gain or loss **16b**		
	c Depletion (other than oil and gas) **16c**		
	d (1) Gross income from oil, gas, and geothermal properties . . **d(1)**		
	(2) Deductions allocable to oil, gas, and geothermal properties **d(2)**		
	e Other adjustments and tax preference items (attach schedule) **16e**		
Foreign Taxes	**17a** Type of income ▶		Form 1116, Check boxes
	b Name of foreign country or U.S. possession ▶		
	c Total gross income from sources outside the United States (attach schedule).. **17c**		⎰ Form 1116, Part I
	d Total applicable deductions and losses (attach schedule) . **17d**		
	e Total foreign taxes (check one): ▶ ☐ Paid ☐ Accrued . . **17e**		Form 1116, Part II
	f Reduction in taxes available for credit (attach schedule) . . . **17f**		Form 1116, Part III
	g Other foreign tax information (attach schedule) **17g**		See Instructions for Form 1116.
Other	**18a** Total expenditures to which a section 59(e) election may apply **18a**		See Partner's Instructions for Schedule K-1 (Form 1065).
	b Type of expenditures ▶		
	19 Tax-exempt interest income **19**	25	Form 1040, line 8b
	20 Other tax-exempt income. **20**		⎰ See Partner's Instructions for ⎱
	21 Nondeductible expenses · **21**		⎱ Schedule K-1 (Form 1065). ⎰
	22 Recapture of low-income housing credit:		
	a From section 42(j)(5) partnerships **22a**		⎰ Form 8611, line 8
	b Other than on line 22a. **22b**		

23 Supplemental information required to be reported separately to each partner (attach additional schedules if more space is needed):

Supplemental Information

....

....

....

....

....

....

....

....

....

....

....

....

....

....

....

....

Form 1120-A (Short-Form)

Rose Flower Shop, Inc., is the corporation for which the sample return is filled out. Rose Flower Shop operates a business that sells fresh cut flowers and plants. It uses an accrual method of accounting and files its returns on the calendar year.

A corporation can file Form 1120-A if it has gross receipts under $500,000, total income under $500,000, total assets under $500,000, and meets certain other requirements. Since Rose Flower Shop met all these requirements for 1992, it filed Form 1120-A.

Page 1

When you prepare your return use the pre-addressed label sent to you by the IRS. It is designed to expedite processing and prevent errors. If you do not have a pre-addressed label, enter your corporation's name, street address, city, state, and ZIP code in the appropriate spaces on the first page. After putting the pre-addressed label at the top of the page, Rose Flower Shop proceeds to report its income and deductions.

Show the name and employer identification number of the corporation in the top margin of schedules and attachments to Form 1120-A.

Fill in all applicable items for income, deductions, tax, and payments listed on page 1. Do not alter, substitute for, or cross out the line captions on the return forms.

Line 1. Gross sales for the year totaled $248,000, using the accrual basis of accounting. After subtracting $7,500 of returned goods and allowances, line 1c shows net sales of $240,500.

Line 2. Cost of goods sold is $144,000. Compute this using the worksheet (not illustrated) in the form instructions.

Line 3. Net sales less cost of goods sold results in gross profit of $96,500.

Lines 4 through 10. Enter other items of income next. During the year, the only other item of income was taxable interest of $942, shown on line 5.

Line 11. Total income is $97,442.

Line 12. Enter the $23,000 salary of the company president.

Line 13. Enter other salaries and wages of $24,320 on line 13a. This includes only sala-

ries and wages neither included on line 12 nor deducted as part of cost of goods sold on line 2. Rose Flower Shop does not have a jobs credit, so enter $24,320 also on line 13c.

Line 16. Rent for Rose Flower Shop's store was $6,000 for the year.

Line 17. Deductible taxes totaled $3,320.

Line 18. Interest expense accrued during the year was $1,340. It does not include interest to carry tax-exempt securities. See Chapter 6 of Publication 535 for a discussion of amounts deductible as interest as well as when to take the deduction.

Line 19. During 1992, Rose Flower Shop contributed $1,820 to various charitable organizations. The $1,820 is less than the limit for deductible contributions, which is 10% of taxable income figured without the contribution deduction.

Line 22. Other deductions consist of $3,000 for advertising. If there had been several expenses included in the total, a supporting schedule would be required.

Line 23. Total of lines 12 through 22 is $62,800.

Lines 24, 25, and 26. Line 24 shows taxable income of $34,642. Since Rose Flower Shop did not have a net operating loss or special deduction, show the same amount on line 26.

Tax summary. Enter on line 27 the total tax ($5,196) from Part I, line 7, page 2. List payments against the tax on line 28. On the Rose Flower Shop return, the only payment is the four estimated tax deposits totaling $6,000. It enters this amount on lines 28b and 28d, and as a total on line 28h. The resulting overpayment is $804, which Rose Flower Shop has credited to its 1993 estimated tax. Rose Flower Shop could have the overpayment refunded.

Signature. An authorized corporate officer must sign the return.

Page 2

Part I–Tax Computation. Use the tax computation schedule in the form instructions to figure the tax on line 1. Lines 3, 5, and 6, the other taxes and credits listed on Part I, do not apply to Rose Flower Shop. Enter the tax of $5,196 on lines 1, 4, and 7.

Part II–Other Information. Answer all applicable questions. Provide the business activity

code number, business activity, and product or service information on lines (a), (b), and (c) of question 1. Purchases of $134,014 appear on line (1) of question 5a. Other costs of $9,466 appear on line (3) of question 5a. These supporting itemization is not illustrated. These costs consist of costs directly related to the sale of flowers, wreaths, and plants, such as flower pots, vases, stands, boxes, and tissue paper.

Part III–Balance Sheets. Provide comparative balance sheets for the beginning and end of the tax year. Entries in Part III should agree with amounts shown elsewhere on the return or included on a worksheet. For example, the figures for beginning and ending inventories must be the same as those appearing on the worksheet in the form instructions for cost of goods sold.

Part IV–Reconciliation of Income (Loss) per Books With Income per Return. All Form 1120-A corporate filers must complete

Part IV unless total assets on line 12, column (b) of Part III are less than $25,000. Since total assets of Rose Flower Shop exceed this amount, it completes Part IV.

To properly complete Part IV, first get additional information from your corporation's books and records. The following profit and loss account appeared in the books of Rose Flower Shop for the calendar year 1992.

Account	Debit	Credit
Gross sales		$248,000
Sales returns and allowances	$ 7,500	
Cost of goods sold	144,000	
Interest income		942
Compensation of officers	23,000	
Salaries and wages	24,320	
Rents	6,000	
Taxes	3,320	
Interest expense	1,340	
Contributions	1,820	
Advertising	3,000	
Federal income tax accrued	5,196	
Net income per books after tax	29,446	
Total	**$248,942**	**$248,942**

Part IV starts with the net income (loss) per books, after reduction for federal income tax accrued, as shown in the corporation's profit and loss account. It provides for necessary adjustments to reconcile this amount with the taxable income shown on line 24, page 1.

Line 1. $29,446 is the net income per books. It is in the profit and loss account previously as net income per books after tax.

Line 2. $5,196 is the federal income tax accrued for the tax year.

Line 8. $34,642 is the taxable income on line 24, page 1.

Form 1120-A

Form 1120-A
Department of the Treasury
Internal Revenue Service

U.S. Corporation Short-Form Income Tax Return

See separate instructions to make sure the corporation qualifies to file Form 1120-A.
For calendar year 1992 or tax year beginning ...., 1992, ending............., 19.....

OMB No. 1545-0890

1992

A Check this box if corp. is a personal service corp. (as defined in Temporary Regs. section 1.441-4T—see instructions) ▶ ☐

Use IRS label. Other-wise, please print or type.	Name Rose Flower Shop, Inc.
	Number, street, and room or suite no. (If a P.O. box, see page 6 of instructions.) 38 Superior Lane
	City or town, state, and ZIP code Fair City, MD 20715

B Employer identification number
10-2134567

C Date incorporated
7-1-82

D Total assets (see Specific Instructions)
$

E Check applicable boxes: **(1)** ☐ Initial return **(2)** ☐ Change in address
F Check method of accounting: **(1)** ☐ Cash **(2)** ☑ Accrual **(3)** ☐ Other (specify) . . ▶

Income

1a Gross receipts or sales `248,000` **b** Less returns and allowances `7,500` **c** Balance ▶		**1c**	240,500
2 Cost of goods sold (see instructions)		**2**	144,000
3 Gross profit. Subtract line 2 from line 1c		**3**	96,500
4 Domestic corporation dividends subject to the 70% deduction		**4**	
5 Interest		**5**	942
6 Gross rents		**6**	
7 Gross royalties		**7**	
8 Capital gain net income (attach Schedule D (Form 1120))		**8**	
9 Net gain or (loss) from Form 4797, Part II, line 20 (attach Form 4797)		**9**	
10 Other income (see instructions)		**10**	
11 Total income. Add lines 3 through 10 ▶		**11**	97,442

Deductions
(See instructions for limitations on deductions.)

12 Compensation of officers (see instructions)		**12**	23,000
13a Salaries and wages `24,320` **b** Less jobs credit **c** Balance ▶		**13c**	24,320
14 Repairs		**14**	
15 Bad debts		**15**	
16 Rents		**16**	6,000
17 Taxes		**17**	3,320
18 Interest		**18**	1,340
19 Charitable contributions (see instructions for 10% limitation)		**19**	1,820
20 Depreciation (attach Form 4562)	**20**		
21 Less depreciation claimed elsewhere on return	**21a**	**21b**	
22 Other deductions (attach schedule) *(Advertising)*		**22**	3,000
23 Total deductions. Add lines 12 through 22 ▶		**23**	62,800
24 Taxable income before net operating loss deduction and special deductions. Subtract line 23 from line 11		**24**	34,642
25 Less: **a** Net operating loss deduction (see instructions)	**25a**		
b Special deductions (see instructions)	**25b**	**25c**	

Tax and Payments

26 Taxable income. Subtract line 25c from line 24		**26**	34,642
27 Total tax (from page 2, Part I, line 7)		**27**	5,196
28 Payments:			
a 1991 overpayment credited to 1992	**28a**		
b 1992 estimated tax payments	**28b** `6,000`		
c Less 1992 refund applied for on Form 4466	**28c** ( ) Bal ▶ **28d** `6,000`		
e Tax deposited with Form 7004	**28e**		
f Credit from regulated investment companies (attach Form 2439)	**28f**		
g Credit for Federal tax on fuels (attach Form 4136). See instructions	**28g**		
h Total payments. Add lines 28d through 28g		**28h**	6,000
29 Estimated tax penalty (see instructions). Check if Form 2220 is attached ▶ ☐		**29**	
30 Tax due. If line 28h is smaller than the total of lines 27 and 29, enter amount owed		**30**	
31 Overpayment. If line 28h is larger than the total of lines 27 and 29, enter amount overpaid		**31**	804
32 Enter amount of line 31 you want: **Credited to 1993 estimated tax** ▶ `804` Refunded ▶		**32**	

Please Sign Here

Under penalties of perjury, I declare that I have examined this return, including accompanying schedules and statements, and to the best of my knowledge and belief, it is true, correct, and complete. Declaration of preparer (other than taxpayer) is based on all information of which preparer has any knowledge.

▶ *George Rose*	2-15-93	▶ President
Signature of officer	Date	Title

Paid Preparer's Use Only

Preparer's signature ▶		Date	Check if self-employed ▶ ☐	Preparer's social security number
Firm's name (or yours if self-employed) and address ▶			E.I. No. ▶	
			ZIP code ▶	

For Paperwork Reduction Act Notice, see page 1 of the instructions.   Cat. No. 11456E   Form **1120-A** (1992)

Part I   **Tax Computation** (See instructions.)

1	Income tax. Check this box if the corporation is a qualified personal service corporation as defined in section 448(d)(2) (see instructions on page 14) ▶ ☐	1	5,196
2a	General business credit. Check if from: ☐ Form 3800 ☐ Form 3468 ☐ Form 5884 ☐ Form 6478 ☐ Form 6765 ☐ Form 8586 ☐ Form 8830 ☐ Form 8826	2a	
b	Credit for prior year minimum tax (attach Form 8827)	2b	
3	**Total credits.** Add lines 2a and 2b	3	
4	Subtract line 3 from line 1	4	5,196
5	Recapture taxes. Check if from: ☐ Form 4255 ☐ Form 8611	5	
6	Alternative minimum tax (attach Form 4626)	6	
7	**Total tax.** Add lines 4 through 6. Enter here and on line 27, page 1	7	5,196

Part II   **Other Information** (See instructions.)

1 Refer to the list in the instructions and state the principal:
  a Business activity code no. ▶ _5995_
  b Business activity ▶ _Flower shop_
  c Product or service ▶ _Flowers_

2 Did any individual, partnership, estate, or trust at the end of the tax year own, directly or indirectly, 50% or more of the corporation's voting stock? (For rules of attribution, see section 267(c).)   ☑ Yes   ☐ No
(Schedule not illustrated)
If "Yes," attach a schedule showing name and identifying number.

3 Enter the amount of tax-exempt interest received or accrued during the tax year   ▶ |$ — 0 — |

4 Enter amount of cash distributions and the book value of property (other than cash) distributions made in this tax year   ▶ |$ — 0 — |

5a If an amount is entered on line 2, page 1, see the worksheet on page 12 for amounts to enter below:
  (1) Purchases   134,014
  (2) Additional sec. 263A costs (see instructions—attach schedule)
  (3) Other costs (attach schedule)   9,466

b Do the rules of section 263A (for property produced or acquired for resale) apply to the corporation?   ☐ Yes ☑ No

6 At any time during the 1992 calendar year, did the corporation have an interest in or a signature or other authority over a financial account in a foreign country (such as a bank account, securities account, or other financial account)? If "Yes," the corporation may have to file Form TD F 90-22.1   ☐ Yes ☑ No
If "Yes," enter the name of the foreign country ▶ _____

Part III   **Balance Sheets**

		(a) Beginning of tax year	(b) End of tax year
Assets	1 Cash	20,540	18,498
	2a Trade notes and accounts receivable		
	b Less allowance for bad debts	( )	( )
	3 Inventories	2,530	2,010
	4 U.S. government obligations	13,807	45,479
	5 Tax-exempt securities (see instructions)		
	6 Other current assets (attach schedule)		
	7 Loans to stockholders		
	8 Mortgage and real estate loans		
	9a Depreciable, depletable, and intangible assets		
	b Less accumulated depreciation, depletion, and amortization	( )	( )
	10 Land (net of any amortization)		
	11 Other assets (attach schedule)		
	12 Total assets	36,877	65,987
Liabilities and Stockholders' Equity	13 Accounts payable	6,415	6,079
	14 Other current liabilities (attach schedule)		
	15 Loans from stockholders		
	16 Mortgages, notes, bonds payable		
	17 Other liabilities (attach schedule)		
	18 Capital stock (preferred and common stock)	20,000	20,000
	19 Paid-in or capital surplus		
	20 Retained earnings	10,462	39,908
	21 Less cost of treasury stock	( )	( )
	22 Total liabilities and stockholders' equity	36,877	65,987

Part IV   **Reconciliation of Income (Loss) per Books With Income per Return** (You are not required to complete Part IV if the total assets on line 12, column (b) of Part III are less than $25,000.)

1	Net income (loss) per books	29,446	
2	Federal income tax	5,196	
3	Excess of capital losses over capital gains		
4	Income subject to tax not recorded on books this year (itemize)		
5	Expenses recorded on books this year not deducted on this return (itemize)		
6	Income recorded on books this year not included on this return (itemize)		
7	Deductions on this return not charged against book income this year (itemize)		
8	Income (line 24, page 1). Enter the sum of lines 1 through 5 less the sum of lines 6 and 7	34,642	

FORM 1120

Tentex Toys, Inc., is the corporation for which the sample return is filled out. Tentex manufactures and sells children's toys and games. It uses an accrual method of accounting and files its returns on the calendar year.

Page 1

When you prepare your return use the pre-addressed label sent to you by the IRS. It is designed to expedite processing and prevent errors. If you do not have a pre-addressed label, enter your corporation's name, street address, city, state, and ZIP code in the appropriate spaces on the first page. After putting the pre-addressed label at the top of the page, Tentex proceeds to report its income and deductions.

Show the name and employer identification number of the corporation in the top margin of schedules and attachments to Form 1120.

Fill in all applicable items for income, deductions, tax, and payments listed on page 1. Do not alter, substitute for, or cross out the line captions on the return forms.

Line 1. Gross sales, line 1a, for the year totaled $2,010,000, using the accrual basis of accounting. After subtracting returned goods and allowances of $20,000, line 1c shows net sales of $1,990,000.

Line 2. Cost of goods sold is $1,520,000. This is the total from Schedule A (line 8) on page 2.

Line 3. Net sales less cost of goods sold results in gross profit of $470,000.

Lines 4 through 10. Show other items of income next. During the year, Tentex received $10,000 of dividends from domestic corporations, $5,000 of tax-exempt interest from state bonds, and $4,000 of taxable interest. It also received $1,500 interest on its business accounts receivable. Enter the gross amount of dividends on line 4 (note you take the dividends-received deduction on line 29b). Line 5 shows total taxable interest of $5,500. Do not include tax-exempt interest in income.

Line 11. Total income is $485,500.

Line 12. Enter the salaries of $70,000 paid to company officers, listed on Schedule E. Complete Schedule E because total receipts (line 1a plus lines 4 through 10 of page 1) exceed $500,000.

Line 13. Line 13a shows other salaries and wages of $44,000. This includes only salaries and wages neither included on line 12 nor deducted as part of cost of goods sold on line 3, Schedule A on page 2. For a manufacturing company such as Tentex, this amount represents nonmanufacturing salaries and wages, such as office salaries. See Chapter 2 of Publication 535 for a discussion of salaries and wages.

Tentex is eligible for a $6,000 jobs credit, figured on Form 5884 (not illustrated). Reduce the deduction for salaries and wages by the $6,000 credit on line 13b . Enter the balance, $38,000, on line 13c.

Line 14. Repairs include only payments for items that do not add to the value of the assets repaired or substantially increase their useful lives. Repairs total $800. See Chapter 13 of Publication 535 for information on repairs, improvements, and replacements.

Line 15. Tentex uses the specific charge-off method of accounting for bad debts. Actual accounts written off during the year total $1,600. See Chapter 12 of Publication 535 for information on bad debt deductions.

Line 16. Rent for Tentex's office facilities is $9,200 for the year.

Line 17. Deductible taxes are $15,000.

Line 18. Interest expense accrued during the year is $27,200. This includes interest both on debts for business operations and debts to carry investments. Do not include interest to carry tax-exempt securities. See Chapter 6 of Publication 535 for a discussion of deductible interest.

Line 19. During 1992, Tentex contributed $11,400 to the United Community Fund and $12,600 to the State University scholarship fund. The total, $24,000, is more than the limit for deductible contributions, which is 10% of taxable income figured without the contribution deduction and special deduction entered on line 29b. The amount allowable on line 19 is $23,150. Carry the excess, $850, not deductible this year, over as explained earlier under *Charitable Contributions*. Also, during 1992, Tentex made nondeductible contributions of $500.

Lines 20 and 21. Depreciation from Form 4562 (not illustrated) is $17,600. Enter it on line 20. Reduce this amount by the depreciation claimed on Schedule A ($12,400) and enter it on line 21a. Deduct the balance ($5,200) on line 21b since it is the depreciation on the assets used in the indirect operations of the business.

Line 22. Tentex does not have a depletion deduction. See Chapter 11 of Publication 535.

Line 23. Advertising expense is $8,700.

Lines 24 and 25. Tentex does not have a profit-sharing, stock bonus, pension, or annuity plan. See Chapter 4 of Publication 535.

Line 26. Other business deductions total $78,300. This includes miscellaneous office expenses, sales commissions, legal fees, etc. Attach a schedule itemizing these expenses to the return, even though this example does not show one.

Line 27. Total of lines 12 through 26 is $277,150.

Lines 28, 29, and 30. Taxable income on line 28 is $208,350. Since Tentex did not have a net operating loss, its only entry on line 29 is

the dividends-received deduction of $8,000 from Schedule C, page 2. Enter this amount on lines 29b and 29c. Taxable income on line 30 is $200,350.

Tax summary. Enter on line 31 the total tax ($55,387) from Schedule J. Line 32 has the payments against the tax. On the Tentex return, the only credit is the four estimated tax deposits totaling $69,117. Enter this amount on lines 32b, 32d, and 32h. The resulting overpayment is $13,730, which Tentex chooses to have credited to its 1993 estimated tax. Tentex could have the overpayment refunded.

Signature. An authorized corporate officer must manually sign the return.

Page 2

Schedule A. Use Schedule A to report your cost of goods sold. This figure is beginning inventory, plus merchandise bought or produced during the year, less ending inventory. Because Tentex is a manufacturer, it must account for its costs of manufacturing as part of cost of goods sold. It valued goods on hand at the beginning of the year at $126,000, using the lower of cost or market.

Add cost of goods manufactured during the year to beginning inventory. This cost consists of three items: direct materials, direct labor, and overhead. List material costs of $1,127,100 on line 2. This includes subcontracted parts as well as raw materials.

Salaries and wages on line 3 is $402,000. This amount includes wages paid to production-line workers and the part of supervisory salaries attributable to actual production of goods. It also includes 30% of the salaries paid to officers. Do not include payments already deducted on line 12 or 13 of page 1.

The $40,000 on line 4 is for indirect general administration costs. Other costs of $123,300 appear on line 5. These costs include factory overhead such as electricity, fuel, water, small tools, and depreciation on production-line machinery. This example does not show the supporting itemization. Note that $12,400 is depreciation on the assets used in the direct operations of the business.

Line 9. Check all applicable boxes.

Schedule C. Dividend income is $10,000, all of which qualified for the 80% dividends-received deduction, line 2, because Tentex is a 20%-or-more owner. Show total dividends both here and on line 4 of page 1. Figure the total dividends-received deduction here and enter it on line 29b of page 1.

Schedule E. Complete this schedule only if your total receipts (line 1a plus lines 4 through 10 of page 1) are $500,000 or more. (Tentex meets this requirement.) Since Tentex has only three officers, these are the only entries on the schedule. Include here only compensation for services rendered. Do not include dividends on stock held by the corporate officers.

Page 3

Schedule J. Use Schedule J to figure the corporation's tax. Applying the rates to Tentex's taxable income of $200,350 results in income tax of $61,387. Decrease this amount by the jobs credit of $6,000, resulting in a total tax of $55,387.

Figure the jobs credit by multiplying $15,000 of wages paid to five qualified employees in their first year of employment by the 40% rate. They are certified members of a targeted group. Each earned $3,000 in salary in 1992. Tentex files Form 5884 (not illustrated) with its return to support this credit.

Other taxes and credits listed on Schedule J do not apply to Tentex for 1992.

Schedule K. Answer all applicable questions.

Page 4

Schedule L. Provide comparative balance sheets for the beginning and end of the tax year. Entries on this page should agree with amounts shown elsewhere on the return. For example, the figures for beginning and ending inventories must be the same as those appearing on Schedule A, page 2. Note that the appropriated retained earnings of Tentex increased from $30,000 to $40,000 during the year, due to the setting aside of $10,000 as a reserve for contingencies. Tentex took this amount out of unappropriated retained earnings, as shown on Schedule M-2.

Tentex completes Schedules M-1 and M-2 because the amount of total assets (line 15, column (d), Schedule L) is over $25,000. To properly complete these schedules, you need additional information from the books and records. The following profit and loss account appeared in the books of Tentex for the calendar year 1992.

Account	Debit	Credit
Gross sales		$2,010,000
Sales returns and allowances	$ 20,000	
Cost of goods sold ...	1,520,000	
Dividends received ...		10,000
Interest income:		
On state bonds	$ 5,000	
Taxable	5,500	10,500
Proceeds of life insurance		9,500
Premiums on life insurance	9,500	
Compensation of officers	70,000	
Salaries and wages–indirect	44,000	
Repairs	800	
Bad debts	1,600	
Rental expense	9,200	
Taxes	15,000	

	Debit	Credit
Interest expense:		
On loan to buy tax-exempt bonds	$ 850	
Other	27,200	28,050
Contributions:		
Deductible $24,000		
Nondeductible 500		24,500
Depreciation–indirect		3,580
Advertising		8,700
Other expenses of operation		78,300
Loss on securities ...		3,600
Federal income tax accrued		55,387
Net income per books after tax		147,783
Total	**$2,040,000**	**$2,040,000**

Tentex analyzed its retained earnings and the following appeared in this account on its books:

Item	Debit	Credit
Balance, January 1, 1992		$238,000
Net profit (before federal income tax)		203,170
Reserve for contingencies	$ 10,000	
Income tax accrued for 1992	55,387	
Dividends paid during 1992	65,000	
Refund of 1990 income tax		18,000
Balance, December 31, 1992	328,783	
Total	**$459,170**	**$459,170**

Schedule M-1. Schedule M-1 starts with the net income per books, after allowance of federal income tax accrued, as shown in the corporation's profit and loss account. It provides for necessary adjustments to reconcile this amount with the taxable income shown on line 28, page 1.

Line 1. $147,783 is the net income per books. It appears in the profit and loss account as net income per books after tax.

Line 2. $55,387 is the federal income tax accrued for the tax year.

Line 3. $3,600 is the excess of capital losses over capital gains. The net loss is from the sale of securities.

Line 4. This would show all income and credits included in income subject to tax but not recorded on the books for this year. This can happen if the corporation valued assets on its books at an amount greater than that used for tax purposes. When it has a sale of such assets, the gain included in taxable income is greater than that recorded on the books. It shows the difference here.

Line 5. Tentex shows expenses recorded on its books that it does not deduct. The $850 listed on line 5b is for contributions over the 10% limit. Tentex itemizes the remaining nondeductible expenses on a statement (not illustrated) attached to the return. These include the following:

Premiums paid on term life insurance on corporate officers		$ 9,500
Interest paid to purchase tax-exempt securities		850
Nondeductible contributions		500
Reduction of salaries by jobs credit		6,000
Total		**$16,850**

Line 6. This is the total of lines 1 through 5.

Line 7. This shows nontaxable income recorded on the corporation's books during the year that is not on the return. This total, $14,500, includes insurance proceeds of $9,500 and interest on state bonds of $5,000.

Line 8. This includes all deductions claimed for tax purposes but not recorded in the corporation's books. Tentex enters $1,620 on line 8a. This is the difference between depreciation claimed on the tax return and the corporation's books. If the corporation had other deductions to itemize on this line but not enough space, it would attach an itemized statement to the return.

Line 9. $16,120 is the total of lines 7 and 8.

Line 10. The difference, $208,350, between lines 6 and 9 must agree with line 28, page 1.

Schedule M-2. Schedule M-2 analyzes the unappropriated retained earnings as shown in Schedule L, the corporation's balance sheets.

Line 1. This is from line 25 of Schedule L for the beginning of the tax year. Tentex enters $238,000.

Line 2. This is the net income per books (after federal income tax), $147,783.

Line 3. This shows all other increases to retained earnings. Enter the $18,000 refund of 1990 income tax.

Line 4. This is the total of lines 1, 2, and 3.

Line 5. This includes all distributions to shareholders charged to retained earnings during the tax year. Enter the $65,000 dividends paid.

Line 6. This shows any decreases (other than those on Line 5) in unappropriated retained earnings. These decreases are not deductible on the tax return at the time of the appropriation, but a deduction may be allowable on a later return. A common example is amounts set aside for contingencies. A customer was injured on company property during 1992 and the company retained an attorney. Tentex set up a contingent liability of $10,000 for the customer's claim. If they settle the claim during 1993 for $5,000 and the attorney's fee is $2,500, Tentex charges $7,500 to the retained earnings (appropriated). It deducts $7,500 in arriving at taxable income for 1993. Another common example of items entered on this line is the payment of prior year's federal tax. Attach a schedule to the return listing all items taken into account for the amount shown on this line.

Line 7. This is the total of lines 5 and 6.

Line 8. $328,783 is Tentex's retained earnings at the end of its tax return year. It determined this figure by subtracting the total on line 7 from the total on line 4. This figure must agree with the amount on Schedule L for the end of the tax year.

Form **1120**	**U.S. Corporation Income Tax Return**	OMB No. 1545-0123
Department of the Treasury Internal Revenue Service	For calendar year 1992 or tax year beginning ...., 1992, ending ...., 19 ... ▶ **Instructions are separate. See page 1 for Paperwork Reduction Act Notice.**	19**92**

A Check if a:	Use IRS label. Other-wise, please print or type.	Name Tentex Toys, Inc.	B Employer identification number 10-0395674
(1) Consolidated return (attach Form 851) ☐		Number, street, and room or suite no. (If a P.O. box, see page 6 of instructions.) 36 Division St.	C Date incorporated 3-1-72
(2) Personal holding co. (attach Sch. PH) ☐			
(3) Personal service corp. (as defined in Temporary Regs. sec. 1.441-4T—see instructions) ☐		City or town, state, and ZIP code Anytown, IL 60930	D Total assets (see Specific Instructions) $ 879,417

E Check applicable boxes: (1) ☐ Initial return (2) ☐ Final return (3) ☐ Change in address

Income

1a	Gross receipts or sales 2,010,000	**b** Less returns and allowances 20,000	**c** Bal ▶	1c	1,990,000
2	Cost of goods sold (Schedule A, line 8)		2	1,520,000
3	Gross profit. Subtract line 2 from line 1c		3	470,000
4	Dividends (Schedule C, line 19)		4	10,000
5	Interest		5	5,500
6	Gross rents		6	
7	Gross royalties		7	
8	Capital gain net income (attach Schedule D (Form 1120))		8	
9	Net gain or (loss) from Form 4797, Part II, line 20 (attach Form 4797)		9	
10	Other income (see instructions—attach schedule)		10	
11	**Total income.** Add lines 3 through 10 ▶		11	485,000

Deductions (See instructions for limitations on deductions.)

12	Compensation of officers (Schedule E, line 4)			12	70,000
13a	Salaries and wages 44,000	**b** Less jobs credit 6,000	**c** Balance ▶	13c	38,000
14	Repairs			14	800
15	Bad debts			15	1,600
16	Rents			16	9,200
17	Taxes			17	15,000
18	Interest			18	27,200
19	Charitable contributions (see instructions for 10% limitation)			19	23,150
20	Depreciation (attach Form 4562)	20	17,600		
21	Less depreciation claimed on Schedule A and elsewhere on return	21a	12,400	21b	5,200
22	Depletion			22	
23	Advertising			23	8,700
24	Pension, profit-sharing, etc., plans			24	
25	Employee benefit programs			25	
26	Other deductions (attach schedule)			26	78,300
27	**Total deductions.** Add lines 12 through 26 ▶			27	277,150
28	Taxable income before net operating loss deduction and special deductions. Subtract line 27 from line 11			28	208,350
29	**Less:** **a** Net operating loss deduction (see instructions)	29a			
	b Special deductions (Schedule C, line 20)	29b	8,000	29c	8,000

Tax and Payments

30	**Taxable income.** Subtract line 29c from line 28			30	200,350
31	**Total tax** (Schedule J, line 10)			31	55,387
32	**Payments: a** 1991 overpayment credited to 1992	32a			
b	1992 estimated tax payments	32b	69,117		
c	Less 1992 refund applied for on Form 4466	32c ( )	**d** Bal ▶	32d	69,117
e	Tax deposited with Form 7004			32e	
f	Credit from regulated investment companies (attach Form 2439)			32f	
g	Credit for Federal tax on fuels (attach Form 4136). See instructions			32g	
				32h	69,117
33	Estimated tax penalty (see instructions). Check if Form 2220 is attached ▶ ☐			33	
34	**Tax due.** If line 32h is smaller than the total of lines 31 and 33, enter amount owed			34	
35	**Overpayment.** If line 32h is larger than the total of lines 31 and 33, enter amount overpaid			35	13,730
36	Enter amount of line 35 you want: **Credited to 1993 estimated tax** ▶ 13,730 **Refunded** ▶			36	

Please Sign Here

Under penalties of perjury, I declare that I have examined this return, including accompanying schedules and statements, and to the best of my knowledge and belief, it is true, correct, and complete. Declaration of preparer (other than taxpayer) is based on all information of which preparer has any knowledge.

▶ James O. Barclay Signature of officer | ▶ 3-7-93 Date | ▶ President Title

Paid Preparer's Use Only

Preparer's signature ▶	Date	Check if self-employed ☐	Preparer's social security number
Firm's name (or yours if self-employed) and address ▶		E.I. No. ▶	
		ZIP code ▶	

Cat. No. 11450Q

Schedule A	**Cost of Goods Sold** (See instructions.)		
1	Inventory at beginning of year	**1**	126,000
2	Purchases	**2**	1,127,100
3	Cost of labor	**3**	402,000
4	Additional section 263A costs (attach schedule)	**4**	40,000
5	Other costs (attach schedule)	**5**	123,300
6	**Total.** Add lines 1 through 5	**6**	1,818,400
7	Inventory at end of year	**7**	298,400
8	**Cost of goods sold.** Subtract line 7 from line 6. Enter here and on page 1, line 2	**8**	1,520,000

9a Check all methods used for valuing closing inventory:

    (i) ☐ Cost   **(ii)** ☑ Lower of cost or market as described in Regulations section 1.471-4

    (iii) ☐ Writedown of "subnormal" goods as described in Regulations section 1.471-2(c)

    (iv) ☐ Other (Specify method used and attach explanation.) ▶ ....

  b Check if the LIFO inventory method was adopted this tax year for any goods (if checked, attach Form 970) ..... ▶ ☐

  c If the LIFO inventory method was used for this tax year, enter percentage (or amounts) of closing inventory computed under LIFO   **9c**

  d Do the rules of section 263A (for property produced or acquired for resale) apply to the corporation? ..... ☑ Yes ☐ No

  e Was there any change in determining quantities, cost, or valuations between opening and closing inventory? If "Yes," attach explanation ☐ Yes ☑ No

Schedule C	**Dividends and Special Deductions** (See instructions.)	(a) Dividends received	(b) %	(c) Special deductions: (a) × (b)
1	Dividends from less-than-20%-owned domestic corporations that are subject to the 70% deduction (other than debt-financed stock)		70	
2	Dividends from 20%-or-more-owned domestic corporations that are subject to the 80% deduction (other than debt-financed stock)	10,000	80 see instructions	8,000
3	Dividends on debt-financed stock of domestic and foreign corporations (section 246A)			
4	Dividends on certain preferred stock of less-than-20%-owned public utilities		41.176	
5	Dividends on certain preferred stock of 20%-or-more-owned public utilities		47.059	
6	Dividends from less-than-20%-owned foreign corporations and certain FSCs that are subject to the 70% deduction		70	
7	Dividends from 20%-or-more-owned foreign corporations and certain FSCs that are subject to the 80% deduction		80	
8	Dividends from wholly owned foreign subsidiaries subject to the 100% deduction (section 245(b))		100	
9	**Total.** Add lines 1 through 8. See instructions for limitation			8,000
10	Dividends from domestic corporations received by a small business investment company operating under the Small Business Investment Act of 1958		100	
11	Dividends from certain FSCs that are subject to the 100% deduction (section 245(c)(1))		100	
12	Dividends from affiliated group members subject to the 100% deduction (section 243(a)(3))		100	
13	Other dividends from foreign corporations not included on lines 3, 6, 7, 8, or 11			
14	Income from controlled foreign corporations under subpart F (attach Form(s) 5471)			
15	Foreign dividend gross-up (section 78)			
16	IC-DISC and former DISC dividends not included on lines 1, 2, or 3 (section 246(d))			
17	Other dividends			
18	Deduction for dividends paid on certain preferred stock of public utilities (see instructions)			
19	**Total dividends.** Add lines 1 through 17. Enter here and on line 4, page 1 ▶	10,000		
20	**Total deductions.** Add lines 9, 10, 11, 12, and 18. Enter here and on line 29b, page 1 ▶			8,000

Schedule E	**Compensation of Officers** (See instructions for line 12, page 1.)

Complete Schedule E only if total receipts (line 1a plus lines 4 through 10 on page 1, Form 1120) are $500,000 or more.

(a) Name of officer	(b) Social security number	(c) Percent of time devoted to business	Percent of corporation stock owned (d) Common	(e) Preferred	(f) Amount of compensation
1 James O. Barclay	581-00-0936	100 %	45 %	%	55,000
		%	%	%	
George M. Collins	447-00-2604	100 %	15 %	%	31,000
		%	%	%	
Samuel Adams	401-00-2611	50 %	2 %	%	14,000
2	Total compensation of officers				100,000
3	Compensation of officers claimed on Schedule A and elsewhere on return				30,000
4	Subtract line 3 from line 2. Enter the result here and on line 12, page 1				76,000

Schedule L — Balance Sheets

Assets	Beginning of tax year (a)	(b)	End of tax year (c)	(d)
1 Cash		98,400		28,331
2a Trade notes and accounts receivable	14,700		103,700	
b Less allowance for bad debts	( )	98,400	( )	103,700
	96,400		245,400	
3 Inventories		126,000		120,000
4 U.S. government obligations				
5 Tax-exempt securities (see instructions)		24,300		17,261
6 Other current assets (attach schedule)				
7 Loans to stockholders				
8 Mortgage and real estate loans				
9 Other investments (attach schedule)		100,000		80,000
10a Buildings and other depreciable assets	272,400		296,700	
b Less accumulated depreciation	(86,300)	184,100	(104,280)	192,420
11a Depletable assets				
b Less accumulated depletion	( )		( )	
12 Land (net of any amortization)		20,000		20,000
13a Intangible assets (amortizable only)				
b Less accumulated amortization	( )		( )	
14 Other assets (attach schedule)		14,800		19,300
15 Total assets		684,300		879,412

Liabilities and Stockholders' Equity				
16 Accounts payable		28,500		34,834
17 Mortgages, notes, bonds payable in less than 1 year		4,300		4,300
18 Other current liabilities (attach schedule)		6,500		2,400
19 Loans from stockholders				
20 Mortgages, notes, bonds payable in 1 year or more		176,700		264,100
21 Other liabilities (attach schedule)				
22 Capital stock: a Preferred stock				
b Common stock	200,000	200,000	200,000	200,000
23 Paid-in or capital surplus				
24 Retained earnings—Appropriated (attach schedule)				
25 Retained earnings—Unappropriated		30,000		40,000
26 Less cost of treasury stock		238,300		328,783
27 Total liabilities and stockholders' equity		684,300		879,412

Note: You are not required to complete Schedules M-1 and M-2 below if the total assets on line 15, column (d) of Schedule L are less than $25,000.

Schedule M-1 — Reconciliation of Income (Loss) per Books With Income per Return (See instructions.)

1 Net income (loss) per books	147,783	7 Income recorded on books this year not included on this return (itemize):	
2 Federal income tax	55,387	Tax-exempt interest $ 5,000	
3 Excess of capital losses over capital gains	3,600	Insurance Proceeds 4,500	
4 Income subject to tax not recorded on books this year (itemize):			14,500
		8 Deductions on this return not charged against book income this year (itemize):	
5 Expenses recorded on books this year not deducted on this return (itemize):		a Depreciation $ 1,620	
a Depreciation $		b Contributions carryover $	
b Contributions carryover $			1,620
c Travel and entertainment $ 850		9 Add lines 7 and 8	14,120
See itemized statement attached 314,850		10 Income (line 28, page 1—line 6 less line 9)	203,350
6 Add lines 1 through 5	224,420		

Schedule M-2 — Analysis of Unappropriated Retained Earnings per Books (Line 25, Schedule L)

1 Balance at beginning of year	238,000	5 Distributions: a Cash	65,000
2 Net income (loss) per books	147,783	b Stock	
3 Other increases (itemize):		c Property	
Refund of 1990 income tax due to IRS examination	18,000	6 Other decreases (itemize): Reserve for Contingencies	10,000
		7 Add lines 5 and 6	75,000
4 Add lines 1, 2, and 3	403,783	8 Balance at end of year (line 4 less line 7)	328,783

Schedule J — Tax Computation (See instructions.)

1 Check if the corporation is a member of a controlled group (see sections 1561 and 1563) ▶ ☐

2 If the box on line 1 is checked:
  a Enter the corporation's share of the $50,000 and $25,000 taxable income bracket amounts (in that order):
  (i) $ (ii) $
  b Enter the corporation's share of the additional 5% tax (not to exceed $11,750) ▶ $

3 Income tax. Check this box if the corporation is a qualified personal service corporation as defined in section 448(d)(2) (see instructions on page 14) . . . . . . ▶ ☐ | 3 | 61,387 |

4a Foreign tax credit (attach Form 1118) | 4a | |
  b Possessions tax credit (attach Form 5735) | 4b | |
  c Orphan drug credit (attach Form 6765) | 4c | |
  d Credit for fuel produced from a nonconventional source | 4d | |
  e General business credit. Enter here and check which forms are attached:
    ☐ Form 3800 ☐ Form 3468 ☐ Form 5884 ☐ Form 6478
    ☐ Form 6765 ☐ Form 8586 ☐ Form 8830 ☐ Form 8826 | 4e | |
  f Credit for prior year minimum tax (attach Form 8827) | 4f | |

5 Total credits. Add lines 4a through 4f | 5 | 6,000 |
6 Subtract line 5 from line 3 | 6 | 55,387 |
7 Personal holding company tax (attach Schedule PH (Form 1120)) | 7 | |
8 Recapture taxes. Check if from: ☐ Form 4255 ☐ Form 8611 | 8 | |
9a Alternative minimum tax (attach Form 4626) | 9a | |
  b Environmental tax (attach Form 4626) | 9b | |
10 Total tax. Add lines 6 through 9b. Enter here and on line 31, page 1 | 10 | 55,387 |

Schedule K — Other Information (See instructions.)

		Yes	No
1	Check method of accounting: a ☐ Cash b ☑ Accrual c ☐ Other (specify) ▶		
2	Refer to the list in the instructions and state the principal:		
	a Business activity code no. ▶ 3945		
	b Business activity ▶ Manufacturing		
	c Product or service ▶ Toys		
3	Did the corporation at the end of the tax year own, directly or indirectly, 50% or more of the voting stock of a domestic corporation? (For rules of attribution, see section 267(c).)		✓
	If "Yes," attach a schedule showing: (a) name and identifying number, (b) percentage owned; and (c) taxable income or (loss) before NOL and special deductions of such corporation for the tax year ending with or within your tax year.		
4	Did any individual, partnership, corporation, estate, or trust at the end of the tax year own, directly or indirectly, 50% or more of the corporation's voting stock? (For rules of attribution, see section 267(c).) If "Yes," complete a, b, and c below.		✓
	a Is the corporation a subsidiary in an affiliated group or a parent-subsidiary controlled group?		
	b Enter the name and identifying number of the parent corporation or other entity with 50% or more ownership ▶		
	c Enter percentage owned ▶		
5	During this tax year, did the corporation pay dividends (other than stock dividends and distributions in exchange for stock) in excess of the corporation's current and accumulated earnings and profits? (See secs. 301 and 316.) If "Yes," file Form 5452. If this is a consolidated return, answer here for the parent corporation and on Form 851, Affiliations Schedule, for each subsidiary.		✓

		Yes	No
6	Was the corporation a U.S. shareholder of any controlled foreign corporation? (See sections 951 and 957.) . . . . If "Yes," attach Form 5471 for each such corporation. Enter number of Forms 5471 attached ▶		✓
7	At any time during the 1992 calendar year, did the corporation have an interest in or a signature or other authority over a financial account in a foreign country (such as a bank account, securities account, or other financial account)? If "Yes," the corporation may have to file Form TD F 90-22.1. If "Yes," enter name of foreign country ▶		✓
8	Was the corporation the grantor of, or transferor to, a foreign trust that existed during the current tax year, whether or not the corporation has any beneficial interest in it? If "Yes," the corporation may have to file Forms 926, 3520, or 3520-A.		✓
9	Did one foreign person at any time during the tax year own, directly or indirectly, at least 25% of: (a) the total voting power of all classes of stock of the corporation entitled to vote, or (b) the total value of all classes of stock of the corporation?		✓
	a Enter percentage owned ▶		
	b Enter owner's country ▶		
	c The corporation may have to file Form 5472. (See page 18 for penalties that may apply.) Enter number of Forms 5472 attached ▶		
10	Check this box if the corporation issued publicly offered debt instruments with original issue discount . . . ▶ ☐ If so, the corporation may have to file Form 8281.		
11	Enter the amount of tax-exempt interest received or accrued during the tax year ▶ $ 5,000		
12	If there were 35 or fewer shareholders at the end of the tax year, enter the number ▶		
13	If the corporation has an NOL for the tax year and is electing under sec. 172(b)(3) to forego the carryback period, check here . . . . ▶ ☐		

FORM 1120S

StratoTech Inc., is a distributor of machinery, equipment, and supplies for the building trades. It uses an accrual method of accounting and files its returns on the calendar year. In December 1991, StratoTech Inc., made a timely and proper election to be treated as an S corporation.

Page 1

When the corporation's return is prepared for 1992, the pre-addressed label sent to the corporation by the IRS should be used. The pre-addressed label is designed to expedite processing and prevent errors. If the corporation does not have such a label, the corporation's name, street address, room number, suite, or unit, and city, state, and ZIP code should be entered in the appropriate spaces on the first page. After entering the identifying information at the top of the page, StratoTech's items of income and deductions are then reported in summary form.

The name and employer identification number of the corporation is shown in the top margin of all schedules and other attachments to Form 1120S.

Line Items. All applicable items for income, deductions, and tax listed on page 1 of Form 1120S are filled in, even though totals may be shown in schedules attached to the return. Do not alter, substitute, or cross out the line captions printed on the official return forms.

Line 1. Gross sales for the year totaled $1,545,700 (line 1a), determined on the accrual method of accounting. After subtracting returned goods and allowances of $21,000 (line 1b), net sales of $1,524,700 are entered on line 1c.

Line 2. Cost of goods sold is deducted on line 2. This figure, $954,700, is the total from Schedule A (line 7) on page 2.

Line 3. Net sales minus cost of goods sold result in gross profit of $570,000.

Line 6. Total income on line 6 is $570,000.

Line 7. The salaries of the company president, vice president, and secretary-treasurer total $170,000 and are included on line 7. Compensation paid to corporate officers must be separated from other salaries and wages and must be entered on line 7 rather than on line 8.

Line 8. Other salaries and wages are entered on line 8a. The entry includes only salaries and wages not included on line 7 and not deducted as part of cost of goods sold. Salaries and wages of $144,000 on line 8a are reduced by $6,000, the amount of the jobs credit, discussed later, passed through to the shareholders on line 8b.

Line 9. Repairs include only payments for items that do not add to the value of the assets repaired or substantially increase their useful lives. StratoTech incurred $800 for repairs.

Line 10. StratoTech must use the specific charge-off method for bad debts. Actual accounts written off during the year total $1,600.

Line 11. Rental expense for StratoTech's office and service building is $9,200 for the year.

Line 12. Deductible taxes total $15,000.

Line 13. Interest expense accrued during the year amounts to $14,200. This includes interest on debts for business operations only. Interest of $850 to carry tax-exempt securities and investments is not included. Interest on the debt to carry investments that produce taxable income is $3,000. It is shown on line 11a of Schedule K and passed through to the shareholders on Schedule K–1.

Lines 14a and 14b. Depreciation of $15,200 is brought forward from Form 4562, *Depreciation and Amortization* (not illustrated). If StratoTech had a section 179 deduction, it would not be included here. It is passed through to the shareholders on Schedule K–1.

Line 16. Advertising expense of $8,700 is entered on line 16.

Line 19. Other ordinary and necessary business deductions total $78,300. These include miscellaneous office expenses, sales commissions, legal fees, etc. A schedule itemizing these expenses must be attached to the return, even though it is not shown.

Line 20. Total deductions are $451,000.

Line 21. Ordinary income (nonseparately stated income) is $119,000.

Corporate officer's signature. The corporation return must be signed manually by the corporate officer authorized to sign. Use of the corporate seal is optional.

Page 2

Schedule A. Schedule A is used to report the cost of goods sold. This figure is beginning inventory plus merchandise bought or produced during the year minus ending inventory.

Line 1. Because it is a distributor, StratoTech accounts for its purchasing costs as part of the cost of goods sold. Goods on hand at the beginning of the year were properly valued at $126,000, using the lower of cost or market valuation method. StratoTech reports this amount on line 1.

Line 2. Purchases cost of $1,127,100 is listed on line 2.

Line 7. StratoTech had goods on hand at the end of the year properly valued at $298,400. StratoTech reports that amount on line 7.

Lines 9a — 9e. All applicable questions on these lines should be answered.

Other information. All applicable questions in this section should be answered and the appropriate boxes checked.

Designation of tax matters person. Information relating to the shareholder designated as the tax matters person should be provided

as indicated at the bottom of page 2, Form 1120S. For information on the rules for designating a tax matters person (TMP), see Temporary Income Tax Regulation 301.6231(a)(7)–1T.

Page 3

Schedule K. Schedule K summarizes the corporation's income, deductions, credits, etc., that are reportable by the shareholders.

Line 1. On line 1, StratoTech shows the ordinary income (nonseparately stated income) of $119,000 from line 21, page 1.

Line 4. Line 4 is used to report portfolio income and loss items. Portfolio items include interest income, dividend income, royalty income, short-term capital gain or loss, and long-term capital gain or loss. StratoTech had the following portfolio items:

1) Taxable interest income of $4,000 reportable on *line 4a,* and

2) Taxable dividends of $16,000 reportable on *line 4b.*

Line 7. Line 7 is for charitable contributions. During 1992, StratoTech contributed $11,400 to the United Community Fund and $12,600 to the State University Scholarship Fund. The total of $24,000, subject to a 50% limitation, is entered in the total column on line 7.

Lines 11a and 11b(1). These lines show the items that must be taken into account by shareholders to figure their interest deduction on investment indebtedness. *Line 11a* is used for investment interest expense. StratoTech had investment interest expense of $3,000. *Line 11b(1)* is for investment income. StratoTech had taxable interest from investments (line 4a) totaling $4,000. StratoTech also had dividends from investments (line 4b) totaling $16,000. Therefore, StratoTech enters $20,000 on line 11b(1). Each shareholder's share of these items must be reported on Schedule K–1.

Line 13. Line 13 is for the jobs credit. StratoTech has $6,000 of jobs credit in 1992. The credit was figured on Form 5884, *Jobs Credit* (not shown here).

Line 17. Tax-exempt interest is entered on line 17. StratoTech earned $5,000 of tax-exempt interest from state bonds.

Line 19. StratoTech had $6,000 of nondeductible salaries due to the jobs credit.

Line 20. Line 20 is for distributions other than those reported on line 22. StratoTech distributed $65,000 in 1992.

Line 23. Taxable income of $112,000 from line 8, Schedule M–1, is entered here.

Schedule K–1. A separate Schedule K–1 is completed by the S corporation for each shareholder.

Generally, shareholders must treat items of income, loss, deduction, credit, etc., on their returns consistent with the way the S corporation reported them on its return. A shareholder who shows the items differently from the way the S corporation reported them on Schedule K–1 should complete Form 8082.

A copy of each shareholder's Schedule K–1 should be filed with Form 1120S. A copy is kept as a part of the corporation's records, and each shareholder receives a copy with instructions attached.

StratoTech must prepare a Schedule K–1 for each shareholder. The illustrated Schedule K–1 is for John H. Green who owns 9,000 shares (45%) of the corporation's stock, which he acquired on March 3, 1974. He devotes 100% of his time to the business for which he is paid $40,000.

Lines 1 through 10 are for each shareholder's distributive share of nonseparately stated income or loss and separately stated income or loss and deductions.

Line 1. Line 1 shows Mr. Green's share of nonseparately stated income of $53,550. It makes no difference whether this income was distributed to him in 1992. He must report $53,550 on Schedule E (Form 1040) when he files his individual income tax return, Form 1040.

Line 4. Line 4 is for portfolio income and loss items. Mr. Green's share of interest income is $1,800. His share of dividend income is $7,200.

Line 7. Line 7 is for Mr. Green's share of StratoTech's charitable contributions for 1992. His share is $10,800. Because all StratoTech's contributions were given to public charities, they qualify for the 50% limitation.

Lines 11a and 11b(1). These lines are used to show each shareholder's share of interest on investment indebtedness. The amounts reported on these lines will be used to complete Form 4952, *Investment Interest Expense Deduction. Line 11a* shows Mr. Green's share of StratoTech's investment interest expense, $1,350 (45% × $3,000). Investment interest expense is that part of StratoTech's total interest for loans made to carry its investment. *Line 11b(1)* shows Mr. Green's share of StratoTech's investment income, $9,000 (45% × $20,000). This represents StratoTech's income from ordinary dividends and interest. It does not include interest on municipal bond investments, which is tax-exempt.

Line 13. Line 13 is for the jobs credit. Mr. Green's share of StratoTech's jobs credit is $2,700 (45% × $6,000).

Line 17. In 1992, StratoTech had $5,000 of tax-exempt interest form state bonds. Mr. Green's 45% share of the tax-exempt interest is $2,250. This amount is entered on line 17.

Line 19. Mr. Green's 45% share of nondeductible expenses due to the jobs credit is $2,700. This amount is entered on line 19.

Line 20. Line 20 is for distributions paid during the year other than those paid from accumulated earnings and profits and reported on Form 1099–DIV. During 1992, StratoTech distributed $65,000. Mr. Green's 45% share of the distribution is $29,250.

Page 4

Schedule L. Comparative balance sheets for the beginning and end of the tax year are shown on Schedule L. The balance sheets should agree with the S corporation's books and records. Entries on this page should also agree with amounts shown elsewhere on the return. For example, the figures for beginning and ending inventories must be the same as those appearing in the analysis of cost of goods sold. In addition, the figures on the balance sheet for the beginning of the tax year will normally agree with the balance sheet figures for the end of the last tax year.

Schedules M–1 and M–2. These schedules must be completed if the total assets (line 15, column (d), Schedule L) are $25,000 or more. To properly complete these schedules, additional information must be obtained from the corporation's books and records.

The following appeared on the books of StratoTech for the calendar year 1992.

Account	Debit	Credit
Gross sales		$1,545,700
Sales returns and allowances	$ 21,000	
Cost of goods sold	954,700	
Dividend income		16,000
Interest income (on state bonds)		5,000
(other—taxable) ...		4,000
Premiums on life insurance	9,500	
Compensation of officers	170,000	
Salaries and wages ..	144,000	
Repairs	800	
Bad debts	1,600	
Rental expense	9,200	
Taxes	15,000	
Interest expense (loan to buy tax-exempt bonds) ... $ 850		
(other) .. 17,200	18,050	
Contributions	24,000	
Depreciation	9,580	
Advertising	8,700	
Other expenses of operation	78,300	
Net income per books	106,270	
Total	$1,570,700	$1,570,700

Schedule M–1. Schedule M–1 starts with the net income per books as shown in the corporation's books and records. It provides for necessary adjustments to reconcile this amount with the taxable income shown on line 23, Schedule K.

Line 1. Line 1 is the net income per books, $106,270, shown on the corporation's books.

Line 2. Line 2 should show all income and credits included in income subject to tax that are not recorded on the books for this year. This can happen if assets are valued on the corporate books at an amount greater than that used for tax purposes. When these assets are sold, the gain included in taxable income is greater than that recorded on the books, and the difference is shown here.

Line 3. Line 3 is for expenses recorded on the corporation's books that may not be deducted. They are shown in an itemized statement attached to the return (not illustrated). It would include the following:

Premiums paid on term life insurance on corporate officers	$ 9,500
Interest paid to purchase tax-exempt securities	850
Reduction of salaries by jobs credit	6,000
Total	$16,350

Line 4. The total of lines 1 through 3, $122,620, goes on line 4.

Line 5. Line 5 shows nontaxable income recorded on the corporation's books during the year that is not on the return. This totals $5,000, the interest on state bonds.

Line 6. Line 6 includes all deductions claimed for tax purposes that are not recorded on the corporation's books. StratoTech enters $5,620 on line 6a. This represents the difference between depreciation claimed on the tax return and the corporation's books. If the corporation had other deductions to itemize on this line and there was not enough space on the line, it would have to attach a statement to the return listing them.

Line 7. The total of lines 5 and 6, $10,620, goes on line 7.

Line 8. The difference, $112,000, between lines 4 and 7 must agree with line 23, Schedule K.

Schedule M–2. Schedule M–2 provides an analysis of certain earned equity accounts of the corporation for the tax year. The schedule shows the changes to the equity accounts for the income, deductions, distributions, etc., that are reported on the return for the tax year.

Column (a), Line 1. The first column is the accumulated adjustments account. For an S corporation's first year beginning after 1982, the initial balance in the account is zero. StratoTech enters zero on line 1.

Line 2. StratoTech's ordinary income for 1992 (page 1, line 21) is $119,000. This is entered on line 2.

Line 3. StratoTech enters $20,000 ($16,000 dividends plus $4,000 interest) on line 3. This is made up of amounts on lines 4a and 4b of Schedule K.

Line 4. Line 4 is for any loss shown on page 1, line 21. Because StratoTech has no losses in 1992, line 4 is zero.

Line 5. StratoTech enters $33,000 on line 5. This is made up of $3,000 interest on a loan to carry investments, $6,000 reduction in salaries and wages due to the jobs credit, and $24,000 charitable contributions.

Line 6. Line 6 is the total of lines 1 through 5, or $106,000.

Line 7. Line 7 is for distributions other than dividend distributions. StratoTech enters $65,000 on this line.

Line 8. Line 8 shows the balance in the accumulated adjustments account at the end of the year. StratoTech subtracts line 7 from line 6 and enters $41,000 here.

Column (b), Line 1. The second column is the other adjustments account. It is for other items, such as tax-exempt income and related expenses. The balance at the beginning of the year is zero. This is entered on line 1.

Line 3. StratoTech had $5,000 of tax-free interest income from state bonds. This amount is entered on line 3.

Line 6. The total of lines 1 through 5, $5,000, is entered on line 6.

Line 7. Because the total distributions, other than dividends, did not exceed the balance in the accumulated adjustments account, none of the distribution is applied to the other adjustments account. StratoTech enters zero on line 7.

Line 8. The balance in the other adjustments account at the end of the year is $5,000. StratoTech enters this amount here.

Column (c). The third column is for undistributed taxable income that was included in shareholders' income for years that began before 1992. Since this is StratoTech's first year as an S corporation, there are no entries in this column.

Form **1120S**

Department of the Treasury
Internal Revenue Service

U.S. Income Tax Return for an S Corporation

For calendar year 1992, or tax year beginning .... , 1992, and ending .... , 19 .....
► See separate instructions.

OMB No. 1545-0130

1992

| A Date of election as an S corporation
12-1-91 | Use IRS label. Other-wise, please print or type. | Name
Strato Tech, Inc. | C Employer identification number
10-4487965 |
|---|---|---|---|
| B Business code no. (see Specific Instructions)
5008 | | Number, street, and room or suite no. (If a P.O. box, see page 8 of the instructions.)
482 Winston St.
City or town, state, and ZIP code
Metro City, OH   43705 | D Date incorporated
3-1-74
E Total assets (see Specific Instructions)
$ 771,334 |

F Check applicable boxes: (1) ☑ Initial return (2) ☐ Final return (3) ☐ Change in address (4) ☐ Amended return
G Check this box if this S corporation is subject to the consolidated audit procedures of sections 6241 through 6245 (see instructions before checking this box) ► ☐
H Enter number of shareholders in the corporation at end of the tax year . . . . ► 6

Caution: Include **only** trade or business income and expenses on lines 1a through 21. See the instructions for more information.

Income

1a	Gross receipts or sales 1,545,700 b Less returns and allowances 21,000 c Bal ►	1c	1,524,700
2	Cost of goods sold (Schedule A, line 8)	2	954,700
3	Gross profit. Subtract line 2 from line 1c	3	570,000
4	Net gain (loss) from Form 4797, Part II, line 20 (attach Form 4797) . . .	4	-0-
5	Other income (loss) (see instructions) (attach schedule)	5	-0-
6	**Total income (loss).** Combine lines 3 through 5 . . . . ►	6	570,000

Deductions (See instructions for limitations.)

7	Compensation of officers	7	170,000
8a	Salaries and wages 144,000 b Less jobs credit 6,000 c Bal ►	8c	138,600
9	Repairs	9	800
10	Bad debts	10	1,600
11	Rents	11	9,200
12	Taxes	12	15,000
13	Interest	13	14,200
14a	Depreciation (see instructions) 14a 15,200		
b	Depreciation claimed on Schedule A and elsewhere on return . 14b -0-		
c	Subtract line 14b from line 14a	14c	15,200
15	Depletion **(Do not deduct oil and gas depletion.)**	15	-0-
16	Advertising	16	8,700
17	Pension, profit-sharing, etc., plans	17	-0-
18	Employee benefit programs	18	-0-
19	Other deductions (see instructions) (attach schedule)	19	78,300
20	**Total deductions.** Add lines 7 through 19 . . . . ►	20	451,000
21	Ordinary income (loss) from trade or business activities. Subtract line 20 from line 6	21	119,000

Tax and Payments

22	**Tax:**		
a	Excess net passive income tax (attach schedule) 22a		
b	Tax from Schedule D (Form 1120S) 22b		
c	Add lines 22a and 22b (see instructions for additional taxes)	22c	-0-
23	**Payments:**		
a	1992 estimated tax payments 23a		
b	Tax deposited with Form 7004 . . . . 23b		
c	Credit for Federal tax paid on fuels (attach Form 4136) . . 23c		
d	Add lines 23a through 23c	23d	-0-
24	Estimated tax penalty (see instructions). Check if Form 2220 is attached. . . . ► ☐	24	-0-
25	**Tax due.** If the total of lines 22c and 24 is larger than line 23d, enter amount owed. See instructions for depositary method of payment . . . . ►	25	-0-
26	**Overpayment.** If line 23d is larger than the total of lines 22c and 24, enter amount overpaid ►	26	-0-
27	Enter amount of line 26 you want: **Credited to 1993 estimated tax** ►	Refunded ►	27	-0-

Please Sign Here

Under penalties of perjury, I declare that I have examined this return, including accompanying schedules and statements, and to the best of my knowledge and belief, it is true, correct, and complete. Declaration of preparer (other than taxpayer) is based on all information of which preparer has any knowledge.

► John H. Green   3-10-93   ► President
Signature of officer   Date   Title

Paid Preparer's Use Only

Preparer's signature ►		Date	Check if self-employed ☐	Preparer's social security number
Firm's name (or yours if self-employed) and address ►			E.I. No. ►	
			ZIP code ►	

For Paperwork Reduction Act Notice, see page 1 of separate instructions.   Cat. No. 11510H   Form **1120S** (1992)

Schedule A   **Cost of Goods Sold** (See instructions.)

1	Inventory at beginning of year	**1**	126,000
2	Purchases	**2**	1,127,100
3	Cost of labor	**3**	-0-
4	Additional section 263A costs (see instructions) *(attach schedule)*	**4**	-0-
5	Other costs *(attach schedule)*	**5**	-0-
6	**Total.** Add lines 1 through 5	**6**	1,253,100
7	Inventory at end of year	**7**	298,400
8	**Cost of goods sold.** Subtract line 7 from line 6. Enter here and on page 1, line 2	**8**	954,700

9a Check all methods used for valuing closing inventory:
  (i) ☐ Cost
  (ii) ☑ Lower of cost or market as described in Regulations section 1.471-4
  (iii) ☐ Writedown of "subnormal" goods as described in Regulations section 1.471-2(c)
  (iv) ☐ Other (specify method used and attach explanation) ▶ ....
  b Check if the LIFO inventory method was adopted this tax year for any goods (*if checked, attach Form 970*) . . . . . ▶ ☐
  c If the LIFO inventory method was used for this tax year, enter percentage (or amounts) of closing
    inventory computed under LIFO . . . . | **9c** |
  d Do the rules of section 263A (for property produced or acquired for resale) apply to the corporation? . . . . ☐ Yes ☑ No
  e Was there any change in determining quantities, cost, or valuations between opening and closing inventory? . . ☐ Yes ☑ No
    If "Yes," attach explanation.

Schedule B   **Other Information**

		Yes	No
1	Check method of accounting: **(a)** ☐ Cash **(b)** ☑ Accrual **(c)** ☐ Other (specify) ▶		
2	Refer to the list in the instructions and state the corporation's principal:		
	(a) Business activity ▶ *5008 - Distributor* **(b)** Product or service ▶ *Heavy Equipment*		
3	Did the corporation at the end of the tax year own, directly or indirectly, 50% or more of the voting stock of a domestic corporation? (For rules of attribution, see section 267(c).) If "Yes," attach a schedule showing: **(a)** name, address, and employer identification number and **(b)** percentage owned.		✓
4	Was the corporation a member of a controlled group subject to the provisions of section 1561?		✓
5	At any time during calendar year 1992, did the corporation have an interest in or a signature or other authority over a financial account in a foreign country (such as a bank account, securities account, or other financial account)? (See instructions for exceptions and filing requirements for form TD F 90-22.1.)		✓
	If "Yes," enter the name of the foreign country ▶		
6	Was the corporation the grantor of, or transferor to, a foreign trust that existed during the current tax year, whether or not the corporation has any beneficial interest in it? If "Yes," the corporation may have to file Forms 3520, 3520-A, or 926		✓
7	Check this box if the corporation has filed or is required to file **Form 8264,** Application for Registration of a Tax Shelter . . . . ▶ ☐		
8	Check this box if the corporation issued publicly offered debt instruments with original issue discount . . ▶ ☐		
	If so, the corporation may have to file **Form 8281,** Information Return for Publicly Offered Original Issue Discount Instruments.		
9	If the corporation: **(a)** filed its election to be an S corporation after 1986, **(b)** was a C corporation before it elected to be an S corporation **or** the corporation acquired an asset with a basis determined by reference to its basis (or the basis of any other property) in the hands of a C corporation, and **(c)** has net unrealized built-in gain (defined in section 1374(d)(1)) in excess of the net recognized built-in gain from prior years, enter the net unrealized built-in gain reduced by net recognized built-in gain from prior years (see instructions) . . . . ▶ $ *37,200*		
10	Check this box if the corporation had subchapter C earnings and profits at the close of the tax year (see instructions) . . . . ▶ ☑	✓	
11	Was this corporation in operation at the end of 1992?		
12	How many months in 1992 was this corporation in operation? *12*		

Designation of Tax Matters Person (See instructions.)

Enter below the shareholder designated as the tax matters person (TMP) for the tax year of this return:

Name of designated TMP ▶	*John H. Green*	Identifying number of TMP ▶	*458-00-0327*
Address of designated TMP ▶	*4340 Holmes Parkway, Metro City, OH 43704*		

Schedule K — Shareholders' Shares of Income, Credits, Deductions, etc.

	(a) Pro rata share items		(b) Total amount
Income (Loss)	1 Ordinary income (loss) from trade or business activities (page 1, line 21)	1	119,000
	2 Net income (loss) from rental real estate activities (attach Form 8825)	2	
	3a Gross income from other rental activities	3a	
	b Expenses from other rental activities (attach schedule)	3b	
	c Net income (loss) from other rental activities. Subtract line 3b from line 3a	3c	
	4 Portfolio income (loss):		
	a Interest income	4a	4,000
	b Dividend income	4b	16,000
	c Royalty income	4c	
	d Net short-term capital gain (loss) (attach Schedule D (Form 1120S))	4d	
	e Net long-term capital gain (loss) (attach Schedule D (Form 1120S))	4e	
	f Other portfolio income (loss) (attach schedule)	4f	
	5 Net gain (loss) under section 1231 (other than due to casualty or theft) (attach Form 4797)	5	
	6 Other income (loss) (attach schedule)	6	24,000
Deductions	7 Charitable contributions (see instructions) (attach schedule)	7	
	8 Section 179 expense deduction (attach Form 4562)	8	
	9 Deductions related to portfolio income (loss) (attach schedule)	9	
	10 Other deductions (attach schedule)	10	3,000
Investment Interest	11a Interest expense on investment debts	11a	20,000
	b (1) Investment income included on lines 4a through 4f above	11b(1)	
	(2) Investment expenses included on line 9 above	11b(2)	
Credits	12a Credit for alcohol used as a fuel (attach Form 6478)	12a	
	b Low-income housing credit:		
	(1) From partnerships to which section 42(j)(5) applies for property placed in service before 1990	12b(1)	
	(2) Other than on line 12b(1) for property placed in service before 1990	12b(2)	
	(3) From partnerships to which section 42(j)(5) applies for property placed in service after 1989	12b(3)	
	(4) Other than on line 12b(3) for property placed in service after 1989	12b(4)	
	c Qualified rehabilitation expenditures related to rental real estate activities (attach Form 3468)	12c	
	d Credits (other than credits shown on lines 12b and 12c) related to rental real estate activities (see instructions) *Jobs Credit*	12d	6,000
	e Credits related to other rental activities (see instructions)	12e	
	13 Other credits (see instructions)	13	
Adjustments and Tax Preference Items	14a Depreciation adjustment on property placed in service after 1986	14a	
	b Adjusted gain or loss	14b	
	c Depletion (other than oil and gas)	14c	
	d (1) Gross income from oil, gas, or geothermal properties	14d(1)	
	(2) Deductions allocable to oil, gas, or geothermal properties	14d(2)	
	e Other adjustments and tax preference items (attach schedule)	14e	
Foreign Taxes	15a Type of income ▶		
	b Name of foreign country or U.S. possession ▶		
	c Total gross income from sources outside the United States (attach schedule)	15c	
	d Total applicable deductions and losses (attach schedule)	15d	
	e Total foreign taxes (check one): ▶ ☐ Paid ☐ Accrued	15e	
	f Reduction in taxes available for credit (attach schedule)	15f	
	g Total foreign tax information (attach schedule)	15g	
Other	16a Total expenditures to which a section 59(e) election may apply	16a	
	b Type of expenditures ▶		
	17 Tax-exempt interest income	17	5,000
	18 Other tax-exempt income	18	6,000
	19 Nondeductible expenses	19	65,000
	20 Total property distributions (including cash) other than dividends reported on line 22 below (see instructions)	20	
	21 Other items and amounts required to be reported separately to shareholders (see instructions) (attach schedule)	21	
	22 Total dividend distributions paid from accumulated earnings and profits	22	
	23 Income (loss). (Required only if Schedule M-1 must be completed.) Combine lines 1 through 6 in column (b). From the result, subtract the sum of lines 7 through 11a, 15e, and 16a.	23	112,000

Schedule L — Balance Sheets

		Beginning of tax year (a)	Beginning of tax year (b)	End of tax year (c)	End of tax year (d)
Assets					
1	Cash		98,400		14,514
2a	Trade notes and accounts receivable	48,400		33,700	
b	Less allowance for bad debts				
3	Inventories		134,000		193,400
4	U.S. Government obligations				
5	Tax-exempt securities		100,000		100,000
6	Other current assets (attach schedule)		24,300		26,300
7	Loans to shareholders				
8	Mortgage and real estate loans				
9	Other investments (attach schedule)		100,000		100,000
10a	Buildings and other depreciable assets	204,700		204,700	
b	Less accumulated depreciation	36,000	168,700	45,580	159,120
11a	Depletable assets				
b	Less accumulated depletion				
12	Land (net of any amortization)		20,000		20,000
13a	Intangible assets (amortizable only)				
b	Less accumulated amortization				
14	Other assets (attach schedule)		14,800		19,300
15	Total assets		663,900		771,334
Liabilities and Shareholders' Equity					
16	Accounts payable		28,500		34,834
17	Mortgages, notes, bonds payable in less than 1 year		4,300		4,400
18	Other current liabilities (attach schedule)				
19	Loans from shareholders				
20	Mortgages, notes, bonds payable in 1 year or more		6,800		7,400
21	Other liabilities (attach schedule)				
22	Capital stock		144,300		215,530
23	Paid-in or capital surplus		2,000		2,000
24	Retained earnings		198,000		198,000
25	Less cost of treasury stock		(268,000)		(307,270)
26	Total liabilities and shareholders' equity		663,900		771,334

Schedule M-1 — Reconciliation of Income (Loss) per Books With Income (Loss) per Return (You are not required to complete this schedule if the total assets on line 15, column (d), of Schedule L are less than $25,000.)

1	Net income (loss) per books	106,270	5 Income recorded on books this year not included on Schedule K, lines 1 through 6 (itemize):	
2	Income included on Schedule K, lines 1 through 6, not recorded on books this year (itemize):	-0-	a Tax-exempt interest $ 5,000	5,000
3	Expenses recorded on books this year not included on Schedule K, lines 1 through 11a, 15e, and 16a (itemize):		6 Deductions included on Schedule K, lines 1 through 11a, 15e, and 16a, not charged against book income this year (itemize):	
a	Depreciation $		a Depreciation $ 5,420	
b	Travel and entertainment $ (Itemized Statement Attached)	5,420	7 Add lines 5 and 6	
4	Add lines 1 through 3		8 Income (loss) (Schedule K, line 23). Line 4 less line 7	

Schedule M-2 — Analysis of Accumulated Adjustments Account, Other Adjustments Account, and Shareholders' Undistributed Taxable Income Previously Taxed (See instructions.)

		(a) Accumulated adjustments account	(b) Other adjustments account	(c) Shareholders' undistributed taxable income previously taxed
1	Balance at beginning of tax year	-0-		
2	Ordinary income from page 1, line 21	119,000		
3	Other additions	-0-	5,000	
4	Loss from page 1, line 21	(20,000)		
5	Other reductions	(33,000)	-0-	
6	Combine lines 1 through 5	106,000	5,000	
7	Distributions other than dividend distributions	65,000	-0-	
8	Balance at end of tax year. Subtract line 7 from line 6	41,000	5,000	

SCHEDULE K-1 (Form 1120S)	**Shareholder's Share of Income, Credits, Deductions, etc.**	OMB No. 1545-0130
Department of the Treasury Internal Revenue Service	▶ See separate instructions.	**19 92**
	For calendar year 1992 or tax year beginning ___, 1992, and ending ___ , 19 ___	

Shareholder's identifying number ▶	Corporation's identifying number ▶
Shareholder's name, address, and ZIP code John H. Green 4340 Holmes Parkway Metro City, OH 43704	Corporation's name, address, and ZIP code StratoTech, Inc. 482 Winston St. Metro City, OH 43705

A Shareholder's percentage of stock ownership for tax year (see Instructions for Schedule K-1) . . . . ▶ _45_ %

B Internal Revenue Service Center where corporation filed its return ▶ _Cincinnati, OH_

C (1) Tax shelter registration number (see Instructions for Schedule K-1) . . . . ▶ ....

   (2) Type of tax shelter ▶ ....

D Check applicable boxes: (1) ☐ Final K-1   (2) ☐ Amended K-1

		(a) Pro rata share items	**(b)** Amount	**(c)** Form 1040 filers enter the amount in column (b) on:
Income (Loss)	1	Ordinary income (loss) from trade or business activities . . .	**1**	53,550	See Shareholder's Instructions for Schedule K-1 (Form 1120S).
	2	Net income (loss) from rental real estate activities	**2**		
	3	Net income (loss) from other rental activities	**3**		
	4	Portfolio income (loss):			
	a	Interest	**4a**	1,800	Sch. B, Part I, line 1
	b	Dividends	**4b**	7,200	Sch. B, Part II, line 5
	c	Royalties	**4c**		Sch. E, Part I, line 4
	d	Net short-term capital gain (loss).	**4d**		Sch. D, line 5, col. (f) or (g)
	e	Net long-term capital gain (loss)	**4e**		Sch. D, line 13, col. (f) or (g)
	f	Other portfolio income (loss) (attach schedule)	**4f**		(Enter on applicable line of your return.)
	5	Net gain (loss) under section 1231 (other than due to casualty or theft)	**5**		See Shareholder's Instructions for Schedule K-1 (Form 1120S)
	6	Other income (loss) (attach schedule)	**6**		(Enter on applicable line of your return.)
Deductions	7	Charitable contributions (see instructions) (attach schedule) . .	**7**	10,800	Sch. A, line 13 or 14
	8	Section 179 expense deduction	**8**		See Shareholder's Instructions for Schedule K-1 (Form 1120S).
	9	Deductions related to portfolio income (loss) (attach schedule) .	**9**		
	10	Other deductions (attach schedule)	**10**		
Investment Interest	11a	Interest expense on investment debts	**11a**	1,350	Form 4952, line 1
	b (1)	Investment income included on lines 4a through 4f above .	**b(1)**	9,000	See Shareholder's Instructions for Schedule K-1 (Form 1120S).
	(2)	Investment expenses included on line 9 above	**b(2)**		
Credits	12a	Credit for alcohol used as fuel	**12a**		Form 6478, line 10
	b	Low-income housing credit:			
	(1)	From section 42(j)(5) partnerships for property placed in service before 1990	**b(1)**		
	(2)	Other than on line 12b(1) for property placed in service before 1990	**b(2)**		Form 8586, line 5
	(3)	From section 42(j)(5) partnerships for property placed in service after 1989	**b(3)**		
	(4)	Other than on line 12b(3) for property placed in service after 1989	**b(4)**		
	c	Qualified rehabilitation expenditures related to rental real estate activities (see instructions)	**12c**		
	d	Credits (other than credits shown on lines 12b and 12c) related to rental real estate activities (see instructions)	**12d**		See Shareholder's Instructions for Schedule K-1 (Form 1120S).
	e	Credits related to other rental activities (see instructions) . .	**12e**		
	13	Other credits (see instructions) . Jobs Credit . . .	**13**	2,700	
Adjustments and Tax Preference Items	14a	Depreciation adjustment on property placed in service after 1986	**14a**		See Shareholder's Instructions for Schedule K-1 (Form 1120S) and Instructions for Form 6251
	b	Adjusted gain or loss	**14b**		
	c	Depletion (other than oil and gas)	**14c**		
	d (1)	Gross income from oil, gas, or geothermal properties. . .	**d(1)**		
	(2)	Deductions allocable to oil, gas, or geothermal properties .	**d(2)**		
	e	Other adjustments and tax preference items (attach schedule)	**14e**		

For Paperwork Reduction Act Notice, see page 1 of Instructions for Form 1120S.   Cat. No. 11520D   **Schedule K-1 (Form 1120S) 1992**

	(a) Pro rata share items		(b) Amount	(c) Form 1040 filers enter the amount in column (b) on:
Foreign Taxes	**15a** Type of income ▶			Form 1116, Check boxes
	b Name of foreign country or U.S. possession ▶			
	c Total gross income from sources outside the United States *(attach schedule)* . . .	**15c**		Form 1116, Part I
	d Total applicable deductions and losses *(attach schedule)* . . .	**15d**		
	e Total foreign taxes (check one): ▶ ☐ Paid ☐ Accrued . .	**15e**		Form 1116, Part II
	f Reduction in taxes available for credit *(attach schedule)* . .	**15f**		Form 1116, Part III
	g Other foreign tax information *(attach schedule)*	**15g**		See Instructions for Form 1116
Other	**16a** Total expenditures to which a section 59(e) election may apply	**16a**		See Shareholder's Instructions for Schedule K-1 (Form 1120S).
	b Type of expenditures ▶			
	17 Tax-exempt interest income	**17**	*2,250*	Form 1040, line 8b
	18 Other tax-exempt income	**18**		See Shareholder's Instructions for Schedule K-1 (Form 1120S).
	19 Nondeductible expenses	**19**	*2,700*	
	20 Property distributions (including cash) other than dividend distributions reported to you on Form 1099-DIV	**20**	*29,250*	
	21 Amount of loan repayments for "Loans From Shareholders" . .	**21**		
	22 Recapture of low-income housing credit:			
	a From section 42(j)(5) partnerships	**22a**		Form 8611, line 8
	b Other than on line 22a	**22b**		

Supplemental Information

23 Supplemental information required to be reported separately to each shareholder *(attach additional schedules if more space is needed):*

....

....

....

....

....

....

....

....

....

....

....

....

....

....

....

....

....

....

APPENDIX 9: TAXPAYERS STARTING A BUSINESS

Introduction

This publication discusses several topics of interest to an individual starting a small business. It looks at some decisions involved in setting up a recordkeeping system, and typical books and records for a small business. Sample records and filled-in forms are illustrated at the end of the publication.

Penalties. To ensure all taxpayers pay their fair share of taxes, the law provides penalties for failure to file returns or pay taxes as required. Other penalties include those pointed out later under *Business Taxes* and *Information Returns*. You may not be charged a penalty if your noncompliance was due to reasonable cause.

However, criminal penalties may be imposed for willful failure to file, tax evasion, or making a false statement.

Ordering publications and forms. To order free publications and forms, call our toll-free telephone number 1-800-TAX-FORM (1-800-829-3676). You can also write to the IRS Forms Distribution Center nearest you. Check your tax package for the address.

Useful Items
You may want to see:

Publication

- ☐ **334** Tax Guide for Small Business
- ☐ **505** Tax Withholding and Estimated Tax
- ☐ **509** Tax Calendars for 1993
- ☐ **533** Self-Employment Tax
- ☐ **538** Accounting Periods and Methods
- ☐ **587** Business Use of Your Home
- ☐ **917** Business Use of a Car
- ☐ **937** Employment Taxes and Information Returns
- ☐ **946** How To Begin Depreciating Your Property

Form (and Instructions)
This publication discusses many different forms that you may have to file with the IRS. We have not listed them separately here. Please see the individual discussions.

Types of Businesses

When beginning a business, you must decide which type of business entity to use. Legal and tax considerations enter into this decision. However, legal considerations are beyond the scope of this publication.

Normally, you conduct a business in the form of a sole proprietorship, partnership, or corporation. If your business is a sole proprietorship or partnership, the business itself does not pay income tax. The sole proprietor or the partners include the profit or loss on their personal tax returns. The profit of a corporation, except for an S corporation, is taxed both to the corporation and to the shareholders when the profit is distributed as dividends. However, except for S corporation stockholders, a stockholder generally cannot deduct any loss of the corporation.

Sole proprietorships. A sole proprietorship is the simplest form of business organization. The business has no existence apart from you, the owner. Its liabilities are your personal liabilities and you undertake the risks of the business for all assets owned, whether used in the business or personally owned.

You must report the profit or loss from each of your sole proprietorships on a separate Schedule C (Form 1040). Enter the combined profit or loss on Form 1040, *U.S. Individual Income Tax Return.*

As a sole proprietor, you may be liable for self-employment tax and estimated tax payments.

For more information on sole proprietorships, see Chapter 28 in Publication 334.

Partnerships. A partnership is not a taxable entity. However, a partnership must figure its profit or loss and file a return on Form 1065, *U.S. Partnership Return of Income.*

A partnership is the relationship existing between two or more persons who join to carry on a trade or business. Each person contributes money, property, labor, or skill, and expects to share in the profits and losses of the business.

For more information, see Publication 541, *Tax Information on Partnerships.*

Corporations. In forming a corporation, prospective shareholders transfer money, property, or both, for the corporation's capital stock. Most corporations file Form 1120, *U.S. Corporation Income Tax Return* or Form 1120-A, *U.S. Corporation Short-Form Income Tax Return.* A corporation generally takes the same deductions as a sole proprietorship to figure its taxable income. A corporation can also take special deductions.

For more information, see Publication 542, *Tax Information on Corporations.*

S corporations. A qualifying corporation may choose to be generally exempt from federal income tax. Its shareholders include in income their share of the corporation's separately stated items of income, deduction, loss, and credit, and their share of nonseparately stated income or loss. A corporation that makes this choice is known as an S corporation.

To make this election, a corporation must have no more than 35 shareholders, in addition to other requirements. An S corporation files its return on Form 1120S, *U.S. Income Tax Return for an S Corporation.*

For more information, see Publication 589, *Tax Information on S Corporations.*

Identification Numbers

You must have a taxpayer identification number so the Internal Revenue Service can process your returns. There are two kinds of taxpayer identification numbers—a social security number and an employer identification number.

Employer Number

A sole proprietor does not need an employer identification number (EIN). However, you do need an EIN if you:

1) Have a Keogh plan.
2) File any of these tax returns:
   a) Employment.
   b) Excise.
   c) Fiduciary.
   d) Alcohol, tobacco, and firearms.

Otherwise, use your social security number.

You are a sole proprietor if you are self-employed (work for yourself) and are the only owner of your unincorporated business.

How To Get an EIN

To get an EIN, file Form SS-4, *Application for Employer Identification Number,* with the IRS Center for your area listed in the instructions to Form SS-4. You can get Form SS-4 at IRS or Social Security Administration (SSA) offices.

When to apply. You should file Form SS-4 early enough to receive the number by the time you must file a return or statement or make a tax deposit. It takes about four weeks to process Form SS-4.

If you do not receive your EIN by the time a return is due, file your return anyway. Write "Applied for" and the date you applied for the number in the space for the EIN. If a tax deposit (discussed under *Business Taxes*) is due before you receive your number, send your payment to the IRS Center where you file your returns. Make your check or money order payable to the Internal Revenue Service. Write your name (as it appears on the Form SS-4 you completed), your address, the kind of tax you are paying, the period covered, and the date you filed Form SS-4 on the check.

How To Use an EIN

You must include your taxpayer identification number (SSN or EIN) on all returns or other documents you send to the IRS. You must also furnish your number to other persons who use your identification number on any returns or documents they send to the IRS. This includes returns or documents they file to report:

1) Interest, dividends, royalties, etc., paid to you.
2) Amounts paid to you (in your business) that total $600 or more for the year.
3) Any amount paid to you as a dependent care provider.
4) Alimony paid to you.

If you fail to furnish your identification number as required, you will be subject to penalties.

More than one EIN. If you have more than one EIN and are not sure which to use, please contact the IRS Center where you file your return. Tell them the numbers you have, the name and address you used on each application, and the address of your main place of business. They will tell you which number to use.

When To Get a New EIN

You may need to get a new EIN if the organization or the ownership of your business changes.

Change in organization. You need a new EIN when any of the following occurs:

1) A sole proprietorship incorporates.

2) A sole proprietorship takes in partners and operates as a partnership.

3) A partnership incorporates.

4) A partnership is taken over by one of the partners and operated as a sole proprietorship.

5) A corporation changes to a partnership or sole proprietorship.

A corporation converting to an S corporation does not need a new EIN.

Change in ownership. You need a new EIN when any of the following occurs:

1) You purchase or inherit an existing business that you will operate as a sole proprietorship. (You cannot use the EIN of the former owner, even if he or she is your spouse.)

2) You represent an estate that operates a business after the owner's death.

3) You terminate an old partnership and begin a new one.

Employee and Other Payee Numbers

In the operation of a business, you will normally make certain payments you must report on information returns, discussed later. You must give the recipient of these payments (the payee) a statement showing the total amount paid during the year. The forms used to report these payments must include the payee's identification number, as well as your identification number.

Employee. If you are an employer, you must get a social security number (SSN) from each of your employees. When you hire an employee, you should give him or her a Form W-4, *Employee's Withholding Allowance Certificate.* The employee must complete the form and return it to you. It will give you his or her SSN and the information needed to figure the income tax to withhold from the employee's salary. You will use the SSN of each employee when you report his or her wages and the withheld social security and income taxes. Using

the SSN will ensure that each employee's account is properly credited.

If your employee does not have an SSN, he or she should file Form SS-5, *Application for Social Security Card,* with the Social Security Administration. Forms are available at SSA offices and by calling 1-800-829-3676.

Other payee. If you make payments to a nonemployee that you report on an information return, get an SSN from each individual (including sole proprietors). If you make payments to an organization such as a corporation or partnership, you must get the EIN of the organization.

To get the payee's SSN or EIN, use Form W-9, *Request for Taxpayer Identification Number and Certification.* A sole proprietor must give his or her individual name on Form W-9, as well as the SSN or EIN. This form is available from IRS offices.

A payee who does not provide you with an identification number may be subject to backup withholding of 20%. For information on backup withholding, see Form W-9 and the 1993 *Instructions for Forms 1099, 1098, 5498, 1096, and W-2G.*

Business Taxes

The type of business you operate determines what taxes you must pay and how you pay them. There are four general kinds of business taxes:

1) Income tax.

2) Self-employment tax.

3) Employment taxes.

4) Excise taxes.

Publication 509 contains a general tax calendar, an employer's tax calendar, and an excise tax calendar. Each calendar explains when to file returns and make tax payments.

Income Tax

Every business must file an annual income tax return. Which form you use depends on how your business is organized.

Organization:	File:
Sole proprietorship	Schedule C (Form 1040)
Farming	Schedule F (Form 1040)
Partnership	Form 1065
Corporation	Form 1120 or 1120-A
S corporation	Form 1120S

If you are a sole proprietor or farmer and have more than one business, file a separate Schedule C or Schedule F for each business.

How to pay. Federal income and self-employment taxes are pay-as-you-go taxes.

Individuals. Income from your business is not subject to withholding. You generally pay the tax during the year as you earn your income. Sole proprietors, partners, or shareholders of an S corporation pay as they go by making regular payments of estimated tax during the year. If your estimated income tax and

self-employment tax will be $500 or more for 1993, you generally have to make estimated tax payments. If you are not required to make estimated tax payments, you may pay any tax due when you file your return. For information on estimated tax, see Publication 505.

Corporations. A corporation must deposit the taxes it owes, including estimated tax payments and any balance due shown on its tax return. For information on how to make tax deposits, see *Depositing Taxes,* later.

Self-Employment Tax

Self-employment tax is the social security and Medicare tax for individuals who work for themselves, including sole proprietors, self-employed farmers and fishermen, and members of a partnership. You figure self-employment tax on Schedule SE and attach it to Form 1040.

For more information, see Publication 533.

Employment Taxes

If you have employees, you will pay employment taxes. These taxes include:

1) Federal income tax withholding.

2) Social security and Medicare taxes.

3) Federal unemployment (FUTA) tax.

Federal Income, Social Security, and Medicare Taxes

You withhold federal income tax from your employee's wages. For social security and Medicare taxes, you withhold part from your employee's wages and you pay a matching amount yourself.

Tax returns. You report and pay social security and Medicare taxes and withheld income tax together. Farm employers report these taxes on Form 943, *Employer's Annual Tax Return for Agricultural Employees.* Other employers use Form 941, *Employer's Quarterly Federal Tax Return.*

Federal Unemployment (FUTA) Tax

You report and pay FUTA tax separately from social security and Medicare taxes and withheld income tax. You pay FUTA tax only from your own funds. Employees do not pay this tax or have it withheld from their pay.

Tax return. You report federal unemployment tax on Form 940, *Employer's Annual Federal Unemployment (FUTA) Tax Return.*

Simplified form. Form 940EZ, *Employer's Annual Federal Unemployment (FUTA) Tax Return,* is a simplified version of Form 940. You can use Form 940EZ if:

1) You pay employment taxes to only one state.

2) You pay all state employment tax by the due date for filing Form 940EZ.

3) The FUTA wages you pay are also taxable for state unemployment tax.

How to Pay

You generally must deposit employment taxes before you file an employment tax return. See *Depositing Taxes*, later, for information on making deposits.

For more information on reporting and deposit requirements for employment taxes, see Publication 15, *Circular E, Employer's Tax Guide*, and Publication 937. Publication 15 also contains withholding tax tables to figure the amount of social security, Medicare, and federal income tax to withhold.

Farmers. For more information on reporting and deposit requirements for employment taxes, see Publication 51, *Circular A, Agricultural Employer's Tax Guide.*

Penalties

If you do not withhold income, social security, or Medicare taxes from employees, or withhold taxes but do not deposit them or pay them to the IRS, you may be subject to a penalty of 100% of the tax. You may also be subject to penalties if you deposit the taxes late. For more information, see Publication 937.

Excise Taxes

If you manufacture or sell certain products, you may have to pay excise taxes. There are also excise taxes on certain kinds of businesses, certain transactions, and the use of various kinds of equipment, facilities, and products.

Form 720. The federal excise taxes reported on Form 720, *Quarterly Federal Excise Tax Return*, consist of several broad categories:

1) Environmental taxes imposed on domestic crude oil, imported petroleum products, and certain chemicals sold by producers, manufacturers, or importers.

2) Facilities and services taxes, including taxes on amounts paid for telephone communications and air transportation.

3) Fuel taxes, including taxes on the sale or use of gasoline, gasohol, diesel fuel, and special motor fuels.

4) Manufacturer's taxes on the sale or use of a variety of different products.

5) Excise tax on the first retail sale of heavy trucks and trailers, and certain luxury items (passenger cars, boats, aircraft, jewelry, and furs).

6) Other excise taxes, including taxes on policies issued by foreign insurers and obligations not in registered form.

File Form 720 generally within one month after the end of a calendar quarter.

You may have to deposit the excise taxes reported on Form 720 before the return is due. For information on making deposits, see *Depositing Taxes*, later. For more information on the excise taxes you report on Form 720 and the deposit requirements, see Publication 510, *Excise Taxes for 1993.*

Form 2290. There is a federal excise tax on certain trucks, truck tractors, and buses used on public highways. The tax applies to vehicles having a gross vehicle weight of 55,000 pounds or more. Report the tax on Form 2290, *Heavy Vehicle Use Tax Return*. For more information, see Publication 349, *Federal Highway Use Tax on Heavy Vehicles.*

ATF forms. If you produce, sell, or import guns, tobacco, or alcohol products, or if you manufacture equipment for their production, you may be liable for one or more excise taxes. Report these taxes on forms filed with the Bureau of Alcohol, Tobacco and Firearms. For more information on these forms, see Publication 510.

Form 730. If you are in the business of accepting bets or running a betting pool or lottery, you may be liable for federal excise taxes on wagering. Use Form 730, *Tax on Wagering*, to report tax on the bets you receive. For more information, see the Form 730 instructions.

Form 11–C. Use Form 11–C, *Special Tax Return and Application for Registry—Wagering*, to pay an annual tax and to register your place of business. For more information, see the Form 11–C instructions.

Depositing Taxes

In some cases, you may have to deposit the tax you owe before you file your return. A return can cover more than one deposit period.

Mail or deliver deposits with completed *deposit coupons* to an authorized financial institution or a Federal Reserve bank for your area. To help ensure proper crediting of your account, include the following on your check or money order:

1) Your EIN.
2) Type of tax.
3) Tax period for the payment.

To be on time, mailed deposits must arrive at the depository by the due date. You may be charged a penalty for not making deposits when due, unless you have reasonable cause.

Deposit the taxes from the forms listed below:

Type of Tax	Reported On
Corporate income tax	Form 1120
Social security and Medicare taxes and withheld income tax (non-agricultural)	Form 941
Social security and Medicare taxes and withheld income tax (agricultural)	Form 943
Federal unemployment (FUTA) tax	Form 940
Excise tax	Form 720

Deposit coupons. Form 8109, *Federal Tax Deposit Coupon Book*, contains coupons for depositing taxes. On each coupon, you must show the deposit amount, the type of tax, the period for which you are making a deposit, and your telephone number. Use a separate coupon for each tax and period. You must include a coupon with each deposit you make.

When you apply for an employer identification number (EIN), as discussed earlier, the IRS will send you the coupon book. If you have a deposit due and there is not enough time to obtain a coupon book, blank coupons (Form 8109–B) are available at most IRS offices. You cannot use photocopies of the coupons to make your deposits.

If you have not received your EIN and must make a deposit, mail your payment with an explanation to the IRS Center where you file your return. Make your check or money order payable to the Internal Revenue Service. On the check, write your name (as shown on Form SS–4), address, kind of tax, period covered, and date you applied for an EIN.

More Information. For more information on when deposits and business tax returns are due, see Publications 15, 51, 509, and 937.

Information Returns

You may make or receive payments in your business that you must report to the IRS.

You must report on information returns various kinds of payments made to, or certain payments received from, persons who are not your employees. The IRS uses information returns to match the payments with each person's income tax return to see if the payments were included in income. You must give each person a statement showing the total amount paid to or received from that person during the year.

Form 1099–MISC. Use Form 1099–MISC, *Miscellaneous Income*, to report certain payments you make in your trade or business. These include payments of $10 or more for royalties, and payments of $600 or more for rents, prizes and awards not for services rendered, and payments to persons who were not your employees (such as independent contractors).

Form 8300. You must file Form 8300, *Report of Cash Payments over $10,000*, if you receive more than $10,000 in cash or foreign currency in one or more related business transactions.

For more information, see Publication 1544, *Reporting Cash Payments of Over $10,000.*

Other returns. In addition to Forms 1099–MISC and 8300, you may use other returns to report certain kinds of payments or transactions. For information on these returns, and on the general requirements for filing information returns, see Publication 937.

Penalties

If you do not follow the requirements for filing, completing, and furnishing information returns, the following penalties may be charged for each failure:

1) $50 maximum penalty if you do not file an information return on time with the IRS.

2) $50 maximum penalty if you do not include all information required on the return, or the correct information.

3) $50 penalty if you do not furnish a copy of an information return to a payee or payer on time.

The penalty for (1) and (2) is reduced if you file the information return or correct the information on a filed return within a specified period. The penalty is $15 per return if you correct the error within 30 days after the due date. If you correct the error by August 1 of the year the return is due, the penalty is $30 per return. However, there is no penalty for a de minimis number of returns (the greater of 10 or one-half of 1% of all information returns filed) if you correct the errors by August 1 of the year the returns are due.

The maximum penalty for (1) and (2) is $250,000 a year. However, if you correct the returns within the periods specified, the maximum penalties are reduced to $75,000 and $150,000 respectively. The maximum penalty for (3) is $100,000 a year.

Waiver of penalty. These penalties will not be imposed if you can show that the failures were due to reasonable cause and not willful neglect.

Checksheet for Employers

You may want to keep the following employment-related forms and publications on hand:

Forms:

☐ SS–5, *Application for a Social Security Card*

☐ W–4, *Employee's Withholding Allowance Certificate*

☐ 940, *Employer's Annual Federal Unemployment (FUTA) Return*

☐ 940EZ, *Employer's Annual Federal Unemployment (FUTA) Return*

☐ 941, *Employer's Quarterly Federal Tax Return*

☐ 8109, *Federal Tax Deposit Coupon Book*

Publications:

☐ 15, *Circular E, Employer's Tax Guide*

☐ 937, *Employment Taxes and Information Returns*

Recordkeeping

Everyone in business must keep records. Good records will help you prepare accurate tax returns so you pay only the amount of tax you owe. Good records are also needed for good management.

Advantages of Good Records

Good records can save you time and money. You need good records to show the progress of your business operations, to prepare credit applications, and to support items of income and expense reported on your tax return.

Identify source of receipts. You will receive money or property from many sources. Your records can identify the source of your receipts. You need this information to separate business from nonbusiness receipts and taxable from nontaxable income.

Keep track of deductible expenses. You may forget expenses when you prepare your tax return unless you record them when they occur.

Figure depreciation allowance. You should record the assets you can depreciate in a permanent record. You need a record of the cost and other information on your assets to figure your depreciation deductions. If you sell the assets or make capital improvements to them, only a permanent record shows how much of their cost you have recovered.

Record details of assets. Good, complete records show the date you acquired an asset, the percentage of its business use, and any changes in the basis of each asset. You need this information to figure (and to know how to report) gain or loss if you sell, trade, or otherwise dispose of it, or it is destroyed.

Determine earnings for self-employment tax purposes. The self-employment tax is the means for providing social security coverage for people who work for themselves. The social security benefits you receive when you retire, or are disabled, or the benefits your family receives when you die, depend on how much you earn. Your records should show how much self-employment tax you pay on your earnings.

Support items reported on tax returns. If the IRS examines any of your tax returns, you may be asked to explain the items reported. A complete set of records will speed up the examination. You support adequate and complete records with sales slips, invoices, receipts, deposit slips, canceled checks, certain financial account statements, and other documents.

Financial account statements as proof of payment. If you cannot provide a canceled check to prove payment of an expense item, you may be able to prove payment with certain financial account statements. This includes account statements prepared by a third party who is under contract to prepare statements for the financial institution. Acceptable account statements include:

1) An account statement showing a check clearing is accepted as proof (depending on your method of accounting) if it shows the:
   a) Check number,
   b) Amount,
   c) Payee name, and
   d) Date the check amount was posted to the account by the financial institution.

2) An account statement prepared by a financial institution showing an electronic funds transfer is accepted as proof if it shows the:
   a) Amount transferred,
   b) Payee name, and
   c) Date the transfer was posted to the account by the financial institution.

3) An account statement prepared by a financial institution showing a credit card charge (an increase to the cardholder's loan balance), is accepted as proof if it shows the:
   a) Amount charged,
   b) Payee name, and
   c) Date charged (transaction date).

These account statements must show a high degree of legibility and readability. For this purpose, legibility is the quality of a letter or number that allows it to be identified positively excluding all other letters and numbers. Readability is the quality of a group of letters or numbers that allows it to be recognized as words or complete numbers. However, this does not mean the information must be typed or printed. For example, the IRS will accept an account statement that reproduces the required information in the account holder's own handwriting from checks or charge slips.

However, proof of payment of an amount alone does not establish that you are entitled to a tax deduction. You should also keep other documents as discussed in *Support items reported on tax returns,* earlier.

Records Required

The law does not require any special kind of records. You may choose any system suited to your business to clearly show your income.

Your permanent books (including inventory records) must show your gross income, as well as your deductions and credits. In addition, you must keep any other records and data necessary to support the entries in your books and on your tax and information returns. File paid bills, canceled checks, etc., that support entries in your books in an orderly fashion and keep them in a safe place. For most small businesses, the business checkbook is the main source for entries in the business records.

The business you are in affects the type of records you need to keep for federal tax purposes. You should set up your books using an accounting method that clearly shows your income for your tax year. If you are in more than one business, you should keep a complete and separate set of books for each business.

The sample records in this publication show the kinds of records a small business operating as a sole proprietorship can use.

Car expense records. If you use your car for business, see Publication 917 for information on the records to keep for your deduction.

Tax Year

You must figure your taxable income and file an income tax return based on an annual accounting period called a tax year. A tax year is usually 12 consecutive months. There are 2 kinds of tax years:

Calendar

Fiscal

If you operate a business as a sole proprietor, the tax year for your business must be the same as your individual tax year.

Calendar year. A calendar year is 12 consecutive months beginning January 1 and ending December 31. If you are a calendar year taxpayer and a sole proprietor, your business must also be on the calendar year basis.

Fiscal year. A fiscal year is 12 consecutive months ending on the last day of any month other than December, or a 52–53 week year. You must keep your books on a fiscal year basis to file a fiscal year tax return.

If you are considering using a fiscal year, see Publication 538.

Short tax year. A short tax year has less than 12 months. You will have a short tax year if your business is not in existence for an entire tax year or you change your tax year. Figuring tax for a short tax year is different for each situation. See Publication 538.

S corporations. All S corporations, regardless of when they became S corporations, must generally use a calendar tax year. An S corporation can use any other accounting period for which the corporation establishes a business purpose to the satisfaction of the IRS or for which it has made a section 444 election. For more information, see Publication 538.

Partnerships. All partnerships, including existing partnerships, must use a tax year that conforms to their partners' tax year, unless the partnership can establish a business purpose for a different period or makes a section 444 election. For more information, see Publication 538.

First-time filer. If you have never filed an income tax return, you can choose either a calendar year or a fiscal tax year. You must choose a tax year by the time set by law (not including extensions) for filing your first return.

You must use the calendar year if you have inadequate records or you have no accounting period, or your annual accounting period does not qualify as a fiscal year.

Accounting Method

An accounting method is a set of rules used to determine when and how to report income and expenses in your books and on your income tax returns.

You can choose any of the following accounting methods if you use it regularly and it clearly shows your income.

1) Cash method.
2) Accrual method.
3) Special methods of accounting for certain items of income and expenses.
4) Combination (hybrid) method using elements of (1), (2), or (3).

If you need inventories to show income correctly, you must generally use the accrual method of accounting for purchases and sales.

You must use the same accounting method from year to year to figure your taxable income and keep your books if that method clearly shows your income. In general, any accounting method that consistently uses accounting principles suitable for your trade or business clearly shows income. An accounting method clearly shows income only if it treats all items of gross income and expense the same from year to year.

Cash method — reporting income. Under this method, you report income when actually or constructively received, and you report expenses when paid.

Constructive receipt. Constructive receipt occurs when an amount is credited to your account or made available to you without restriction as to the time or manner of payment. You do not need to have possession of it.

Holding checks or similar property from one tax year to another does not put off payment of tax on the income. Include this income in the year the check or other property is set aside for you and subject to your demand.

Example 1. The bank credits interest to your account on December 30, 1992. You withdraw the interest on January 3, 1993. You must include the interest in income for 1992, the year it is credited to your account, not the year it is withdrawn or entered in your passbook.

Example 2. You received a check for $250 on December 31, 1992, for an item you sold. You did not cash the check until January 2, 1992. You must include the $250 in gross receipts in 1992, the year you received the check.

Example 3. On January 2, 1993, you received and deposited a check dated December 28, 1992, for payment of goods. You must include this amount in gross receipts for 1993, the year you received the check.

Cash method—deducting expenses. You usually deduct expenses in the tax year you pay them. However, you can deduct prepaid expenses only in the year to which they apply.

Example. You are a calendar year taxpayer and pay $3,000 for an insurance policy effective July 1, 1992, for a 3-year period. You can deduct $500 in 1992, $1,000 in 1993, $1,000 in 1994, and $500 in 1995.

Limits on use of cash method. Corporations (other than S corporations) and certain partnerships with average yearly gross receipts of more than $5,000,000, and all tax shelters, cannot use the cash method of accounting. For more information, see Publication 538.

Accrual method — reporting income. Under the accrual method, you generally report income when you earn it, even though you may receive payment in a later year. It is not the receipt of payment that is important, but the right to receive it. All events that fix your right to receive the income must have occurred, and you must be able to figure the amount with reasonable accuracy.

Example. You are a calendar year taxpayer. You sold a radio in November 1992. You billed the customer 2 days later, but you did not receive payment until February 1993. You must include the amount of the sale in income for 1992 because you earned the income in that year.

Accrual method—deducting expenses. Under this method, you deduct expenses as you incur them, whether or not you pay them in the same year. All events that set the amount of the liability must have occurred, and you must be able to figure the amount with reasonable accuracy.

Economic performance rule. Business expenses are generally not deductible until economic performance occurs. If the expense is for property or services provided to you, or for property you use, economic performance occurs as the property or services are provided, or as you use the property. If the expense is for property or services you provide to others, economic performance occurs as you provide the property or service. You can treat certain recurring expenses as incurred during a tax year even though economic performance has not occurred. For a discussion of the economic performance rule, see Publication 538.

Example. You are a calendar year taxpayer and buy office supplies in December 1992. You received the supplies and the bill for them in December, but you pay for them in January 1993. You can deduct the expense in 1992 because all events that set the amount of the liability and economic performance occurred in

General Journal

Date	Description of Entry	Post Ref.	Debit	Credit
Oct. 5	Rent Expense		780 00	
	Cash			780 00

that year. Your office supplies qualify as a recurring expense and you can deduct the expense in 1992, even if delivery of the supplies (economic performance) does not occur until 1993.

Cash or accrual. If you use the accrual method of accounting for purchases and sales, you can use the cash method for figuring all other income and expenses. However, if you use the cash method for figuring gross income from your business, you must use the cash method for figuring business expenses. If you use an accrual method for figuring business expenses, you must use an accrual method for figuring all items that affect the gross income from your business.

You can account for business and personal items under different accounting methods. You can figure the income from your business under the accrual method even if you use the cash method to figure personal items.

More than one business. When you own more than one business, you can use a different accounting method for each separate business if the method you use for each clearly shows your income. When you use different accounting methods, you must keep a complete and separate set of books and records for each business.

Example. You run a personal service business and a manufacturing business. You can use the cash method for the personal service business. However, you must use the accrual method or a hybrid method for the manufacturing business because inventories are required to account for your income.

Changing your method of accounting. Once you have set up your accounting method, you must get the consent of the IRS before you can change to another method. A change in accounting method not only includes a change in your overall system of accounting, but also a change in the treatment of any material item. For examples of changes that require consent and information on how to get consent for the change, see Publication 538.

Bookkeeping System

You must decide whether to use a single- or a double-entry bookkeeping system. The single-entry system of bookkeeping is the simplest to maintain, but it may not be suitable for everyone. You may find the double-entry system better because it has built-in checks and balances to assure accuracy and control.

Single-entry. A single-entry system is based on the income statement (profit or loss statement). It can be a simple and practical system if you are starting a small business. For tax purposes, the system records the flow of income and expenses through the use of:

1) A daily summary of cash receipts.
2) Monthly summaries of cash receipts and disbursements.

Double-entry. A double-entry bookkeeping system uses journals and ledgers. Transactions are first entered in a journal and then posted to ledger accounts. These accounts show income, expenses, assets (property a business owns), liabilities (debts of a business), and net worth (excess of assets over liabilities). You close income and expense accounts at the end of each accounting period. You keep asset, liability, and net worth accounts open on a permanent basis.

In the double-entry system, each account has a left side for debits and a right side for credits. It is self-balancing because you record every transaction as a debit entry in one account and as a credit entry in another. An example of a journal showing a payment of rent in October is shown in this publication.

Under this system, the total debits must equal the total credits after you post the journal entries to the ledger accounts. If the amounts do not balance, you have made an error and you must find and correct it.

At the end of each accounting period, you prepare financial statements. These are generally the income statement and the balance sheet. The income statement reflects current operations for the year. The balance sheet shows the financial position of the business in terms of assets, liabilities, and net worth on a given date.

Automatic data processing system. You can use a computer accounting system if it maintains adequate permanent records and produces a legible printout.

Additional information. You can get more information on accounting systems and basic accounting terms and procedures from various Small Business Administration (SBA) publications. Write for the free *Directory of Business Development Publications* at the following address:

SBA Publications
P.O. Box 1000
Fort Worth, TX 76119

Recordkeeping System

You do not have to keep your records in bound books. Records are adequate if they show current income on the basis of an annual accounting period.

A recordkeeping system for a small business might include the following:

Business Checkbook

Daily Summary of Cash Receipts

Monthly Summary of Cash Receipts

Check Disbursements Journal

Depreciation Worksheet

Employee Compensation Record

You must have the books and records of your business available for inspection by the IRS.

How long to keep records. You must keep your records as long as they may be needed for the administration of any provision of the Internal Revenue Code. Keep records that support an item of income or deduction on a return until the statute of limitations for that return runs out. Usually, the statute of limitations for an income tax return is the later of 3 years after the return is due or filed, or 2 years from the date the tax is paid.

If you have employees, you must keep all employment tax records for at least 4 years after the date the tax becomes due or is paid, whichever is later.

Keep records that verify your basis in property for as long as they are needed to figure the basis of the original or replacement property. Also, new laws may provide tax benefits to taxpayers who can prove from their records they are entitled to the benefits.

Copies of tax returns. You should keep copies of your filed tax returns. They help in preparing future tax returns and making computations if you later file a claim for refund. They may also be helpful to the executor or administrator of your estate, or to the IRS, if your original return is not available.

The Business Checkbook

The business checkbook is your basic source of information for recording your business expenses. You should deposit all daily receipts in your business checking account. You should check your account for errors by reconciling it. See *Reconciling Your Checking Account* under the *Sample Record System,* later.

Consider using a checkbook that allows enough space to identify the source of deposits as business income, personal funds, or loans. You should also note on the deposit slip the source of the deposit and keep copies of all slips.

You may need a petty cash fund for small expenses. See *Petty cash fund* under the *Sample Record System*, later. You must clearly support all business expenses paid by cash with documents that show their business purpose.

You should make all payments by check to document business expenses. Write checks payable to yourself only when making withdrawals from your business for personal use. Avoid writing checks payable to cash. If you must write a check for cash to pay a business expense, include the receipt for the cash payment in your records. If you cannot get a receipt for a cash payment, you should make an adequate explanation in your records at the time of payment.

Sample Record System

The bookkeeping system illustrated on the following pages uses the principles described earlier. This is a single-entry system used by Henry M. Brown, the sole proprietor of a small automobile body shop. Henry uses part-time help, has no inventory of items held for sale, and uses the cash method of accounting.

These sample records should *not* be viewed as a recommendation of how to keep your records. They are intended to show one way to keep business records and how to use the records to complete Schedule C (Form 1040).

The design of Schedule C may change from year to year. Make sure you enter all items on the correct line of the current form.

Amounts on Schedule C have been rounded to the nearest dollar.

The following explanations are keyed to the numbers and letters on the sample records and the Schedule C. Use the bracketed numbers to help relate the text to the illustrations. The bracketed letters and related discussions identify and explain the progression of certain transactions throughout the sample system.

[1] Daily Summary of Cash Receipts. This summary records cash sales for the day and accounts for the cash over the amount in your Change and Petty Cash Fund at the beginning of the day.

You may take the Cash Sales entry from your cash register tape. If you have no cash register, you may simply total your cash sale slips and any other cash received that day.

[A] Enter the total receipts ($267.80) including cash sales ($263.60) and sales tax ($4.20) for January 2, 1992, from the *Daily Summary of Cash Receipts* [1] in the *Monthly Summary of Cash Receipts* [2]. This gives you the total monthly receipts to figure the total monthly taxable income.

Petty cash fund. You can use a petty cash fund to make small payments without having to write checks for small amounts. Each time you make a payment from this fund, you should make out a petty cash slip and attach it to your receipt as proof of payment. You should set up a fixed amount in your petty cash fund ($50 is the amount shown for this example). The total of the unspent petty cash

and the amounts on the petty cash slips should equal the fixed amount of the fund. When the totals on the petty cash slips approach the fixed amount, bring the cash in the fund back to the fixed amount by writing a check to "Petty Cash" for the total of the outstanding slips. (See the *Check Disbursements Journal* [4] entry for check number 91). This restores the fund to its fixed amount of $50. Then summarize the slips and enter them in the proper columns in the monthly check disbursements journal.

[2] Monthly Summary of Cash Receipts. This shows the income activity for the month with such items as net sales, sales tax, daily receipts, and deposits in separate columns. The net sales figure for the year is the principal income item (Gross receipts or sales) on Schedule C.

[B] The total monthly net sales ($4,865.05) is carried to the *Annual Summary for Schedule C Entries* [5] to figure gross receipts for the year.

To figure total monthly net sales, reduce the total monthly receipts by the sales tax to be turned over to the state. You cannot take a deduction for sales tax turned over to the state because you only collected the tax. You did not include the tax in your income.

As an alternative, you can include the total sales tax collected in gross receipts and take a deduction for sales taxes paid to the state on the taxes line of Schedule C. Various states and local jurisdictions have different requirements for the collection of sales taxes. You should contact the taxing authorities in your area for sales tax regulations.

[3] Employee Compensation Record. This record shows the number of hours the employee worked in a pay period and the employee's total pay for the period. It also shows withheld deductions used to compute the employee's net pay.

[C] The employee compensation record also records the monthly gross payroll, which is carried to the *Annual Summary for Schedule C Entries* [5].

[4] Check Disbursements Journal. You should enter checks drawn on the business checking account in the *Check Disbursements Journal* each day. All checks should be prenumbered, and each check number listed and accounted for in the column provided in the journal.

Frequent expenses have their own headings across the sheet. You should enter in a separate column expenses that require comparatively numerous or large payments each month, such as materials, gross payroll, and rent. Under the general account column, you can enter small expenses that normally have only one or two monthly payments, such as licenses and postage.

You should not pay personal or nonbusiness expenses by checks drawn on the business account. If they are drawn on the business account, you should record them in the journal, even though you cannot deduct them as business expenses.

[D] Carry the monthly total of materials ($1,083.50) to the *Annual Summary for Schedule C Entries* [5]. Similarly, enter monthly expenses for telephone, truck, auto,

etc., in the appropriate columns of this summary.

[5] Annual Summary for Schedule C Entries. This annual summary of monthly cash receipts and expense totals provides the final amounts to enter on your tax return. Figure the annual summary from the total of monthly cash receipts items, such as [B], which is from the *Monthly Summary of Cash Receipts* [2], and from monthly expenditures like [D], which is from the *Check Disbursements Journal* [4]. As in the journal, keep each major expense in a separate column.

[E] Enter the cash receipts total ($47,440.95) from the annual summary on line 1, Part I of Schedule C.

[F] Carry the total for materials ($10,001.00) from the annual summary to the supplies line of Part II.

There are no inventories of materials and supplies in this example. Henry buys parts and supplies on a per-job basis and uses them only for body work services. A business that carries materials and supplies on hand, unless they are incidental and records of use are not kept, must complete the inventory lines in Part III of Schedule C.

Enter annual totals for interest, rent, taxes, and wages on the appropriate lines of Schedule C. The total for taxes and licenses includes the employer's share of social security and Medicare taxes, the federal unemployment (FUTA) tax, and the business license fee. Enter other annual business expense totals as miscellaneous items on line 27 of Schedule C.

[6] Depreciation Worksheet. Another major item entered on Schedule C is the depreciation allowed on assets used in your trade or business. The sample depreciation worksheet shows examples of items depreciated using the modified accelerated cost recovery system (MACRS). Depreciation is discussed in Chapter 3 of Publication 534, *Depreciation*, and Chapter 3 of Publication 946.

You must take depreciation in the year it is allowable. You cannot deduct in the current year the allowable depreciation you failed to take in a prior year. You must amend the prior year's tax return to take the depreciation deduction.

You can deduct up to $10,000 of the cost of certain depreciable property purchased and placed in service in your trade or business during 1992. This is the "section 179 deduction." For each dollar of investment in section 179 property over $200,000 in a tax year, the $10,000 maximum is reduced (but not below zero) by one dollar. The section 179 deduction is discussed in Publications 534 and 946.

[G] The amount of depreciation you can claim for the tax year is shown on your depreciation worksheet. Carry the deduction for the tax year ($12,724) from line 20, Part IV of Form 4562, to line 13, Part II of Schedule C (Form 1040).

Reconciling Your Checking Account

When you receive your bank statement, you should make sure the statement, your checkbook, and your books agree. The statement balance may not agree with the balance in your checkbook and books because the statement:

1) May include bank charges you must enter in your books and subtract from your checkbook balance, or

2) Does not include deposits made after the statement date or checks that did not clear your account before the statement date.

By reconciling your checking account, you will:

1) Verify how much money you have in the account.

2) Ensure your checkbook and books reflect all bank charges and the correct balance in the checking account.

3) Correct any errors in the bank statement, your checkbook, and books.

You should reconcile your checking account each month.

Before you start to reconcile your monthly bank statement, check your own figures. Begin with the balance shown in your checkbook at the end of the prior month. To this balance, add the total cash deposited during the month and subtract total cash disbursements. The *Monthly Summary of Cash Receipts* [2] shows the monthly total of your bank deposits. The total cash disbursements is in the "Amount of Check" column of your *Check Disbursements Journal* [4].

After checking your figures, the result should agree with your checkbook balance at the end of the month. If the result does not agree with your checkbook balance at the end of the month, you may have made an error in recording check or deposit amounts. You can find such errors by doing the following.

1) Add the amounts on your check stubs and compare that total with the total in

the "Amount of Check" column of your *Check Disbursements Journal* [4]. If the totals do not agree, check the individual amounts to see if an error was made in your check stub record or in the related entry in the "Amount of Check" column of your *Check Disbursements Journal.*

2) Add the deposit amounts in your checkbook. Compare that total with the monthly total of "Daily Receipts" in the *Monthly Summary of Cash Receipts* [2]. If the totals do not agree, check the individual amounts to find any errors.

If your checkbook and journal entries still disagree, then recompute the running balance in your checkbook to make sure additions and subtractions are correct.

Steps to reconcile your checking account. When your checkbook balance agrees with the balance figured from the journal entries, you may begin reconciling your checkbook record with the bank statement. Many banks print a reconciliation worksheet on the back of the statement.

To reconcile your account:

1) Compare the amounts on all canceled checks and other debit slips (such as service charges) with the amounts listed on the statement. Make sure you issued all checks correctly and charged correct amounts against your account.

2) Compare the deposits listed on the bank statement with deposit amounts shown in your checkbook. Account for all differences. List in the first section of the reconciliation any deposits entered in your checkbook that do not appear on the bank statement. In the sample reconciliation, the bank prepares the statement near the end of the month and the deposits of $701.33 and $516.08 do not appear on the bank statement.

3) Put all the canceled checks in numerical order.

4) Compare each canceled check, including both check number and dollar amount, with the entry on your check stub. If correct, mark that number on the checkbook as having cleared the bank. After accounting for all checks returned by the bank, those not marked on your checkbook are your outstanding checks. List in the next section of the reconciliation these outstanding checks. In the sample reconciliation, checks numbered 89, 90, 93, and 94 are still outstanding.

5) Enter any errors you find in the preceding steps in the last section of the reconciliation under "Add" or "Subtract."

6) Enter service charges and other bank debits, determined in step (1) in the last section of the reconciliation, under "Add" or "Subtract."

7) Update your checkbook by entering items on the reconciliation but not recorded (such as service charges). At this point, the adjusted bank statement should equal your adjusted checkbook balance. If you still have differences, check to find errors in the prior steps.

In the illustrated sample reconciliation, Henry must decrease the checkbook balance to reflect the net adjustment of $4 ($10 minus $6). The only book adjustment needed is to the *Check Disbursements Journal* [4] for the $10 bank service charge. No adjustment is needed on the *Monthly Summary of Cash Receipts* [2] because the January 8 deposit of $600.40 was correctly entered in that record.

[1]—Daily Summary of Cash Receipts

January 2, 1992

Cash Sales			263 60
Sales Tax			4 20
Total Receipts			267 80
Cash on Hand			
Cash in Register (Including unspent petty cash)			
Coins	23 75		
Bills	143 00		
Checks	134 05		
Total Cash in Register			300 80
Petty Cash Slips			17 00
Total Cash			317 80
Less: Change and Petty Cash			
Petty Cash Slips	17 00		
Coins and Bills (unspent petty cash)	33 00		
Total Change and Petty Cash Fund			50 00
Total Cash Receipts			267 80

[2]— Monthly Summary of Cash Receipts

Date 1992	Net Sales	Sales Tax	Daily Receipts	Deposit	
Jan 2	263 60	4 20	267 80		[A]
3	212 00	3 39	215 39		
4	194 40	3 10	197 50	680 69	
6	222 40	3 54	225 94		
7	231 15	3 68	234 83		
8	137 50	2 13	139 63	600 40	
9	187 90	2 99	190 89		
10	207 56	3 31	210 87	401 76	
11	128 95	2 05	131 00		
13	231 40	3 77	235 17		
14	201 28	3 21	204 49		
15	88 01	1 40	89 41	660 07	
16	210 95	3 36	214 31		
17	221 80	3 53	225 33	439 64	
18	225 15	3 59	228 74		
21	221 93	3 52	225 45		
22	133 53	2 13	135 66	589 85	
23	130 84	2 08	132 92		
24	216 37	3 45	219 82	352 74	
25	220 05	3 50	223 55		
27	197 80	3 15	200 95		
28	272 49	4 34	276 83	701 33	
29	150 64	2 40	153 04		
30	224 05	3 56	227 61		
31	133 30	2 13	135 43	516 08	
[B]	4865 05	77 51	4942 56	4942 56	

[3] — EMPLOYEE COMPENSATION RECORD

NAME: John E. Marks
ADDRESS: 1 Elm St., Newark, NJ
PHONE: 555-6075

FULL TIME _____
PART TIME ___X___

SOC. SEC. NO. 567-00-8901
DATE OF BIRTH 12-21-65
NO. OF EXEMPTIONS Single - 1

Pay Period Ending	Hours Worked S M T W T F S	Hours Worked S M T W T F S	Total Reg. Hours	Over-time	Earnings Regular Rate	Earnings Overtime Rate	Earnings Total	Deductions Social Security	Deductions Medicare	Deductions Fed. Income Tax	Deductions State Income Tax	Deductions Other	Net Pay
1-4-92	5 5 5	5 5 4 6	40		6.50		$260.00	$16.12	$3.77	$20.00	$6.00		$214.11
1-18-92	4 4 4 4 2	4 3 4 4 3	40		6.50		260.00	16.12	3.77	20.00	6.00		214.11
QUARTERLY TOTALS			80				$520.00	$32.24	$7.54	$40.00	$12.00		$428.22

[C]

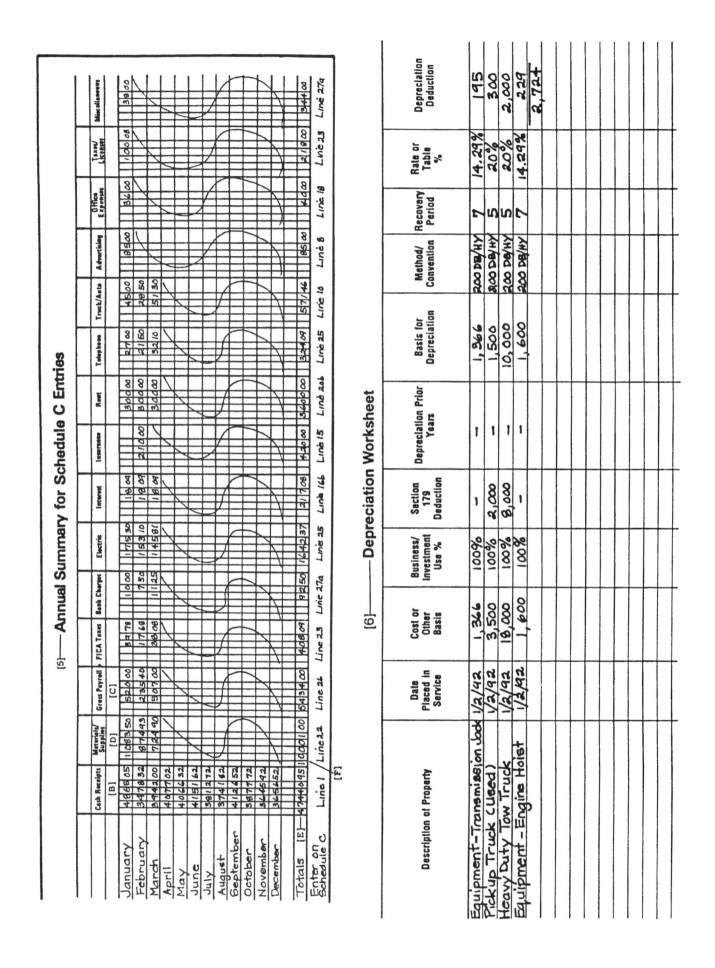

[5] —— Annual Summary for Schedule C Entries

	Cash Receipts [B]	Materials/ Supplies [D]	Gross Payroll [C]	FICA Taxes	Bank Charges	Electric	Interest	Insurance	Rent	Telephone	Truck/Auto	Advertising	Office Expense	Taxes/License	Miscellaneous
January	4866.05	1083.50	520.00	39.78	10.00	175.50	18.09		300.00	27.00	45.00	85.00	36.00	100.00	39.00
February	3478.32	874.43	235.40	17.60	7.50	153.10	18.09	210.00	300.00	31.60	28.50				
March	3942.00	724.90	507.00	38.08	11.25	145.81	18.09		300.00	32.10	51.30				
April	4077.02														
May	4064.32														
June	4151.62														
July	3812.72														
August	3741.62														
September	4124.52														
October	3877.72														
November	3645.42														
December	3652.52														
Totals [E]	47440.95	10000.00	5434.00	408.09	92.50	1644.37	217.08	420.00	3600.00	324.09	571.46	85.00	44.00	219.00	344.00
Enter on Schedule C	Line 1/Line 22	Line 22	Line 26	Line 23	Line 27a	Line 25	Line 16b	Line 15	Line 20b	Line 25	Line 10	Line 8	Line 18	Line 23	Line 27a

[F]

[6] —— Depreciation Worksheet

Description of Property	Date Placed in Service	Cost or Other Basis	Business/ Investment Use %	Section 179 Deduction	Depreciation Prior Years	Basis for Depreciation	Method/ Convention	Recovery Period	Rate or Table %	Depreciation Deduction
Equipment-Transmission Jack	1/2/92	1,366	100%	—	—	1,366	200 DB/HY	7	14.29%	195
Pickup Truck (used)	1/2/92	3,500	100%	2,000	—	1,500	200 DB/HY	5	20%	300
Heavy Duty Tow Truck	1/2/92	18,000	100%	8,000	—	10,000	200 DB/HY	5	20%	2,000
Equipment – Engine Hoist	1/2/92	1,600	100%	—	—	1,600	200 DB/HY	7	14.29%	229
										2,724

[4]——Check Disbursements Journal

199**2**		Paid To	Ck. No.	Amount of Check		Materials		Gross Payroll		Federal Withheld Income Tax		FICA Social Security Reserve		Medicare Reserve	
Jan	2	Dale Advertising	74	85	00										
	4	City Treasurer	75	35	00										
	4	Auto Parts, Inc.	76	203	00	203	00								
	4	John E. Marks	77	214	11			260	00	(20	00)	(16	12)	(3	77.
	6	Henry Brown	78	250	00										
	6	Mike's Delicatessen	79	36	00										
	6	Joe's Service Station	80	74	50	29	50								
	6	ABC Auto Paint	81	137	50	137	50								
	7	Henry Brown	82	225	00										
	14	Telephone Co.	83	27	00										
	18	National Bank	84	90	74										
	18	Auto Parts, Inc.	85	472	00	472	00								
	18	Henry Brown	86	275	00										
	18	John E. Marks	87	214	11			260	00	(20	00)	(16	12)	(3	77.
	21	Electric Co.	88	175	30										
	21	M.B. Ignition	89	66	70	66	70								
	21	Baker's Fender Co.	90	9	80	9	80								
	21	Petty Cash	91	17	00	15	00								
	21	Henry Brown	92	225	00										
	25	Baker's Fender Co.	93	150	00	150	00								
	25	Enterprise Properties	94	300	00										
	25	National Bank (Tax Deposit)	95	119	56					40	00	32	24	7	54
	25	State Treasurer	96	12	00										
	25	State Treasurer	97	65	08										
				3,477	40	1,083	50	520	00	–0–		–0–		–0–	
		Bank Service Charge		10	00										
				3,489	40	1,083	50	520	00	–0–		–0–		–0–	
						[D]		[C]							

State Withheld Income Tax	Employer's FICA Tax	Electric	Interest	Rent	Telephone	Truck/ Auto	Drawing	General Accounts	
								Advertising	85 00
								License	35 00
(6 00)									
							250 00		
								Shop Holiday Party	36 00
						45 00			
							225 00		
					27 00				
			18 09					Loan	72 65
							275 00		
(6 00)									
		175 30							
								Postage	2 00
							225 00		
				300 00					
	39 78								
12 00									
								Sales Tax	65 08
—0—	39 78	175 30	18 09	300 00	27 00	45 00	975 00		295 73
									10 00
—0—	39 78	175 30	18 09	300 00	27 00	45 00	975 00		305 73

SCHEDULE C
(Form 1040)

Department of the Treasury
Internal Revenue Service | (T)

Profit or Loss From Business
(Sole Proprietorship)

▶ **Partnerships, joint ventures, etc., must file Form 1065.**

▶ Attach to Form 1040 or Form 1041.   ▶ See Instructions for Schedule C (Form 1040).

OMB No. 1545-0074

1992

Attachment
Sequence No. **09**

Name of proprietor	Social security number (SSN)
Henry M. Brown	123 : 00 : 6789

A Principal business or profession, including product or service (see page C-1)
Auto Repair Service

B Enter principal business code (from page 2) ▶ 8 9 5 3

C Business name
Brown's Auto Body Shop

D Employer ID number (Not SSN)
1 0 9 9 9 9 9 9 9

E Business address (including suite or room no.) ▶ ......5 Amherst Avenue......
City, town or post office, state, and ZIP code   Newark, NJ   07103

F Accounting method: (1) ☑ Cash   (2) ☐ Accrual   (3) ☐ Other (specify) ▶ ....

G Method(s) used to value closing inventory: (1) ☐ Cost   (2) ☐ Lower of cost or market   (3) ☐ Other (attach explanation)   (4) ☑ Does not apply (if checked, skip line H)

		Yes	No
H	Was there any change in determining quantities, costs, or valuations between opening and closing inventory? If "Yes," attach explanation	N/A	
I	Did you "materially participate" in the operation of this business during 1992? If "No," see page C-2 for limitations on losses	✓	
J	Was this business in operation at the end of 1992?	✓	
K	How many months was this business in operation during 1992? ▶	12	
L	If this is the first Schedule C filed for this business, check here ▶ ☑		

Part I   Income

1	Gross receipts or sales. Caution: If this income was reported to you on Form W-2 and the "Statutory employee" box on that form was checked, see page C-2 and check here ▶ ☐	1	47,441	[E]
2	Returns and allowances	2		
3	Subtract line 2 from line 1	3	47,441	
4	Cost of goods sold (from line 40 on page 2)	4		
5	Gross profit. Subtract line 4 from line 3	5	47,441	
6	Other income, including Federal and state gasoline or fuel tax credit or refund (see page C-2)	6		
7	Gross income. Add lines 5 and 6 ▶	7	47,441	

Part II   Expenses (Caution: *Do not enter expenses for business use of your home on lines 8–27. Instead, see line 30.*)

8	Advertising	8	85		21	Repairs and maintenance	21	
9	Bad debts from sales or services (see page C-3)	9			22	Supplies (not included in Part III)	22	10,001 [F]
10	Car and truck expenses (see page C-3—also attach Form 4562)	10	571		23	Taxes and licenses	23	626
11	Commissions and fees	11			24	Travel, meals, and entertainment:		
12	Depletion	12			a	Travel	24a	
13	Depreciation and section 179 expense deduction (not included in Part III) (see page C-3)	13	12,724		b	Meals and entertainment		
14	Employee benefit programs (other than on line 19)	14			c	Enter 20% of line 24b subject to limitations (see page C-4)		
15	Insurance (other than health)	15	420		d	Subtract line 24c from line 24b	24d	
16	Interest:				25	Utilities	25	1,966
a	Mortgage (paid to banks, etc.)	16a			26	Wages (less jobs credit)	26	5,434
b	Other	16b	217		27a	Other expenses (list type and amount):		
17	Legal and professional services	17				Bank service charge 93		
18	Office expense	18	40			Miscellaneous 344		
19	Pension and profit-sharing plans	19						
20	Rent or lease (see page C-4):							
a	Vehicles, machinery, and equipment	20a						
b	Other business property	20b	3,600		27b	Total other expenses	27b	437

28	Total expenses before expenses for business use of home. Add lines 8 through 27b in columns ▶	28	36,121	
29	Tentative profit (loss). Subtract line 28 from line 7	29	11,320	
30	Expenses for business use of your home. Attach Form 8829	30		
31	Net profit or (loss). Subtract line 30 from line 29. If a profit, enter here and on Form 1040, line 12. Also, enter the net profit on Schedule SE, line 2 (statutory employees, see page C-5). If a loss, you MUST go on to line 32 (fiduciaries, see page C-5)	31	11,320	
32	If you have a loss, you MUST check the box that describes your investment in this activity (see page C-5). If you checked 32a, enter the loss on Form 1040, line 12, and Schedule SE, line 2 (statutory employees, see page C-5). If you checked 32b, you MUST attach Form 6198.	32a ☐ All investment is at risk. 32b ☐ Some investment is not at risk.		

For Paperwork Reduction Act Notice, see Form 1040 instructions.   Cat. No. 11334P   Schedule C (Form 1040) 1992

Form **4562**		**Depreciation and Amortization**		OMB No. 1545-0172

Depreciation and Amortization

(Including Information on Listed Property)

Department of the Treasury
Internal Revenue Service

► See separate instructions. ► Attach this form to your return.

1992

Attachment Sequence No. **67**

Name(s) shown on return: Henry M. Brown

Identifying number: 123-00-6789

Business or activity to which this form relates: Auto Repair Service

Part I Election To Expense Certain Tangible Property (Section 179) (Note: If you have any "Listed Property," complete Part V before you complete Part I.)

1	Maximum dollar limitation (see instructions)	1	$10,000
2	Total cost of section 179 property placed in service during the tax year (see instructions)	2	24,466
3	Threshold cost of section 179 property before reduction in limitation	3	$200,000
4	Reduction in limitation. Subtract line 3 from line 2, but do not enter less than -0-	4	-0-
5	Dollar limitation for tax year. Subtract line 4 from line 1, but do not enter less than -0-	5	10,000

	(a) Description of property	(b) Cost	(c) Elected cost	
6				

7	Listed property. Enter amount from line 26.	**7** 10,000	
8	Total elected cost of section 179 property. Add amounts in column (c), lines 6 and 7	8	10,000
9	Tentative deduction. Enter the smaller of line 5 or line 8	9	10,000
10	Carryover of disallowed deduction from 1991 (see instructions)	10	-0-
11	Taxable income limitation. Enter the smaller of taxable income or line 5 (see instructions)	11	10,000
12	Section 179 expense deduction. Add lines 9 and 10, but do not enter more than line 11	12	10,000
13	Carryover of disallowed deduction to 1993. Add lines 9 and 10, less line 12 ►	**13** -0-	

Note: Do not use Part II or Part III below for automobiles, certain other vehicles, cellular telephones, computers, or property used for entertainment, recreation, or amusement (listed property). Instead, use Part V for listed property.

Part II MACRS Depreciation For Assets Placed in Service ONLY During Your 1992 Tax Year (Do Not Include Listed Property)

(a) Classification of property	(b) Month and year placed in service	(c) Basis for depreciation (business/investment use only—see instructions)	(d) Recovery period	(e) Convention	(f) Method	(g) Depreciation deduction
14 General Depreciation System (GDS) (see instructions):						
a 3-year property						
b 5-year property						
c 7-year property		2,966	7	HY	200 DB	424
d 10-year property						
e 15-year property						
f 20-year property						
g Residential rental property			27.5 yrs.	MM	S/L	
			27.5 yrs.	MM	S/L	
h Nonresidential real property			31.5 yrs.	MM	S/L	
			31.5 yrs.	MM	S/L	
15 Alternative Depreciation System (ADS) (see instructions):						
a Class life					S/L	
b 12-year			12 yrs.		S/L	
c 40-year			40 yrs.	MM	S/L	

Part III Other Depreciation (Do Not Include Listed Property)

16	GDS and ADS deductions for assets placed in service in tax years beginning before 1992 (see instructions)	16	
17	Property subject to section 168(f)(1) election (see instructions)	17	
18	ACRS and other depreciation (see instructions)	18	

Part IV Summary

19	Listed property. Enter amount from line 25.	19	2,300
20	Total. Add deductions on line 12, lines 14 and 15 in column (g), and lines 16 through 19. Enter here and on the appropriate lines of your return. (Partnerships and S corporations—see instructions)	20	12,724 [G]
21	For assets shown above and placed in service during the current year, enter the portion of the basis attributable to section 263A costs (see instructions)	**21**	

For Paperwork Reduction Act Notice, see page 1 of the separate instructions. Cat. No. 12906N Form **4562** (1992)

Part V | Listed Property—Automobiles, Certain Other Vehicles, Cellular Telephones, Computers, and Property Used for Entertainment, Recreation, or Amusement

For any vehicle for which you are using the standard mileage rate or deducting lease expense, complete only 22a, 22b, columns (a) through (c) of Section A, all of Section B, and Section C if applicable.

Section A—Depreciation (Caution: *See instructions for limitations for automobiles.*)

22a Do you have evidence to support the business/investment use claimed? ☑ Yes ☐ No   22b If "Yes," is the evidence written? ☑ Yes ☐ No

(a) Type of property (list vehicles first)	(b) Date placed in service	(c) Business/ investment use percentage	(d) Cost or other basis	(e) Basis for depreciation (business/investment use only)	(f) Recovery period	(g) Method/ Convention	(h) Depreciation deduction	(i) Elected section 179 cost
23 Property used more than 50% in a qualified business use (see instructions):								
Pickup Truck	1/2/92	100 %	3,500	1,500	5	200 DB/HY	300	2,000
Tow Truck	1/2/92	100 %	18,000	10,000	5	200 DB/HY	2,000	8,000
		%						
24 Property used 50% or less in a qualified business use (see instructions):								
		%				S/L –		
		%				S/L –		
		%				S/L –		

25 Add amounts in column (h). Enter the total here and on line 19, page 1 . . . . . | **25** | 2,300
26 Add amounts in column (i). Enter the total here and on line 7, page 1 . . . . | **26** | 10,000

Section B—Information Regarding Use of Vehicles—*If you deduct expenses for vehicles:*
- *Always complete this section for vehicles used by a sole proprietor, partner, or other "more than 5% owner," or related person.*
- *If you provided vehicles to your employees, first answer the questions in Section C to see if you meet an exception to completing this section for those vehicles.*

	(a) Vehicle 1		(b) Vehicle 2		(c) Vehicle 3		(d) Vehicle 4		(e) Vehicle 5		(f) Vehicle 6	
27 Total business/investment miles driven during the year (DO NOT include commuting miles)	10,000		20,000									
28 Total commuting miles driven during the year	–0–		–0–									
29 Total other personal (noncommuting) miles driven	–0–		–0–									
30 Total miles driven during the year. Add lines 27 through 29	10,000		20,000									
	Yes	No	Yes	No	Yes	No	Yes	No	Yes	No	Yes	No
31 Was the vehicle available for personal use during off-duty hours?		✓		✓								
32 Was the vehicle used primarily by a more than 5% owner or related person?		✓		✓								
33 Is another vehicle available for personal use?	✓		✓									

Section C—Questions for Employers Who Provide Vehicles for Use by Their Employees
Answer these questions to determine if you meet an exception to completing Section B. **Note:** *Section B must always be completed for vehicles used by sole proprietors, partners, or other more than 5% owners or related persons.*

	Yes	No
34 Do you maintain a written policy statement that prohibits all personal use of vehicles, including commuting, by your employees?		
35 Do you maintain a written policy statement that prohibits personal use of vehicles, except commuting, by your employees? (See instructions for vehicles used by corporate officers, directors, or 1% or more owners.)		
36 Do you treat all use of vehicles by employees as personal use?		
37 Do you provide more than five vehicles to your employees and retain the information received from your employees concerning the use of the vehicles?		
38 Do you meet the requirements concerning qualified automobile demonstration use (see instructions)? . .		

Note: *If your answer to 34, 35, 36, 37, or 38 is "Yes," you need not complete Section B for the covered vehicles.*

Part VI | Amortization

(a) Description of costs	(b) Date amortization begins	(c) Amortizable amount	(d) Code section	(e) Amortization period or percentage	(f) Amortization for this year
39 Amortization of costs that begins during your 1992 tax year:					
40 Amortization of costs that began before 1992				40	
41 Total. Enter here and on "Other Deductions" or "Other Expenses" line of your return . . .				41	

Check Reconciliation as of
January 31, 1992

Balance shown on bank statement							1	458	12
Add deposits not credited:									
1/28				70	1	33			
1/31				51	6	08			
							1	217	41
							2	675	53
Subtract outstanding checks:									
No. 89				6	6	70			
90					9	80			
93			1	50		00			
94			3	00		00			
								526	50
Adjusted balance per bank statement							2	149	03
Balance shown in checkbook							2	153	03
Add: Deposit of $600.40 for 1/8									
entered as $594.40 (difference)								6	00
							2	159	03
Subtract:									
Bank service charge								10	00
Adjusted checkbook balance							2	149	03

How to Get IRS Forms and Publications

You can order tax forms and publications from the IRS Forms Distribution Center for your state at the address below. Or, if you prefer, you can photocopy tax forms from reproducible copies kept at participating public libraries. In addition, many of these libraries have reference sets of IRS publications that you can read or copy.

Alaska, Arizona, California, Colorado, Hawaii, Idaho, Kansas, Montana, Nevada, New Mexico, Oklahoma, Oregon, Utah, Washington, Wyoming — Western Area Distribution Center Rancho Cordova, CA 95743-0001

Alabama, Arkansas, Illinois, Indiana, Iowa, Kentucky, Louisiana, Michigan, Minnesota, Mississippi, Missouri, Nebraska, North Dakota, Ohio, South Dakota, Tennessee, Texas, Wisconsin — Central Area Distribution Center P.O. Box 8903 Bloomington, IL 61702-8903

Connecticut, Delaware, District of Columbia, Florida, Georgia, Maine, Maryland, Massachusetts, New Hampshire, New Jersey, New York, North Carolina, Pennsylvania, Rhode Island, South Carolina, Vermont, Virginia, West Virginia — Eastern Area Distribution Center P.O. Box 85074 Richmond, VA 23261-5074

Foreign Addresses—Taxpayers with mailing addresses in foreign countries should send their requests for forms and publications to: Eastern Area Distribution Center, P.O. Box 85074, Richmond, VA 23261-5074; or Western Area Distribution Center, Rancho Cordova, CA 95743-0001, whichever is closer.

Puerto Rico—Eastern Area Distribution Center, P.O. Box 85074, Richmond, VA 23261-5074

Virgin Islands—V.I. Bureau of Internal Revenue, Lockharts Garden, No. 1A, Charlotte Amalie, St. Thomas, VI 00802

Detach at This Line

Order blank—We will send you 2 copies of each form and 1 copy of each publication or set of instructions you circle. Please cut the order blank on the dotted line above and **be sure to print or type your name and address accurately on the bottom portion.** Enclose this order blank in your own envelope and address your envelope to the IRS address shown above for your state. To help reduce waste, please order only the forms, instructions, and publications you think you will need to prepare your return. Use the blank spaces to order items not listed. If you need more space, attach a separate sheet of paper listing the additional forms and publications you may need. You should either receive your order or notification of the status of your order within 7-15 work days after we receive your request.

1040	Schedule EIC (1040A or 1040)	Schedule 2 (1040A)	2119 & Instructions	8332	Pub. 463	Pub. 529	
Instructions for 1040 & Schedules	Schedule F (1040)	Schedule 3 (1040A) & Instructions	2210 & Instructions	8582 & Instructions	Pub. 505	Pub. 590	
Schedule A&B (1040)	Schedule R (1040) & Instructions	1040EZ	2441 & Instructions	8822	Pub. 508	Pub. 596	
Schedule C (1040)	Schedule SE (1040)	Instructions for 1040EZ	3903 & Instructions	8829	Pub. 521	Pub. 910	
Schedule C-EZ (1040)	1040A	1040-ES (1993)	4562 & Instructions	Pub. 1	Pub. 523	Pub. 917	
Schedule D (1040)	Instructions for 1040A & Schedules	1040X & Instructions	4868	Pub. 17	Pub. 525	Pub. 929	
Schedule E (1040)	Schedule 1 (1040A)	2106 & Instructions	8283 & Instructions	Pub. 334	Pub. 527		

Internal Revenue Service

Name
Number and street
City or town, State, and ZIP code

APPENDIX 10: THE SMALL BUSINESS DIRECTORY

Published by the U.S. Small Business Administration. Used by kind permission.

DIRECTORY Effective August 5, 1993 (Prices subject to change)

VIDEOTAPES

VT1 - $30.00   Marketing: Winning Customers With a Workable Plan
VT2 - $30.00   The Business Plan: Your Roadmap To Success
VT3 - $39.00   Promotion: Solving the Puzzle
VT4 - $39.00   Home-Based Business: A Winning Blueprint
VT5 - $30.00   Basics of Exporting

COMPUTER SOFTWARE

CS1 - FREE   Review for Business Loans
CS2 - $5.00   Cash Flow Statement
CS3 - $5.00   Profit and Loss Statement
CS4 - $5.00   Business Plan

PUBLICATIONS

NEW PRODUCTS/IDEAS/INVENTIONS

PI1 - $3.00   Ideas, Inventions and Innovations
PI2 - $2.00   Avoiding Patent, Trademark and Copyright Problems
PI3 - $1.75   Trademarks and Business Goodwill

FINANCIAL MANAGEMENT

FM1 - $1.25   ABCs of Borrowing
FM1S - $1.25   ABCs of Borrowing (Spanish)
FM2 - $1.25   Profit Costing and Pricing For Manufacturers
FM4 - $1.25   Understanding Cash Flow
FM5 - $1.00   A Venture Capital Primer For Small Business
FM8 - $1.25   Budgeting In a Small Service Firm
FM10 - $2.00   Record Keeping In a Small Business
FM13 - $1.25   Pricing Your Products
FM14 - $3.00   Financing for the Small Business

MANAGEMENT AND PLANNING SERIES

MP2 - $1.25   Locating or Relocating Your Business
MP3 - $1.75   Challenges In Managing a Family-Owned Business
MP4 - $3.50   Business Plan For Small Manufacturers
MP5 - $3.50   Business Plan For Small Construction Firms
MP6 - $1.75   Planning and Goal Setting For the Small Business
MP9 - $3.50   Business Plan For Small Retailers
MP11 - $3.25   Business Plan For Small Service Firm

MP12	-	$1.25	Checklist For Going Into Business
MP12S	-	$1.25	Checklist For Going Into Business (Spanish)
MP14	-	$2.00	Computerizing Your Business
MP15	-	$2.50	The Business Plan For Homebased Business
MP16	-	$2.25	How To Buy or Sell a Small Company
MP20	-	$1.75	Insurance Options For Business Continuation Planning
MP21	-	$3.00	Introduction to Strategic Planning
MP22	-	$1.25	Successful Inventory Management
MP25	-	$1.00	Selecting the Legal Structure For Your Business
MP26	-	$1.00	Evaluating Franchise Opportunities
MP28	-	$3.00	Small Business Risk Management Guide
MP29	-	$5.00	How To Start a Child Care Business
MP30	-	$5.00	Child Day-Care Services
MP31	-	$5.00	Handbook for Small Business
MP32	-	$2.50	How To Write A Business Plan

MARKETING SERIES

MT1	-	$1.25	Creative Selling: The Competitive Edge
MT2	-	$1.00	Marketing For Small Business: An Overview
MT8	-	$2.00	Researching Your Market
MT9	-	$1.75	Selling By Mail Order
MT10	-	$1.75	International Trade: A Global Opportunity
MT11	-	$1.25	Advertising

CRIME PREVENTION

CP2	-	$3.25	Curtailing Crime — Inside and Out
CP3	-	$3.00	A Small Business Guide To Computer Security

PERSONNEL MANAGEMENT

PM2	-	$2.00	Employees: How To Find and Pay Them
PM3	-	$2.25	Managing Employee Benefits

EMERGING BUSINESS

EG1	-	$3.00	Transferring Management in a Family-Owned Business
EG2	-	$5.00	Marketing Strategies For the Growing Business
EG3	-	$2.00	Management Issues For the Growing Business
EG4	-	$2.25	Human Resources Management For the Growing Business
EG5	-	$3.25	Audit Checklist For the Growing Business
EG6	-	$2.00	Strategic Planning
EG7	-	$4.50	Financial Management For the Growing Business

APPENDIX 11: THE ABC'S OF BORROWING

Published by the U.S. Small Business Administration. Used by kind permission.

INTRODUCTION

All businesses, no matter what size, will at some time need to raise more money. For small businesses, the owner may be able to dip into his or her personal savings, or friends may be able to lend the needed money. Usually, however, the owner will have to look to outside sources for financing.

IS YOUR FIRM CREDIT WORTHY?

Obtaining money when you need it is as necessary to the operation of your business as a good location or an adequate labor force. Before a bank will lend you money, the loan officer must feel satisfied with the answers to the following questions.

What is your character will you want to repay the loan? How capable are you in managing the businesswill you be able to repay the loan?

What is the specific purpose of the loan? Is it a short- or long-term need?

Do you have a clear financial plan and forecast showing why you need the loan and how you will pay it back?

Is the loan request large enough to cover any unexpected change in your situation, but not so large that its repayment will be a heavy burden?

What is the general economic outlook for your business and industry?

Do you have a reasonable amount at stake in the business?

What collateral is available to secure the loan amount?

FINANCIAL INFORMATION REQUIRED BY LENDERS

The two basic financial documents that lenders require are the balance sheet and the income statement. The balance sheet is the major yardstick for solvency and the income statement is the common measure of profits. Using these and other sources, lenders ask the following questions.

General Questions

Are the business's books and records up-to-date and in good condition?

Does the business have a lawyer and/or accountant?

Who are the customers and what percentage of total sales do the largest customers represent?

Are all obligations paid promptly?

What is the insurance coverage?

Accounts Receivable

What is the quality of the accounts receivable?

Have any been pledged to another creditor?

Are customers paying you promptly?

Is there an allowance for bad debts?

Inventory

Can the merchandise be sold at full price?

How much raw material is on hand?

How much work is in progress?

How much of production is finished goods?

Is too much money tied up in inventory?

Is the inventory turnover in line with industry norms?

Fixed Assets and Equipment

What is the type, age and condition of the equipment?

What are the depreciation schedules?

What are the details of mortgages or leases?

What are the future fixed asset and equipment needs for the company?

The lender scrutinizes the cash flow of the business to determine whether or not the owner-manager is providing sufficient cash to meet the firm's obligations. The lender also makes sure that cash needed for working capital is not being diverted to other areas, such as the acquisition of fixed assets, thereby reducing liquidity.

WHAT TYPE OF LOAN?

When you set out to borrow money for your firm, it is important to know the type of loan you want and its duration. There are two basic kinds of loans—lines of credit and installment loans—and two general categories of loan length—short-term and long-term.

The purpose for which the funds are to be used is a very important factor in deciding what kind of loan to request. There is also an important connection between the length of the loan and the source of repayment.

Generally, short-term loans are repaid from the liquidation of the current assets (i.e., receivables, inventory) that are financed, while long-term loans are generally repaid from earnings.

Line of Credit
A line of credit is an arrangement in which the bank disburses funds as they are needed, up to a predetermined limit. The customer may borrow and repay repeatedly up to the limit within the approved time frame (usually one year).

Installment Loan
An installment loan is an agreement to provide a lump sum amount of money at the beginning of the loan. The loan is paid back in equal amounts over the course of a number of years.

Short-term Loan
A short-term bank loan can be used for purposes such as financing a seasonal buildup in accounts

receivable or inventory. Lenders usually expect these loans to be repaid after their purposes have been served: for example, accounts receivable loans when the outstanding accounts have been paid by the customers and inventory loans when the inventory has been sold and cash collected. Short-term loans are generally repaid in less than a year.

Long-term Loan
A long-term loan is usually a formal agreement to provide funds for more than one year, and most are for an improvement that will benefit the company and increase earnings. An example is the purchase of a new building that will increase capacity or of a machine that will make the manufacturing process more efficient and less costly. Long-term loans are usually repaid from profits.

COLLATERAL

Sometimes your signature and general credit reputation are the only collateral the bank needs to make a loan. This type of loan is called unsecured. At other times, the bank requires a pledge of some or all of your assets as additional assurance that the loan will be repaid. This is called a secured loan. The kind and amount of collateral depends on the bank and on variables in the borrower's situation.

Many types of collateral can be pledged for a secured loan. The most common are endorser, warehouse receipts, floor planning, purchase money security interest (PMSI) in furniture and/or equipment, real estate, accounts receivable inventory, savings accounts, life insurance policies, and stocks and bonds.

Endorser, Co-maker, Guarantor
A borrower may ask another person to sign a note in order to augment his or her credit. This endorser is then liable for the note: if the borrower fails to pay, the bank expects the endorser to pay. Sometimes the endorser may also be asked to pledge assets.

A co-maker is an endorser who assumes an obligation jointly with the maker, or borrower. In this arrangement, the bank can collect directly from either maker or co-maker.

A guarantor is an endorser who guarantees the payment of a note if the borrower does not pay. Both private and government lenders often require guarantees from officers of corporations in order to assure continuity of effective management.

Warehouse Receipts

A bank may take commodities as collateral by lending money on a warehouse receipt. The receipt is usually delivered directly to the bank and shows that the merchandise has either been placed in a public warehouse or has been left on your premises under the control of one of your employees who is bonded. Such loans are generally made on staple or standard merchandise that can be readily marketed. The typical loan is for a percentage of the cost of the merchandise.

Floor Planning

Merchandise such as automobiles, appliances and boats must be displayed to be sold, but the only way many small marketers can afford displays is by borrowing money. Such loans are often secured by a note and trust receipt. The trust receipt is used for serial numbered merchandise. It acknowledges receipt of the merchandise, shows agreement to keep the merchandise in trust for the bank and verifies the promise to pay the bank as the goods are sold.

Purchase Money Security Interest

If you buy expensive equipment, such as a cash register or a delivery truck, you may be able to get a loan using the equipment as collateral. (This kind of loan is also called a chattel mortgage.) The bank assesses the present and future market value of the equipment and makes sure it is adequately insured.

Real Estate

Real estate is another form of collateral, usually for long-term loans. In evaluating a real estate mortgage, the bank considers the market and foreclosure value of the property and its insurance coverage.

Accounts Receivable

Many banks lend money against accounts receivable; in effect, counting on your customers to pay your loan. The bank may take accounts receivable on a notification or nonnotification plan. Under the notification plan, the purchaser of the goods is informed by the bank that the account has been assigned and is asked to make payments directly to the bank. Under the nonnotification plan, customers continue to pay you and you pay the bank.

Inventory

Inventory is the merchandise, wares and any assets that can be liquidated of a retail, wholesale or manufacturing business that will provide a form of financial guarantee against the loan proceeds. Unless otherwise specified in the loan documents, plant and equipment (e.g., computers, cash registers, manufacturing equipment, telephones and other fixtures) can also be included as inventory to be held as collateral.

Savings Accounts and Certificates of Deposit

It is possible to get a loan by assigning a savings account to the bank. You assign the account and the bank keeps the passbook.

If you assign an account at another bank as collateral, the lending bank asks the other bank to mark its records to show that the account is held as collateral.

Life Insurance

Another kind of collateral is the cash value of a life insurance policy, in which you assign the policy to the bank. Some people prefer to use life insurance as collateral rather than borrowing directly from the insurance company because a bank loan generally is easier to obtain and carries a lower interest rate.

Stocks and Bonds

Marketable stocks and bonds are also sources of collateral. Banks usually lend 75 percent or less on the value of high-grade stocks and up to 90 percent on government securities. The limits leave a cushion or margin for protection against declines. If the market value of the collateral does fall below a certain level, the bank may ask for additional collateral or a partial payment of the loan.

THE LOAN AGREEMENT

A loan agreement is a tailor-made document, fully stating all the terms and conditions of the loan. It gives the amount of the loan and terms of repayment, identifies the principle parties and lists any restrictions placed on the borrower.

Limitations
Banks often include limitations in a loan agreement that restrict what an owner can do. These limitations depend to a great extent on the company. If the company is a good risk, the limitations will be minimal. A higher risk company, on the other hand, will have greater limitations. The three principle limitations involve repayment terms, the use of collateral and periodic reporting. Limitations are spelled out in the covenant section.

Covenants: Negative and Positive
Negative covenants are restrictions placed on the borrower by the lender. Some examples are limitations on the borrower's total debt, agreement not to pledge assets to other creditors and limitations on the amount of dividends that may be issued.

Positive covenants are all actions the borrower must agree to.

They include maintaining a minimum working capital, carrying adequate insurance, adhering to the repayment schedules and supplying the lender with regular financial statements and reports. Loan agreements can be amended from time to time and exceptions made. Certain provisions may be waived from year to year with the consent of the lender.

Negotiating with the Lender
Ask to see the papers before the loan closing. Reputable lenders will be glad to comply. While you're mulling over the terms you may want to get the advice of your associates and advisors.

Discuss and negotiate the lending terms before you sign the loan agreement—it is good practice, no matter how much you need the money. Chances are the lender may be willing to give on some of the terms; try to get terms with which you know your company can live. Remember, though, that once the loan is made, you are bound by it.

THE LOAN APPLICATION

Banks and other lending institutions, including the SBA, require a loan application on which you list certain information about your business.

SBA Form 4 is an example of a loan application. It is more detailed than most bank forms, because the bank usually has the advantage of prior knowledge of the applicant and his or her activities, while SBA usually does not have such knowledge. Also, the longer maturities offered on SBA loans ordinarily require more information about the applicant.

Before you fill out a loan application, you should talk with an SBA representative, or your accountant or banker, to make sure that your business is eligible for an SBA loan. Because of public policy, SBA cannot make certain types of loans, nor can it make loans under certain conditions. For example, if you qualify for a loan on reasonable terms from a bank, SBA cannot lend you money.

You also are not eligible for an SBA loan if you can get funds by selling assets that your company does not need in order to grow.

Most sections of the SBA loan application are self-explanatory; however, some applicants have trouble with certain sections because they do not know where to get the necessary information requested.

The collateral section is an example. Collateral is the borrower's assets that are pledged to the lender to guarantee the loan. Your company's books should show the market value of assets such as business real estate and business machinery and equipment. (Market means what you paid for such assets less depreciation.) If your records do not contain detailed information on these assets, the bank sometimes can get it from your federal income tax returns. Reviewing the depreciation that you have taken for tax purposes on such assets can help to ascertain their value.

If you are a good manager, you probably balance your books every month. Some businesses, however, prepare balance sheets less regularly. In filling out your Balance Sheet as of _____,

19___, Fiscal Year Ends_____, remember that you must show the condition of your business within 60 days of the date on your loan application. It is best to get expert advice when working up this vital information. Your accountant or banker can help you.

Again, if your records do not show the details necessary for working up income (profit and loss) statements, your federal income tax returns may be useful in getting together facts for a loan application.

APPENDIX 12: ADDITIONAL FORMS
TO HELP YOU GET ORGANIZED

SMALL BUSINESS DIRECTORY OF FREQUENTLY CALLED PHONE NUMBERS AND CONTACTS

	Contact	Phone No.
Fire Department		
Police Department		
Rescue Department		
Security Company		
Accountant/Lawyer		
Business Forms		
Insurance Agent		
Bank		
OSHA Compliance		
Local Newspaper		
Internal Revenue		
Social Security Administration		
State Chamber of Commerce		
Local Chamber of Commerce		
State Department of Corporations and Taxation		
A. State Unemployment		
B. State Incorporation Tax		
C. Sales Tax		
D. Meals Tax		
E. Inspectors/Licenses		
F. Other		
City Hall/Town Hall		
A. Sales Tax		
B. Real Estate Tax		
C. Zoning		
D. Licenses/Inspectors		
E. Other		

OTHER KEY BUSINESS CONTACTS

NAME	ADDRESS	PHONE NUMBER	
		Business	Home

THE MEMORY PAD

DATE	CONCERN OF IDEA	CONTACT	MUST BE COMPLETED OR IMPLEMENTED BY

GET ORGANIZED

Key Planning for:
Month _____

	MONDAY	TUESDAY	WEDNESDAY	THURSDAY	FRIDAY	SATURDAY	SUNDAY
Week of							
Week of							
Week of							
Week of							

GLOSSARY

Accounting cycle (simplified):	1. Business transactions occur. 2. Analyze transactions by rule of Dr and Cr. 3. Journalize. 4. Post to ledger. 5. Prepare trail balance. 6. Prepare income statement. 7. Prepare balance sheet.
Accounting equation:	Assets – Liabilities + Owner Equity
Accounts payable:	A liability indicating an amount owed to creditors.
Accounts payable subsidiary ledger:	A book or file that contains, in alphabetical order, individual creditors and the amounts owed them. This book or file is not found in the journal or general ledger.
Accounts receivable:	An asset showing an amount customers owe us.
Accounts receivable subsidiary ledger:	A book or file that contains, in alphabetical order, the individual records of amounts owed by various customers to us.
Accumulated depreciation:	A contra asset that accumulates the amount of depreciation taken on an asset. This contra asset is recorded on the balance sheet.
Acid test ratio:	$\dfrac{\text{Current assets} - \text{Inventory}}{\text{Current liabilities}}$
Assets:	Things of value owned by a business.
Asset turnover:	$\dfrac{\text{Net sales}}{\text{Total assets}}$
Average days collection period for accounts receivable:	$\dfrac{\text{Accounts receivable}}{\text{Sales/360 days}}$
Balance sheet:	A financial report prepared as of a particular date that shows a "history" of assets, liabilities, and equity.
Bank reconciliation:	The process of explaining the difference between the balances in the bank statement and the company's checkbook (ledger).
Bookkeeping:	The recording function of accounting.
Break-even chart:	A graph that shows the relationship between volume of sales, costs, and profit.

Break-even point:	The level of business at which revenues for the period are equal to cost incurred—no profit, no loss.
Break-even point in units:	$$\frac{\text{Fixed costs}}{\text{Unit sales price} - \text{Unit variable expense}}$$
Budget:	A tool that aids in planning by setting benchmarks and by allowing you to measure performance.
Calendar year:	January 1 to December 31.
Cash budget:	A tool that aids in planning for: 1. a cash deficiency period; 2. the bank repayment schedule; and 3. plant expansion.
Cash payments, expenses and purchase journal:	A combined journal that reflects the features of the cash payments and purchase journal.
Cash payments journal:	A special journal that records the outward flow of money.
Cash receipts journal:	A special journal that records the inward flow of money.
Check outstanding:	Check written but not yet processed or received by the bank before the bank statement is sent.
Contribution margin:	Total revenue less variable cost.
Corporation:	A form of business organization owned by shareholders. The corporation is considered a separate legal entity.
Current assets:	Those assets of a business that are expected to be converted into cash or used up within a one-year period, such as cash, accounts receivable or inventory.
Current liabilities:	Debts or obligations of a business that come due within one year.
Current ratio:	$$\frac{\text{Current assets}}{\text{Current liabilities}}$$
Debt/total assets:	$$\frac{\text{Total liabilities}}{\text{Total assets}}$$
Deposits in transit:	Deposits made but not yet received or processed by the bank before the bank statement is sent.
Depreciation:	The allocating of the cost of an asset over its period of usefulness. The IRS has guidelines to estimate depreciation. Keep in mind that taking depreciation is an indirect cash savings.

Double-entry bookkeeping:	A self-balancing system that concentrates on both the income statement and the balance sheet. See the Accounting cycle entry for specifics.
Employee individual earnings record:	A card or file for each individual employee that summarizes by quarterly periods the wages paid, as well as the deductions taken.
Exempt:	Not taxable.
Expenses:	Sacrifices in running your business. They represent a potential or outward flow of assets.
Federal unemployment tax (FUTA):	The employer pays this tax to the federal government. If cumulative total is less than $100, payment is due by January 31 of the following year. If the cumulative total due is more than $100, quarterly payments are due.
FICA:	Federal Insurance Contribution Act. This tax is paid by both the employer and the employee.
Fixed assets:	Assets that are not for resale whose life extends beyond one year and will aid in producing revenue (sales).
Fixed asset turnover:	$\dfrac{\text{Net sales}}{\text{Fixed assets}}$
Fixed costs:	Costs that remain constant through a volume of sales.
Form 941:	Employer's quarterly federal tax return. This report is filed each quarter by the employer. This form deals with FWT and the contributions of FICA by the employee and employer. Depending on the amount of tax owed, weekly or monthly deposits (Form 501) may be required.
FWT:	Federal withholding tax. This tax is better known as federal income tax.
Gross pay:	Net pay + Deductions
Gross profit:	Sales - cost of goods sold
Income statement:	A financial report that is prepared for a specific period of time and compares inward flows (revenue) to outward flows (expenses).
Inventory:	Cost of goods for resale.
Inventory turnover:	$\dfrac{\text{Net sales}}{\text{Inventory}}$
Journal:	A book of original entry in which are recorded business transactions in chronological order.

Ledger:	A book of final entry in which is accumulated information about business transactions. This accumulated information will aid in preparing financial reports.
Liabilities:	What a business owes creditors.
Limited liability:	Potential loss is limited to your investment. Investment into a corporation results in limited liability.
Long-term liabilities:	Debts or obligations of a business that will not come due for at least one year.
Merit rating:	A state assigns a percentage rate to a business for calculating the state unemployment tax. The tax rate is based upon the unemployment "track record" of the employer.
Net profit margin:	$$\frac{\text{Net income after tax}}{\text{Sales}}$$
Net sales:	Sales – Sales discounts - SRA
NSF check:	Bounced check; insufficient funds.
Owner's investment (capital):	The difference between assets and liabilities. What the owner has invested into the business.
Partnership:	A form of business organization owned by two or more people through a legal association.
Payroll register:	The journal used to record payroll information about the employee. Eventually this information is summarized into the ledger.
Petty cash:	A fund set up to minimize check writing.
Petty cash voucher:	A slip of paper used to verify taking money out of petty cash. The petty cash custodian approves payment, and the recipient signs for it.
Posting:	The process of transferring information from the journal to the ledger.
Projected financial reports:	The building of financial reports in the present for the future. It is estimating or "building" income statements and balance sheets through past experience, trends, forecasts, and so forth.
Purchases journal:	A special journal that records the purchase of merchandise or other items on account.
Retained earnings:	An account that shows the profit or net income that is kept or "retained" in the business.

Return on equity:	$\dfrac{\text{Net income after tax}}{\text{Stockholders' equity}}$
Return on investment:	$\dfrac{\text{Net income after tax}}{\text{Total assets}}$
Revenue:	The inward flow of assets (cash and/or accounts receivable) that come into a business from the sale of goods and services.
Rules of debit and credit:	Arbitrary rules to accumulate information about business transactions in the ledger: Assets: Debit for increase or Credit for decrease Liabilities: Debit for decrease or Credit for increase Capital: (owner's investment) - Debit for decrease or Credit for increase Revenue: Debit for decrease or Credit for increase Expense: Debit for increase or Credit for decrease Drawing (withdrawal): Debit for increase or Credit for decrease
Sales journal:	A special journal that only records sales on account.
Single-entry bookkeeping:	Simplest bookkeeping system. Major limitation is its concentration on the income statement and not the balance sheet. Does not have a self-balancing feature.
Sole proprietorship:	Form of business organization owned by one person.
Special journals:	Books of original entry that record similar transactions. Examples: CRJ, sales journal. These special journals replace much of the need for general journals.
SS-4:	Application for employer identification number.
Stockholders' equity:	Assets – liabilities
S-type corporation:	For tax purposes, this is a domestic corporation with one class of stock held by no more than fifteen shareholders. A company that chooses to be taxed by an S-type corporation provides tax benefits of a proprietorship or partnership but retains the limited liability of the corporation.
SWT:	State withholding tax.
Target profit:	Sales – Variable cost + Fixed cost + Net income
Tax calendar:	A detailed list of taxes that are due and of when they are due.
Trial balance:	A list of the ledger to prove accuracy in recording debits and credits.

Unlimited liability: Potential loss of personal assets, if one owns a proprietorship or partnership that goes bankrupt. On the other hand, investors in a corporation have a limited liability.

Variable costs: Costs that vary with the volume of sales.

Wage bracket table: From Circular E; tables are available for calculating employee deductions for FWT and FICA.

W-2:   Wage and tax statement sent to each employee by end of first month following the end of the calendar year. This shows the employee's total earnings and deductions for the year. This form must be attached to individual tax returns.

W-4:   Employee's withholding allowance certificate. This form is filled out by employees for determining deductions the employer will take out of employees' paychecks.

RESOURCES FOR SMALL BUSINESS

Upstart Publishing Company, Inc. These publications on proven management techniques for small businesses are available from Upstart Publishing Company, Inc., 12 Portland St., Dover, NH 03820. For a free current catalog, call (800) 235-8866 outside New Hampshire, or 749-5071 in state.

The Business Planning Guide, 6th edition, 1992, David H. Bangs, Jr. and Upstart Publishing Company, Inc. A manual that helps you write a business plan and financing proposal tailored to your business, your goals and your resources. Includes worksheets and checklists. (Softcover, 208 pp., $19.95)

The Market Planning Guide, 1990, David H. Bangs, Jr. and Upstart Publishing Company, Inc. A manual to help small-business owners put together a goal-oriented, resource-based marketing plan with action steps, benchmarks and time lines. Includes worksheets and checklists to make implementation and review easier. (Softcover, 160 pp., $19.95)

The Cash Flow Control Guide, 1990, David H. Bangs, Jr. and Upstart Publishing Company, Inc. A manual to help small-business owners solve their number one financial problem. Includes worksheets and checklists. (Softcover, 88 pp., $14.95)

The Personnel Planning Guide, 1988, David H. Bangs, Jr. and Upstart Publishing Company, Inc. A 176-page manual outlining practical, proven personnel management techniques, including hiring, managing, evaluating and compensating personnel. Includes worksheets and checklists. (Softcover, 176 pp., $19.95)

The Start Up Guide: A One-Year Plan for Entrepreneurs, 1989, David H. Bangs, Jr. and Upstart Publishing Company, Inc. This book utilizes the same step-by-step, no-jargon method as *The Business Planning Guide*, to help even those with no business training through the process of beginning a successful business. (Softcover, 160 pp., $19.95)

Managing By the Numbers: Financial Essentials for the Growing Business, 1992, David H. Bangs, Jr. and Upstart Publishing Company, Inc. Straightforward techniques for getting the maximum return with a minimum of detail in your business's financial management. (Softcover, 160 pp., $19.95.)

Buy the Right Business—At the Right Price, 1990, Brian Knight and the Associates of Country Business, Inc., Upstart Publishing Company, Inc. Many people who would like to be in business for themselves think strictly of starting a business. In some cases, buying a going concern may be preferable—and just as affordable. (Softcover, 152 pp., $18.95)

Borrowing for Your Business, 1991, George M. Dawson, Upstart Publishing Company, Inc. This is a book for borrowers and about lenders. Includes detailed guidelines on how to select a bank and a banker, how to answer the lender's seven most important questions, how your banker looks at a loan and how to get a loan renewed. (Hardcover, 160 pp., $19.95)

The Home-Based Entrepreneur, 1993, Linda Pinson and Jerry Jinnett, Upstart Publishing Co., Inc. A step-by-step guide to all the issues surrounding starting a home-based business. Issues such as zoning, labor laws and licensing are discussed and forms are provided to get you on your way. (Softcover, 192 pp. $19.95)

Keeping the Books, 1993, Linda Pinson and Jerry Jinnett, Upstart Publishing Co., Inc. Basic business recordkeeping both explained and illustrated. Designed to give you a clear understanding of small business accounting by taking you step-by-step through general records, development of financial statements, tax reporting, scheduling and financial statement analysis. (Softcover, 208 pp., $19.95)

Target Marketing for the Small Business, 1993, Linda Pinson and Jerry Jinnett, Upstart Publishing Co., Inc. A comprehensive guide to marketing your business. This book not only shows you how to reach your customers, it also gives you a wealth of information on how to research that market through the use of library resources, questionnaires, demographics, etc. (Softcover, 176 pp., $19.95)

On Your Own: A Woman's Guide to Starting Your Own Business, Second edition, 1993, Laurie Zuckerman, Upstart Publishing Company, Inc. *On Your Own* is for women who want hands-on, practical information about starting and running their own business. It deals honestly with issues like finding time for your business when you're also the primary care provider, societal biases against women and credit discrimination. (Softcover, 320 pp., $19.95)

Steps to Small Business Start-Up, 1993, Linda Pinson and Jerry Jinnett, Upstart Publshing Co., Inc. A step-by-step guide for starting and succeeding with a small or home-based business. Takes you through the mechanics of business start-up and gives an overview of information on such topics as copyrights, trademarks, legal structures, recordkeeping and marketing. (Softcover, 256 pp., $19.95)

Problem Employees, 1991, Dr. Peter Wylie and Dr. Mardy Grothe, Upstart Publishing Company, Inc. Provides managers and supervisors with a simple, practical and straightforward approach to help all employees, especially problem employees, significantly improve their work performance. (Softcover, 272 pp., $22.95)

The Woman Entrepreneur, 1992, Linda Pinson and Jerry Jinnett, Upstart Publishing Co, Inc. Thirty-three successful women business owners share their practical ideas for success and their sources for inspiration. (Softcover, 244 pp., $14.00)

INDEX

251